CU00951195

■ The Son of God in the Roman World

The Son of God in the Roman World

Divine Sonship in Its Social and Political Context

Michael Peppard

OXFORD
UNIVERSITY PRESS

OXFORD
UNIVERSITY PRESS

Oxford University Press, Inc., publishes works that further
Oxford University's objective of excellence
in research, scholarship, and education.

Oxford   New York
Auckland   Cape Town   Dar es Salaam   Hong Kong   Karachi
Kuala Lumpur   Madrid   Melbourne   Mexico City   Nairobi
New Delhi   Shanghai   Taipei   Toronto

With offices in
Argentina   Austria   Brazil   Chile   Czech Republic   France   Greece
Guatemala   Hungary   Italy   Japan   Poland   Portugal   Singapore
South Korea   Switzerland   Thailand   Turkey   Ukraine   Vietnam

Published by Oxford University Press, Inc.
198 Madison Avenue, New York, New York 10016

www.oup.com

Oxford is a registered trademark of Oxford University Press

Library of Congress Cataloging-in-Publication Data
Peppard, Michael.
The Son of God in the roman world : divine sonship in its social and political
context / Michael Peppard.
    p.   cm.
Includes bibliographical references and index.
ISBN 978-0-19-975370-3
1. Son of God—History of doctrines—Early church, ca. 30–600.   2. Rome.
3. Adoption—Rome.   4. Jesus Christ—Divinity—History of doctrines—
Early church, ca. 30–600.   5. Son of Man—History of doctrines—
Early church, ca. 30–600.   6. Theological anthropology—Christianity.   I. Title.
BT198.P467 2012
231'.209015—dc22   2011015623

9 8 7 6 5 4 3 2 1

Printed in the United States of America
on acid-free paper

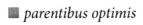 *parentibus optimis*

■ CONTENTS

Imagine yourself in the first century, a Jewish resident of the burgeoning Roman Empire. Perhaps you live in Rome itself, the eternal city. Or perhaps you live in Alexandria, that other bastion of high culture around the Mediterranean. If you live in Jerusalem, your perspective is slightly different, as the Roman military presses in on you from all sides. From there, it seems like the world is about to end. Regardless of exactly where you live, you have a different perspective on the cosmos, a different worldview, than that of a modern Western person. You are not an autonomous individual with guaranteed liberties, but your entire life transpires as a subject of an empire. You have never actually seen your emperor, but you know a great deal about him. You have heard stories about him from everyone, about what he says and does, about what his childhood was like, about his many triumphs. You know his face from coins and the faces of his whole family from statues; you know them almost as well as your own. In fact, in this era before mirrors in every room, you probably know his face better than your own. He is the most famous, the most powerful person in the world.

But there is someone else, also whom you have never seen, that you know even better than the emperor. You first heard of Jesus from people who actually did know him. They told you all kinds of stories about him, too many to remember, accounts of what he said and did, about his tragic end and his glorious appearing. You believe the stories, they give you life, and you want to share the stories with as many people as you can. You decide to write a narrative. But where do you begin? You don't know about his childhood or what he looked like. You met his brother once—maybe he looked a bit like him? Then again, you think of yourself also as his "brother." Those who knew him passed on his chief teachings, and they proclaimed him as the "son of God." He prayed to his "father" and inaugurated a new "family" of God. You believe this and you live by it, but believing and living are different than narrating. Again, where do you begin? One main problem you have, as a Jew, with portraying God's "son" is that your God does not have a partner. For this reason, among others, your God is unusual in the Roman world. But if the paternal God does not procreate, how do you portray the divine sonship of Jesus? Again, where do you begin? Put yourself in Mark's shoes—how do you narrate the life of God's son?

■ ACKNOWLEDGMENTS

My sincere gratitude goes first to Harold Attridge. At the beginning of graduate work, he persuaded me to study at least two languages at a time, and at the end, he helped me to see this book through to completion. I thank him for many conversations and look forward to more. Equally formative on stages of this project have been Adela Yarbro Collins, Dale Martin, Steve Davis, and Bentley Layton. For various points of advice, encouragement, and correction, I would like to thank Siobhán Garrigan, Julia Prest, Judy Gundry, John Collins, Skip Stout, Carlos Noreña, David Kelsey, Jeremy Hultin, Shane Berg, Ward Blanton, Yonder Gillihan, Bryan Spinks, and Fr. Peter Walsh. Working for (and with) Lou Martyn was uniquely beneficial to my growth as a young scholar. My undergraduate professors introduced me to the fields of religious studies, theology, and philosophy, and to these I owe belated thanks: Greg Sterling, Al Neiman, Blake Leyerle, Fr. David Burrell, Fr. John Jenkins, and Rabbi Michael Signer (זכר צדיק לברכה). At Fordham University, Terry Tilley, Larry Welborn, and Ben Dunning have greatly eased my transition from doctoral student to professor—and from New Haven to the Bronx. Graduate students Allan Georgia, John Penniman, and Patrick Burns provided assistance in manuscript preparation. At Oxford University Press, Cynthia Read and others expertly guided the manuscript into a completed book.

For financial support I am grateful to a Fordham University faculty research grant and at Yale University, the Graduate School, Divinity School, Institute of Sacred Music, Department of Religious Studies, and Department of Classics for various monies. The Catholic Biblical Association also provided generous financial aid during my Ph.D. program. Portions of this book were previously published in different form. Material from chapters 2 and 4 appeared in "The Eagle and the Dove: Roman Imperial Sonship and the Baptism of Jesus (Mark 1.9–11)," *NTS* 56 (2010): 431–51; material from chapter 5 appeared in "Adopted and Begotten Sons of God: Paul and John on Divine Sonship," *CBQ* 73 (2011): 92–110. Thanks to Cambridge University Press and the Catholic Biblical Association of America for permission to reprint this material here.

Numerous friends and colleagues have supported me over years of study and research, especially Steve and Pat Ahearne-Kroll, Alice Kearney Alwin and Scott Alwin, Joshua Ezra Burns, Ryan Carlin, Joshua and Kristi Garroway, Khurram Hussain, Steve and Rachael Jungkeit, Tim and Christie Luckritz-Marquis, Luke Moorhead, Candida Moss, Brent Nongbri, John Oksanish and Devon Mackay, Chris Pramuk, Patrick Redding and Kathryn Reklis, Mark Roschewski, Lauren and John Steele, Linn Tonstad, Raymond Ward, Natalie Wigg-Stevenson, Kevin and Warrena

Wilkinson, Molly Worthen, Linda Zenner, and Courtney Zenner. Shelly and Paul Russell have been supportive of my career throughout, in ways they likely don't recall. Tyler Wigg-Stevenson was part of this project since its inception, and he joined me for a final, grueling editing session.

Final thanks go to those closest to me: Christiana, Montana, and my parents. During the research and writing, Christy consistently reminded me of the ideas with which I began the project and kept me honest to them. In the last phases, she often sacrificed her own scholarly work to help me out, and she provided a coffee, a joke, or a bolt of seriousness—whatever was needed. I really can't believe how often she allowed me to read bits of this book to her while we made dinner. Thanks to her for the habits of close companionship. Montana has renewed my spirit every day. She never lets me take anything too seriously. Now if she would only learn to sit still on my lap while I type.

Parentibus optimis: this work is dedicated to my parents, Gerard and Linda, who are the best. My mom unwittingly guided me toward biblical studies long ago, through her own faith and devotional practices. And in the end, she made sure we had a good restaurant reservation to celebrate the completion of this book. My dad was not sure about my career path but always supported my ambitions nonetheless, this book project included. And with those two weeks of childcare in the middle of a New England winter, he enabled me finally to finish it off. As a Roman might say: *Bene te*, Dad.

■ The Son of God in the Roman World

Introduction

Over time and through repeated use, metaphors die. A metaphor dies when its meaning becomes stable for its audience, when it stops being considered, when everyone knows what it means. That insight from literary theory is an impetus for this book: the metaphor "son of God"—a central expression of ancient Christians— has died for most contemporary interpreters of early Christianity. We think we know what it means.

But the divine sonship metaphor is rarely considered in the Roman sociopolitical environment of the first and second centuries, which is a key context of the New Testament and other early Christian literature. Most interpreters instead analyze divine sonship and the term "son of God" using conceptions from elite theological debates of later centuries. Furthermore, divine sonship is customarily discussed only in reference to the person that became known uniquely as the Son of God, Jesus of Nazareth, without reference to other people who were considered sons and daughters of God.

How did early Christians imagine the filial relationship between Jesus and God? To whose divine sonship would his have been compared? Moreover, how did Christians understand Jesus' divine sonship vis-à-vis their own relationships to God as sons and daughters? What models of sonship did they use to understand his status and their own? Why did divine sonship come to be distinguished as "begotten" or "made," and why was the former eventually considered to have higher status than the latter? When we try to answer these questions, we find ways to bring the sonship metaphor back from the dead. All metaphors die, but some can be resurrected.

■ AN OVERVIEW

The chief objectives of this book are (1) to critique the conceptual framework within which the term "son of God" has usually been construed in biblical scholarship and (2) to reinterpret divine sonship in the sociopolitical context of early Christianity. The method by which I resurrect the metaphor works toward both objectives simultaneously. It is a well-known method but has not yet been applied to this topic—namely, to interpret a concept by examining the social practices with which that concept interacts. Concepts, especially metaphors, are almost always rooted in practices. Human beings do not think in isolation from their cultural practices: the metaphor of *divine* father-son relations only *means* in the context of *actual* father-son relations. Yet actual father-son relations have rarely been examined as a way to understand divine sonship. Examining social practices from the first and second centuries allows us to critique a conceptual framework drawn from later eras, which is exactly what chapter 1 sets out to do.

Chapter 1, "Divine Sonship Before Nicea: Biblical Scholarship on 'Son of God,'" argues that scholarship on divine sonship in the New Testament has relied anachronistically on the philosophical and theological categories of fourth-century Christianity, especially the key distinction, "begotten not made." In the Roman world before Nicea, begetting and making sons was not primarily a philosophical distinction. On the contrary, the father-son relationship was at the heart of all Roman *social* relationships—the crux of Roman kinship and politics. My argument critiques the Nicene approach to biblical texts, which is often an unconscious combination of fourth-century Christological categories with first-century texts. It further assesses what can be gained for the study of divine sonship from narrative, historical-critical, and audience-oriented methods. My own approach is characterized by a concern for social practices, an ear for political ideology, and a focus on the singular figure of the Roman emperor.

The next two chapters break down the term "son of God" into its constitutive concepts. In order to think differently about divine sonship in early Christianity, we need to acknowledge the shifts in scholarly perspective on divinity ("god") and family ("son") in the Roman world. The figure of the emperor—the first famous "son of god" in the Roman Empire—lies at the heart of the changes in perspective. Chapter 2, "Divinity and Divine Sonship in the Roman World," engages scholarship on divinity in Roman religion, with special attention to significant studies of emperor worship. Recent work in Roman history and religious studies has critiqued previous modern understandings of ancient divinity as being mistakenly grounded in elite philosophical ideas. The use of archaeological research and nuanced theories of power has allowed scholars to incorporate into a coherent worldview some previously anomalous data—not least the widely attested worship of the Roman emperor as a god. Taken together, the changes in the study of Roman religion and emperor worship have invited fresh comparisons with early Christianity and the worship of Jesus Christ. Chapters 4 and 5 will fill out some of those comparisons.

Chapter 3, "Begotten or Made? Adopted Sons in Roman Society and Imperial Ideology," investigates father-son relationships in the Roman family, emphasizing the practices of adoption and inheritance among elites. In the Roman worldview, sonship did not primarily point *backward* to begetting, but *forward* to inheritance, often through the medium of adoption. For emperors, this observation is especially crucial, since these "fathers" of the Empire had no small trouble propagating their family lines through natural begetting. These divine fathers usually had to adopt their divine sons. Therefore, I analyze the transmission of power from father to son in the imperial family and the competing family ideologies of natural ("begotten") sons and adopted ("made") sons. My analysis shows that scholarship on divine sonship has been hampered by mistaken assumptions about adopted sons. Far from being second-class family members, they were pivotal and often favored. The adoption of adult males helped to stabilize ruling families and formed a key part of imperial ideology. When read in the light of Roman social practices, emperor worship, and imperial ideology, several early Christian texts take on new meaning. We can hear new resonances in the same old texts.

One of these "same old texts" is the Gospel of Mark, which has long been linked to Rome and has sometimes been read in connection with Roman political ideology. Chapter 4, "Rethinking Divine Sonship in the Gospel of Mark," demonstrates the ways in which Mark's image of Jesus and his followers interacts with that of the Roman emperor and the imperial family. The practice of adoption in the political ideology leading up to Mark's era allows us to reimagine his Christology in unexpected ways. Reading the baptism of Jesus through the lens of imperial ideology encourages one to hear the divine voice as an adoption, the beginning of Jesus' accession as a son and heir. The dove functions as an omen of this grace and counter-symbol to the eagle, which was a public portent of divine favor and election in Roman culture. The adoptive relationship can be traced later in the gospel and understood to relate to the divine sonship offered by God to all people through the Spirit. Based on the arguments of chapter 3, I contend that the supposedly "low" connotations of such an adoption are a misconstrual of ancient evidence. Viewed in its Roman sociopolitical context, Mark's Christology was as high as humanly possible. When facing the novel challenge of narrating the divine sonship of a human being—in relation to a God that did not procreate—Mark crafted a portrayal that was theologically coherent and also resonated in its cultural context. The resurrected metaphor enables us to read Mark anew.

The arguments of chapters 1 through 4 try to take the reader back before Nicea to the first and second centuries. What options had been available for characterizing and narrating divine sonship? The book concludes by bringing the reader forward from the Christologies of the New Testament all the way through to Nicea, the triumphant philosophical Christology. Chapter 5, "Begotten and Adopted Sons of God—Before and After Nicea," synthesizes a broad range of texts in order to show the shifting relationship between begotten and adoptive metaphors during the first four centuries of Christianity. These texts anchor the previous chapter's interpretation of Mark's Christology, while they also show how the resonance of "son of God" changed over time. Many authors of the first and second centuries, when describing the divine sonship of Christ and Christians, mixed the begotten and adoptive metaphors. But by the fourth century, adoption was no longer a crucial, visible component of imperial ideology and thus lost some (but not all) of its appeal as a metaphor of power and exaltation. Moreover, with the predominance of philosophical categories among Christian leaders, the terms "begotten" and "made" changed in meaning: they ceased functioning as metaphors linked to human practices. They became increasingly abstract concepts, until the watershed debates of the Nicene era established them finally as the property of theologians alone. Jesus was now the begotten one, and everything else was made—and made now meant "created," not "adopted." By the time of the fourth-century controversies, adoption had become the Christological idea *non grata* among bishops and other theologians. The chapter is roughly chronological and thus offers a clear view of several interweaving themes on the road to Nicea: begotten and adoptive metaphors of divine sonship; the sonship of Christ and the sonship of Christians; Christ as unique and Christ as exemplar; philosophy and narrative; theological doctrine and liturgical practice. In the end, with revised understandings of several ancient phenomena—especially divine status, adoption, and baptism—this book aims toward an ambitious goal: to rethink the Son of God in the Roman world.

▪ CHRISTOLOGICAL QUESTIONS

While working on this book, I encountered more than a few quizzical expressions when I explained its topic, especially if I was speaking with colleagues educated in Christian theology. I would explain that I was examining Jesus' status as son of God, as expressed by a selection of early Christian texts, in relation to the divine sonship of the Roman emperors, who were usually adopted. Furthermore, I was bringing that knowledge to bear on the understanding of Christian divine sonship developing in the first few centuries of theology and ritual practice. Then came the reply: "Do you think Mark was adoptionist?" or "Are you doing an Arian reading of early Christian texts?" Depending on who was asking, the question was accompanied by either (a) raised eyebrows and a confused look that said, "Good luck," or (b) squinted eyes and a steely glare that said, "Get away from me, you heretic."

There is some measure of intrigue at being accused of heresy; paradoxically, the label sounds both ancient and urgent at the same time. I think it is inaccurate, however, and I would rather it did not stick. I feel compelled to provide some defense of my topic in advance. First, I do not think that Mark was an adoptionist, at least not in any sense of the word commonly in use. Second, I am not doing an Arian reading of early Christian texts, as if I were some Arian pastor doing sermon preparation for a long-lost branch of Christianity. But both of these accusations do provide opportunities to discuss what I am actually doing in this book. I try to understand the Roman worldview of divine status and divine sonship and also the singular role of the emperor figure in that worldview. These points of emphasis allow me to articulate a new way (as far as I am aware) of understanding the metaphor of adoption in early Christianity, specifically by grounding it in the actual adoptive practices and concomitant family ideology of the Roman Empire. In chapters 1, 2, and 3, I hope the reader will see where biblical scholarship has fallen short in its analysis of ancient "son of God" concepts and how scholarship on Roman religion and social practices can help chart a new path. Through the arguments of chapters 4 and 5, I hope the reader will come to imagine why certain manifestations of Christology—now labeled pejoratively as "low" or "adoptionist"—might have resonated culturally with many Christians in the Roman world. I ask my readers to try to read part of the Gospel of Mark anew, in a differently emphasized historical context. Mark's ingenuity in crafting the first narrative Christology ought to be understood independently, rather than in contrast to other "high" narrative Christologies or in the terms of later theological debates. Therefore, my readings of Mark and other ante-Nicene texts are neither Arian nor proto-Arian nor crypto-Arian. What I want to emphasize is the irrelevance of fourth-century philosophical concerns to the milieu of first-century Christianity. My readings of the early texts attempt to imagine nascent Christology before the cosmologies of the Nicene era were relevant. In the third and fourth centuries, when these cosmologies do become relevant, the understanding of divine sonship changes accordingly, as I elaborate in my final chapter.

By this book I do not intend to make any criticism of or contribution to systematic or constructive Christian theology. The Gospel of Mark and most of the other texts I interpret play limited roles in those enterprises anyway. Rather, I intend to offer historically informed and, I think, new interpretations of these texts for scholars of the New Testament and early Christianity, while hopefully adding analysis of some benefit to Roman historians along the way. These interpretations will stand or fall based on their appeal to the practitioners of historical-critical methods. If theologians want to consider them, that is their prerogative, but it is not my intention. In any case, whether theologians consider my arguments or not, they should have nothing to fear from them. The early Christian perspective on Jesus' divine sonship did change over time, but this fact should not impede theological discourse or orthodox faith. As Raymond Brown once affirmed: "orthodox Christians need have no conflict with such a thesis of a growing retrospective evaluation of Jesus, provided it is understood that the evaluation involves an appreciation of a reality that was already there—Jesus was who he was during his lifetime, even if it took his followers centuries to develop a partially adequate theological vocabulary in which to articulate his greatness."[1]

■ THE WRITING ON THE WALL

A few years ago, before he passed away, I had the honor and pleasure of sharing a lunch conversation with Jaroslav Pelikan, an inimitable scholar and teacher. When he found out that I was both Catholic and a biblical scholar, he smiled and asked, "Now what do you have hanging over your desk where you work?" I described the icon that hangs there, portraying Jesus as ἡ ἄμπελος, "the vine," and the disciples as the branches. "Well that's fine," he retorted, "but what you *should* have is a framed copy of *Divino Afflante Spiritu*! It's your Magna Carta!" Prof. Pelikan was referring to the 1943 encyclical of Pope Pius XII, which promoted biblical studies in the Roman Catholic Church. Among other things, the encyclical endorsed what has come to be called "historical criticism," which was encouraged in this way: "Let the interpreter, then, with all care and without neglecting any light derived from recent research, endeavor to determine the peculiar character and circumstances of the sacred writer, the age in which he lived, the sources written or oral to which he had recourse, and the forms of expression he employed."[2]

In my work, I follow this tradition and, employing the "light derived from recent research," explore in a new way the historical context within which the life of Jesus was first narrated, interpreted, and celebrated. But first I must offer a belated apology to Prof. Pelikan. I am sorry to say that I never had *Divino Afflante Spiritu* framed and hung over my desk. The text is just too long, and I like the icon besides. However, to the side of my desk is another document close to the heart of Prof. Pelikan. In parallel columns of Greek and Latin hangs the Nicene Creed, one of the texts that inspired Prof. Pelikan's four-volume work, *Creeds and Confessions of Faith in the Christian Tradition*, the last of his *magna opera*. If the aforementioned encyclical undergirds my work, perhaps the Nicene Creed hangs over it. For it was through reflection on three of that text's words—γεννηθέντα οὐ ποιηθέντα, *natum non factum*, begotten not made—that I began to ask the questions leading to this book.[3] How did the issue of "begotten" or "made" arise as a chief dispute concerning divine sonship? Before Nicea, how would the terms "begotten" and "made" have resonated in the Roman context? What worldview might have encouraged some committed Christians to think of Jesus as an "adopted" or "made" son of God? How did that view relate to their own sense of themselves as sons and daughters of God? Is there ancient evidence we have overlooked? By pursuing these questions, we can breathe new life into a dead metaphor.

1   Divine Sonship Before Nicea

Biblical Scholarship on "Son of God"

> Son of God ... eternally begotten of the Father ... begotten, not made.
> —NICENE CREED

> In the earliest period of Christianity "Son of God" was not an obvious
> vehicle of a christology of incarnation or pre-existence.
> —JAMES D. G. DUNN

The meaning of "son of God" has become stable over time and through repeated use by Christians. We all think we know what it means, and indeed, we do know what it meant for the theologians gathered at the Council of Nicea. Scholars have at least agreed on the conceptual meanings of the key phrases in that fourth-century debate: the Son was eternally begotten of the Father, begotten not made, and though they were two, they are also one-in-being. I argue, however, that our understanding of divine sonship in early Christianity—especially in the Roman world before Nicea—relies on some false assumptions and untested anachronisms. That is to say, when examining the term "son of God" and the concept of divine sonship in the New Testament era, biblical scholars have too often conducted their research within the later framework of fourth-century Christian thought. The elite philosophical debates of the Nicene era have so dominated scholarly discourse about divine sonship that it has been difficult to examine "son of God" language in its first-century context. Instead of searching for the most relevant meaning of the term in the immediate milieu of nascent Christianity, scholars have often posed the questions that Athanasius and Arius asked centuries later: Did "son of God" imply absolute divinity? When did the son come into existence? But these questions were not relevant—indeed, were hardly even considered—in the first-century Roman world, the sociopolitical context of nascent Christianity. And though the central Nicene question, "Was the son begotten or made?," *was* relevant in the first-century context, it meant something quite different at that time.[1]

In this chapter and the next, I will argue that our understanding of divine sonship in the first-century context of early Christianity can be rejuvenated by setting aside the Nicene framework and interacting with current scholarship on Roman religion and emperor worship. I contend that the most relevant single datum that would help to illuminate divine sonship in early Christianity—the divine sonship of the Roman emperor—has been ignored or rejected by most biblical scholars. The argument begins with a critique of biblical scholarship on "son of God" language. By organizing and evaluating previous interpretations of divine sonship in the New Testament, this chapter begins to rethink the "son of God" in the Roman world.

In order to explain how my work fits in to the long history of scholarship on the New Testament and early Christianity, I have grouped selected scholars into four categories. The review will not march diachronically through a long series of authors and books, since that approach can prove soporific, but will instead classify scholars according to the method by which they deal with the "son of God" concept in the texts they interpret. I discuss the Nicene approach, narrative criticism, and the history-of-religion methods of Wilhelm Bousset, Martin Hengel, James Dunn, and Larry Hurtado. Then I explain a fourth method, employed by Adela Yarbro Collins, which listens for how the term "son of God" might have resonated in various cultural contexts of the ancient world. This will not be only a history of scholarship, but also an overture for my own scholarly argument. It will outline how this book builds on the research of the third and fourth groups but also attends to the ancient social practices undergirding father-son metaphors. That is to say, my argument begins presently, through the following re-appraisal of the available options for interpreting "son of God" in the historical contexts of early Christianity.

■ THE NICENE APPROACH

The first group includes scholars who write as if the concept of divine sonship no longer needs interpreting. For them, the "son of God" metaphor has become "dead," in the terminology of Paul Ricoeur. Like the dead metaphors, "foot" of a chair or "foot" of a mountain, everyone knows what "son of God" means—its meaning is stable. These same scholars can be quite careful and critical, however, about other terms of New Testament Christology, such as "son of man." This difference occurs because the term "son of man" is no longer in common use by Christians as a title for Jesus. Like "son of God," the term "son of man" is also dead, but not from repeated use. It is dead because it is *never* used. Therefore, scholars bring it to life again for modern readers of the New Testament, using all the exegetical methods available. For this, Christians and other interested readers are rightfully thankful. The term "son of God," on the other hand, is often treated *un*critically because its meaning has been stabilized through sixteen centuries of theological and liturgical use. It is not usually regarded as a metaphor at all, but as plain, nonfigurative speech.[2] By default, then, in the vast majority of interpretive moments, and unless an author makes a case otherwise, the term carries with it the philosophical and theological categories of the Nicene era.

For many scholars, Nicene christological thinking has become second nature and thus guides their analyses of New Testament texts. William L. Lane, for example, evokes the language of the Creed when interpreting the divine sonship portrayed by the Gospel of Mark: "Jesus did not *become* the Son of God, at baptism or at the transfiguration; he *is* the Son of God," and it is "an eternal and essential relationship."[3] Clear echoes of the Creed resound in Lane's analysis—the relationship is "eternal" (*eternally* begotten of the Father) and "essential" (*homoousios*, "one-in-being" or "of the same essence"). What is more, this quotation emphasizes the fundamentally Platonic concerns of Nicene-era theologians and their modern recapitulators. For Plato and his philosophical heirs, the chief metaphysical distinction divides the static world of Being from the dynamic world of Becoming. By the time of Nicea, many Christian theologians had embraced this philosophical distinction and, having all agreed that God the Father belonged on the side of Being, were then concerned with where the Son belonged.[4] Lane pronounces in favor of the orthodox: the Son *is*, he did not *become*.

More recently, Simon Gathercole has taken up the Platonic debate anew with regard to divine sonship in the Synoptic Gospels. In *The Preexistent Son*, he argues that "the preexistence of Christ can be found in the Synoptic Gospels," precisely the place where most biblical scholars would not look for such a doctrine.[5] When commenting on the Gospel of Mark, Gathercole describes Jesus' divine sonship with the following terms: it is "beyond a merely functional sonship possessed by someone with otherwise entirely natural origins," having instead a "supernatural, transcendent origin."[6] The Son "participates in the same reality as the angels and the Father."[7] His concern here is thus metaphysical in Platonic terms: is the Son natural or supernatural, mundane or transcendent, earthly or heavenly?[8] (The language of "participation in reality" would find a perfect home in a philosophy course on Plato.) In Gathercole's own words, on which side of the "God/Creation divide" does Jesus exist? Being or Becoming?

But such questions are anachronistic when asked of the New Testament era (with the possible exceptions of John and Hebrews). Do we have any reason to believe that the Synoptic authors or original audiences thought about Jesus in such terms? At the conclusion of his "prolegomena," Gathercole attempts this *reductio ad absurdum* argument: "it would in fact be strange," he writes, "if Jesus were not regarded as preexistent. He would then be a divine, heavenly, space-transcending figure who was somehow not preexistent."[9] Indeed, in a Platonic philosophical worldview, his *reductio* argument works. But in the New Testament era, and among every non-philosopher in the Roman world, the argument fails. In *this* worldview, there were figures regarded as divine, heavenly, and even space-transcending who were not considered preexistent or eternally existent. The problem of Jesus' divine sonship has been created by our seeing that sonship only in the terms of Nicea.

Another way of framing my critique is by contrasting protological and eschatological divine sonship. Some biblical scholars rightly interpret the divine sonship of Jesus in eschatological terms; what mattered to first-century followers of Jesus was not the (protological) origin of his divine sonship, but its (eschatological) power. As son of God, Jesus had power to usher in God's kingdom and to populate it with other sons and daughters of God. In the words of Richard Bauckham, "Jesus understood the Fatherhood of God as the eschatological relationship of God to men."[10] The divine sonship of Jesus means precisely his making other sons and daughters for God. Bauckham also argues, perhaps unintentionally, against the Platonic framework by saying, "Neither in the Synoptics nor in John do we find that sonship is static being: sonship is a relationship to be fulfilled in mission. . . . Christology may not conceive of the sonship of Jesus simply as the timeless being of the eternal Son. Jesus cannot be said to be the Son independently of his mission: the two are inseparable."[11] Eschatological sonship is grounded in the New Testament texts and provides a more cogent interpretative framework than that of Nicea. As we will see later, it also coheres with the understanding of divine sonship in the Roman worldview.

In short, most biblical scholars use the term "son of God" without explaining what they mean by it, thus leaving readers to infer that it means for them basically what it has come to mean from Nicea to the modern day. I have offered only a couple examples to represent a large segment of New Testament scholarship. This Nicene position, though usually implied unknowingly in the process of exegesis, is also consciously defended by a small cadre of scholars.

▪ INSIGHTS FROM NARRATIVE CRITICISM

A second group of scholars treats divine sonship in the Gospels through narrative criticism. By narrative criticism of the Gospels, I mean a method that regards each Gospel as a finished, whole story, whose meaning is best articulated through precise analysis of the story's narrative features (plot, characterization, point of view, etc.), with minimal reference to data external to the story.[12] This method focuses on the hermeneutical stance of the "implied reader," described by Jack Dean Kingsbury as "the imaginary person in whom the intention of the text is to be thought of as always reaching its fulfillment."[13] I will review here exemplary applications of this method to divine sonship in each of the Synoptic Gospels. Each of these offers a challenge to the Nicene "son of God" concept passed down through theology and liturgy.

Donald Verseput's analysis of divine sonship in Matthew begins with research questions similar to my own: although the title "son of God" is universally regarded as important for Christology, Verseput expresses surprise that "the actual *content* of this expression has of late received comparatively little attention from many of those concerned to establish its importance."[14] Verseput then persuasively argues— contrary to the untested assumptions of most readers—that divine sonship for Matthew is not related to his distinctive narration of Jesus' conception and birth. "Although possessing every opportunity to do so, the First Evangelist actually avoids drawing any direct connection between the miraculous conception and the divine Sonship of Jesus."[15] The son of God is *not* "he who was begotten by God"—at least, not in *this* text, not in *this* century.

By examining the entire narrative, Verseput's exegesis challenges the *status quo* and coheres with several criticisms outlined above. He shows how Matthew's vision of divine sonship does not look primarily backward to begetting but forward to the eschaton. The Gospel "appears unconcerned with the pre-temporal existence of Jesus," but he is indeed "the eschatological representative of the Father . . . qualified to bring eschatological deliverance to men."[16] This eschatological sonship is not a metaphysical essence. Contradicting the Platonic framework, Verseput writes, "the *primary* function which leads the Evangelist to exalt Jesus' Sonship role is not to be found in such static speculations, but rather in the opportunity which the divine Sonship offered to witness to the reality of the messianic mission."[17] Jesus' divine sonship is a functional, superhuman power—a power over the inheritance of God's kingdom and to make other sons and daughters for God in the new age.[18] This clarification of Jesus' divine sonship as dynamic is not to deny, however, the "intimate" and "unique" relationship between Father and Son, which Matthew has emphasized. In Matthew's worldview, the intimacy between Father and Son is expressed and proven through Jesus' obedience to the will of his Father. Jesus is uniquely endowed with spirit and power, uniquely sent to make children for the kingdom, and intimately bonded to God in will.

So is Matthew not interested in the origins of Jesus? To be sure, Matthew is very interested in where Jesus came from, his *genesis*.[19] But his Davidic sonship is more important than his divine sonship, at least as far as the narrative itself permits us to see. The crucial account of Jesus' infancy narrative emphasizes his legitimacy as a son of David, and its ending reveals "the crux of the Matthean concern: Jesus is adopted into the kingly line of David at the behest of God."[20] Matthew never defends that Jesus is rightly called God's son, though he certainly assumes his audience will agree with that designation. But he does labor to show how Jesus is rightly David's son, a relationship legitimized through his adoption by Joseph, himself a "son of David" in this text (1:16, 20, 24–25).[21] The focus on Davidic sonship does not stop after the family leaves Bethlehem. Scholars consistently show how "Matthew has from the beginning to the end of his Gospel thrust the image of Jesus as the royal Davidic Messiah to the forefront."[22]

Scholarly attention to the Gospel of Mark has taken a different tack, with consensus that the characterization of Jesus as God's son is crucial to Mark's overall portrayal. In *The Christology of Mark's Gospel*, Jack Dean Kingsbury argues that, despite the greater quantity of the terms "son of man" and "messiah," the term "son of God" best captures the thrust of Jesus' characterization throughout the narrative.[23] Previous scholars had downplayed divine sonship in Mark, contending that Mark depicted a suffering son of man, thereby trying to oppose or correct his readers' idea of a glorious son of God. Kingsbury responds, however, that "God's understanding of Jesus is normative in Mark's story," so God's declarations of his sonship at the baptism and transfiguration govern the characterization of Jesus throughout.[24] Kingsbury is less concerned with the content of the term "son of God" than with its proclaimers—*who* calls Jesus God's son? Throughout the life of Jesus, human beings do not. Kingsbury therefore considers the famous "messianic secret" to be an inadequate description of Mark's point of view.[25] The secret of Jesus' identity was not his messiahship but his sonship; it is the *sonship* secret.

The Roman centurion, as the only human character to make the declaration of divine sonship, thus takes center stage at the Gospel's conclusion. The secrecy motif "is so to guide the action of the story that the way God 'thinks' about Jesus" during his life should ultimately "be espoused at the end by human characters."[26] To the question, "But why a Roman centurion?," Kingsbury unfortunately does not offer a response. He had brought divine sonship to the foreground of Mark's Gospel but leaves its further interpretation open to future scholars.

Charles G. Dennison uses the baptism narrative of Luke as a key witness to divine sonship and asks the question, "*How* is Jesus the Son of God?"[27] His narrative-critical approach draws out a crucial tension in the portrayal of Jesus' sonship: it is a *unique* relationship and yet *unifies* him with those who would become the church. From birth to baptism, from humiliation to exaltation, Luke depicts Jesus as the exemplar of the divine sonship available to his followers. Jesus was not a static being but one who traveled a path of salvation. Dennison goes so far as to interpret Jesus' divine sonship with the outline of traditional Reformed soteriology:

> In his union with the people, Jesus travels their road of humiliation to glory; . . . Their need dictates his experience. According to the traditional formulation of the *ordo salutis*, their need is calling (regeneration), faith, repentance, justification, *adoption*, sanctification and glorification. All of this Jesus undergoes in the work of salvation; the baptism is a proleptical experience which comprehends the character of his mission. In his baptism we see a picture of Jesus' vicarious experience of redemption. If then baptism is related to redemption and therefore adoption, it can be said that the word of the Father, "Thou art My beloved Son . . .," suggests adoption even for Jesus. In the resurrection, Jesus became Son in a way he never was before.[28]

Yet his is no "low" Christology, nor is it adoptionist in the classical sense, since Dennison affirms Jesus' uniqueness as God's Son and as God. "In Jesus, God has given himself," he writes, and yet "[Jesus'] Sonship is replete with humanity. Jesus is the Son of God as we are and as we shall be in conformity to him."[29] This tension in Luke's narrative, which exhibits a "both-and" vision of Jesus' divine sonship, is not welcome in the "either/or" dichotomies of later, Nicea-inspired Christology.[30] Dennison's narrative interpretation imagines divine sonship as far richer and more complex than Platonic philosophical categories allow. Narratives are never easily transferred into dogmas, and Luke's is no exception.[31] Furthermore, Dennison points out that "neither Justin [Martyr] nor Clement [of Alexandria]" saw Luke's understanding of Jesus' baptism as "a threat to orthodoxy."[32] It is only after Nicea that Jesus' divine sonship has been construed as the marker of a static, preexistent being.

■ THE *RELIGIONSGESCHICHTLICHE SCHULE* AND ITS HEIRS

A third group of scholars has examined "son of God" language as a key aspect of early Christology by using the so-called history-of-religion method. Historical analysis had been sporadically brought to biblical texts through the eighteenth and nineteenth centuries, and a seminal focus of historical inquiry was achieved at the beginning of the twentieth. A particular group of scholars at Göttingen, who straddled the turn of that century, shared enough data, methods, and presuppositions to be characterized together as the *religionsgeschichtliche Schule*, or "history-of-religion school."[33] New data—in the form of manuscript discoveries and philological research on Greek, Egyptian, Iranian, and other "Hellenistic" religions—partially fueled the school of thought. These data were incorporated into a comparative method, through which certain terms, concepts, and narratives of Hellenistic religions were isolated and magnified according to their perceived resemblances to the New Testament. Perceived resemblances were rarely left as such, though, but were framed as decisive influences on the development of early Christianity. The method was thus undergirded by two key presuppositions: first, the historical scholar ought to arrange resemblances between terms and concepts into an orderly process of *influence*;[34] second, the final result of historical analysis should provide a narrative of *Christian* religious development.[35] That is, the one "religion" of the history-of-religion school was Christianity, a great river that accumulated the influx, both water and silt, from many tributaries.[36]

The "brightest star in the galaxy of the history of religion school" was Wilhelm Bousset.[37] His greatest and most lasting work, *Kyrios Christos*, charts the development of early Christian veneration for Jesus, from the primitive Palestinian community's acclamation of the "son of man" as a preexistent, heavenly Messiah to the later Gentile communities' confession of Jesus as "Lord."[38] The "son of God" title is not neglected, though, since Bousset interprets it as a less frequent but important concept. He begins his chronology with "the primitive Palestinian community," to which he gains access through the Synoptic Gospels. For them the "son of man" concept is dominant, and divine sonship is less important. Though he admits its importance for the Gospel of Mark, it is not for Bousset the dominant feature of earliest Christology. The term "son of God" is used rarely by Jesus; according to Bousset, it contradicts "the sensitivities of Old Testament piety. It has a much too mythical ring which stands in contradiction with the rigid monotheism of the Old Testament."[39] Bousset dismisses the evidence of the concept in pious Jewish texts like the Psalms and the Wisdom of Solomon; and when he cannot dismiss "son of God" language easily, he argues for its origin in a "servant of God" tradition (the Hebrew עבד and Greek παῖς can mean both "servant" and "son").[40]

In the Gentile community, however, the title "son of God" achieves "undisputed dominance."[41] According to Bousset, the term is both metaphysical, satisfying the theological speculations of Paul and John, and mythological, satisfying the popular imagination. Though he does not phrase it in this way, Bousset seems to argue that "son of God" gained prominence as Christianity spread because it performed wide-ranging rhetorical work; more than other concepts, it allowed Jesus to be many things to many people.[42] Turning to the "son of God" concept in Paul's letters, Bousset conjectures that the term "could be an independent creation of Paul" because it "points to theological reflection" on "the relation of the two beings, God and Christ."[43] Whether Paul drew on older Jewish ideas in his articulation of divine sonship is unimportant for Bousset. What is crucial for him is how Paul presents the son of God as "a supraterrestrial being who stands in the closest metaphysical connection with God," who has a "heavenly nature."[44] Bousset does not give much evidence from Paul's letters to defend such assertions; as the prooftext for his definition of divine sonship, he footnotes Romans 1:4 ("appointed son of God in power"), a phrase which on its own cannot bear the weight of Bousset's claim (and some scholars would say contradicts it, as I discuss in chapter 5). His argument for metaphysical divine sonship is made more confusing when he admits Paul is *not* concerned with Jesus' "divine pretemporal essence" but rather with Jesus' *death* as God's son.[45] If Paul is more focused on Jesus' "actuality" than his "essence"—the analysis itself is built on a Platonic heritage—then how can Paul be said to portray divine sonship as supraterrestrial and metaphysical?[46] Is it not eschatological and actual?

Furthermore, Bousset states that "son of God" was chosen by Paul to inform "his Hellenistic congregations, in a formula current among them, how the relation of God the Father and Christ was to be grasped conceptually."[47] I applaud Bousset's openness to formulas current among Paul's Greco-Roman audience, but there are at least two problems with his analysis: First, the majority of people designated as "sons of gods" in Greek were not heavenly beings in the philosophical sense that Bousset implies. Egyptian worship practices do provide some evidence for heavenly divine families, but most sons of gods were heroes and rulers who accrued such titles during their lives. Second, Bousset dismisses the evidence of Roman emperor worship, even though he admits *divi filius* / θεοῦ υἱός was a "well-known formula." He does not address the evidence because he believes emperor worship was not prominent at the time of Paul and the title had "a very concrete and well-defined content" for the emperor.[48] Recent scholarship on Roman religion shows, however, that the emperor was venerated much earlier than was thought in Bousset's era. Furthermore, chapter 2 will argue that the concrete content of emperor worship is not irrelevant to the divine sonship of Jesus. For Bousset, the "son of God" is "the present exalted Lord . . . venerate[d] in the cultus."[49] That description also fits the Roman emperor.

Regarding the Johannine writings, Bousset considers divine sonship to be the central christological characterization. "Son of God" is "the actual title with which John paraphrases Jesus' position of honor"; it is "at the center of the proclamation"; and with it "the Christian confession is summarized."[50] Yet Bousset's argument about the content of the term is surprisingly sparse.[51] He presumes from the outset that the title has "a metaphysical significance" for a "supraterrestrial" being, just as he had presumed with the Pauline writings.[52] He then focuses on texts indicating the unity of Father and Son, but does not entertain ways in which "unity" could mean something other than the preexistent, metaphysical, essential unity clarified at Nicea centuries later.[53] Instead, he presumes the argument has been made already and moves on to reflect on Johannine piety, a "mystical piety" sharing "a common soil" with texts from the *Corpus Hermeticum*.[54] The son of God, while sojourning on earth, is the mystical mediator of present salvation between the Father and the world.[55] Most importantly for Bousset's historical chronology, the Johannine writings signify the time when divine sonship and divinity "move very close together."[56] Through Paul and John, "the dogma of the deity of Christ is on the march."[57]

While the ideas of Paul or John might titillate theological minds, the popular imagination is kindled instead by the narrative of the miraculous birth, which Bousset consigns to the late first century (Matthew, Luke, and Ignatius).[58] As a contrast to the "supernaturally, metaphysically structured Christology" proper to Paul and John, the miraculous birth story is a "natural, crudely drawn interpretation which suggests itself to the simple mind, in particular on the basis of Hellenistic mythology."[59] For him, it "represents a popular coarsening of the idea of the supraterrestrial Son of God."[60] Bousset's language implies disdain for the materiality of the myth—how dare they take the term "son of God" so literally? The myth of this *enfant* is so *terrible*, the mature Bousset becomes embarrassed and cannot bring himself to blame early Christians for it: "one will not be able to avoid the conclusion that influences of the surrounding Hellenistic milieu were exerted upon this folk theology of the infant Christianity."[61] A crude Hellenistic influx had muddied the pure waters of the Christian river—infancy narratives for the infantile *Volk*. Bousset was certainly pleased that the perspectives of Paul and John, which he viewed as more mature, eventually came to dominate Christian thought.

After Bousset, the next major work on divine sonship and the origins of Christology came from Martin Hengel.[62] His inaugural lecture at Tübingen, which later became a short, pithy monograph, criticizes the findings of the *religionsgeschichtliche Schule* from Bousset to Bultmann.[63] He strongly rejects their theories of Hellenistic influence on the development of early Christology. In repudiating their data and conclusions, Hengel does not, however, challenge the methods undergirding the work. On the contrary, he retains the *religionsgeschichtlich* methods and presuppositions of his forebears but applies them to a different set of data—the texts of early Judaism.

Using the data from the Hebrew Bible and Hellenistic Judaism, Hengel's analysis seeks a point of origin for "son of God" and a historical process of its development through the New Testament era—where did the term come from and how did it travel through time? The book's subtitle is "The Origin of Christology and the History of Jewish-Hellenistic Religion," and its stated task is "the difficult question of the historical derivation of the title Son of God."[64] He seeks to chart this "development"—an "inner trend in christological thought"—by "moving back from Paul to the origins of Christian belief."[65] He checks and rejects the older *religionsgeschichtlich* parallels offered as precursors to the Pauline doctrine, such as mystery cults, ruler cults, θεῖος ἀνήρ traditions, and Gnostic redeemer myths. "All this gets us no closer to the origin of christology."[66]

Most of his deft arguments against supposed parallels hit the mark, but his dismissal of the imperial "son of God" title is based on rather flimsy reasoning. He initially grants some importance to the imperial title, correctly noting that the term "son of God" is "relatively rare in the Hellenistic world and, with one exception [the emperor], is never used as a title."[67] He then contends, however, that the *divi filius* / θεοῦ υἱός title "was no more a serious influence on the conceptuality of the earliest Christianity . . . than the title Kyrios used of the ruler, . . . or the εὐαγγέλια which appears on individual imperial inscriptions. This official, secular state religion was at best a negative stimulus, not a model."[68] The first problem with this very brief argument is how it treats "son of God" and "kyrios" as if they were used similarly in the Roman world. Hengel himself acknowledges how rare the term "son of God" was in the Greco-Roman world, whereas "kyrios" was a matter of everyday speech, from the simplest master/slave relationship all the way up to rulers and gods. The imperial use of "son of God" is relevant because of its rarity as a title for an individual combined with its wide dissemination as a title used by the emperor. As for the εὐαγγέλια inscriptions, recent scholars disagree with Hengel's dismissal of their relevance. Many argue that Christian usage of the term εὐαγγέλιον was influenced by the public announcements of imperial activities and travels;[69] but even if it was not a source of Christian usage, it was certainly "*the background against which distinctively Christian usage was forged and heard.*"[70] Finally, Hengel admits that the imperial title, described unusually as part of a "secular religion," was perhaps a "negative stimulus" of Christian usage. I interpret him to mean that Christians disagreed with and challenged the titles of emperor worship; imperial usage was not a model to be emulated but perhaps a foil to be rejected.[71] If I am correct in how to interpret Hengel here, he has granted imperial usage much more power than scholars before him did. A "negative stimulus" is negative not because it lacks formative power, but because it repels.[72] If early Christian usage of "son of God" or "kyrios" developed in part because Christians found imperial usage repulsive, then imperial usage certainly had an influence.

Hengel rejects Greco-Roman parallels to early Christology; instead he finds Hellenistic Jewish texts to be the primary sources for early Christian thinking.[73] He follows "son of God" language as it pops up periodically in Sirach, Wisdom of Solomon, Joseph and Aseneth, 3 Enoch, various wisdom traditions, and especially Philo. From these examples, Hengel draws out three streams of influence: the "thought-patterns" of "pre-existence, mediation at creation, and sending into the world."[74] Using a "mosaic collection of Jewish sources," he cobbles together "a hypothetical reconstruction of the development of the Son of God christology in the brief twenty years" between the death of Jesus and the ministry of Paul.[75] When he applies the "thought-patterns" of Hellenistic Judaism to the New Testament evidence, Hengel concludes that "son of God" is "primarily an explicit expression of Jesus' *exaltation.*"[76] If that is so, how did the notions of pre-existence enter the stream of Christian doctrine? He argues that the Son's pre-existence developed as a matter of "consistency": because the exalted status of Jesus needed to be distinguished from all the other intermediary figures in early Jewish cosmology (angels, Logos, Wisdom, etc.), there was "an inner necessity" to bring Jesus as far backward in time, and as close to God, as possible.[77]

Hengel's contribution is, on the whole, deeply learned and contributes positively for our continued study of the topic. If we take Bousset's analysis (gradual development, rooted in Hellenistic sources) together with Hengel's (rapid development, rooted in Hellenistic Jewish sources), we have the raw material to create an overview of the best theories of early Christology.

Thanks to James Dunn, such a synthesis exists. The foundational chapter of *Christology in the Making* manages to incorporate the most relevant data from Jewish and Greco-Roman texts into a clear history of the divine sonship concept in the New Testament.[78] Among this third group of scholars, Dunn is the most self-aware regarding his own method: he combines the search for "historical context of meaning" with the chronological interest in "conceptuality in transition."[79] Thus, although he is critical of the original *religionsgeschichtliche Schule*, his method bears some similarities. The focus on "historical context of meaning" is familiar enough, and Dunn explains it better than most. He interprets texts in their broad cultural contexts and their narrower particular circumstances of composition and delivery. Later theological considerations are especially to be avoided, as much as possible. By "conceptuality in transition," Dunn means to acknowledge the changing meanings of words over time. To trace how the term "son of God" travels through time is necessarily to chart the conceptual changes associated with the term. This is done best when interpreters attempt to limit themselves to "the possibilities available at the time of writing, to take a stand within the inevitably limited horizon of writer and readers, who did not and could not know how the words written were going to be taken and understood in subsequent years and decades."[80] In other words, Jesus did not know there would be a Paul to proclaim his divine sonship; Paul did not know that the divine sonship he *proclaimed* would come to be *narrated*; Mark did not know that Logos Christology would become the most prominent corollary of divine sonship, and so on.

The product of this method is a detailed description of how the term "son of God" and the concept of divine sonship developed in the first century of Christianity. First, Dunn establishes the most relevant "historical context of meaning." He mines the same raw materials as previous scholars did, noting especially his debt to Hengel, but finds more similarities between Jewish and Hellenistic "son of God" usage than had been previously noted.[81] Usage in diverse cultures overlapped especially with regard to kings or rulers, who were considered divine sons in many ancient societies. Furthermore, royal divine sonship frequently intermingled with notions of divine status. According to Dunn, "divine" and "god" were amply applied to human beings in Greco-Roman and Jewish contexts, such that "son of God," "divine," and "god" were interrelated and not infrequent ascriptions of human beings. He finds, in the end, "little or no good evidence from the period prior to Christianity's beginnings that the Ancient Near East seriously entertained the idea of a god or son of god descending from heaven to become a human being," but he does portray a diverse usage of "son of God" language that tends toward exaltation and blurs our modern distinctions between humanity and divinity.[82]

His trajectory of "conceptuality in transition" begins with the historical Jesus and carries through the New Testament era. Using the Synoptic Gospels as his initial data, Dunn describes Jesus' divine sonship as "intimate," "distinctive," and "eschatological"; it was also a relationship upon which the sonship of his disciples depended. Jesus' sonship was "unique" precisely in the sense that it was eschatological.[83] Next Dunn moves to the earliest post-Easter confessions, which he finds preserved in Romans 1:3 and Acts 13:33. These imply that "the first Christians thought of Jesus' divine sonship principally as a role and status he had entered upon, been appointed to at his resurrection."[84] Paul's own teaching did not change this view very much. Divine sonship is still eschatological, and the "God sent his son" texts should be read in that light; Dunn interprets "sent" as a divine commission and not as a sending from heaven.[85] As for the narrative characterizations in the Synoptic Gospels, Jesus' divine sonship means progressively an "anointing with the Spirit ... with a view to his suffering and dying" (Mark); a focus on "his conception and attributing that to the (creative) power of the Spirit" (Matthew); and a confirmation of divine sonship from the moment of conception without denying other traditional moments of emphasis, such as resurrection and baptism (Luke-Acts).[86] Up to this point, as Christianity has traveled forward through time, Jesus' divine sonship has moved backward—from resurrection to death to baptism to birth.[87] Next, with the Epistle to the Hebrews, Dunn thinks discussions of pre-existence may be appropriate; he concludes, however, that this supposed pre-existence is not a "personal" pre-existence and must "be set within the context of [the author's] indebtedness to Platonic idealism."[88] For the concept of a personal pre-existence of God's Son, only the Gospel of John satisfies Dunn's critical judgments. For John, Jesus' divine sonship existed before his birth and is neither "given" nor "enhanced," neither "interrupted" nor "disturbed," by resurrection, death, baptism, or birth.[89] Jesus' intimate relationship with God, as Son to Father, existed before his birth, continued undisturbed on earth, and endures eternally.

Through this *Geschichte* of divine sonship, Dunn makes some noteworthy advances. First, he demonstrates the diversity of perspectives on divine sonship in the New Testament and cautions against leveling their differences. Second, he persuasively argues that, in the historical context of meaning, the term "son of God" was "not an obvious vehicle of a christology of incarnation or pre-existence."[90] For almost all of the New Testament authors, the idea of pre-existent divine sonship "does not yet seem to have crossed the threshold of thought, is neither affirmed nor denied."[91] We ought not assume that Johannine or other Christologies were available to Paul or Mark and rejected by them. In the final analysis, Dunn is careful to point out that his christological narrative does not simply ascend over time from "low" to "high" Christology. The earliest versions of Jesus' divine sonship may not delineate later orthodox dogma, but neither do they proclaim a "mere man."[92] From the beginning, Jesus had a cosmos-altering significance as "son of God": his sonship was uniquely intimate and eschatological, inaugurating a new and eternal family of God through the resurrection.

After Dunn's major contribution to New Testament Christology, what remained to be done? The final scholar to be reviewed in this group is Larry Hurtado, whose many publications address similar questions to those of Bousset, Hengel, and Dunn. He is concerned above all with early Christology, in which divine sonship plays a key role. Specifically, Hurtado has tried to demarcate first-century Jewish monotheism and articulate how "devotion" to Jesus came to be incorporated into what he calls "binitarian" monotheism. As a method, he claims to be interested in the "practices" or "religious experience" of the earliest Christians. Since he wants to recover the earliest possible Christian practices, he looks almost exclusively at Jewish, not gentile, practices as his data. The focus on early Judaism aligns him with Dunn and especially Hengel. Hurtado's chosen predecessor, however, is Bousset; the title of his massive *Lord Jesus Christ* plainly invokes the former's *Kyrios Christos*. He obviously reveres Bousset's work, even as he intends his own work to supersede it. Taken as a whole corpus, Hurtado's work is representative of "a new *religionsgeschichtliche Schule*," which appropriates most of the aims of the old one but focuses instead on the "Jewish religious matrix of the Christian movement."[93] What is more, if the old *Schule* breathed the air of modern liberalism, the new one is imbued with a spirit of neo-orthodoxy. Hurtado's work is, if not apologetics, unapologetically Christian, with an emphasis on orthodox Christology. Such convictions are present on the first page, as it were, since he dedicates *Lord Jesus Christ* to the "EHCC" (acronym for "Early High Christology Club"), an informal group of scholars of which he is a co-founder.

The content of *Lord Jesus Christ* has been summarized in dozens of scholarly reviews and need not be rehearsed in detail here.[94] Overall Hurtado has three interweaving theses to demonstrate. First, devotion to Jesus arose "phenomenally early" and "cannot be restricted to a secondary stage of religious development or explained as the product of extraneous forces."[95] He describes Jesus-devotion as a "volcano-like" eruption, at the earliest period possible.[96] (For Hurtado, perhaps the Christian 'river' is better portrayed as a lava flow.) Second, "devotion to Jesus was exhibited in an unparalleled intensity and diversity of expression, for which we have no true analogy in the religious environment of the time.... [It] is not one example of a class of analogous religious phenomena in comparable groups."[97] The comparative approach of the old *Schule* will be avoided. Third, devotion to Jesus, "which includes reverencing him as divine, was offered and articulated characteristically within a firm stance of exclusivist monotheism."[98]

Was divine sonship a force in this christological eruption? Yes, but in a different way than that depicted by the old *Schule*. Though Hurtado does not dispute that "divine sonship was a category in the pagan religious environment of the Roman era," he dissents from Bousset's interpretation of this fact.[99] The "son of God" idea was not "a clever marketing device used by Paul" for the Gentiles—in Hurtado's rather reductionistic summary of Bousset's analysis—but actually "derive[d] its meaning from *biblical and Jewish traditions*."[100] For Paul, according to Hurtado, divine sonship "communicated Jesus' unique status and intimate relationship with God" by alluding especially to the enthronement of the Israelite king and the binding of Isaac.[101] In addition, Hurtado rightly follows Bauckham and Dunn on two key points: he emphasizes the eschatological aspect of divine sonship[102] and also describes Jesus' divine sonship as "the pattern for, and basis of, the enfranchisement of Christians as 'sons of God.'"[103]

Hurtado is less persuasive in his treatment of divine sonship in the Gospels, especially the Synoptics. He approaches them chronologically, and already in Q he argues for a surprising construal of "son of God." Despite claiming to emphasize the Jewish tradition of divine sonship, which he admits has a "diverse background" and application, Hurtado declares that "son of God" in Q "connotes a transcendent status."[104] I am not certain where he finds this in the Jewish tradition, but in Q he finds it in the temptation narrative and the so-called "Johannine thunderbolt."[105] In the Gospel of Mark, divine sonship again equates to "transcendent status," "transcendent significance," or "even his 'intrinsic divinity.'"[106] A Platonic framework undergirds the analysis, such as when Hurtado concludes, regarding all the canonical Gospels, that 'son of man' "designates Jesus operating in the human/historical sphere," and 'son of God,' on the other hand, "discloses the higher significance of who this human figure really is."[107] Does Hurtado mean to imply that Jesus operating as a human, in history, is not who he *really* is? Such a claim would verge on docetism.

Hurtado's view of all four Gospels seems to be governed by the Christology of John's. Indeed, this is the only of the four to receive detailed analysis of sonship language in his book. As in the Synoptics, divine sonship language in John means "who [he] *really* is" and "from *whence* he really comes"; but with John's Gospel, at least Hurtado provides exegetical defenses for giving divine sonship "transcendent significance."[108] His analysis of John is mostly laudable, but it still seems, in the end, only to serve Nicene Christology. The crucial Jewish use of "son of God" as an earthly, royal title is mentioned but subordinated to texts supporting a heavenly characterization.[109] More importantly, Hurtado does not elaborate on the most distinctive aspect of divine sonship in the Johannine writings—the fact that Christians too have a begotten divine sonship.[110] Hurtado argues that John distinguishes the unique divine sonship of Jesus, "the Son" (ὁ υἱός), from the divine sonship of Christians, "the children" (τὰ τέκνα). Yet the term "children" is different from "the Son" in number and gender, not nature. Hurtado does not explore how, for John, the same metaphor of begetting is used for both Jesus and his followers.[111] The tension in the dialogue with Nicodemus, for instance, should not be so easily resolved: Jesus is called "unique" (μονογενής, 3:16, 18), but others are also "begotten" from above (3:3–10). Thus, how can Jesus' begottenness be his uniqueness, according to John? This tension is not acknowledged by Hurtado because, in the end, he does not deal with "son of God" as a metaphor—for him its meaning is stable. The Platonic-Nicene conception of divine sonship provides the framework for his history of Christology.

Getting back to Hurtado's main theses: of the three, I can support the first. His book goes a long way toward challenging the "gradual development" narratives of previous scholars. I have strong objections, however, to his second and third theses. In both cases, Hurtado's shortcomings are errors of omission; however, they cannot be absolved by the customary "one can't cover everything" excuse. His book is exceptionally long, but more importantly, these omissions are crucially significant to his argument. By omitting well-known facts from the arguments toward his second and third theses, Hurtado has smoothed the path toward his own conclusions.

The third thesis omits contravening evidence when characterizing the Jewish context of Christ-devotion as maintaining "a firm stance of exclusivist mono-theism." My own criticisms on this point have been expressed well by other reviewers of Hurtado's work. William Horbury finds the line drawn by Hurtado between humanity and divinity to be too sharp. For example, Horbury criticizes him for "a series of interpretive decisions which tilt Jewish conceptions that might suggest complexity in the godhead" and "a neglect of the importance of spirits, divine and human, in the Jewish as well as gentile thought of the time."[112] Most people, whether Jews or Gentiles, did not have a Platonic conception of God's absolute transcendence; moreover, the intermediary beings common in the Greco-Roman world were too a part of Judaism, including spirits, angels, and demons—but also rulers, whether Jewish and Hellenistic kings or Roman emperors. With Bousset, Deissmann, and others, Horbury finds the "cultic praise of deities and rulers in the ancient world" to be of "comparable exuberance" to early Christian devotion.[113] The hints of this comparison have instigated my own work.

Regarding the "Jewish context of Christ-devotion," Hurtado's narrative usage of ancient "Jews" bears a peculiar resemblance to the narrative of John's Gospel. In that text, the infamous "Jews" appear about eighty times, as is well known. Everywhere Jesus goes, "the Jews" are there, usually to antagonize him. Hurtado also has a composite character popping up throughout his book: the "scrupulous Jews" or, more frequently, "devout Jews."[114] In previous work, Hurtado had tried out different characterizations; they were also "conscientious Jews" or "faithful Jews."[115] But by the time of his major work, and in subsequent work,[116] he has settled on the term "devout." (It is a good choice for his purposes—"conscientious" is too cumbersome, "faithful" too Christian, "scrupulous" too pejorative.) Though the moniker of these Jews is changeable, their essence is not: these are the "exclusivist monotheists," who are crucial to his argument, but the reader never finds out who they were historically or how representative they are of early Judaism. If, for John, "the Jews" were Jesus' foil—the negative "religious environment"—are "devout Jews" the positive "religious environment" for Hurtado?

Paula Fredriksen takes Hurtado to task on his idealization of early Judaism, arguing that the monotheism he imagines did not exist: "Ancient monotheism is about the imagined architecture of the numinous, not (certainly) its absolute population. [Hurtado] knows this, but when he turns to describing ancient Christologies or later heretics, he seems to forget."[117] In the same vein as my argument later in chapter 2, she writes: "Divinity was on a gradient all throughout this period and before and long after—probably up until the Scientific Revolution. That may make 'devotion to Jesus' seem less explosive or startling or revolutionary. Its oddness survives intact, I think, without the false impression created by defining monotheism as Hurtado does."[118] Both Horbury and Fredriksen thus encapsulate my criticisms of the third thesis vis-à-vis the "Jewish context." My analysis of the Greco-Roman context brings us to his second thesis.

Hurtado's second thesis, that there was "no true analogy" for Jesus-devotion "in the religious environment," also omits too much data. The main question is: *which* religious environment? Hurtado hardly engages the gentile religious environment, which was the environment of most early Christians for whom we have evidence. Even if we were hypothesizing only about the regions visited by Jesus in the first years of the Christian movement, most scholars have robust descriptions of Hellenization and Romanization in those locales.[119] Was not a Roman imperial temple towering over Peter's confession at Caesarea Philippi—a temple which was built there because of the adjacent Hellenistic sanctuary of Pan? What is more, if we were to limit ourselves only to Jewish practices as relevant, what would be our evidence for the first century? Josephus, Jewish-Roman historian? Philo, Jewish-Greek philosopher? There is little evidence of the first-century Jewish environment unmediated by the Greco-Roman world. Many would contend that the New Testament, the very chronicle of Jesus-devotion, is itself actually the best evidence of Judaism in the first century. But then Hurtado's argument would circle back on itself.

Late in Hurtado's history of early Christology, the metaphor of the river returns, and his use of it highlights his neglect of Christianity's Greco-Roman environment. Bousset was not the first to chart the influence of non-Christian sources on Christianity; already in the second century, Clement of Alexandria taught, "There is only one way of truth, but various things from various places come into it, just like tributaries discharging into an ever-flowing river."[120] However, since Hurtado ignores the gentile environment of early Christianity, the river metaphor functions much differently for him than for earlier historians.[121] Like others, he looks "upstream" to discern the "tributaries" that influenced the "mainstream" Christian river up to its early-second-century "confluence."[122] But whereas Bousset and the *religionsgeschichtliche Schule* tried to chart how foreign, non-Christian matter was introduced into the Christian river, Hurtado has instead reinforced its banks. Though the book's introduction pays lip service to non-Christian influences, stating that "the Christian movement was not hermetically sealed from the cultures in which it developed," this statement is not elaborated in the ensuing argument.[123]

Rather, Hurtado fashions a history of early Christianity of which Irenaeus would be proud—an orderly progression of original doctrines and practices. He ignores the influential thesis of Walter Bauer, that Christian orthodoxy developed over several centuries through a diverse process of distillation and exclusion.[124] On the contrary, in Hurtado's river metaphor, the tributaries bolstering Christianity are neither *non*-Christian nor proto-heterodox influences but are actually forms of canonical Christianity (especially Hebrews and the disputed Pauline Epistles). The great orthodox river welcomes proto-orthodox ideas, of course, by definition. But the foreign matter of heterodox Christianity has been shut out completely—Valentinus, Marcion, and others have been dammed. In the end, the basin of Hurtado's river system comprises only Christian streams, and the heterodox rivulets do not even reach the main. One wonders, in this image, where on earth is everyone else, the entire Roman Empire not yet inundated in Christianity? Across a continental divide, flowing to a distant shore? Or in the desert, parched and dead?

Hurtado's analysis ignores just about everything religious going on in the Roman world. I am mostly concerned, though, with the avoidance of cultic practices devoted to divine humans and divine sons—heroes, ancestors, rulers, gods.[125] Ruler cults were widespread in antiquity, and Roman emperor worship confronted Jews not only in the Diaspora. By the time of nascent Christianity, it had a presence for several generations in Judea, Samaria, and Galilee. (Under Gaius Caligula, it approached the temple itself.) The Roman emperor was a prominent feature of the "religious environment," in the words of Hurtado's second thesis, and I hope to show his relevance as an "analogy," (though I will leave its "true"-ness to be assessed by my readers).

When Hurtado does briefly engage the worship of the emperor, his arguments are strained. For example, in the course of addressing challenges by Crispin Fletcher-Louis to his "exclusivist monotheism" thesis, Hurtado discusses the gesture of "bowing down" (προσκύνησις) before various figures.[126] He admits that ancient people, including Jews, performed this gesture to "any superior person or being, whether human or heavenly . . . to any victor in battle and by subject peoples to those who subdued them."[127] But he does not admit such evidence as "'worship' in the 'hard' sense of reverencing a figure as a deity" because "the specific connotation of the prostration or other gestures depended entirely on what kind of honor the person offering the reverence intended to attribute to the figure receiving the gesture." In this rebuttal, Hurtado moves—either unintentionally or sophistically—from discussing gestures to intentions. Not only is it methodologically tricky to discern the intention of ancient figures when they bowed before their rulers or masters, but it also goes against Hurtado's own stated emphasis on practices. Practices have a logic of their own; intention does not always, or even usually, play a part.[128] If Jews engaged in some of the same practices toward rulers and masters as they did toward the God of Israel, this fact should register strongly within Hurtado's own system of analysis. Yet he remains committed to the "no true analogy" thesis, strongly worded as it is.

The omissions that clear the path for Hurtado's second thesis should give us pause. Since he demonstrates such thoroughness elsewhere in his scholarship, why this particular lacuna? Though it receives scant mention in his book, he undoubtedly knows of emperor worship. He prefers to relegate its importance for divine sonship, however, to a later date: "I contend that the rising frequency in the christological use of divine sonship language that we see in the Christian writings of the late first century and thereafter may very well reflect a reaction against the contemporaneous increase in the use of the same rhetoric in the emperor cult under the Flavians and thereafter."[129] A charitable interpretation of this view is that Hurtado has relied on older scholarship on emperor worship,[130] thereby remaining unaware of scholarship that dates emperor worship as earlier and more widespread. Regarding divine sonship in the Roman world, he thus follows Hengel's argument and reproduces its mistakes. But a more skeptical interpretation is that the titles, tales, and images shared by both Jesus and the Roman emperor render emperor worship "too close for comfort" and complicate Hurtado's defense of Jesus-devotion as *sui generis*. On the whole, his presentation of Jesus as *sui generis*—the "no true analogy" thesis—is successful in this work only because he avoids the primary analogies to Jesus Christ: other powerful human beings considered divine by those receiving their benefactions. I agree with Hurtado that Jesus came to be regarded quickly as a divine human son of God, but in the Roman world, "a world full of gods," he was not alone in that status.[131]

Through ingenuity, labor, and mettle, the *religionsgeschichtliche Schule* and its heirs have established a formidable hoard of historical data concerning the New Testament's environment. But there is more than historical data (or *Historie*) in their work; as we have seen, they also narrate historical processes (or *Geschichte*) according to which certain terms and concepts were imagined to have traveled through time. Scholars like Bousset, Hengel, Dunn, and Hurtado have told gripping stories of conceptual development, and the *geschichtlich* part of their moniker is aptly given. The disagreements among them largely concern not whether but how quickly transition happened: did "son of God" gain prominence gradually (so Bousset and Dunn) or rapidly (so Hengel and Hurtado)? When viewing the members of this group together, the affinity between their method and their object of inquiry is unmistakable: using a genealogical method, they seek the origin of a son.

▪ LISTENING FOR RESONANCE

A fourth kind of scholar has been drawing on the third group's indisputable treasury of merit but avoiding its stemmatic reconstructions of the past. This fourth method rejects the *religionsgeschichtlich* construal of linguistic and conceptual development, which organizes terms and concepts diachronically along a root-and-branch model, as with a family tree or the stemma of a manuscript tradition. Instead of looking for the origin of a term, for example, this fourth method listens primarily for its *resonance*. Regardless of where or when a word came from, how would it have sounded to its different audiences? What meaningful connections would listeners likely have made, connections both intended and unintended by speakers? If the *religionsgeschichtliche Schule* sought the meaning of terms and concepts in their origins, this method judges meaning by use. The meanings develop over time not like a stemma or family tree, but like a multifaceted culture. No one person in a culture can determine the meaning of a term or concept, even its originator. Once released into the culture, its meaning develops through innumerable moments of being used; it is defined by everyone and no one at the same time.

As applied to the terminologies and ideologies of the cultural environments of the New Testament, the method can be traced back at least to Adolf Deissmann and continues through the recent work of John Dominic Crossan and Jonathan L. Reed.[132] For our purposes, the method is best exemplified by Adela Yarbro Collins in her twin studies of how "son of God" language would have been heard in the various historical milieux of the Gospel of Mark.[133] Her point of departure is to imagine the Gospel's audiences: it was "read aloud in gatherings of Christians," but the listeners "were not all equally committed to the Christian faith." Therefore, they "probably assimilated and interpreted the instruction that they received in various ways." What is more, though Mark was "written primarily for insiders," it is also "likely that copies were available to interested or critical outsiders." Over the course of two articles, Yarbro Collins lays out a wide array of concepts and figures with which Mark's "son of God" portrayal could have interacted to make meaning for original audiences. She does not argue for one meaning of "son of God"; rather, many compelling options are presented. The words and images in Mark do not establish meanings, but they evoke meanings as they resonate in their audiences.[134] This approach, more open-ended than that of the second or third group, is manifested in the rhetoric of her work. It often follows a form like this: "those who link A with B" will interpret "son of God" one way, while "those who hold that all C are D" will be led to see it another way.[135] This openness does not lead to vacuousness, however; it allows her to clarify many scholarly positions and draw sound conclusions.

In the first study, she asks how "son of God" might have resonated among "those members of Mark's audience who were knowledgeable about and preferred Jewish traditions."[136] For them, the term and concept would have called to mind the Israelite royal ideology established through David and Solomon, the prophetic servant of the Lord traditions, the spiritual endowment of Elijah and Elisha, or the Qumran messianic expectation, among other traditions. The summary "force" of the "ancient mythical language" was "to express the ideas that God will choose the messiah, appoint him as God's agent, and endow him with divine power."[137]

In the second study, Yarbro Collins takes soundings of the Greek and Roman cultural environs. Its method is similar to that of the first—she focuses on "diversity of meaning" in the "reception" of Mark. But she is open in this study to even the unconscious connections made by certain listeners, namely "those members of Mark's audience who were more familiar with Greek and Roman religious traditions than with Jewish traditions and who preferred, consciously or unconsciously, to interpret the Christian proclamation about Jesus in Greek or Roman terms."[138] What did "son of God" mean, when heard by these listeners? Those imbued with the tales of the Greek gods might have associated Jesus with various sons of Zeus or Apollo, especially the many kings and rulers who appropriated such titles. Divine sonship might also have brought to mind great poets, sages, heroes, or healers like Asclepius, among other figures. But above all, the term "son of God" would have resonated with a common acclamation of the most famous person in the world—the Roman emperor, *divi filius*. This "most striking parallel" reinforces the general connection between divine sonship and kings or rulers found in Jewish, Greek, and Roman usage.[139] While Yarbro Collins does not single the emperor out as the only relevant comparison to Jesus' divine sonship, she does depict him as the most compelling figure with which Mark's image of Jesus would have interacted in a Greco-Roman worldview.

■   METHODS AND PRESUPPOSITIONS GOING FORWARD

I am now in a position to articulate how this book fits into the above categories. As for the first group, the general lack of critical attention to divine sonship in biblical scholarship is what led me to this research; I hope this book partially fills in that lacuna. I have benefited greatly from the narrative-critical work of the second group, and I employ its focus on whole, individual documents in my analyses of the Gospels and Acts. When appropriate I incorporate insights from literary criticism and postmodern epistemologies into my analysis, as Foucauldian and postcolonial interpretations of power have guided some of my research questions. But this book, while not *religionsgeschichtlich* in the sense of the third group, is fundamentally historical-critical, and I hope it will be judged as such.

My argument builds on the method of the fourth group in two ways. First, it examines the resonance of "son of God" in the Roman worldview and asks how this resonance affects our understanding of the Gospel of Mark and other selected Christian texts.[140] As I will argue, the Roman worldview was not limited to the city of Rome or Roman citizens; it pervaded the Empire, even as did the visage and presence of the emperor. So how did "son of God" resonate? The only titular use of "son of God" in the New Testament era, outside of the New Testament itself, was for the Roman emperor, who was *divi filius* in Latin and θεοῦ υἱός in Greek (regarding these terms, see chapters 2 and 3). Besides its application to the emperor, the term "son of God" was almost nonexistent in Latin and Greek because gods typically have names. Someone might be called "son of Zeus" or "son of Hercules" to express an affiliation to one of those gods.[141] But the plain "son of God" was used for the emperor and, of course, for Jesus Christ. My argument thus emphasizes the Empire-wide recognition of the emperor as "son of God," a fact which makes imperial divine sonship a relevant, though neglected, historical *comparandum* for divine sonship in early Christianity.

Second, this book provides a "thick description" of divine status and divine sonship in the Roman worldview. Clifford Geertz used that term as shorthand for his way of doing ethnography, which offered rich details of context so that outside observers could better participate in the meanings of foreign behaviors.[142] His famous essay encouraged me to try to describe more thickly what "god" and "son of God" meant in the Roman world and how emperors came to be acclaimed as both. In recent years, Roman historians have already been describing more and more thickly what "god" meant in the Roman world. The scholars treated in the next chapter have gotten away from the "map" of Roman divinity offered by Cicero and other philosophically inclined thinkers. By examining instead the "territory" of Roman religion—temples, inscriptions, processions, jewelry, omens, sacrifices— they show, among other things, that there was no absolute dividing line between humanity and divinity in the Roman worldview. Few Romans were Platonists. Another fruit of their research has been a renewed perspective on ruler cults in antiquity. Previously thought to be mere political flattery, scholars have now focused on them as crucial features of ancient religion. Before, the question was asked whether the emperor was viewed as a man or a god. But if the entire cosmos is a spectrum or gradient of honor, this "problem" of the ruler cult ceases to be a problem. Though the emperor was certainly a man, he was also, as one scholar notes, the only universal deity in the Roman world.[143]

While the concept of "god" has received some thick description, the "son of God" concept still needs attention. Roman historians have not treated it in much detail, and descriptions of Roman divine sonship in biblical scholarship have also been too "thin," usually describing the mere *datum* of the emperor's *divi filius* title. Though almost every scholarly introduction to the New Testament will mention that the emperor was called "son of God," almost none of them pursue the matter beyond a footnote. My work puts a magnifying glass to that footnote. Or, to use a more technologically current metaphor, if that footnote is a hyperlink, my work might open up in a new window.

My approach to the study of divine sonship seeks to complement the "resonance" method by examining in more detail the social practices of sonship in the Roman world. Concepts, especially metaphors, are almost always rooted in practices. Human beings do not think in isolation from their cultural practices; the metaphor of divine father-son relationships only *means* in the context of actual father-son relationships. However, the social practices surrounding fathers and sons—even divine fathers and sons—in the Roman Empire are not usually brought into scholarship on divine sonship in early Christianity.[144] Instead, as stated above, most scholars treat the first-century concept of divine sonship with a Nicene-era disdain for adoptive or "made" sonship. As I will discuss in chapter 5, the dichotomy of "begotten" vs. "made" had a particular conceptual meaning for the two sides of the Arian controversy, functioning to distinguish whether there was ever a time (at the beginning of time) when the Son did not exist. Stated philosophically, the Nicene question was, "On which side of the Being/Becoming line did the Son fall?" But in the first century, begetting and making sons was not primarily a philosophical distinction. On the contrary, the father-son relationship was the center of all Roman social relationships—the crux of Roman politics and kinship. In chapter 3, I investigate father-son relationships in the Roman family, emphasizing the practices of adoption and inheritance. In the Roman worldview, sonship did not point primarily backward to begetting, but forward to inheritance, often through the medium of adoption. More specifically, I analyze the transmission of power from father to son in the imperial family and the competing family ideologies of natural ("begotten") sons and adopted ("made") sons. As I will argue, scholarship on divine sonship has been hampered by mistaken assumptions about adopted sons. Far from being second-class family members, they were pivotal and often favored; they stabilized ruling families and formed a key part of imperial ideology. The close examination of Roman fathers and sons will allow us to hear new resonances of divine sonship in early Christian texts (chaps. 4 and 5).

A presupposition stands behind my method. By examining the political-family ideology of Roman society together with the Christian theology that grew and eventually flourished in that society, I presuppose fundamental connections between them. I presume that political ideology and religious theology are almost always related; at the same time, they are almost never related in a simplistic way.[145] Throughout the book, I will examine the interface between divine status in the Roman worldview and early Christian theology, and between divine sonship in the Roman worldview and early Christian Christology.

To conclude this chapter, I would like to recall my earlier assessment of Larry Hurtado's major work on Christology. As stated above, Hurtado rejects the gradualism of the *religionsgeschichtliche Schule* and argues instead for a "volcano-like" eruption of devotion to Jesus in earliest Christianity.[146] I do not see reason to challenge that first of his theses; I find it quite compelling. I respond, however, that the term "son of God" also had a volcano-like eruption in the Roman world, namely when Octavian claimed it as the title which most legitimated his imperial power. His new status as "son of God" spread throughout the Empire, via every medium of Roman communication. By the end of Tiberius's principate, the mantle of divine sonship had been laid upon each *princeps*, the most famous person in the world, for about eighty years. Therefore, the divine sonship of the emperor—how it was acquired, how it was portrayed, what it meant—is of utmost relevance for understanding the divine sonship of Jesus. Stated most succinctly, my ultimate critique of biblical scholarship on divine sonship is this: its field of vision has a blind spot the size of the Roman emperor. To interpret the term "son of God" in the Roman world without discussing the emperor shows a neglect of his importance and a lack of sensitivity to how language functions in society.[147] It is like interpreting the "American dream" without discussing the world-changing speech of Martin Luther King.

2 Divinity and Divine Sonship in the Roman World

> Caesar, god from god . . . .
>
> — P.OXY. XII 1453

The twin powers of Platonism and Christianity have governed the intellectual traditions of the Western world with lasting authority. It has been almost impossible for a resident of that world to think independently from their metaphysical and theological systems. But the postmodern era—defined perhaps most clearly as incredulity toward those two metanarratives—has enabled scholars to reassess the constitutive concepts of the human perspective on the cosmos. In the fields of Roman history and religious studies, some scholars have begun to incorporate new perspectives into their understanding of divinity in the Roman world. For example, scholars such as Simon Price, Ittai Gradel, and Clifford Ando articulate interpretations of divinity that confound the categories customarily used by Roman historians and scholars of religion. In their view, divinity in the Roman world was not an essence or a nature, but a concept of *status* and *power* in a cosmic spectrum that had no absolute dividing lines. The realm of the gods was not, in the famous maxim of Rudolf Otto, "wholly Other." In this chapter, I survey and synthesize the current conclusions of this burgeoning field of research, in order to encourage fellow scholars to question their presuppositions about divinity in the Roman world, just as I have scrutinized and reoriented my own. My approach to the matter draws especially from recent studies of emperor worship, while also making some analogies to scholarship on Judaism and Christianity in their Roman context. The synthetic viewpoint of the chapter allows us to see the scope of the changes that have occurred in the last generation—from the bird's eye view, perhaps we can also see the way forward.

▪ DIVINITY IN THE ROMAN WORLD

Investigating what the term "son of God" meant in the Roman world necessitates a reassessment of its constitutive concepts. This section uses recent scholarship on Roman religion to elucidate some aspects of the concept of "god" prevalent in the Roman world, especially as it came to be applied to the emperor. Since this book is not primarily about Roman religion, my treatment of Roman divinity will contain more synthesis than analysis; enough innovative work has recently been done on the topic, however, that a survey of old and new perspectives should still prove beneficial to both Roman historians and scholars of early Christianity. The final section and the subsequent chapter then address the concept of "son" as it functioned in the Roman family and specifically the imperial family.

Divinity and Religion: Perspectives Old and New

When surveying a field of information as large as the scholarship on Roman divinity and emperor worship, a chart of key features may be helpful. The accompanying chart (see table 2.1) of old and new perspectives on Roman divinity and emperor worship has emerged from my study of the most recent work on the topic, and I offer it to aid my necessarily brief prose description of the *status quaestionis*. What I call the "old perspective" on Roman divinity was first generated by philosophical and other intellectual opinions about the gods, such as those expressed in Cicero's *De natura deorum*. The data of Roman divinity were what

TABLE 2.1

Divinity in the Roman World	
Old	New
—data: the "map" of divinity provided by philosophical sources —interpretation: a Christian "lens" and an anachronistic view of monotheism → these combine to undergird a presupposition of absolute division between material world / divinity	—data: the "territory" of religious practices provided by artifacts and accounts of practices —interpretation: the "lenses" of anthropology, cultural studies, ritual studies → these reveal a gradient of honor or status in the cosmos

Emperor Worship	
Old	New
—viewed from the top, emperor worship was political manipulation; from the bottom, it was flattery or empty formality → as to his divinity, the people did not really believe it —power: a top-down imposition of a new cult; characterized by domination and excess → "imperial cult" as centrally controlled monolith · —*deus/divus* distinction: divinity manufactured only after death → no worship of the living emperor	—evidence of practices reveals the vibrancy of devotion; widespread geographically and over time → their beliefs, even if accessible, are not the best way to judge emperor worship —power: worship arose substantially from local initiatives by subjects negotiating complex systems of power; excess of a couple emperors was the exception, not the rule → worship studied by region; diverse local manifestations, but with enough resemblances to cohere —*deus/divus* distinction not stable in actual Latin usage and nonexistent in Greek (both rendered by θεός) → worship of living emperor, especially his *genius* and *numen*, suggested by the archaeological evidence

*This chart is my own compilation but indebted to many scholars. A helpful survey of some of these shifts can be found in Rives, "Roman Religion Revived."

intellectuals thought about the gods.[1] Not only was this corpus deemed a convenient place to learn about Roman divinity, but it was also consulted to address the question posed most often by modern scholars of the old perspective: what did the Romans *believe* about the gods? I call this set of data the "map" of divinity—it was compact, organized, free of obstacles, and could be drawn with knowledge gleaned from just a few volumes of the Loeb Classical Library.

But through the incorporation of archaeological research, the first shift in perspective took place. When the "territory" of Roman divinity emerged as a complex, if partially preserved, landscape, newer scholars discovered that the compact "map" was insufficient. The imagined religion of the *urbs* had sprawled—and they needed more than Cicero to navigate it. Already a generation or two ago, scholars such as Fergus Millar propounded the study of material artifacts and records of ritual practices, evidence of what Romans *did* with respect to the gods: temples, priesthoods, inscriptions, papyri, milestones, amulets, jewelry, oaths, sacrifices, libations, hymns, pilgrimages.[2] The focus on religious practices continued in the next generation and shows no signs of abating in current scholarship. John Scheid's popular primer on Roman religion is so grounded in material evidence and ritual practices that the intellectual systems of Cicero and Varro appear only briefly at the very end of his book. "Obviously, to most Roman citizens," he writes, "these systems meant nothing at all."[3] When commenting on Varro's learned portrayal of the Roman religious system, Cicero himself said that it was unfamiliar to most Romans.[4] Perhaps he would have admitted the same of his own system. Then Ittai Gradel would not be too bold in warning, "Only with extreme caution should philosophical treatises, such as Cicero's *De Natura Deorum* or *De Divinatione* be employed in the study of Roman religion; and as for its interpretation, they are best left out of account altogether."[5]

The shifting of focus from map to territory has not been the only change in the new perspective on Roman religion.[6] Recent scholars are also using different lenses to examine and interpret the data—lenses ground most precisely by Simon Price, whose seminal *Rituals and Power* galvanized new interpretive trends by applying them so brilliantly to the erstwhile "imperial cult." His thick description of ritual practices in Asia Minor—with indebtedness to Geertz explicit throughout—turned out to be the perfect catalyst for new modes of analysis because the historical fact of emperor worship transgresses so many of the categorical boundaries presumed by the old perspective. In order to describe the evidence, Price *needed* to jettison old assumptions and introduce new methods. He explicitly points to several "Christianizing assumptions": religion necessarily involves emotional participation; internal beliefs are more real than external practices; individual/private relations to divinity are more important than communal/public expressions.[7] By identifying and rejecting these assumptions, Price was able to incorporate data that had been previously de-emphasized: the well-known and continuously growing set of archaeological evidence for emperor worship.[8] Indeed, if communal, public practices are regarded as proper and legitimate data for the study of religion, then the evidence for emperor worship is as broad as for almost any other ancient religion.[9]

The new data—because it was ritual, communal, public—also opened up Roman religion to social-scientific modes of analysis. Price explicitly employs the theories of Foucault and Bourdieu, for example, at crucial points of his argument; in truth, their influences teem beneath the surface of every chapter. Foucault enables Price to collapse the dichotomy of religion and politics—both are means of symbolically constructing power.[10] Bourdieu enables him to collapse the dichotomy of belief and ritual—both have structures *and* create them.[11] With binaries collapsing all around, one begins to wonder whether "Christianizing assumptions" were actually the problem in the first place. Could something more ancient, even more ingrained than Christianity, have been governing the assumptions of older scholars?

In recent years, Clifford Ando has argued that it is actually the philosophical binaries inherited from Plato that have made our interpretation of ancient religion difficult and imprecise. Deeper than the dichotomies of religion/politics or belief/ritual lie the root Platonic binaries: reality/appearance; form/matter; object/name; being/becoming. In a trenchant essay on the ancient critique of idolatry, for instance, Ando demonstrates how Platonic epistemology and ontology hinder us from understanding the Roman stance toward statues of the gods ("idols").[12] His master example concerns the question of what Romans thought they were doing when, following a military conquest, they transported a foreign god back to Rome. The Platonic worldview would have us decide: either they believed the statue *really* was the god, in which case the god would no longer exist if the statue were lost at sea or otherwise destroyed, or the statue *represented* the god, in which case that particular statue is no different than other statues of the same god. But neither pole of this dichotomy adequately explains the ancient evidence.[13] The "problem" of the ancient evidence is created by the binaries of reality/appearance and being/representing. As with Price's use of Geertz, Foucault, and Bourdieu, Ando's rejection of Platonism is no mere submission to current philosophical trends (though Plato has no doubt been under attack in the postmodern era). More important, the Platonic-Christian lens fails to help us interpret central practices of ancient religion, such as those involving statues of gods or rulers, and for our purposes, the practice of emperor worship. Therefore other lenses, with more explanatory power, must be used. When this shift occurs, one gains nothing less than a different perspective on humanity and divinity in the Roman world.

In the old view of Roman divinity, the data of Roman intellectuals (many of them Platonists) were read through a Platonic-Christian framework, a combination which undergirded two key presuppositions: First, there was an absolute dividing line between the realm of the divine and the realm of the human. For example, Otto Weinreich's seminal article on divine humans in antiquity begins: "If we speak of 'divine humanity,' then we bring together two concepts between which a world-wide distance seems to lie: God and Human. The more absolute the essence of God, the more frail the essence of the human is felt, so much deeper gapes the abyss, the larger is the tension between the two poles."[14] In short, divinity was absolute. God was *das ganz Andere,* or "Wholly Other," in the famous words of Rudolf Otto.[15]

Correlated to this presupposition was an anachronistic view of monotheism among scholars of the ancient world.[16] Previous scholars had too often accepted the argument of early Christian apologists—that Christians, like Jews, were monotheists, and pagans were polytheists—as a basically accurate portrayal of religion in the Roman Empire.[17] But this neat division is problematized by all kinds of evidence. Ancient Christians (or Jews) cannot uniformly be categorized as monotheistic.[18] In the world of practices, even if one manages to incorporate early Christian devotion to Jesus into monotheism, one would still have to discount too many cults of the martyrs and saints and other superhuman beings to construct a clearly monotheistic version of early Christianity.[19] In the world of ideas, some intellectuals—especially those influenced by Platonism—were gesturing toward monotheism in the first and second centuries. But on the whole, early Christians struggled to articulate a coherent monotheistic view amid a multitude of superhuman forces—heroes, martyrs, rulers, angels, saints, demons, spirits, along with gods and their mothers and sons. The complexity of Sethian and Valentinian theological systems is the paramount and most famous example of this challenge. It took proto-orthodox theology centuries to find a partially adequate vocabulary to express Christian monotheism. For Christianity, as for Judaism earlier and Islam later, the challenge to construct divine unity in belief and practice was ongoing.[20]

Building on new data and new presuppositions, research on emperor worship has led many scholars to a new understanding of divinity in the Roman world: it was not an essence but a status—a status honored because of powerful benefactions. Few first-century listeners would have understood a claim of divinity apart from some enactment of power. When continuous benefactions led to continuous honors, that process could admittedly lead to a kind of ontology—a status solidified because of a god's perpetual benefactions. But this was a process nonetheless: divinity was dynamic.

Divinity was also relative. Contrary to the view expressed by Weinreich, divinity and humanity were not best expressed as fixed "poles" stationed across a "gaping abyss" of "world-wide distance." As Arthur Darby Nock observed, "to the ancients the line of demarcation between god and man was not as constant and sharp, or the interval as wide, as we naturally think."[21] Hans-Josef Klauck sees the supposed abyss as "not completely unbridgeable"—the emperor was the *pontifex maximus,* after all—and he employs the category of "myth" to deal with the evidence of the emperor's divinity; it is "the work of myth" to mediate between contrasting concepts.[22] Other scholars have abandoned the abyss metaphor altogether and opted instead for images of continuous change: divinity exists along a cosmic gradient or spectrum.[23] The "problem" of emperor worship, using these new interpretations of divinity, ceases to be a problem.

The most recent and forceful expositor of this perspective is Ittai Gradel, but the idea has an older history among a small cadre of scholars. Over sixty years ago, one art historian observed the relative aspect of Roman divinity as if it should be obvious: "Men and gods were not on two completely separate and differentiated levels, the one on the natural, the other on the supernatural, plane. They occupied either end, as it were, of a sliding scale."[24] Some years later, but before Price's work, J. Rufus Fears further noted how divinity was not an essential property but a status honored because of benefactions: "[The Greeks and Romans] were ready at all times to recognize a newly manifested divine force capable of rendering supernatural benefits to the community or the individual."[25] But what a few earlier scholars had noted in passing, Gradel has featured as a foundation of his major work, *Emperor Worship and Roman Religion.* He begins and ends his reassessment of the material evidence for emperor worship in Italy with the new perspective on Roman divinity, which finds its most succinct expression in his discussion of Roman sacrifice:

> One may stress these demarcations between sacred and profane, between men and gods, and thus neatly isolate Graeco-Roman religion from secular society as an independent category. Such an approach, convenient because it will make the ancient world fit into our own categories, may not be entirely wrong, but is far too narrow. One should rather stress the fact that the sacrificial system formed an integral part of a larger social context, which should be examined as a whole to become intelligible in contemporary terms. Temples, priests, and sacrifices were the ingredients of the highest or divine or heavenly honours (*summi, divini, caelestes honores*), and such were the most prestigious honours known to men. But they differed in degree, not in kind, from lower, terrestrial, or—as we would say—secular honours. They were ultimately an aspect of the honours-for-benefactions structure found in all relationships between parties of vastly unequal power and social standing in Roman society, such as in the interplays between subjects and ruler, cities and benefactors, dependants and patrons, slaves and masters.[26]

Gradel's methodological commitments to material evidence, ritual practices, and the interpretation of Roman religion with a scale of relative divinity allow him to situate the worship of the emperor within the normal functioning of Roman religious practice.[27] The worship of the emperor, both man and god, becomes less perplexing to modern interpreters.

With the new perspective on Roman divinity, what is most important to Roman historians is that crucial ancient evidence can be read anew. Old anomalies no longer seem so strange. By way of conclusion, consider the following inscription: in 27 B.C.E., the city of Mytilene on Lesbos established many honors for Augustus, sent ambassadors to Rome with the news, and had their decree inscribed in other major cities for all to see. After explaining in the decree the new honors by which they would worship Augustus as a god, they also went on to promise that "if something more splendid should be found later on, the city [of Mytilene's] eagerness and piety will not neglect whatever can be done *to deify him even more.*"[28] Whatever could that have meant, if divinity was absolute?

Emperor Worship: Perspectives Old and New

> Under the Roman Empire, from the time of Augustus to that of
> Constantine, the cult of the emperor was, according to the patterns of
> "religion" (not in a Christian sense but in the sense of Roman
> religion), the most important type of worship.
>
> —GÉZA ALFÖLDY

The outlines of the old and new perspectives on emperor worship have been drawn already in the previous pages and accompanying chart, but here let us fill in some detail and color.[29] The most easily identified tendency among older scholars on emperor worship is this: they could not imagine that it was genuine. The emperor was clearly a human being and not a god; for most twentieth-century scholars, attempting to imagine the emperor as the object of genuine divine worship produced a cognitive dissonance that was difficult to rectify. (Their trouble with imagining a *divine human* is more than a bit ironic, considering the "Christianizing assumptions" governing older scholarship.) Viewed from the top, emperor worship was interpreted as political manipulation. Lily Ross Taylor, whose book *The Divinity of the Roman Emperor* defined a field of inquiry, concludes that "for Augustus the imperial cult was primarily an instrument of politics.... He found in the worship an effective instrument of government."[30] Viewed from the bottom, it was empty flattery, a vacant formality. The people could not have believed it—they just played along for the sake of expediency.

Some scholars barely corral their disdain for the practice and place themselves alongside the cultured despisers from the Roman elite. A century ago, J. S. Reid proclaimed, "No men of culture, and of the emperors only crazy men like Gaius and Elagabalus, regarded the superhuman powers as anything but accompaniments and attestations of power."[31] His attitude was matched in German scholarship of the early- and mid-twentieth century.[32] But years later, and surprisingly at the same conference where the shift in perspectives was beginning, Glen Bowersock echoed Reid's incredulity.[33] According to his reading of the "Greek intellectuals," emperor worship was comprised of "civic duties suitable for the wealthy and ambitious but in no sense a display of piety," a "routine part of the Roman administrative machinery" with "no evidence at all for such religious emotion." Pliny, for example, "was an intelligent person" so he could "hardly" have believed Trajan to be a god—"no thinking man" would believe that! The Greek intellectuals learned to "accept" and "ignore" the divinity of the emperor. As long as such literary and philosophical sources were the data, it was difficult for modern scholars—with their aforementioned presuppositions—to imagine that the Romans genuinely worshipped the emperor.

The evidence from material artifacts and ritual practices, however, reveals the vibrancy of devotion to the emperor. As a counterpoint to Bowersock, Fergus Millar drew these conclusions from his preferred evidence: "firstly that the conception of a human attaining divine status had already long been integral to ancient paganism; and secondly that the Imperial cult was fully and extensively integrated into the local cults of the provinces, with the consequence that the Emperors were the object of the same cult-acts as the other gods."[34] The evidence of rituals and artifacts (especially inscriptions) for emperor worship was widespread geographically and over time. Other scholars who focused on practices, such as H. W. Pleket and Keith Hopkins, blazed new interpretive trails in the years leading up to Price's work. Pleket was the first to take emperor worship seriously in comparison with other "mystery" cults in antiquity.[35] Hopkins was among the first to get beyond "belief" as the main category for evaluating the topic.[36] The question "Did they really believe it?" had been answered with an emphatic "No" for too long because of an over-reliance on philosophers—and occasionally misinterpretations of philosophers.[37] Hopkins thinks the question is not the most useful one to ask, but his answer, more or less, is: "They certainly acted like it." The conclusion to his essay pointed the way forward:

> Sophisticated Romans may not have believed that the emperor was a god, nor did the courtiers who saw him, but they sacrificed to him, as though he was a god, and perhaps they covered the conflict of evidence with a metaphysical metaphor—god made manifest, son of god, the least of gods but highest of mortals, son of Apollo, Hercules on earth. Most people probably did not bother with the demarcation; the emperor was clearly both man and god.[38]

If Hopkins sketched the guidelines of how emperor worship enacted the "symbolic unity" of the Roman Empire, Géza Alföldy was able later to paint the details of its universal appeal. In his analysis of the evidence, emperor worship became all things to all people over time; it spread horizontally throughout the Empire's lands and, more surprisingly, vertically through different social strata. This, his summary assessment of a major conference on emperor worship, radically overturns the older perspective:

> Practically everybody was involved [in emperor worship]. This is true in a double sense. Spatially, the ruler-cult was carried out at Rome as well as in all the towns of Italy and the provinces, and even in private houses. Socially, it was spread through all classes and groups. The *fratres Arvales* and the *collegia* of *sodales Augustales, sodales Flaviales*, etc. represented the participation of the senatorial aristocracy in this cult; the *flamines* or *sacerdotes provinciae*, coming from the equestrian order and other local élites, represented the whole population of their province; the *flamines* of the towns represented the élites of the *municipia* and *coloniae*; the *seviri Augustales* the "second class" of the urban population, especially rich freedmen; the *magistri* and the *ministri* of the *Lares Augustorum* etc. were freedmen and slaves.[39]

In short, the scholarship that emerged from a new focus on material artifacts and ritual practices shared a relatively simple underlying insight: the actions of many speak louder than the words of a few.

A second limitation of the old perspective on emperor worship was its unilateral understanding of power. The divinity of the emperor was construed as a top-down imposition, centrally controlled by the emperor himself, upon people powerless to reject it. The older term "imperial cult" helped to manifest this view, carrying as it did the connotations of organization and unity. Again, reliance only on literary sources played a role in propagating the idea, since they tended to focus on the domination and excess of a few emperors (e.g., Gaius Caligula and Domitian).[40] But there were also unstated theories of power and ideology at work. Rome was thought to have ruled only by force—if they wanted an "imperial cult," by Jove, they would get it!

New archaeological data and new theories of power have altered these views. The past thirty years have broadened the available evidence of emperor worship; in fact, there is so much data that research has progressed through local and regional studies. Major scholarly contributions have covered Iberia (Étienne), Asia Minor (Price), the Latin West (Fishwick), the Germanic provinces (Liertz), Italy (Gradel), Judea and Galilee (Bernett), and Greece (Kantiréa).[41] These are no mere antiquarian collections either; most of them offer nuanced and detailed interpretations of emperor worship in its diverse local contexts. Yet the local manifestations of emperor worship share enough resemblances to cohere as a group, about which some general conclusions can be drawn. Emperor worship was not a top-down phenomenon but was usually initiated by local subjects—in Kantiréa's eloquent phrasing, "*Le prince ne se faisait pas adorer, il se laissait adorer.*"[42] Emperor worship offered a unique opportunity for local elites to express their relationships to their distant Roman benefactor, while simultaneously building clout within their proximate social hierarchies.[43] Emperor worship was not only, or even primarily, directed to the dead emperors and their relatives, as some of the literary sources would have us believe; but the living emperor was also worshipped, often in the form of his *genius* or *numen*, as were other members of the imperial family (see below). Those who spend time with the material evidence of temples, sacrifices, and priesthoods conclude that the emperors received worship as gods.

Both Gradel and Kantiréa reach similar conclusions about how ultimately to understand the divine status of the emperor. His divinity made sense as a part of the honors-for-benefactions structure of Greco-Roman society. In the old perspective on divinity in the Roman world, the honors-for-benefactions structure had led scholars to discount the divinity of the emperor—he wasn't *really* a god because he had to *earn* it. Bowersock, channeling the satirist Lucian, uses exactly this criterion to disparage emperor worship.[44] But interpretations of divinity as a status, not an essence, allow us to see things differently. Before the Platonic worldview became dominant, all gods were gods because of their benefactions. How else would a god come to be regarded as such? Even the Jewish worship of the God of Israel developed in this way: the Exodus was the great benefaction that engendered worship.[45] In short, gods don't first tell you they're gods; they *show* you, and then *you* tell *them*—this is one reason why the supposed self-aggrandizements of Gaius Caligula and Domitian might have been viewed as appalling and unbelievable.

Benefactions were what led to worship, and continuous benefactions led to continuous worship. Benefactions deemed superhuman eventually led to superhuman status. Regarding the emperor specifically, the initial divine honors for Julius Caesar and Augustus were rooted in their benefactions (euergetism). But over time, and "without ever departing from its principal framework of euergetism, [emperor worship] was crystallized in a dynastic ideology"—a subject of the next chapter.[46] Over the course of about three generations (from the battle of Actium to the principate of Claudius), one can say that emperor worship expanded—and now I am using Christian labels—from a "soteriology" of the emperor to a "theology" of the imperial family.[47] This is not conceptually different from the trajectory of Christian thought about Jesus Christ: the path from the Crucifixion to the Gospels to Nicea was a soteriology in search of a theology. As with the worship of the emperor, the worship of Jesus Christ began by proclaiming his divine power to save and then moved toward situating his power among the other accepted divine powers.

In some cases, scholars of emperor worship use distinct theories of power and ideology to explain their evidence. Price interprets the rituals of emperor worship à la Foucault and, to a limited extent, Bourdieu, in order to elucidate how they constitute a "public cognitive system" of power.[48] Ando also relies on French social theory but extends his work to incorporate the theories of Weber and especially Habermas. In his analysis, the worship of the emperor was a constitutive aspect of an overall "imperial ideology," which was "the product of a complex conversation between center and periphery," between Rome and the provinces.[49] He uses the communicative theories of Habermas to demonstrate meticulously the Roman achievement of "*consensus*, a unanimous intersubjective agreement about social, religious, and political norms," which allowed the Empire to last as long as it did.[50] The emperor was the key to imperial ideology and, in a real sense, *was* the Empire. Most recently, insights from postcolonial theory have enabled scholars to describe societal power structures with more nuance than previous models allowed. The study of formerly colonized peoples around the world—specifically, the texts and practices developed by them as responses to their colonization—has generated a body of social theory distinct from that suggested by the colonizers' perspectives alone. This body of theory is now being applied to power relations more generally speaking, in contexts not properly "colonial," with mixed but generally positive results. Briefly stated, postcolonial theory allows us to see that sustained relationships of power are never simply imposed from one culture onto another. Power that lasts never comes unilaterally from the top, and there are many points on the spectrum between domination and resistance. The colonized always retain agency, though it is an agency enacted, in part, through the particular modes of expression by which they have been oppressed. The Roman Empire, probably the most famous (if not the most recent) colonial power in world history, is beginning to be studied fruitfully with this theoretical lens.[51]

Another way of understanding the new perspective on emperor worship is to connect it with a new consensus on the *terminology* of divinity in the Roman world: specifically, what was meant by *deus, divus,* and θεός? (And how were *genius* and *numen* related to these?) The consensus on *deus, divus,* and θεός is that all three terms should be translated as "god" without qualification, and they exhibited wide flexibility in actual ancient usage. Regarding the *deus/divus* distinction, the word *divus* had been usually and mistakenly interpreted as denoting a lower status than *deus*—a *divus* was considered a god that had been a human, while a *deus* is, well, a *real* god. But before the consecration of Julius Caesar as *divus*, that distinction did not exist at all, nor did it exist for many Latin speakers afterward. In fact, Varro, the grammarian who tried to distinguish the terms etymologically, had argued in the first century B.C.E. that *divus* was the *more* honorable of the two terms—exactly the opposite of how it came to be understood.[52] In his view, *divus* denotes "a subcategory . . . the 'elite division,' so to speak, of the gods," which "implied the noblest condition, that of the eternal gods, and was therefore the more dignified term."[53] But because of its continued application to members of the imperial family, *divus* eventually came to mean "gods that had been humans" and thus came to carry a *lower* connotation than *deus*. What is more, neither did *deus* only denote gods that were *not* humans. As J. Rufus Fears notes, the term *deus* was amply applied to living humans:

> It is too often forgotten that for the pagan Roman *deus* was not charged with the absolute meaning which it has for the Christian. Anyone could establish his own cult to any force which seemed superhuman in its power to benefit him. In this sense, Tityrus could say of the young Octavian: *Ille mihi semper deus* ["He is always a god to me"] (Verg. *Ecl.* 1.6–8); and Cicero could call Lentulus Spinther *parens ac deus nostrae vitae* ['parent and god of our life']. (*Red. in Sen.* 4.8)[54]

In recognition of their unique power, the term *deus* was applied to emperors often by poets and in some inscriptions from the Latin West.[55] Therefore, both *divus* and *deus* could refer to a god, whether a living human or not.

In parts of the Empire where Latin was not predominant—and that was an enormous portion—the *deus/divus* distinction was thus not relevant, even in the few cases when it was known.[56] For example, a neo-Punic inscription from the province of Africa refers to Augustus as *elim*, from the main Semitic word-group meaning "god" (*el, elim, elohim*).[57] More importantly, the Greek word θεός was generally used to translate both *deus* and *divus* across the Empire. Like the Latin terms, the Greek could be applied to humans, confirming the inadequacy of a stark divine/human dichotomy as a framework for interpreting the ancient world.[58] Regarding the Roman emperor in the early and high Empire, imperial titulature that contained *divus* would have been rendered as θεός; every *divi filius* would have been θεοῦ υἱός (or a close variant). In addition, the emperor was called θεός on many occasions independently of titulature, and all emperors of the first century C.E. were called θεός, even though they were not all *divi*. Therefore, as Simon Price has correctly argued, historians should not try to get "behind" the Greek usage of θεός to uncover an intended meaning of *divus*.[59] On the one hand, *divus* itself did not always mean "dead emperor"; on the other hand, even in the time period when it did, it cannot be presumed always to have been behind the articulation of θεός. Like ritual practices, linguistic practices matter, and they have a logic of their own—often independent of intentions. What we do know as historians, and what we can say with certainty, is that θεός was applied to the emperor broadly throughout the Empire, and by all social classes. The evidence comes in diverse forms: literature, coins, inscriptions, papyri, *et cetera*.[60] All these uses of θεός should be interpreted as such, and not as substitutions for either *deus* or *divus*. In Price's words, "The predication of *theos* of the emperor, though it is in certain contexts equivalent to *divus* in Latin, has meaning in the context of general Greek usage of *theos*."[61]

Some scholars have pointed to various emperors' refusal of divine honors as a way of arguing that they were not really considered as gods.[62] However, as stated above, the worship of the emperor was not centrally controlled, and divine honors were heaped upon emperors whether they accepted them or not. Furthermore, the linguistic situation in Greek does not allow simple conclusions to be drawn about the supposed imperial refusal of divinity. For example, in his "Embassy to Gaius," Philo praises Augustus's refusal of divinity as a way to chastise the self-righteous current emperor: "That [Augustus] was never elated or puffed up by the vast honours given to him is clearly shown by the fact that he never wished anyone to address him as a θεός but was annoyed if anyone used the word."[63] On the contrary, Philo claims that Gaius really thought he was a θεός, having been encouraged in this belief by the Alexandrians, who used the term for him just as they did for many other powerful beings.[64] But Philo's arguments make sense only in one particular perspective on the cosmos, in which someone cannot be both god and human. (Elsewhere, Philo does not himself seem to maintain the stark division.)[65] Augustus's refusal of the term θεός did not necessarily mean he was refusing *divinity*, since there were many other ritual expressions of divinity he *did* accept, and on Philo's own admission, θεός was a term used for all sorts of powerful beings. Augustus might have disliked the connotations of the term, but that does not mean he rejected worship of himself. Moreover, even when emperors explicitly refused the term, that did not stop anyone from using it—even the emperors' own spokesmen. The glaring example of this paradox comes from Claudius's letter to the Alexandrians (*P. Lond.* 1912).[66] In the body of the letter, the emperor delineates which honors he accepts and which he rejects from the Alexandrians. He specifically rejects the establishment of a priesthood and temples to himself, thus refusing to be worshipped as a god there.[67] But what often goes unnoticed is how the letter itself is introduced.[68] The Roman prefect of Egypt posts the letter publicly so that all may read it and "admire the greatness of Caesar, our θεός," namely Claudius, the very living emperor that asks not to be worshipped in the body of the letter!

This brings us to the final shift in the new perspective on emperor worship: the acknowledgment that the emperor was worshipped while he was alive. Older scholars had thought—relying on the *deus/divus* distinction, a strong divine/human dichotomy, a top-down view of emperor worship, and a neglect of archaeological evidence—that the emperor was worshipped in Rome and Italy only after death, though he was possibly worshipped while alive in the eastern provinces (due to their history of divine rulers).[69] Based on new data and new presuppositions, recent scholars have strongly challenged that view. The old view relied mostly on literary sources, especially Dio's claim that emperors, even Augustus, were not worshipped in Italy while alive.[70] When archaeological evidence did not line up with this claim, the errant data were incorporated into the "*genius* theory" of imperial worship. According to Lily Ross Taylor, the theory's most eloquent proponent, worship in Italy "was directed not to the emperor as a god on earth but to his shadowy attendant spirit [*genius*]. But the cult given his attendant spirit had taken on the character of the Hellenistic ruler cult, and the Genius was but a thin veil for the emperor himself."[71] This theory has been found wanting by Gradel, whose argument establishes a reasonable way of construing worship of the living emperor in Italy itself.[72] The emperor's *genius* was indeed worshipped, but for a separate reason—it was proper to do so for the *paterfamilias* of the Empire. As chapter 3 will explain, his own family life-force had invaded neighborhoods and homes and superseded that of other *patresfamilias*.[73] People also worshipped the emperor's *numen*, or divine power, widely in the Empire.[74] According to Fishwick, a *numen* is "what all gods possess, and by virtue of which they manifest their efficacy, . . . [it is] the quintessential property of a god: that which makes a god a god."[75] An emperor's *numen* was the immanent power of his divinity, a property that distinguished him from other humans. The collection of evidence overall thus attests to the worship of the emperor himself, his *genius*, and his *numen*—in addition to the worship of other members of the imperial family or the whole *domus divina*.[76] The work of Fishwick and Gradel in English is supported in German by that of Manfred Clauss, probably the most vigorous defender of the divinity of the living emperor. In his bold words, "The *princeps* was god. He was so from the beginning, since Caesar and Augustus, he was so during his lifetime, he was so even in the Western parts of the Roman Empire, in Italy, in Rome."[77]

In conclusion, recent scholarship on emperor worship has catalyzed a new understanding of divinity in the Roman world. A focus on material culture and ritual practices, combined with a rejection of old presuppositions, illuminates a conception of divinity as a status based on power, not an essence or nature. The old "problem" of emperor worship—was he a man or a god?— has turned out to be a mirage, which vanishes when the background horizon is altered. In her study of emperor worship in Greece, Maria Kantiréa encapsulates the resolution of the old "problem":

> The *raison d'être* of the imperial cult was not limited to persuading the subjects of their rulers' divine nature—indeed, a pseudo-problem, to which the older bibliography has attached a great importance—but it existed above all to propagate, in a way much more subtle than the coinage, the preeminent ideas upon which the *princeps* based the moral support of his legitimation, and consequently, to conceal under a civic form the historical necessity of this type of monarchy. And yet, the more characteristic aspect of the imperial honorific system was the coexistence of civic honor and cultic veneration. The enactment of two types of sacrifices, those which were offered to the gods for the well-being of the emperors and those which were directed to the emperors as gods, reflected the bipolarity of the nature of the *princeps*—as much divine as human—and the double character of his power—*dominus et deus*—in the Greek world.[78]

In the new perspective, several dichotomies have collapsed—not least the supposed abyss separating humanity and divinity. On the contrary, the worship of the living emperor as a god appealed broadly throughout the Empire. His reach transcended space and time, since he was present at his temples, shrines, and statues in distant provinces, even while he mediated between heaven and earth.[79] It is not surprising, then, that the worship of the emperor, as it is now understood, has invited fresh comparisons to the worship of Jesus Christ. Clifford Ando is characteristically astute in juxtaposing them, the only two gods that reached the whole Empire:

> In the end, Rome gave to the Empire as a whole two very different gods, who shared one essential quality. So long as his power endured, the emperor's immanence in his ubiquitous portraits made him ἐπιφανέστατος, "the most manifest," of the numinous powers of this world. His chief rival, who became his chief patron, was likewise present everywhere in potentiality and promise: *Ubi enim sunt duo vel tres congregati in nomine meo, ibi sum in medio eorum*, "Wherever two or three of you are gathered in my name, there I am in your midst."[80]

Emperor Worship and Early Christianity

> The new age has a savior figure, the greatest benefactor of all times, the *divi filius* . . . the victorious Augustus.
>
> —HELMUT KOESTER

At the end of chapter 1, when I criticized the guild of biblical scholarship for having "a blind spot the size of the Roman emperor," I noted that exceptions to this sweeping criticism would be forthcoming. Clifford Ando's comparison of the space-transcending presence of the emperor and Jesus Christ is a clever, but not unique, example of reading old evidence in new ways. Among biblical scholars too, there have been notable exceptions to Hurtado's "no true analogy" thesis. Indeed, the exceptions will soon become mainstream through new reference works such as *The Cambridge History of Christianity*, whose "Prelude" seems to counter Hurtado directly: "The earliest and most insistent analogy between the way Christ was celebrated and pagan cultic activity is to be found in the use of language from the ruler-cult tradition, by then associated with the divinization of the Roman emperor."[81] In what follows, I can cite only a small sample of representative types, as the research on emperor worship, imperial ideology, and early Christianity is currently proliferating through conferences and publications.[82]

Some scholars have assessed the relationship of early Christianity to the Roman emperor and imperial ideology through text-specific studies on the Gospels,[83] the Epistles,[84] or Revelation,[85] asking how particular texts have resisted or accommodated the demands of Empire. Other scholars have addressed a certain topic or theme that spans different texts and centuries, such as the titles or narratives shared by Jesus Christ and the emperor,[86] the worship of the emperor and the worship of Jesus Christ,[87] conceptions of the imperial family and the Christian family,[88] and the relationship between imperial power structures and Christian communal self-understanding.[89] A few noteworthy scholars have tried to issue a general wake-up call to their colleagues about the importance of all these topics for historians of early Christianity.[90]

Yet despite this excellent work, which brings the historical fact of emperor worship to bear on diverse aspects of early Christianity, some of the most fascinating connections between the Roman emperor and Jesus Christ have still yet to be analyzed in detail. As I stated in a previous section, "son of God" has received some treatment as a topic that connects Jesus Christ and the emperor, but the studies have been thin; the imperial "son of god" title has been often noted but rarely elaborated.[91] The aspects of imperial divine sonship that are most provocative for the study of early Christianity have only begun to be addressed—if noticed at all. Consider, for example, a papyrus which shows, in the first year of Caesar Augustus (30/29 B.C.E.), a group of Egyptian temple "lamplighters" swearing by "Caesar" as "god from god" (θεὸν ἐκ θεοῦ).[92] Though the lamplighters' duty to make "light from light" must be judged an amusing coincidence, the "god from god" connection to identical Nicene language is scintillating. What did such language mean 350 years earlier, when already in the first year of Augustan rule, residents of the Empire were inspired to address the emperor as "god from god"? Clearly the emperor was both "god" and "son of god," but how did this succession of gods begin? From father to son and beyond—again in the unavoidable language of the Creed—how did divinity *proceed*? And most importantly for our topic, did it matter that Augustus, *divi filius*, was not actually the begotten son of *divus Iulius*?

■ ROMAN EMPEROR AS "SON OF GOD"

> To the Emperor Caesar, God, Son of God, Augustus
> —*Inscriptions throughout the Roman Empire*

Origin and Propagation of the Title

According to standard encyclopedic resources, the origin of the "son of god" title in the Roman Empire is simply explained. Julius Caesar was considered divine during his lifetime by some and was, in any case, declared a god of the Roman state—*divus Iulius*—after his assassination.[93] During the ensuing battle for power with Mark Antony, Octavian (later "Augustus") used his status as Caesar's son to bolster his legitimacy—a status that Antony had desired for himself.[94] Octavian was therefore able to call himself, and was called, *divi filius* or "son of god." This claim of continuity with Caesar was sufficient to rouse troops and public support for the defeat of his rivals and consolidation of imperial powers. So goes the handbook version, and it is correct, as far as it goes.

But there is much more to say, a series of questions to be explored. Why did Octavian choose this particular claim to portray his legitimacy? To what social mores was he appealing? Did it matter that he was not a biological son of Caesar, but an adopted son? Within what matrix of cultural practices was that intelligible? After Augustus, how did divine sonship propagate through later emperors? These are the questions—normally left unasked—that drive the remainder of this chapter and the argument of the next.

The adoption of Octavian by Julius Caesar is described by several ancient sources, some of which date from the Augustan age.[95] Although Caesar had a biological son, Caesarion, by Cleopatra, he had long showed favor for Octavian, his great-nephew. Before he died, he had adopted Octavian in his will—a quasi-legal practice usually called "testamentary adoption" (cf. ch. 3)—but kept this fact secret from Octavian.[96] While alive, however, Caesar's special fondness for Octavian, and even his treatment of him as a son, was clear to those who spent time with them together.[97] His decision to make Octavian his heir was further strengthened by favorable omens.[98] It was also said that Octavian's mother, Atia, had been visited and impregnated by Apollo.[99] Just as Caesar's own divinity was supported by divine ancestry, traced to Venus through Aeneas, so would Octavian's be secured as a "son of Apollo." If anyone was to carry on the charismatic leadership of Caesar, it was this young man.

Octavian, for his part, preferred to be "son of god" (i.e., the son of *divus Iulius*) rather than "son of Apollo," though both lineages helped establish his augustness. Surprisingly, after his divine adoptive father had been assassinated, he seems to have been only briefly vexed by the burden of inheriting the name, property, *genius*, and status of *divus Iulius*. Some relatives encouraged him to refuse the adoption out of fear for his safety amid political turmoil. But he decided that now, as Caesar's son, he must avenge his father's murder and carry on the noble Julian *gens*.[100] He called himself, "Caesar, son of Caesar," and most famously, *divi filius*. His filial connection to Caesar won him great public support,[101] not to mention a vast entourage of clients, so the *divi filius* title was disseminated in coins, inscriptions, and monuments as part of official titulature.[102] Aside from the name "Caesar" itself, the "son of god" title was what most enabled the transition to Octavian's rule to be interpreted in the terms of Roman dynastic ideology.

And yet a paradox lies at the core of this ideology: after Octavian secured sole rule over the Empire, the so-called Julio-Claudian "dynasty" had no small amount of trouble propagating itself through natural, begotten sons. The emperor was actually made "son of god" through the act of adoption, and this fact caused tension between ideologies of natural (begotten) sons and adopted (made) sons throughout the first century of the principate. Moreover, the fact that subsequent emperors (after Augustus) used and were called by the title might lead one to ask whether it denoted anything at all about sonship (either natural or adoptive). Perhaps the "son of god" title was just honorific. Or, to reframe the issue for the purposes of this book: in the mid-first century, as the "son of god" title was also starting to be used for Jesus Christ, did it refer to an actual process of imperial sonship, whether begetting or adoption, or was it merely one of the emperor's titles of exaltation?

It is tempting at first to see the title as just one among many honorific expressions. However, as the next chapter elaborates, the evidence suggests that the begetting and making of imperial sons was charted quite carefully by residents of the Empire, especially during the Julio-Claudian "dynasty." People took note of who was born and adopted in the imperial family. Furthermore, a helpful inscription noting Nero's divine sonship comes from the time *after* his adoption by Claudius but *before* his accession to imperial power (between 50–54 C.E.), thus showing that the "son of god" title was connected more to his adoption than to his rule.[103] At the end of the Julio-Claudian "dynasty," the fictive lineage of sons experienced a rupture—the "Year of Four Emperors" (69 C.E.). When Vespasian and the Flavians rose to power, the "son of god" title still drew on images of divine lineage, but the new era necessitated a shift in understanding. That is to say, the fact that Vespasian could be called "Caesar" and "son of god," although he had neither divine begetting nor imperial adoption to justify the titles, demonstrates how the terms could sometimes stand as honorifics that could be divorced from their origins.[104]

Begotten or Made?

The tension between begotten and made divine sonship began with Julius Caesar and Augustus. As a segue to the detailed investigations of the next chapter, it will be helpful here to summarize briefly the foundation of divine sonship in the Augustan age. During his ascendancy to divine status, Julius Caesar relied upon and propagated the image of his divine ancestry. He traced his genealogy to Aeneas, son of Venus, and her importance in Rome was starkly augmented by Caesar's new temple to *Venus Genetrix* (dedicated 46 B.C.E.) in his *Forum Iulium*.[105] In this grand building project, he honored Venus as a divine ancestor and invoked her patronage on the whole city. Such claims of divine ancestry were common among nobility from republican times, even if they were not always believed.[106] But Caesar's *own* achievement of divine status changed the tenor of subsequent claims. When Octavian trumpeted himself as "son of god," he needed only to appeal to his divine adoptive father, not a distant figure from hoary antiquity. Divine ancestry shifted to divine sonship.

In fact, Octavian wanted to have it both ways—he was a "son of god" by Caesar's adoption and a "son of Apollo" by divine begetting. (Add in his divine ancestry from Mars and the claims that he was a "new Romulus" refounding Rome, and one can see how his divine connections were diverse and powerful.)[107] In his competition with Antony for sole possession of Roman *imperium*, he used both aspects of his divine sonship: the filial connection to Caesar swayed the troops and much of the public, while the patronage of Apollo served to rival Antony's self-presentation as Dionysus or Hercules.[108] Ultimately, though, the connection to Caesar proved most powerful, and it was this particular divine relationship—*divi filius*—that was propagated by adoption through the Julio-Claudian "dynasty."

As the divinity of the emperors—and of the whole imperial house as *domus divina*[109]—became a central aspect of imperial ideology over time, claims to divine ancestry diminished in number and power. Olivier Hekster has persuasively argued that the Augustan preference for sonship to a divine emperor, rather than a distant divine genealogy, continued and intensified for subsequent emperors.[110] He concludes, "The impact of Empire, through the centrality and divinity of the Roman emperor, had made emphasis on divine genealogies a practice of the remote past."[111] To be "son of god" in the Roman Empire, in the time period under consideration, meant primarily to be the son of the emperor—whether begotten or made. The next chapter uses that fact as its point of departure; for the divine sonship of the Roman emperor, both begetting and adoption functioned to grant legitimacy, though in different modes. In the terms of a previously explained methodology, both have "resonance" in a Roman understanding of father-son relations. Most scholars, however, have focused almost exclusively on natural, begotten, dynastic relationships in the study of Roman imperial ideology; the next chapter attempts to shed light on the role of adoption in that ideology.

For Augustus, the different expressions of divine sonship were mutually beneficial, as stated above. For the other famous "son of God," the situation was surprisingly similar. In the first century, before the philosophically rooted conception of divine sonship became the standard, Jesus' status as "son of God" was grounded in multiple claims: there were dynastic considerations in depicting him as a son of David, who himself was a royal son of God; his miraculous infancy and childhood narratives suggested a divine begottenness from birth; and his baptismal experience suggested an adult divine election or adoption.[112]

Yet it is not surprising that a concept as challenging to grasp as divine sonship should be expressed in diverse, and even mutually exclusive, ways. One ancient scholar, well known for grappling with the concept of divine sonship, expressed the tension of the begotten/made distinction in these words: "concerning subjects that are obscure, and which require advancement toward understanding, often not only different but even contradictory demonstrations can become clarifications of the things sought for." The source of this quotation is Athanasius, who favorably excerpted these words while defending a colleague's beliefs about the divine sonship of Jesus Christ.[113] Even Athanasius himself, champion of Nicene orthodoxy *par excellence*, acknowledged the complexity of portraying divine sonship. It is the task of the rest of this book to reach further into that complexity and draw out some fresh interpretations of the "son of God" in the Roman world.

3 Begotten or Made?

Adopted Sons in Roman Society and Imperial Ideology

> All the emperors who took the imperial throne through hereditary
> succession, with the exception of Titus, were bad; those who did so
> through adoption were all good, as were those five from Nerva to
> Marcus; and when the empire lapsed into hereditary succession, it
> came again to ruin.
>
> —NICCOLÒ MACCHIAVELLI

George H. Bush and George W. Bush represented the first American presidential dynasty in almost two hundred years. Most pundits speculated that Bill Clinton would eventually be followed by Hillary Clinton, and some championed the electability of Jeb Bush. Might it have been Bush, Clinton, Bush, Clinton, Bush? Things did not work out that way, but even the close possibility suggests that Americans need to look no further than their own government to see the resilience of dynastic ideology amid a supposedly meritocratic system of succession.[1] Roman familial and political succession also exhibited a tension between meritocratic and dynastic ideologies. However, the Romans had a technique at their disposal—the adoption of adult men—that enabled the different ideologies of succession to coexist for hundreds of years.[2] To read a list of powerful Roman men is necessarily to read a list of *adopted* Roman men: Scipio Africanus the Younger, Caesar Augustus, Tiberius, Germanicus, Gaius Caligula, Nero, Pliny the Younger, Trajan, Hadrian, Antoninus Pius, Marcus Aurelius, Lucius Verus, and Constantius I, to name only the most famous.

This chapter analyzes the idea and practice of adoption in Roman society and especially in the burgeoning ideology of the emperor during the early principate.[3] It first surveys the ancient evidence for Roman adoption in law and in actual practice; adoption was a crucial technique for sustaining the peculiarly Roman perspective on fathers and sons, in which every Roman was under the *patria potestas* or "paternal power" of the eldest male in the family. Adopted sons were *chosen* for the job and then assimilated into new families as natural sons through text and image. An adopted son became literally "affiliated" with his adoptive family. In the early principate, Romans began to live not only under the *potestas* of their proximate fathers, but also under the emperor, who was *pater patriae*—the "father of the fatherland." We will examine what cultural changes were necessitated by refashioning the entire Empire as a large family under the emperor. Within the imperial family, as elsewhere in Roman culture, adoption constituted a chief mode of sustaining family lines. The evidence of adoption as a method of imperial succession, of transmitting power from father to son, will be addressed in some detail.

Regardless of whether such adoptions were private or public in their ceremony, they were highly publicized in coins, portraits, texts, and tales. The Empire was a family, after all, and the family needed to know what was going on at the top. The chapter concludes with treatments of some key imperial adoptions, analyzing how the adopted sons were "affiliated" into their roles and whether Roman observers accepted them as natural members of the ruling "dynasty."

■ ADOPTION IN ROMAN SOCIETY

> One great difference between Roman families and those of the modern
> West is the former's readiness to extend relationships.
>
> —SUZANNE DIXON

> The Romans seem to have been always ready to create kinship
> and affinity.
>
> —MIREILLE CORBIER

In *The Law of the Ancient Romans*, Alan Watson describes *patria potestas* as "the most fundamental and most peculiarly Roman part of family law."[4] All children born to a father lived under the power of their father (*in potestate*) as long as he lived; that is, the father had complete power over each child, even the power of life and death. In theory, a Roman *paterfamilias* could do whatever he wanted to those under this power, and fathers did make decisions about their *familiae* which modern Western readers find deplorable. When speaking of *patria potestas*, the Roman jurist Gaius proclaimed, "there are hardly any other men who have such authority over their children as we have."[5] Yet historians have also argued that, in practice, Roman fathers were not usually the despots that the law permitted them to be.[6] The power of the father was used most frequently not to administer beatings, but to distribute goods. For this reason, the power of the father came to a head, so to speak, in the matter of the family's inheritable goods. As in the modern West, these included land and wealth, but also—sometimes more importantly—the family name, honor, and cult.[7] Those fathers with the most to pass on were the ones most concerned with their heirs. What could a Roman father do when he did not have male sons to carry on the family wealth, name, honor, and cult? He could adopt.

The issue of inheritance brings into focus the chief differences between adoption in Roman culture and in the modern West. In modern Western countries, adoption often springs from a concern for child welfare, as a way to situate orphans or otherwise parentless children in stable and loving homes. It does not only provide children with homes, but often provides childless couples with "social progeny" to pass on their culture.[8] Only thirdly is modern adoption construed as a means of securing heirs. But this third reason to adopt, which is almost absent from modern minds, was the most prominent cause of adoption on the minds of Roman fathers. It will be difficult for many modern readers to comprehend, first, the real sense of duty that Romans felt to their ancestors and, second, the way in which such duty to the past was manifested in the future continuity of the familial *gens*, name, glory, and cult. All of these needed an heir.

The focus on inheritance explains other peculiar features of Roman adoption. For example, they adopted adults more frequently than children; an adult would have already proved himself as a viable and trustworthy heir, but children could easily die or prove otherwise unsuitable. By adopting an adult, a father had confidence in the security of his inheritable goods. Furthermore, those with the most to bequeath were most likely to adopt. Those with little property or status had little cause for adoption; but for patricians and emperors, the stakes were high indeed.

The relationships between fathers and sons were the primary connections governing the systems of politics and kinship, which were the two dominant and overlapping "social spheres" of Roman society.[9] The modern "nuclear family" was hardly a concern because, in most cases, only the father-son relationship mattered for politics and kinship; in fact, scholars have persuasively argued that there is no term in either Greek or Latin which corresponds to the modern Western concept of "family."[10] Therefore, adoption was performed neither for the sake of a child's welfare nor to satisfy a "nuclear" couple's desire to nurture, but for the sake of a father, who needed to pass on his wealth, name, honor and family cult. Since all property and status were concentrated in the *paterfamilias*, even bachelors could adopt in Roman culture. On the whole, "adoption of adult men was a convenient resource for childless aristocrats and for emperors in need of successors."[11]

Adoption in Law and Literature

Our understanding of adoption in the Roman Empire comes from a few descriptions by Roman authors, the family law sections of the Roman civil codes, legal declamations, and some documentary papyri. In his compilation of miscellanies, *Noctes Atticae* or "Attic Nights," Aulus Gellius provides the earliest explicit description (mid-late second century) of the practice in Rome.[12] He distinguishes two forms of adoption: *adoptatio* (usually called simply *adoptio*) and *adrogatio* (also spelled *arrogatio*). The former is the process by which a man already under the power of a father is transferred to the power of a different father. It is enacted through a thrice-repeated formula by the former father and an acceptance by the new father in front of a Roman official. The latter is the process by which men who are their own masters deliver themselves into a father's control and are accepted into the other's family. It is enacted through the consideration of a *comitia curiata* (an assembly comprised of Rome's constituent tribes and families) and under the auspices of the *pontifices*. In addition to these forms reported by Aulus Gellius and confirmed by legal codes, the late Republic and principate also give evidence of testamentary adoption, when fathers would declare adoptions posthumously in their testaments.

The legal codes of Gaius and Justinian chart the details of adoption laws and practices, some of which are germane to our topic.[13] Roman adoption was different from that of the modern West in the irrelevance of the adopter's wife to the transaction and the ensuing family structure. "If I adopt a son, my wife does not occupy the place of a mother to him" (*Dig.* 1.7.23). The adopted son does, however, become related as a sibling to the other children of the father. "But he whom I have adopted becomes the brother of my daughter, since my daughter is a member of my family" (*Dig.* 1.7.23). The irrelevance of the wife/mother explains the Roman allowance for bachelors to adopt (*Dig.* 1.7.30). Some further details are: the good news that a son's former liabilities and debts are taken from him and transferred to his adoptive father (*Dig.* 1.7.45), but also the bad news that the adopted son, being of the same status as a biological son, cannot obtain release from under the power of his new father (*Dig.* 1.7.31).

Buried in the legal codes one finds a small reference to illegal practices: any adoption "not legally made" could later be confirmed by the emperor (*Dig.* 1.7.38). But when a Roman historian looks under the rock of those three words, he or she finds a confusing swarm of crisscrossing data. Indeed, modern scholars have compiled and analyzed evidence demonstrating that Roman adoption law, though an important source for understanding the idealized vision of society, does not begin to describe the variety of adoptive family relations that existed in the Empire. Patricians in the late Republic and emperors in the principate often ignored or flagrantly violated the rules of adoption. The documentary evidence from papyri further depicts instances of adoption that do not map on to the legal sources. The preeminent study of those data concludes that papyrus contracts for "adoption" (υἱοθεσία) do not have an obvious connection to Roman laws of adoption and should be considered rather as local manifestations of a "common law" form of adoption.[14]

In her landmark study, *Römische Adoption*, Christiane Kunst concurs, arguing that the performance and social acceptance of various kinds of adoptive or quasi-adoptive relationships—other than those legalized according to the Roman codes—was much more common than previous scholarship acknowledged.[15] As a point of departure, Kunst articulates the distinction between the narrow sense of the noun *adoptio* and the wide semantic range of the verb *adoptare*, a linguistic distinction which symbolizes a real difference between adoption in the law and adoption in Roman practice: "This divergence between verb and noun provides cause for the supposition that adoption in the strict sense indeed denoted the formal legal acceptance of a child, but as an occurrence it was carried over into a much larger spectrum of social reality."[16] The Greek terminology for adoption during the Roman era was even less regular than the Latin, as one would expect: adoptions were described using diverse verbs (such as ποιέω, εἰσποιέω, ἐκποιέω, υἱοποιέω, τίθημι, υἱοθετέω, etc.) and their related nouns.[17] Moreover, Kunst shows that even Roman authors writing in Latin do not properly distinguish forms of *arrogatio* and *adoptio*, nor do they distinguish formal adoptions from what she labels "quasi-adoptions."[18] The social practice of adoption seems to be least regulated in the era under consideration by the present study, the first two centuries of the principate. On the whole, the "stark mixture of terminology" for adoption in the Roman era reveals a highly adaptable social practice, which fits the Roman family's ubiquitous "readiness to extend relationships."[19]

The legal and historical sources make clear that those to whom family relations had been extended were not supposed to be thought of as inferior to biological kin. In most cases, Romans did not regard the status of adopted sons as lower than that of biological sons. As Watson states, "The adopted person not only entered the family of the adopter; he acquired the status in the community which he should have as a son of the adopter."[20] His adoption was precisely the legal and cultural construction which allowed him to take over the social position of his adoptive father.[21] Certainly some Roman authors record opinions that denigrate adopted sons, which will be considered later, but many sing the praises of adoption as a cultural practice, especially as a method of imperial succession.[22] The Roman civil law proclaims that "adoption imitates nature" (*Inst. Iust.* 1.11.4), and "the rank of a person is not diminished by adoption, but is in fact increased" (*Dig.* 1.7.35). Cicero could readily rely on this legal evaluation of adoption to elaborate a philosophical point. When discussing his hometown with Atticus, he favorably compares the Roman citizenship of someone not born in Rome to an adoptive relationship. Though one still honors a bond with his natural fatherland (*patria*), the adoptive fatherland of Rome has increased his status and "must stand first in [his] affection."[23] Kunst summarizes these ideas as a conclusion of her thorough study: "The adopted son was really to become the son and agent of the adoptive father; he was not a substitute son, nor some kind of second-class son. The adopted son also exchanged his own [status] and took over the status of the adoptive father."[24]

As implied in the discussion of inheritance above, adoption occurred most frequently among Roman elites—those with the most wealth and status to pass on. Patricians and emperors often got themselves entangled in intricate webs of adoptions and marriages in order to control their familial property and name for the future. Much was permitted to these Roman fathers, each of whom had a "recognized right . . . to reshape his relationships," according to Mireille Corbier; adoption was a strategy used for regulating "the formation of alliances between families and between individuals" and providing "the definition of legitimacy in the context of political power."[25] In his monograph on the topic, *Les Adoptions politiques à Rome*, Marcel-Henri Prévost agrees with Corbier, arguing that the legal consequence of adoption (securing an heir), though important, was only a small feature of the overall role adoption played in Roman political culture. Prévost surveys the political adoptions of the Republic and principate to conclude that issues of social status, especially the continued extension of patron-client relationships, trumped the legal matters of inheritance. During both the Republic and the Empire, the social reality [of adoption], which is covered by—and sometimes risks being hidden by—the constitutional contingencies, is the same. Whatever the legal technique used to allocate powers under public law, these [powers] are always entrusted, practically speaking, to the holder of a social power which is made real by the possession of various clienteles and whose cohesion requires the assurance of a continuous line of successive patrons.[26]

Regardless of the legal techniques used or the inheritances involved, the status or "social power" of the father was made real by the possession of clients gained through adoption. In the ancient Roman economy of status, which was a zero-sum system, a father needed always to maintain or bolster the status of his family line as a patron. Through the process of adoption, the new clients were also elevated. The Stoic philosopher Epictetus even warned that the sudden acquisition of status through adoption could go to a person's head. For him, imperial adoption is a ready example of the constant temptations for the aspiring philosopher: "If Caesar were to adopt you as a son, no one would be able to put up with your arrogance."[27]

With immense wealth and status at stake, it is not surprising that Roman sons wrangled with their fathers and brothers over inheritances and favors. Examples of this strife and its attempted resolution are on display in several extant Roman declamations (especially the *Controversiae*, or "legal case studies"), a genre which has long been dismissed by most Roman social historians as a kind of school-boy rhetoric. However, the rhetoric of these speeches trenchantly explores the faultlines in Roman society and the liminal spaces in which Roman identity or "Romanness" was produced. The orators also offer frequent epigrams and commonplaces designed to appeal to the "epistemological unconscious" of their intended audiences.[28] One can thus interpret the kind of "common sense" that an orator expects from his audience. The intended audiences, moreover, are not aptly depicted by the image of school boys. S. F. Bonner situates the declamations of the Elder Seneca in this way: "the whole atmosphere of the Senecan declamations is that of men of standing who found therein a means of sharpening their wits, elaborating and exhibiting their legal knowledge, and spending their leisure hours in a friendly, amusing, and by no means futile intellectual exercise."[29]

Utilizing the work of Bonner and the more recent critical editions of declamations by the Elder Seneca, Quintilian, and Calpurnius Flaccus, historians Mary Beard and Erik Gunderson have helped usher in "an emerging consensus . . . that the connection between declamation and Roman society is profound and that it cannot be ignored."[30] In his book, *Declamation, Paternity, and Roman Identity*, Gunderson offers a cogent and sophisticated argument about how declamation relates to social reality. He endorses Beard's interpretation of declamation as "myth," in which "Romans construct and reconstruct for themselves questions of their Romanness," but investigates it from the supplementary perspective of social psychology, "beyond mere social practice and into the space where society and psyche intersect."[31] Gunderson finds that the Roman psyche is most concerned with how to negotiate social inequality, and the declamations manifest this in their portrayal of asymmetrical father-son relationships.[32]

As mentioned above, the Roman father-son relationship came to a head in the issue of inheritable goods—specifically, who would be the son to inherit them? The declamations are thus outfitted with legal case studies concerning disinheritance (abdication) and adoption. Such are fitting topics for the noble and the upwardly mobile in Roman society, who are trying to negotiate the many "transformations of the family and corresponding alterations in social station" necessary to propagate an elite *familia*.[33] Among the extant *Controversiae* of the Elder Seneca, five deal with adoption in some way and three are germane to our topic.[34] These references bolster and augment the construal of adoption advanced already through analysis of Roman law and literature. One of Seneca's orators makes an analogy to adoption during a speech treating a different issue. In order to elaborate an argument about how one should scrutinize a woman before deciding to marry her, the orator compares the situation to a youth being requested for adoption. "If [the young man] wants to go, he should inquire how many ancestors the old man who seeks him has, what rank they are, what the old man's wealth is—whether he can auction himself off at a sufficient price" (1.6.6).[35] This pursuit of "due diligence" about the wealth and status of one's future parents highlights the dispassionate, businesslike character of the transaction. It also supports the earlier interpretation of Roman adoption as a vehicle for social prestige and upward mobility.

The second and third examples deal with adoption more directly, posing case studies about its proper use. In a speech taking the side of a poor father, who has tried to convince his recalcitrant son to be adopted by a rich man, Porcius Latro (Seneca's favorite orator) offers a rhetorical commonplace on the social benefits of adoption. "The family portraits of the Fabricii found room for the Metelli. Adoption merged the families of the Aemilii and the Scipios. Even names that age has blotted out shine in the person of new heirs. That is how the nobility of the patricians has survived to this day from the founding of the city. Adoption is the remedy for chance" (2.1.17).[36] Latro appeals to classic Roman families, several of whom have used adoption to continue their lines and merge with others. And he concludes with the eminently quotable epigram, "*Adoptio fortunae remedium est.*" Here adoption is a force for good, sustaining great families and protecting them against the vicissitudes of nature.

Latro provides further memorable material in a different speech about an uncouth adoption, whose details are these: A father disinherited a son (1), who himself proceeded to go and have a son (2) of his own with a prostitute. When son (1) fell ill and died, his father came and adopted son (2). But now the brother of the deceased son (1) has become outraged because his father has adopted the son (2) of a prostitute. When speaking on the side of the brother, questioning the appropriateness of his father's adopting son (2), Latro uses another commonplace about adoption—this time, a negative one. Seneca reports: "Latro was speaking on the side of the [brother], and when he got to the part about adoption, he said: 'Now through adoption, this [child] from the very bottom is grafted on to the nobility,' and made other remarks to this effect" (2.4.13).[37] It is clear from Seneca's context that the image of "grafting" was not interpreted as a positive one; this was a figurative way of challenging someone's "genetic" purity. Being one of the finest orators, Latro could thus provide the perfect images either to defend (as above, 2.1) or reject (as here, 2.4) a particular adoption.[38]

At one instance of publicly declaiming on this case study, Latro probably wished he had taken a more positive stance toward adoption than he did. Seneca reports that Latro had declaimed on the subject "in the presence of Caesar Augustus and Marcus Agrippa, whose sons—[Gaius and Lucius,] the emperor's grandsons—the emperor seemed to be proposing to adopt at that time" (2.4.12).[39] Latro's line that portrayed adoption as "grafting" and raising up someone "from the very bottom" insinuated that the adopted son was not really noble; this comment would have struck a dissonant note with both Augustus and Marcus Agrippa. (To make matters worse, one of Latro's rhetorical opponents made a gesture to make certain that Augustus noticed the slip-up.) One problem was that "Agrippa was one of those who were not begotten noble, but made noble" (2.4.12), so Latro was accidentally insulting Agrippa himself.[40] Furthermore, his remark risked insulting Augustus too, by comparing Gaius and Lucius to the son of a prostitute and thus challenging their worthiness as imperial heirs. This was an example *par excellence* of the failure to adapt one's argument to one's audience, resulting in a *faux pas* of imperial proportions. Seneca concludes from the example that Augustus deserves admiration for allowing such a comment to go unpunished— the emperor's *clementia* on public display.

On the whole, the declamations uphold the general depiction of adoption in Roman law and literature and expand our understanding of how adoptions could be construed. As in Roman law, the father reigns supreme; he uses adoption as a means to reshape his relationships and secure a future for his inheritable goods. Though we learn little to support or contradict the summary observations of Gellius, we do find a keen awareness of the social status involved in Roman adoptions. A son could be raised up from the bottom of society and installed among the nobility; furthermore, an adopted son could supersede a natural son in favor and inheritance. Finally, several rhetorical commonplaces about adoption help situate the Roman "common sense" about adoption: it was of great benefit to families and a remedy for chance, but it could be used inappropriately to blur the lines between patricians and plebeians.

Adoption Procedures?

Despite the abundant evidence of adoptions in Roman society, the actual procedure by which fathers adopted sons remains obscure and seems not to have been uniform in the Empire. The Roman law codes are silent concerning rituals or formulae; some authors do, however, describe the practice, and extant papyri and inscriptions provide limited evidence. According to Aulus Gellius, *adoptio* occurs through a thrice-repeated declaration by the former father, releasing the son or sons into the custody of the new father, who accepts them in the presence of a Roman *praetor*. An *arrogatio* requires the additional confirmation of the afore-mentioned *comitia curiata*, which represents the will of the people to approve the transaction. Gellius even cites the language of an *arrogatio* ceremony, in which the question is put to the Roman people for approval: "May it please you to command that N^1 be the son of N^2 as justly and lawfully as if he had been born of that father [N^2] and the mother of his family, and that N^2 have the power of life and death over N^1 which a father has over a son."[41] The will of the Roman people is necessary for the *arrogatio* ceremony because it has more drastic effects than an *adoptio*. By sub-suming an independent man, who was under his own legal power, into the power of another man as father, an *arrogatio* effectively annihilates the former *gens* of the adopted son. His former name, status, and family cult are gone, everything having been brought under the power of his new father.

Extant papyri and inscriptions do not corroborate Gellius's description of a Roman adoptive formula; rather, they demonstrate the diversity of terminology and ideas involved. As noted above, Kurylowicz concludes that the papyri reflect neither the terminology nor law of Rome but reveal a "common law" situation in Greco-Roman Egypt.[42] The terminology and implications of adoption were not uniform there, and moreover, the Greek-speaking eastern provinces used a differ-ent vocabulary from both Rome and Egypt. The epigraphic evidence, though more abundant than the papyrological, does not allay our uncertainty about finding a standard language or formula for adoptive practices in the Roman Empire. Martin Smith charts more than ten different linguistic descriptions of adoptive relation-ships in Greek inscriptions.[43] Yet this diversity is a boon for research when con-trasted with the paucity of explicit references in Latin inscriptions; as Smith explains, "apart from the extremely rare occurrences of *filius adoptivus* and the like, we are forced to make inferences chiefly from cognomina in *-ianus*. As soon as this type of name comes to be commonly used for purposes other than adoption we are left with no reliable guide."[44] In short, we are not lacking evidence of adop-tion in the Roman Empire, but we are restricted from describing the terminology or ritual of the event in a simple way that fits the extant data. Adoption was cer-tainly happening in diverse regions of the Empire, but there does not seem to have been knowledge of the formulae preserved in Gellius's description or concern for the details of the legal codes.

Indeed, Roman elites—the most prolific and prominent adopters—did not always abide by the laws they had established. There were some famously trans-gressive adoptions, such as when the patrician Clodius had himself adopted by a plebeian *younger* than himself, ostentatiously violating the principle that "adoption imitates nature."[45] One of the Elder Seneca's declamation case studies, in which a man tries to adopt his brother while their father was still alive, seems less fanciful in light of Clodius's real-life maneuver.[46] And then there were the testamentary adoptions, in which a father would adopt a son or sons through his last will and testament; though absent from the legal codes, they were used widely by patricians and emperors. These posthumous adoptions express quite clearly the connection between adoption and inheritance in the Roman worldview. Furthermore, one can behold in them the potency of the Roman *paterfamilias*: he could sire children even from beyond the grave.

Sometimes extenuating circumstances necessitated a brief, informal adoption ceremony, such as happened with several imperial adoptions. An example of intrigue comes from the principate of Gaius Caligula. In his "embassy to Gaius," a sharp invective speech against the rule of Gaius Caligula, Philo of Alexandria describes the situation which led Gaius to adopt Tiberius Gemellus, his cousin. Gaius had come to fear the claims that Tiberius Gemellus might have on imperial power, "since Gaius was the grandson of [the emperor] Tiberius by adoption while the other was by nature."[47] As a conniving way to dispose of his rival claimant, Gaius decided to *adopt* Tiberius Gemellus as his son, thus enabling Gaius (legally, at least) to have power over his life and death. Philo described the adoption as "a snare to assure not the sovereignty which [Tiberius Gemellus] expected, but the loss of that which he held already, . . . for the Roman laws assign absolute power over the son to the father."[48] Once adopted, Gaius would order him killed (though he ended up committing suicide instead).[49] This tension and violence between natural and adoptive sons foreshadows the latter portion of this chapter; at this point, I would only emphasize the brief, *ad hoc* nature of the adoption procedure. It occurred through these words: "I will be more than a tutor, teacher, and guardian. I will presently appoint myself to be his father and him to be my son."[50] Later, in the tumultuous "Year of Four Emperors," the adoption of Piso by Galba seems to have been enacted just as hastily, introduced by the simple declaration of the word "son." Nerva's adoption of Trajan was similarly terse, requiring barely a sentence. The memory and evaluation of these imperial adoptions will be analyzed later in this chapter.

Despite the stark repercussions of Roman adoptions, entailing the permanent transfer of wealth and status, Kunst points out that the transactions seem to have been free of pageantry. The urbane Roman sensibility considered it barbaric to associate adoption with any kind of birth ritual, and they "did without any distinctive gestures, such as setting on the knees or hugging," examples of adoptive rituals from other ancient cultures.[51] A point of contrast is provided by Diodorus Siculus, when he describes the apotheosis and adoption ritual performed on Heracles by Zeus and Hera.

> We should add to what has been said about Heracles, that after his apotheosis Zeus persuaded Hera to adopt him (υἱοποιήσασθαι) as her son and henceforth for all time to cherish him with a mother's love, and this adoption (τέκνωσις), they say, took place in the following manner. Hera lay upon a bed, and drawing Heracles close to her body then let him fall through her garments to the ground, imitating in this way the actual birth

(τὴν ἀληθινὴν γένεσιν); and this ceremony is observed to this day by the barbarians whenever they wish to adopt a son (ὅταν θετὸν υἱὸν ποιεῖσθαι βούλωνται).[52]

Just as Ancient Near Eastern cultures used an imitation ritual of nursing or rearing (setting on the knees) to enact adoption, Diodorus Siculus reports that "barbarians" of his own time used an imitation ritual of "actual birth" to enact adoption. But for Roman adoptive parents, such expressions neither were built into the adoptive ritual nor do they seem to have been spontaneous reactions of the parent. This portrayal coheres with the overall picture of Roman parent-child relations, which are totally foreign to a modern Westerner; the role of the Roman parent had almost nothing to do with what we consider a parent's proper functions.

Lack of pageantry is not the only feature distinguishing Roman adoption from its cultural parallels. When examined cross-culturally, two other features stand out. First, as mentioned above, Roman adoption was not a fosterage or child welfare system but rather a method of passing on wealth and status to heirs, to secure the continued existence of a family line.[53] From the perspective of the adopted son, Roman adoption was not for a child to gain a home of love and care but for an adult to gain an inheritance of wealth and status. Stated another way, it was not enacted to stabilize the life of a child, but to stabilize the future of a father. Second, Roman adoption, as with most other Roman family relations, was unusually focused on the *paterfamilias*. At issue were his name, his wealth, his status, and his sacred rites; without a son, his divine spirit (*genius*) would perish. One could say that all laws led to the Roman father.

▩ EMPEROR AS FATHER, EMPIRE AS FAMILY

> "*Augusto, patri patriae, feliciter!*"
> "*Bene te, patriae pater, optime Caesar.*"
> —*Invocations of the emperor, after a meal*

On a winter's day in 2 B.C.E—February 5, to be exact—the Roman family changed forever. The city brimmed with excitement because the Senate had a celebratory announcement to make. But it's not what you might think. No important birth occurred that day. Proclamations of "It's a boy!" did not resound on the Palatine hill or in the Forum. On the contrary, a new *father* was born that day, when Caesar Augustus was declared *pater patriae*—father of the fatherland. In lieu of gifts, the new father requests honors instead.

And honors he would receive. In his *Res Gestae*, a public résumé of accomplishments, Augustus himself describes the events of 2 B.C.E: "In my thirteenth consulship the Senate, the equestrian order, and the whole people of Rome gave me the title of *pater patriae*, and resolved that this should be inscribed in the porch of my house and in the *Curia Julia* and in the *Forum Augustum* below the chariot that had been set there in my honor by decree of the Senate."[54] But what was this honor? What did it mean for the Senate and the Roman people to consider Augustus as a father?

Augustus was actually not the first to be honored with such a title, but its ramifications were more explicitly fleshed out under his rule than at any previous time. The titles *parens patriae* and *pater patriae* had occasionally been bestowed on heroic individuals "to equate the role of a benefactor with that of a father."[55] That is to say, because someone had acted powerfully for the benefit of Rome, as a father exercises his power for the benefit of his family, he was honored with such a title. For his defense against the Catilinarian conspirators, Cicero was hailed as *parens patriae*; for his victory at the battle of Munda, Julius Caesar was called *pater patriae*.[56] Neither of these leaders developed an overall fatherly image, however. With the long reign of Augustus and concomitant shifts in political ideology, *pater patriae* did shift from an honorific title to an authentic role.[57] Romans throughout the Empire began to consider Augustus as a *paterfamilias*—of the largest family on earth. After his death, the fatherly image of the divine Augustus was distributed on the legend of a new coin issue: "*Divus Augustus Pater*."[58] Besides Tiberius, who did not accept the title of "father," every emperor thereafter was known by it.[59]

But didn't the Roman people already have a *pater*—the god Jupiter? Indeed, the fatherly role of Jupiter has been documented and analyzed in the study of Roman religion, and it frequently played a role in the official political ideology of Roman rulers during Republic and Empire. In his monograph on "Jupiter and Roman Imperial Ideology," J. Rufus Fears offers an astute, chronological analysis of how Roman rulers used Jupiter in their official ideology and how that usage was reflected back in the unofficial piety of the people. He argues that "the concept of Jupiter as *pater* clearly predates the Capitoline cult" of Roman Jupiter, stretching back to the Indo-European roots which engendered the Vedic *Dyaus Pitar*, the Greek *Zeus Pater*, and the Roman *Iuppiter*.[60] Crucial to note for our topic is Fears's observation that "the implication of the epithet Father is not generation but rather rule and dependence, the dependence of the human worshiper upon his divine protector who can supply his needs and protect him and under whose power he stands as one inferior in age and status."[61] In the Roman worldview, the father-son relationship did not primarily connote "generation" or a "begotten" relationship; if this fact is kept in mind, our interpretations of father-son language in the Roman Empire can be deepened and expanded.

When investigating the political appropriation of Jupiter throughout Roman history, Fears isolates a specific time when the fatherly god is absent from official political ideology: the principate of Augustus. "If we consider the implications of Augustus' official acts and of such official testimony as the coinage, it becomes clear that after 27 B.C. Jupiter was relegated to a position of honored insignificance."[62] The absence was "marked and intentional," and it made room for the new political ideology of the Augustan age. This was the main point: *Augustus* was now the father of the Roman people, he himself with divine lineage through his adoptive father, and his family would now preside in the fatherly role over the Empire.

In reconceiving the principate as the inheritable property of one man, and the entire Empire as a large family under the patronage and power of that man as a father, Augustus incarnated (or even displaced) Jupiter's traditional fatherly role. The Julio-Claudian family dynasty, perpetuated through adoption, was the manifest divine order of fathers and sons.[63]

Roman writers of the first and second centuries commented on the new role played by Augustus and his successors. For example, from his position of exile, Ovid uses the titles of "parent" and "father" to laud Augustus's family line and also to appeal to his mercy. He praises the Roman "fatherland" to be "safe and secure" under the "parental" care of Augustus because he has established (the adopted son) Tiberius and (the grandsons) Germanicus and Drusus the Younger to continue the imperial family.[64] This interpretation of "father" was shared by Strabo, who interprets Augustus's fatherly status as both a metaphor for good authority and a literal assurance of political stability: it would be "a difficult thing to administer so great a dominion otherwise than by turning it over to one man, as to a father."[65] Furthermore, Ovid invokes Augustus's fatherly mercy: he begs for "a milder and nearer place of exile" with the cry, "Spare me, *pater patriae*! Do not, forgetful of this name [*pater*], take from me the hope that I may appease you!"[66] For Ovid, the title of *pater* connoted authority over a solid line of family descendants and a merciful demeanor toward all under his power.

Seneca the Younger provides an example of how, after two generations of Julio-Claudian reinforcement, the title had become clearly indicative of a role. It now seemed natural to speak of the *princeps* as a *pater*. When articulating the ideal vision of an emperor's *clementia*, Seneca explains:

> This [*clementia*] is the duty of a *parens*, and it is also the duty of a *princeps*, whom not in empty flattery we have been led to call "*pater patriae*." For other designations have been granted merely by way of honor; some we have styled "the great" and "the fortunate" and "the august," and we have heaped upon pretentious greatness all possible titles as a tribute to such men. But to the *pater patriae* we have given the name in order that he may know that he has been entrusted with *patria potestas*, which is most forbearing in its care for the interests of his children and subordinates his own to theirs.[67]

According to Seneca, the title of "father" is not simply an honorific title like "Augustus," which acknowledged past actions (as the title "father" did for Cicero and Caesar). This title instead denotes a present and future *function* of the emperor; he will continue to act as the *paterfamilias*, entrusted with *patria potestas*. Seneca exhorts the emperor not to use the full powers allotted to him, but to deal with his children mercifully.[68]

Imagining the emperor as father did not only affect the imagery of Latin high literature; this reconfiguring of the fundamental Roman social unit had practical consequences. For example, Suetonius encapsulates the event of 2 B.C.E and its repercussions throughout the Empire (*Aug.* 58–60). Some of the events described by Suetonius were generic gestures of adulation for a heroic ruler, such as the redating of municipal calendars, the establishment of temples and games, and the renaming of cities. But others were rather specific responses to the new Augustan role as father. Upon the new declaration, many Roman family heads altered their testaments—the symbols of their fatherly statures—to include offerings to Augustus. By including him in their wills, these previously independent Roman fathers indicated their obeisance to the emperor's overall paternity. The rulers of the various provinces were also sure to situate themselves as members of his family entourage and "show him the attentions usual in dependents" (*more clientium*). Most importantly, the Empire swiftly developed an innovative devotion to the emperor's *genius*, starting with a large-scale enterprise to complete the temple to Jupiter Olympius at Athens and dedicate it to the *genius* of Augustus. Though some scholars have viewed the explosion of dedications and offerings to the emperor's *genius* as a way of honoring the emperor without giving in to direct worship of him, the focus on the *genius* should be interpreted in its proper role as the tutelary spirit of a family line (*gens*).[69] If Augustus had become the father of all, the Roman worldview necessitated an honoring of the family *genius*.[70] John Scheid situates this development in the overall program of the Augustan principate:

> Creating this kind of cult [to the *genius* of Augustus] extended to the public persona of the emperor domestic forms of cult (such as that of the *genius* of the *paterfamilias*), or forms previously reserved for particular Roman surroundings (the *genius* of Rome or some other place). Augustus exploited this ambiguity, for he was always keen to resort to categories of the family and to the symbolism of the powers of the *paterfamilias* in order to define his own relations with the citizens.[71]

Refashioning the Empire as a large family thus engendered a shift in cultic practices, both in public and private. Using the sacrificial record of the *Acta Fratrum Arvalium* as his main source, Gradel completely rewrites the scholarly history of the emperor's *genius* in the Roman state cult.[72] Taylor had previously argued that the *genius* and *numen* of Augustus were both worshipped during Augustus's lifetime and were incorporated into official state cult.[73] Gradel's presentation takes seriously, however, the servile implications of honoring someone's *genius*; that is to say, participating in the family cult of another man's *genius* is to put oneself under that man's power in a poignant way. Roman elites, each with his own status concentrated in his *patria potestas*, would be loath to submit to such an activity, much less enshrine it in state cult. This conflict with high-ranking Roman men was likely the reason that Tiberius initially refused the title of *pater patriae*. It was only under Claudius that the *genius Augusti* entered the state cult. In Gradel's own words:

> The decisive development [in adding the ruling emperor's *genius* to the state cult] took place under Claudius, who joined this cult to that of his deified ancestress Livia and her husband Augustus. The ideological connotations were obvious, stressing Claudius as the true heir of Augustus. With the worship of his *Genius*, the emperor's position in the state

was for the first time clearly expressed in constitutional terms as that of a *paterfamilias* for the whole Roman people .... By implication, if the emperor was a mega-*paterfamilias*, his fellow senators would be his *clientes* ... [Claudius] linked the title [*pater patriae*] with its logical consequence in practice, namely state worship of his own *Genius*, as the *Genius* of a *paterfamilias* was worshipped by his *familia* in the Roman household.[74]

By studying the sacrificial practices of the Arval brethren, Gradel concludes that, after Claudius, the installation of the living emperor's *genius* in state cult was on-and-off for over a century, corresponding roughly to the senatorial characterization of each emperor.[75] The emperor's *genius* was officially worshipped by the state only if the Senate had good relations with that particular emperor.

The argument that worship of the *genius* did not immediately enter the state cult and was not always embraced by Roman elites should *not* be interpreted as a diminution of Augustus's and his successors' power to penetrate public and private spaces in less official ways, through practices not sponsored by the Senate. On the contrary, Augustus was honored throughout the city of Rome and beyond, especially by those who had more to gain by his fatherly patronage than to lose of their own status. The best evidence of honoring the *genius* of Augustus in Rome are the so-called compital altars, of which several are extant.[76] Roman residents in the Augustan era imagined their city as a collection of neighborhoods (*vici*), with each *vicus* being centered on a *compitum*.[77] An urban *compitum* was a kind of "crossroads," larger than a simple intersection and smaller than a *piazza*—it might now be called a *piazzina*. During the Republic, the neighborhood *collegia*, each of which was oriented around an individual *compitum*, had developed a reputation for political unrest, specifically during the holiday of *Compitalia*. The holiday and its games were thus abolished in the late Republic. Augustus resurrected them, however, as part of his plan for restoration and innovation of traditional cults.[78] Instead of excluding the plebeian leaders of each *vicus* from the closed system of status, he adapted the neighborhood cults in distinct ways. The cults had previously been devoted to the *Lares compitales,* a pair of guardian spirits which ensured the well-being of a particular place (whether house, neighborhood, or entire city, as with the Augustan temple of the *Lares*). Augustus invited leaders from among the freedmen (*vicomagistri*), with slaves to assist, to rededicate altars to the *Lares*, with the added benefit of gaining permanent status for themselves as dedicators.

But the extant altars from Augustan Rome also depict a third figure honored—the *genius Augusti*—alongside the *Lares*, who were themselves renamed *Lares Augusti* in most examples. The altars depict neighborhood freedmen and slaves engaged in sacrifice to the *Lares* and the *genius*, surrounded by Augustan family symbols and, in some cases, portraits of the imperial family itself. This linkage of the twin *Lares* and the *genius* had been noted by Ovid, when he described the Augustan restoration. In times past, says Ovid, he had "sought for images of the twin gods"; sadly they had fallen into disrepair. But now, in the Augustan restoration: "The city has a thousand *Lares* and the *genius* of the leader who delivered them, and the neighborhoods worship three divine powers."[79] Though this threesome of divine powers was bound together as a restoration of a republican cult, Gradel astutely observes that among the sacrifices offered, the sacrifice of a bull to the *genius* indicates that it had become "the main divinity of the cult."[80] The local leaders of the neighborhoods were thus symbolically bringing themselves and their constituents under the familial headship of Augustus.

The penetration of Augustus and his successors did not stop there, but extended into the private homes of the Empire's residents.[81] Though ancient home life is extremely difficult to assess, there is some evidence of honoring the imperial family in home altars and especially libations. For example, writing after the death of Augustus (and still from exile), Ovid describes how his piety is evident to his foreign neighbors by virtue of his household altar:

> Nor is my piety unknown: a strange land sees there is a shrine to Caesar in my house. Beside him stand the pious son and priestess wife, divine powers not less important than himself who has now been made a god. To make the household group complete, both of the grandsons are there, one by the side of his grandmother, the other by that of his father. To these I offer incense and words of prayer as often as the day rises from the east.[82]

Ovid is clearly concerned to articulate the completeness of the imperial *domus* that resides in his own *domus*. Has the shrine to Ovid's biological family been replaced with this *sacrum Caesaris*? He goes on to explain how he celebrates "the birthday of the god" on this "altar," as one would the birthday of one's own *paterfamilias*.[83] And though he obviously describes his *pietas* in order to be noticed by Roman elites and hopefully brought back from exile, he also claims that he is not too worried about their attention, because news of his piety "shall sometime reach the ear of Caesar from whom nothing which occurs in the whole world is hidden."[84] Caesar, who has been "adopted in the ranks above" and made "a new member of the heavens," can see everything and answer prayers from his place among the stars.[85] Ovid concludes by appealing to the overarching image which governs his entire perspective: "thus I prophesy that your divine power [*numen*] is yielding to these prayers, for not undeservedly do you have the gracious name *parens*."[86] Augustus, adopted as son by Caesar on earth, exalted to father of the Empire, has now been adopted by heaven, and his parental mercy is thus widened by his universal gaze.

Tantalizing though examples like this may be, the private invocation of Augustus and his successors is more frequently encountered in less ornate contexts— specifically, the practice of invoking the emperor at all meals, public and private. Dio describes the institution of the practice: "The priests and priestesses were instructed, when they prayed on behalf of the Roman people and the Senate, to pray likewise for him [Augustus]. And at banquets—not only public but also private—everyone was to pour a libation for him."[87] One finds a spontaneous instance of this libation during the famous dinner of Trimalchio. When a bizarre and enticing dessert was presented to the dinner guests, they perceived a sacredness in its flavor and ornamentation. Therefore they stood up and said, "Cheers to Augustus, *pater patriae!*" Presently two attendants brought in images of the *Lares* and another carried around a bowl of wine, crying out, "May the gods be gracious!"[88] Here we find the emperor hailed as *pater* and offered a libation alongside the household gods, the *Lares*. Though the *genius* of the emperor is not explicitly invoked, the paternity of Augustus is connected with the Lares, just as on the compital altars.

Horace and Ovid adduce more florid portrayals of the libation at meals. Their descriptions are undoubtedly stylized, due to their affections for Augustus, but they nonetheless provide food for our rumination about idealized conceptions of how the emperor could fit into the private home. In one of his *Odes* to Augustus, composed while awaiting his return from abroad, Horace describes a pastoral scene: after a full day's work in the field, a vintner "returns happily to his wine and invites you to the second course of the meal, O god. He honors you with many a prayer, pouring libations from the dish, and combines your divine power with the *Lares*."[89] Augustus is clearly invited to the table as a god (*te ... deum*), and his divine power (*numen*) is mixed with the guardian household spirits (*Laribus*), just as his own spirit was juxtaposed to them on the compital altars.[90]

Ovid also links the emperor with the *Lares* in his depiction of libations at a family feast, the *Caristia* of February 22. For the home liturgy, one should:

> Make a libation of sacrificial food, an acceptable pledge of honor, so that the girt *Lares* may feed at the offered platter. And now, when the damp night is about to induce peaceful slumber, fill up the wine with an abundant pour for the prayer, and say, "May it be well with you, [Lares]! May it be well with you, *pater patriae*, best Caesar!," pouring out the wine with these sacred words.[91]

Again the title *pater patriae* is the chosen form of address, which this chapter has shown to be intimately linked with the *genius* of the emperor. Ovid's description corroborates the argument, as he links the family *Lares* with the family *genius* through the invocation of the emperor as head of the family. In all these examples, scholars have debated whether the invocation of the emperor was direct worship of the man as a god, the beseeching of his *numen* as a divine power, or rather the honoring of his *genius* as a guardian spirit. Though such distinctions could be made for purposes of analysis, all three interpretations congeal together within the emperor's role as *pater patriae*.

In sum, Augustus and his successors established the emperor's role as father of the Empire, the *paterfamilias* of a large family. Roman authors regarded the image as befitting Augustan stability, and they hoped it would portend continued imperial *clementia*. The *genius Augusti*, the guardian spirit of the imperial *gens*, thus radiated out from the Palatine hill, filled the neighborhoods of Rome, and reached household altars and *triclinia* at the frontier of the Empire. The provinces responded with loyalty to their new father, demonstrating the successful inculcation of imperial ideology. The emperor was not only the father of Rome, as Romulus was, but "the father of the whole human race," as he was called in the province of Asia.[92]

Augustus had indeed become the father of fifty million people—but in a great irony, he himself had trouble rearing a natural, begotten son to inherit his power. Instead, he would have to make a son. Augustus, the great father, had to adopt.

■ ADOPTION AND IMPERIAL SUCCESSION

> The desire at all levels of the [Roman] population to see stability in the history of the empire was expressed first and foremost by the fiction of dynastic continuity on the throne.
>
> —CLIFFORD ANDO

Adoption as Transmission of Power

Roman historians have acknowledged the crucial function of adoption in imperial successions at least since the work of Mason Hammond.[93] In a masterful series of monographs, and especially in his essay on "the transmission of powers" in the Roman principate, Hammond highlights the indispensability of adoptions, whether formal or informal, for the legitimation of emperors.[94] He isolates three sources of possible legitimation that each gain a hearing at the death of an emperor and accession of an heir. First, the Senate held the constitutional control to assign specific powers to Roman citizens, such as priesthoods, consulships, and other public offices; however, already in the early first century, the historical sources make clear that the "senate had in fact no choice as to the new *princeps*."[95] The various public powers granted to Augustus had been consolidated into the figure of the man, whose quite absolute power swallowed up the distinctions among his diverse offices.[96] The Senate may have been the body to acknowledge imperial authority in a symbolic and documentary sort of way, but the actual social power or *auctoritas* of a new emperor came from elsewhere. The second source of legitimation was "the support of the troops," both the legions and the praetorian guard, which "came to be recognized openly as the real source and mainstay of the imperial power not only in cases of violent change but even when the succession was peaceful and prearranged."[97] One can perceive the clout of the troops especially in the "Year of Four Emperors," when Galba, Otho, Vitellius, and Vespasian successively claimed the imperial power, based almost entirely on various troop allegiances secured through battle. Vespasian's dating of his *imperium* to the date of the army's acclamation "recognized what had from the beginning been true, that the army could in fact make or unmake emperors and that 'constitutional' succession was possible only by its sufferance."[98] The entire drama of that year caused Tacitus to wax poetic: "the secret of empire was now disclosed, that an emperor could be made elsewhere than at Rome."[99] Hammond further demonstrates that the troops were not only important in a time of civil war, but their influence continued into times of peace. (Though, in a sense, such "times of peace" are themselves not aptly named, since the Roman frontier was ever-expanding for the years under our consideration, and emperors were often engaged in battle at great distances from Rome.) Finally, Hammond subordinates even the support of the troops to a third source of legitimation: above all, "the status of destined successor was consolidated through heredity, either natural or adoptive"—and most successors were adopted.[100] In a thorough examination of the transmission of imperial power from the Julio-Claudians through the Severans, he concludes that the adopting of sons, whether through a legal procedure, an informal emergency ceremony, a testamentary adoption, or a deathbed proclamation, undergirded the entire system of imperial power. The emperor's "choice of a successor, as indicated by adoption, by conferring special privileges or powers, and by designation as his personal heir, was *the determining factor* in securing the support of the army and the confirmation of the senate."[101] The most powerful son in the world gained his power by adoption.

In his analysis of the relationship between Roman imperial ideology and provincial loyalty, Clifford Ando also examines the principles by which emperors legitimated their claims to power. He goes far beyond the work of Hammond and other modern historians, though, by his attempts to re-present the classic texts and artifacts with refreshing theoretical sophistication. Drawing from sociological and philosophical theorists—especially Weber, Habermas, and Bourdieu—Ando emphasizes the central importance of adoption in the burgeoning ideology of the Roman emperor. He argues that the adoption of imperial heirs is a paradigmatic case of a "Roman political ritual" which appealed to multiple *strata* of society and could be viewed according to different principles of legitimation.

> The use of adoption to designate a successor appealed on one level to those who interpreted the Principate as a legal institution: after all, the bureaucracy had started out as the personal *familia* of one man, and, as such, it had to be willed by the emperor to his successor, although in practice its fate was never in doubt. To the extent that adoption announced a specific heir to the charisma of the current emperor, it also might appeal to those who wished to see dynastic succession at the heart of imperial rule; even if the designated successor then required the acclamation of his subjects, this need should not distract from the charismatic power that accrued to the adopted heir from the mere fact of his designation. Without doubt few if any people assigned their loyalties through a single principle of legitimation, but nothing about a Roman adoption precluded an individual from viewing it from many perspectives simultaneously.[102]

Ando deftly employs the Weberian categories of "legal authority" and "charismatic authority" to illuminate how the practice of adoption helped Augustus navigate the uncertain waters of imperial succession.[103] The uncertainty arose because the "constitutional fiction" of Augustus's unique *statio* as the *princeps* did not "provide an explicit mechanism to oversee the succession."[104] Adoption allowed him to satisfy the legal conceptions of inheritance and the charismatic conceptions of *auctoritas*. Through the mechanism of adoption, Augustus successfully solved what Weber identified as the primary problem with charismatic authority—its transmission to another individual. Augustus's successors then continued to procure sons through adoption, generating a fictive linear succession of power through the Julio-Claudian family; it was "a multivalent system for concretizing the transfer of charisma between generations."[105] Even the Flavians, who *were* related through natural kinship, affiliated themselves with the Augustan line of succession. This was most evident in Vespasian's formal titulature: *Imperator Caesar Augustus Vespasianus*. The name *Flavius* is nowhere to be found. The High Empire, with its long chain of "good and adoptive emperors," allowed for the ultimate communication of the imperial ideology of adoption, though still in the terms of dynasty.[106] In Ando's words, "the stability and concord of the Antonine house, then, provided time for all to familiarize themselves with the language appropriate to the fiction."[107]

In the first two centuries of the Empire, how widespread was the knowledge of imperial adoptions? How did the imperial family "get the news out" about its changes, and to whom did the news go out? Though we do not have abundant evidence for every imperial adoption, there is enough to conclude that the emperors utilized a wide range of media to advertise key adoptions. They used images and legends of coins; construction and dissemination of portraiture and other monuments; official texts and religious commemorations; and displays at public events. Through these various means, residents of the Empire in diverse locales and social classes learned about imperial adoptions and how to construe them.

Imperial coins were struck to advertise adopted sons,[108] from those of Gaius and Lucius Caesar early in the principate[109] to the Trajan-Hadrian "ADOPTIO" coins in the High Empire.[110] Such media were reinforced by portraiture and other monuments. Statues of imperial family members were instrumental in shaping the dynastic "grammar" by which (especially provincial) residents of the Empire could track its changes in leadership.[111] In Rome itself, permanent monuments to adoption were debated (and probably commissioned) by the Senate, such as whether Livia-*cum*-Julia Augusta should have an "altar" established to commemorate her testamentary adoption by Augustus.[112] Moreover, the *Acta Fratrum Arvalium*, the best extant sources for Roman state cult during the principate, record the official religious honoring of adoptions.[113] For example, on January 10, 69 C.E., the occasion of Galba's adoption of Piso was honored by the Arval brethren at the Capitol with a host of sacrifices "on account of the adoption" (*ob adoptionem*), including cows offered to *providentia* and *securitas*—which the adoption was thought to have ensured—and also "a bull offered to the *genius* of Galba himself" (*genio ipsius taurum*).[114] A decade earlier, the Arval brethren had used a similar sacrificial liturgy to honor the adoption of Nero by Claudius (February 25, 58 C.E.) and its anniversary the following year (59 C.E.).[115] Finally, Roman historians recount the public proclamations or introductions of adopted sons to the people, some of which will be treated later.[116] Through all these means, the news of adoptions spread and became part of the gossip network. A proximate observer like Suetonius offers glimpses into such Roman tales about high-profile adoptions—whether they were auspicious, what precedents they followed, and what the "word on the street" was. More distant observers like Philo, Josephus, and Epictetus knew enough of the imperial adoptions to incorporate them into their works without much explanation. Residents of the Empire did not always agree about the appropriateness of imperial adoptions, but they did know what was going on at the top of the family.

The Role of Divine Election

At various points in the political history of Rome, emperors and those who propagated their ideology expressed their rise to power as the result of a specific divine election. Though the powers of the principate were granted nominally by the Senate and the Roman people, the actual forms of legitimation came from elsewhere. As Hammond has already argued, both the support of the army and the securing of imperial heirs by adoption were methods far more important than the constitutional niceties of the Senate. In times of Roman political crisis, especially when rule had transitioned to a new family, the gods also got involved in the process, carrying out a divine "electoral college" and then choosing an emperor—usually by telling the current emperor whom to adopt. These divine elections were made known to the Empire's inhabitants through reports of omens, auspices, and other specific revelations, in addition to concrete portrayals in coins, portraits, and liturgies.

In his thorough study, *Princeps a diis electus*, J. Rufus Fears surveys and analyzes how divine election functioned as a political concept in the Roman Empire and its relevant antecedents. By his definition, the concept of divine election means that "the ruler has been elected by the gods of the state to serve as their minister on earth and, by virtue of this divine investiture, he insures the prosperity of the temporal community."[117] Previous historians assumed that divine election was not a part of Greek or Roman political ideology until the second century C.E., but Fears demonstrates that "the divine election of kings was well-known in Greece from the time of Homer and that, in various periods, it played an important role in practical political ideology in Greece and in the late Roman republic and early Empire."[118] Alexander the Great, for example, was adept at using the concept of divine election to shore up support for his rule; and once each particular victory had been presented as chosen by the gods, Alexander paid careful "attention to the native ceremonies of kingship" in each conquered culture in order "to rule as a legitimately chosen divine king."[119] The divine election of Augustus was a common theme in early imperial literature, such as the works of Horace, Ovid, and Vitruvius. Fears is careful, though, to separate literary tropes from what he calls the "official ideology" of coins, monuments, and "quasi-official proclamations," such as imperial panegyrics.[120] Both types of evidence support a concept of divine election in Roman politics, but they do so in different ways and at different times. In the end, Fears depicts Roman political ideology as oscillating between two contrasting modes of legitimation: on the one hand, the Roman people appreciated the stability of (good) dynasties, and dynastic rulers preferred to emphasize their human lineage rather than superhuman election; on the other hand, each time a dynasty failed—creating a power vacuum and political crisis—a new ruler would look to divine election for legitimacy. Therefore, Fears identifies divine election as "a major theme in official imperial ideology only in eras of constitutional crisis: the foundation of the Augustan principate, the civil wars of 68–69 and 193–194, the reigns of Domitian, Trajan, and Hadrian, in which principate was transformed into monarchy, and again in the late third century. In a sense, divine election remained a doctrine to justify illegal power."[121]

Fears's elegant argument is, on the whole, persuasive. On one crucial point, however, he has not inspected carefully enough the dynasties about which he reports. Many of the imperial successions which he considers "dynastic" are enacted through adoption. Fears seems to have been swayed by the rulers' own propaganda, since, at least in the early Roman Empire, most of the sons were sons by adoption. His inattentive characterization of these "made" sons as "begotten" sons shows to what extent the propagandists of imperial heirs have successfully shaped our perceptions of them. For example, Fears passes over the Julio-Claudian emperors from Augustus to Nero; by his reckoning, election did not play a role here because the so-called dynasty was stable. However, several key adoptions took place in this period, some of which were tenuous and most of which received divine election in the form of omens and auspices. If these adoptions had not been portrayed and construed by the people as a legitimate— though fictive—succession of fathers and sons, the "dynasty" would never have been interpreted as such. Whereas Fears sees the Empire as an oscillation back and forth between political ideologies of human dynasty and divine election, I find the two ideologies continuously throughout. Sometimes they cohere; sometimes they conflict.

Among the many examples of divine election, two examples bear special relevance for our topic. Each one explicitly connects the events of adoption and divine election. The first comes from Plutarch's treatise, "On the Fortune of Alexander," in which he analyzes the cause of Alexander's momentous achievements—whether they arose because of his virtue or his good fortune.[122] According to Plutarch, the two powers of Fortune and Virtue had mutually generative effects on Alexander,[123] and the treatise reads as part philosophical exploration of these effects and part encomium to Alexander's greatness. At the conclusion of a section delineating Alexander's virtue, Plutarch reports how Darius III, the last king of the Achaemenid Empire of Persia, eventually succumbed to Alexander on account of his virtue. In fact, Darius was so impressed that he wanted Alexander as his own son and successor. He confessed that, if his own fortune and virtue should fail, he would choose Alexander to take over: "'But if my power should be lost—O Zeus, paternal god of the Persians, and the ruling gods—may none other than Alexander sit on the throne of Cyrus.' With the gods as his witnesses, this was Darius's adoption of Alexander."[124] Darius invokes the fatherly god as chief witness over his own expression of fatherhood to Alexander. On the one hand, the use of adoption in this text may simply express a new relationship between Darius and Alexander, who married Darius's daughter Stateira in a political union.[125] On the other hand, it may also serve as a fascinating challenge to the common portrayal of royal ideology in the Hellenistic monarchies, which have been normally construed as consistently dynastic and not open to adoptive modes of succession. Since he lived and wrote at the height of adoptive imperial ideology, Plutarch's own knowledge of adoptive succession in the Roman Empire probably influenced his interpretation of Darius's speech as an adoption.

The second example comes from a fascinating papyrus known as *P.Giss.* 3.[126] The well-preserved text contains part of the script for a specific liturgical celebration of Hadrian's accession, a celebration that took place in Heptakomia, the metropolis of the Apollopolite nome in Egypt.[127] From another papyrus (*P.Oxy.* 3781), we know that the Egyptian prefect had ordered such celebrations to take place, in either 117 or 118 C.E., to inform the people of the new emperor and, apparently, to legitimate him in their eyes. The *libretto* is a call and response for two voices, a dialogue between the god Phoebus [Apollo] and the responding voice of the people. My translation follows:[128]

> [Phoebus Apollo:] Having just ascended with Trajan in a white-horsed chariot,
> I, the not unknown god Phoebus [Apollo],
> have come to you, proclaiming Hadrian as the new ruler,
> to whom all are subject on account of his virtue
> and the *genius* of his father, a god.

> [The people:] Rejoicing, therefore, let us light up the altars for sacrificing,
> lifting up our souls with laughter and drinks from the well
> and the ointments of the *gymnasia*—
> for all of which we are indebted
> to the reverence of our governor for the lord [emperor]
> and his beneficence to us.

In the first part, Apollo announces that Trajan has just become divine, having died and ascended heavenward in Apollo's chariot. But Apollo has chosen a new ruler, Hadrian, and everyone should be subject to him, just as they were to Trajan. In the second part, the people thank their governor, the aptly named Apollonios (who is known to us from other papyri in his archive, published in *P.Brem.* and *P.Giss.*), for his financial support of the festivities honoring their lord.

The divine election portrayed here in words was later symbolized on Hadrian's coinage (*sestertii* and *dupondii*) of 119 C.E., which depicted an eagle flying down to Hadrian with a scepter in its talons.[129] Fears interprets the eagle as the messenger of Jupiter, delivering imperial power to Hadrian, while Arthur Darby Nock interprets it as the apotheosized Trajan.[130] In either case, the legend "*PROVIDENTIA DEORUM*" evokes the divine participation in Hadrian's election. Jupiter and Divus Trajan were working together.

Divine election thus constituted a major part of Hadrian's official imperial ideology. And although I am presenting this example under the rubric of divine election, there is rather more achieved by the pithy rhetoric of Apollo's speech. In addition to this direct legitimation from Apollo, Hadrian's rule is further bolstered through his virtue and through his adoption by a divine father, whose *genius* he now possesses (ἀρετὴν κ[αὶ] πατρὸς τύχην θεοῦ). Therefore, Hadrian is legitimated by three separate means: his divine election, his human merits, and his adoption by Trajan, the human-*cum*-divine father. Since Hadrian's position as emperor would be under serious scrutiny, causing him to issue the *ADOPTIO* and *PROVIDENTIA* coins, he had to defend its legitimacy with all available means in these liturgies.

■ IDEOLOGICAL TENSIONS: NATURAL DYNASTY OR ADOPTIVE MERITOCRACY?

> Now there is a distinction between natural and adopted sons: for a begotten son (τὸ γεννώμενον) becomes whatever kind of person seems appropriate to the heavenly powers, but a man takes an adopted son (τὸ ποιούμενον, a "made" son) to himself through a deliberate selection. The result is that, through natural processes, a man is often given a deformed and incompetent son, but through a process of judgment, one of sound body and mind is certain to be chosen.
> —HADRIAN, *according to Cassius Dio,* Roman History *69.20*

In the foregoing presentations of imperial ideology, some tensions between competing and often mutually exclusive modes of legitimation remain unresolved. Is imperial power conferred by birth or by adoption? By victory in battle or by divine election? The remainder of this chapter will analyze in some detail the tension between natural ("begotten") sonship and adopted ("made") sonship in the transmission of Roman imperial power from Augustus to Trajan. Though the tension cannot be easily resolved, since the tension itself is what generates the complex ideology of Roman familial power, it can nonetheless be examined more closely than previous scholars have done.[131] On the one hand, as argued above, adoption functioned as a dynastic necessity: a childless emperor could use adoption to procure a son or sons for which he would try to orchestrate the smooth transmission of imperial power. The vast majority of these adoptions stayed roughly "within the family"—the emperor would adopt a grandson, a nephew, a stepson, or a son-in-law as his son to keep the power in the same dynasty. On the other hand, adoption offered a meritocratic ideal: an emperor could forestall the vicissitudes of biological chance by instead choosing the "best" man for the job. Biological sons were not necessarily reliable, and an emperor might prefer to select his successor based on his proven merits. These different conceptions of adoption did not develop historically in a simple linear fashion, from "necessity" at the beginning to "ideal" in the High Empire. Some authors of the early second century do, however, maintain a very high view of imperial adoption—even idealizing it as a mode of succession. Nevertheless, my analysis will demonstrate that an ideology of adopting successors did not cleanly supersede the dynastic ideology that pervaded Roman culture. A pure meritocratic system of imperial succession never won the day. Close readings of Roman authors, with occasional reference to the images of imperial ideology, will demonstrate that imperial adoption was inexorably bound up with the logic and rhetoric of dynasty.

This section cannot, of course, analyze every imperial adoption. Instead, we will first gather a brief synchronic analysis of certain recurring topics: the prioritization of natural family lines and the various techniques of "affiliation" for adopted sons. Then we consider some crucial moments from Augustus to Galba that highlight the tension between differing ideologies. Tacitus and Suetonius constitute our principal sources, and other texts and images will be used as appropriate. Finally we turn to the most illustrious expression of adoptive meritocratic ideology, Pliny's *Panegyric*, to see whether it is the exception that proves the rule.

Despite all that has been said so far about adoption, natural family lines were often definitive of one's political future in Roman society—the examples of this are so manifest that the historian can almost miss them. For instance, Suetonius's work on the twelve Caesars has often been construed as a characterization of twelve individuals, and indeed it purports to be that. But each individual characterization begins (and sometimes ends) with a characterization of that person's family. Within the first sentence, and usually in the opening words, of each life, Suetonius invokes a family and begins to evaluate its attributes:

> *gentem Octaviam . . . patricia gens Claudia . . . Germanicus, Gaius Caesaris pater, . . . Patrem Claudi Caesaris Drusum . . . ex gente Domitia . . . Progenies Caesarum in Nerone defecit . . . Maiores Othonis . . . Vitelliorum originem . . . gens Flavia . . . Titus, cognomine paterno,* and *Domitianus . . . gentis Flaviae.*

The function of these ancestral genealogies is not merely informational. Suetonius traces virtues and vices to one's progenitors and identifies them also in one's children. His characterization of the Claudian family (*Tib.* 2) sets up for that of Claudius himself later on (*Claud.* 15–16). "There are on record many distinguished services of the Claudii to their country, as well as many deeds of the opposite character" (*Tib.* 2).[132] Claudius exemplifies that ancestral inconsistency by his behavior (*Claud.* 15–16). On the flip side, the daughter of Gaius Caligula was irrefutably identified as his offspring by her "savage temper" and behavior with other children (*Cal.* 25).

The lineage of natural sons bears special relevance. The thorny relationship of Britannicus (the natural son) and Nero (the adopted son) will be discussed below. But even after the fictive line of "Caesars" ended with Nero, natural sons still carried importance. (And the Flavians adopted the name "Caesar" anyway, even without a legal fiction of adoption.) Vitellius had issued coins of his two children to try to establish his line as a viable dynasty.[133] And Vespasian's two natural sons were considered a boon for his accession to the principate.[134] Tacitus has Mucianus, governor of Syria, deliver a speech of loyalty to Vespasian on precisely these grounds: "your house . . . possesses two young men, one of whom is already equal to ruling the empire; . . . It would be absurd for me not to bow before the throne of a man whose son I should adopt if I myself held it."[135] Ando argues that a dynastic imperial ideology, represented by the logic of Mucianus's concession, formed part of the "generative grammar dictated by Rome to its provincial audiences."[136] But this observation should *not* weigh against the arguments advanced earlier about the importance of adoption in Roman culture; on the contrary, the centrality of family lines was precisely what necessitated these high-profile adoptions. The adoptive practices, although they seem *prima facie* opposed to a dynastic ideology, actually prop up that ideology. The *making* of sons was usually a substitute for the *begetting* of sons in order to secure successors, but the grammar of "sons and fathers"—the grammar of dynasty—perpetuated throughout.

Emperors utilized several techniques of "affiliation" to uphold and disseminate the fictive kinship of their adopted sons—to "affiliate" a new *filius*. The changing of a name simply and clearly represented a new status, as happened with every imperial successor. Even Otho was awkwardly called "Nero" in his brief principate.[137] Overall, the name "Caesar" exhibited unbelievable staying power and bore much of the burden of affiliating successors to the absolute *pater patriae*. For Dio, the names "Caesar" and "Augustus" are sufficient to demonstrate "the succession of their family."[138] For those in and outside of Rome, adopted sons were affiliated to new fathers through statues and portraiture. By the features of their faces and hair and by their positioning vis-à-vis their adoptive fathers, artisans could naturalize these sons into an appearance of biological kinship.[139] Finally, coins covered the most ground in imperial dynastic publicity. William Metcalf has opined that most imperial coinage in the period covered by this chapter served two functions: to "get your face out" to the Empire, and to "establish legitimacy, either forward or backward."[140] An adopted son could validate his new status "backward" in the imperial family, and adoptive and natural fathers could establish their legitimacy "forward" by advertising the existence of their sons. Such "forward" publicity fostered an image of *providentia*, an imperial virtue that the first emperor had a rather tough time fulfilling.

Augustus and His Adopted Sons

Augustus's travails in securing a successor are well known: he prepared Marcellus, Gaius and Lucius, and Agrippa before ultimately settling with Tiberius.[141] We have both textual and material sources to examine the adoption of his grandsons, Gaius and Lucius, and how they were affiliated into Augustan dynastic ideology. When recording Augustus's public appointments and honors, Suetonius explains that he demanded a thirteenth consulship, "wishing to hold the highest magistracy at the time when he introduced each of his [adopted] sons Gaius and Lucius to public life upon their coming of age" (*Aug.* 26.2). He wanted to be in the highest legal position in order to anchor for the Roman audience the image of Gaius and Lucius as his imperial successors. He also held public performances and games in their honor (*Aug.* 43.5). Josephus knew of the adoption of Gaius and reports that his first appearance at an important meeting was when Augustus received the embassy of the various claimants to Herod the Great's territory.[142] The adoptions and their implications for imperial power came to be widely known.

Beyond these ephemeral actions, Augustus established permanent dedications to his adopted sons, such as the portico and basilica of Gaius and Lucius (*Aug.* 29.4), and minted coins to introduce their faces to the wider Empire. These were the largest issues of gold and silver coins up to that time.[143] What is more, the adoptive relationship was portrayed in portraiture throughout the Empire. In his detailed study of the extant portraiture, *Dynastic Commemoration and Imperial Portraiture in the Julio-Claudian Period*, Charles Brian Rose emphasizes the role that such images played in the naturalization of adopted sons into the Augustan dynasty. The production of statuary groups was often prescribed "from the top down" through senatorial decrees sent to the provinces, commissioned to acknowledge "adoptions, marriages, and deifications.... Such a system ensured that changes in the Imperial family received extensive publicity, and the decrees themselves served as potential blueprints for the designs of dynastic groups."[144] The relationships between members of the Augustan family were potentially confusing to a viewer, especially because, in the case of Gaius and Lucius, their natural father (Agrippa) was a man of status and was also depicted in the portraiture. Rose explains that an Eastern audience would not have been accustomed to a situation in which an heir had *two* powerful fathers, one natural and one adoptive.[145] (This confusion would return a century later when Trajan also had two fathers of high status.) Thus the portraiture was designed with sophistication, to highlight the priority of Augustus's paternal relationship.

The specifics of this early imperial portraiture demonstrate the deliberate goal of distancing the adopted sons from their natural father, Agrippa. When analyzing the portraiture from Thespiae, Rose notes that this goal would have required expert artistic diplomacy because Agrippa's presence in the East at the time would have allowed him to see the completed monument.[146] So Agrippa is still cast in the role of a father, but the father of his daughter, Agrippina. Meanwhile, Gaius (the eldest adopted son) is placed between Julia and Livia, and Lucius remains near the Agrippan side. Furthermore, the inscription records Gaius and Lucius with the name "Caesar," but they are the only two without patronymics. "Agrippa's role as natural father of Gaius and Lucius was therefore subtly minimized while the legal [adoptive] connection of the two boys to Augustus was quietly emphasized."[147]

The presentation of Gaius and Lucius as sons and successors did not all come "from the top down." At least two of the compital altars of Augustan Rome, probably products of local artisans in particular Roman *vici*, feature these adopted sons and heirs on their panels.[148] The adopted status of Gaius and Lucius had been sufficiently publicized so that these local leaders felt encouraged to honor them at the altars of their neighborhood *compita*. The "Belvedere Altar" has been variously interpreted, but Paul Zanker surmises that the main panel of this altar features Gaius and Lucius with Augustus as he delivers statues of the *Lares* to the *ministri* of the neighborhood.[149] Another panel seems to depict the apotheosis of Caesar with Augustus, Livia, and the two heirs looking on. If these interpretations are correct, the Belvedere Altar portrays Gaius and Lucius as key members of the household of Caesar and coworkers with Augustus in his *liberalitas* to the Roman *vici*.

The altar from the *vicus Sandalarius* emphasizes more clearly the elder adopted son, Gaius. This altar has also been variously interpreted, but most scholars agree that the augural observation of the sacred chicken on the front panel manifests a good omen for the departure of Gaius Caesar on his military campaign to the east. The *lituus* and the chicken identify him as an augur and commander with *imperium* to hold the *tripudium*, the augury that portended the success or failure of the army.[150] This altar was dedicated in 2 B.C.E, also the year Augustus became *pater patriae*. J. Bert Lott argues that this altar "recalled the importance of Gaius's entry into public service" and reveals how local leaders perceived and honored the precise movements of the imperial family.[151] He concludes thus: "The care that the Vicus Sandalarius paid to the precise ideological nuances of the events of 2 B.C.E demonstrates an astonishing desire on the part of the new neighborhoods to participate in the new imperial scheme and to demonstrate their loyalty to Augustus and his family."[152]

Since both Gaius and Lucius died before they could accede to imperial power, the adoption of Tiberius and the subsequent transfer of power to him became the most important topic of Augustan publicity. Suetonius reports that, once he was adopted, Tiberius ceased to act as a *paterfamilias* or to keep any particular privileges of that position. "He neither made gifts nor freed slaves, and he did not even accept an inheritance or any legacies, except to enter them as an addition to his *peculium*. From this time on nothing was left undone which could add to his prestige, especially after the disowning and banishment of Agrippa made it clear that the hope of the succession lay in him alone" (*Tib.* 15.2). But another remark of Suetonius shows the salience of dynastic ideology for Augustus and the common people. "Augustus's will began in this way: 'Since a cruel fate has bereft me of my sons Gaius and Lucius, let Tiberius Caesar be heir to two-thirds of my estate'" (*Tib.* 23). Even though all three men were adopted as sons, Augustus only refers to the first two as "my sons." Presumably this is because only they were in his direct bloodline, although personal affection may also have played a role. In the will, Tiberius is connected to his family only by the name "Caesar," and Suetonius reports the common interpretation of the will: "These words in themselves added to the suspicion of those who believed that he had named Tiberius his successor from necessity rather than from choice, since he allowed himself to write such a preamble" (*Tib.* 23). He provides further corroboration that the Roman people dishonored Tiberius's adopted status by citing their verse of mockery: "You are no knight. Why so? The hundred thousands you are lacking; If you want to know the whole story, you were an exile at Rhodes" (*Tib.* 59). The first line of this verse implies that he cannot be an *eques* ("knight") because, as the adopted son of Augustus, he had no power over money or property. Another translation presents the mockery more plainly: "You are no knight—Caesar's adopted son / May own no cash to qualify as one; / And banishment in Rhodes cancelled your right / To be a citizen—far less a knight."[153]

Tiberius was certainly cognizant of his questionable status. He was cautious about assuming power in the immediate wake of Augustus's death (Tac. *Ann.* 1.7), so he made a clear public declaration in three coin issues after his accession, the most prominent of which features his own visage on the obverse and the image of *divus Augustus* on the reverse.[154] He was the first member of the imperial family to have an obverse coin type with all of his titles on it.[155] After these coin issues, Tiberius would have hoped his relationship to Augustus was unambiguous. But a century later, Suetonius still felt it necessary to defend the adoption of Tiberius as legitimate.[156] In fact, the legitimation of this particular adoption, which procured a son from outside the immediate bloodline, set the historical precedent for all subsequent imperial adoptions. For this author, writing from the era of the adoptive emperors, the defense of adoption was critical. Therefore he cites at least five excerpts from Augustus's private epistolary correspondence, in order to show that Augustus "was adopting Tiberius for the good of the *res publica*" (*Tib.* 21.3). Suetonius speculates that Augustus weighed "the faults and the merits of Tiberius" and decided that the merits were greater (*Tib.* 21.3). From these excerpts, we get the sense that Roman citizens from the plebs up to Augustus were predisposed to value a natural dynastic lineage over a fictive one; but in Suetonius's brief *apologia*, we glimpse an argument for meritocracy.

Britannicus versus Nero

Claudius's adoption of Nero constitutes another key moment in the tension between natural and adoptive sons. Tacitus narrates the events soberly, while Suetonius provides a colorful evaluation. Tacitus first reports how Pallas, a freedman of Claudius, was "goading" Claudius to adopt Domitius (who took the name "Nero"), in order to "place a protective cordon of maturity around the boyhood of Britannicus," the natural son (*Ann.* 12.25).[157] Pallas refers to previous imperial adoptions to strengthen his case, notably invoking the adoptions performed by Augustus and Tiberius. Tacitus further records that at the time, "experts noted that no previous adoption could be discovered among the patrician Claudii and that they had lasted continuously from Attus Clausus" (*Ann.* 12.25.2). Later he calls it a "ruinous adoption," in which Claudius "had destroyed himself" and the purity of his lineage (*Ann.* 13.2.2). The common people lamented the fate of Britannicus, who, being younger than Nero, was now second to Nero in his father's line. "There was no one so devoid of pity that he was not affected by sorrow at Britannicus's fortune" (*Ann*. 12.26.2). The divergent destinies of Britannicus and Nero were then advertised through their titles, garb, statues, and coins. Britannicus does appear with Nero in coins and portraiture, but he appears so only in the provinces and often in a clearly subordinate role.[158] It is no wonder that Nero did not want Britannicus's face all over the Empire: Agrippina herself admitted that his face was "the true likeness of his father's" (*Ann*. 12.68.2). One can see the unequal status of Nero and Britannicus in a relief from the Sebasteion at Aphrodisias. Nero holds a globe and aplustre, symbols of dominion over land and sea; Britannicus has no such attributes.[159] Furthermore, Nero's physical features have been likened to those of Britannicus—his affiliation as adopted son was on display.

Nevertheless, the presence and appearance of Britannicus caused difficulty for manipulating public opinion about Nero. Tacitus recounts how, after Claudius died, the will was not read out by Nero, "lest the preference of [adopted] step-son to natural son should, by resentment at its injustice, disturb the disposition of the public" (*Ann*. 12.69.3). This testifies yet again to the public preference, at least as Tacitus represents it, for dynastic ideology over adoptive. Suetonius assesses Claudius's behavior in his usual direct manner: "Just before his adoption of Nero, as if it were not bad enough to adopt a stepson when he had a grown-up son of his own, he publicly declared more than once that no one had ever been taken into the Claudian family by adoption" (*Claud*. 39.2). The adoption was also reported by Josephus, who seems to have understood the sensitivities aroused by preferring an adopted son to a natural son.[160] Although adoption could be rationalized as merit-ocratic when necessary, the dynastic ideology seemed to dominate public opinion when natural sons were available.

Tacitus again grants credence to the dynastic ideology when reporting about Agrippina's contrivance against Junius Silanus, proconsul of Asia. "Agrippina . . . dreaded an avenger, given the frequent reports from the public that in preference to Nero . . . there should be someone of settled years, guiltless, noble, and (*something for which there was regard at that time*) belonging to the posterity of the Caesars" (*Ann*. 13.1.1). Why does Tacitus add the aside, italicized above? He indicates that the public opinion had more regard for natural than adopted sons, at least when the imperial family was concerned. The aside could be read as merely informative, but it may also be evaluative. Is Tacitus here evoking "the good old days," when a particular bloodline got the respect it deserved? It is difficult to be sure because, as this chapter will soon demonstrate, Tacitus reflects quite positively on the adoption of Piso by Galba. Again, Suetonius addresses the matter less subtly. He characterizes Claudius's repentance for his adoption of Nero, and when Claudius intended to give Britannicus the toga of manhood, he supposedly said, "That the Roman people may at last have a legitimate [*verus*] Caesar" (*Claud*. 43). He later explains how Nero attempted to murder Britannicus "from fear that he might sometime win a higher place than him-self in the people's regard because of the memory of his father" (*Nero* 33.2). But if only a natural son could be a *verus Caesar*, as Suetonius's quotation of Claudius implies, then the Empire had been full of false Caesars.

Both authors report Britannicus's reaction to Nero's adoption. Obviously humiliated by the adoption and immediate elevation of Domitius (now Nero), Britannicus could not contain his contempt. "When meeting each other, Nero hailed Britannicus by name, the latter him as 'Domitius.' Agrippina, with many a complaint, denounced this to her husband as being the start of disaffection: [she thought] the adoption was being spurned" (*Ann.* 12.41.3). Though the adoption of Nero was legally binding, and he legally acquired the status proper to a natural son, such a change was hardly acceptable to the natural son himself. Suetonius reports that Nero had a response to his brother's jibe: "For merely because his brother Britannicus had, after his adoption, greeted him as usual as Ahenobarbus [his other natural name], he tried to convince his [adoptive] father that Britannicus was a *subditivus*," that is, a 'mix-up at the hospital' (*Nero* 7). Nero thus reacted to Britannicus's taunt of his biological lineage with a clever accusation of his own.

Finally, Tacitus reports Britannicus's act that made Nero ultimately arrange his murder, an act that publicly scorned his adopted status. Conscious that Britannicus would soon be approaching manhood, Nero seized an opportunity to make a spectacle of him while still a youth. At the Saturnalia he achieved through a game the right to compel an embarrassing task from another player. He ordered Britannicus to rise in the midst of everyone and sing a song, "thereby hoping for ridicule of a boy ignorant of even sober, to say nothing of drunken, gatherings," but Britannicus "embarked steadfastly on a poem in which it was indicated that he had been turned out of his paternal abode and the supremacy" (*Ann.* 13.15.2). This aroused an outpouring of pity from the crowd, and Nero, having been thwarted in his attempt at humiliation, proceeded with the arrangements to poison him. On the whole, we must grant the possibility that Tacitus and Suetonius shape and color their narratives in these ways because of the egregious legacy of Nero. However, the details reveal part of the ideological unconscious of Roman culture: despite the legal equivalence of natural and adopted sons and the real options for social advancement through adoption, the appropriateness of a natural son's inheritance continued to hold the attention of the Roman *populus*.

Galba and Piso

The beginning of the end for the short-lived principate of Galba happened when the army in upper Germany refused to swear allegiance to him and demanded another emperor instead (Tac. *Hist.* 1.12; Suet. *Gal.* 16). The army despised him primarily because he had failed to reward them adequately for their services. However, both Suetonius and Tacitus report that Galba understood matters differently. He thought the army disapproved of him because he did not have a son.[161] Suetonius narrates his ensuing actions:

> When this was reported to Galba, thinking that it was not so much his age as his lack of
> children that was criticized, he picked out Piso Frugi Licinianus from the midst of the

throng at one of his morning receptions, a young man of noble birth and high character, who had long been one of his special favorites and always named in his will as heir to his property and name. Calling him "son," he led him to the praetorian camp and adopted him before the assembled soldiers. (*Gal.* 17)

What constituted the adoption ceremony in this case? Was it the simple pronouncement of the word "son," as seemed also to be enough in Gaius Caligula's adoption of Tiberius Gemellus? Hammond doubts "the legal validity of this procedure," but it did acknowledge "the *de facto* importance of securing the favor of the [praetorian] guard."[162]

Tacitus describes the adoption in a similarly *ad hoc* way, but he appends a substantial speech that rationalizes the choice of Piso. He first connotes the irony of the proceedings by calling it an "imperial *comitia*, which he regarded as his only remedy" (*Hist.* 1.14).[163] By this, he attempted to substitute for both the *comitia curiata* necessary for an *arrogatio* and the consular *comitia* that would govern a normal election.[164] The speech itself contains a defense of the meritocratic method of adoption and a strong rejection of dynastic succession (even if the former still relies on the grammar of dynasties, of "fathers" and "sons"). After some opening praise of Piso's birth and character, Tacitus's Galba quickly moves to rationalization by connecting his action with the adoptions of Augustus. However, he boldly transcends Augustus's adoptive practices: "Herein I follow the example of *divus Augustus*, . . . but Augustus looked for a successor within his own house [*domus*], I in the whole state [*res publica*]" (*Hist.* 1.15). Galba thus takes a logical step. Once the hope for a natural son is lost, why not search for the best possible candidate? Next he elucidates how completely he has rejected dynastic ideology by his behavior. The rejection is twofold: Galba did not choose one of his own relatives ("I do this not because I have not relatives or associates in arms," *Hist.* 1.15); but moreover, he also passes over the older brother of Piso, saying, "You have a brother as noble as yourself and older, worthy indeed of this fortune, if you were not the better man [*potior*]" (*Hist.* 1.15). In place of this doubly rejected dynastic ideology, Galba substitutes the idea of meritocracy. With the word *potior*, Galba prepares the listener for his next rhetorical move.

Tacitus's Galba has now *rationalized* his adoption of an emperor from outside his family. Then, after a section of general exhortation about leadership, he attempts also to *universalize* this adoption—to establish it as a model for the future of the principate. The words are audacious and deserve a full quotation:

> Under Tiberius, Gaius, and Claudius we Romans were the heritage, so to speak, of one family; the fact that we emperors are now beginning to be chosen will be for all a kind of liberty; and since the houses of the Julians and the Claudians are ended, adoption will select only the best; for to be begotten and born of *principes* is mere chance, and is not reckoned higher, but the judgment displayed in adoption is unhampered; and, if one wishes to make a choice, common consent points out the individual.[165]

With these words, Galba attempts not only to defend his particular actions, but to establish adoption as the preferred method of future imperial succession. What was once merely a dynastic necessity ought to become a meritocratic ideal. Galba delineates some stark contrasts: by praising the liberating aspect of this new method (*libertatis*), he judges the dynastic ideology as restrictive. He also criticizes the *fortuitus* aspect of natural birth, whereas adoption occurs through "unhampered judgment" (*iudicium integrum*). This observation resonates with the rhetorical commonplace about adoption, preserved already by the Elder Seneca: "Adoption is the remedy for chance."[166] Moreover, although Piso himself is only *potior* than other men, Galba predicts that this method should hypothetically search the *res publica* for the *best* man. Tacitus undoubtedly reflects the spirit of his own age—illumined by Trajan, the *optimus princeps*—by this choice of words: *optimum quemque adoptio inveniet.*

Galba closes his speech with a brave flourish: "For with us there is not, as among people where there are kings [*ut gentibus quae regnantur*], a fixed house of masters [*dominorum*] while all the rest are slaves; but you are going to command [*imperaturus*] people who can endure neither complete slavery nor complete liberty" (*Hist.* 1.16). It is known that throughout the principate, emperor after emperor disdains the language of *rex, regius,* or *regnum.* And at first glance, Galba's invocation of distant kingdoms seems to be only a foil for his commendation of the dignity of Roman citizens. But in light of his previous censure of dynastic ideology and "fixed houses" of rulers, Galba's allusion to kingdoms constitutes a sharp comparison of the Julio-Claudian house to a succession of kings. In truth, if the historical Galba said anything remotely like this, it is not surprising Piso and he ended up as they did.

Other elements from this section of the *Histories* betray Tacitus's own attraction to the adoptive ideology. Piso comes off quite well in the narrative. He has a good reputation and noble birth, though bad luck (*Hist.* 1.14, 1.48); he received the principate without anxiety or exaltation (*Hist.* 1.17); he spoke with *comitas* ("affability," *Hist.* 1.19) and seemed like one "who had the ability more than the desire to be emperor" (*Hist.* 1.17). Tacitus also has Piso commend the adoptive process as a stabilizing force in the Empire; Piso declares that "adoption seemed *to provide,* lest there be any occasion for war even after Galba's death" (*Hist.* 1.29). He claims that "*provisum adoptione videbatur,*" a passage which I have translated to emphasize the word "provide," since this word group has often been associated with the stability of *dynastic* succession.[167] Ando explains the importance of the emperor's *providentia,* a quality displayed "above all in his taking thought for the stability of the empire after his death, and that act had its most concrete realization in the designation of a successor."[168] Tacitus puts this key concept in the speech of Piso, as he tries to rationalize the adoptive ideology to the soldiers.

Finally, we should notice that, in the responses to the speeches of Galba and Piso, Tacitus does not have Otho denounce adoptive ideology in principle. He does not positively refute the idea of adoptive succession. Rather, he opts for an *ad hominem* argument against the supposed gloominess and greed of Piso, whose "ill-starred adoption" [*infaustam adoptionem*] was disapproved by the gods through a remarkable storm (*Hist.* 1.38).[169] On the whole, Tacitus forcefully expresses an adoptive ideology of imperial succession—detached from dynastic considerations—through the speeches of Galba and Piso. What is more, he leaves this ideology open and available for future use by not having Otho or anyone else reject it in principle. Of course, for Tacitus, the pseudo-hypothetical "future use" occurred in his own era, to which we now turn.[170]

Pliny's *Panegyric*

The emperor Nerva was old and feeble already at his accession to the principate and was "thus despised on account of his age."[171] As a solution to his image problem, and to promote the virtue of *providentia*, Nerva secured a transmission of power to Trajan, who was a victorious military commander on the frontier. After hearing of Trajan's victory over the Germans and sensing his own impending demise, Nerva ascended the Capitol, proclaimed prayers for the Senate and the people, and announced, "I adopt Marcus Ulpius Nerva Trajan."[172] He later appointed him "Caesar" before the Senate. With little evidence on which to verify the details of this adoption scene, one can only say, "perhaps, as in the case of Galba and Piso, strict legality was neglected in view of the emergency and the authority of the emperor."[173] What *can* be deduced from the event is the priority of the adoption for the imperial succession. Before any dealings with the Senate, before the granting of any other powers proper to the emperor, Nerva saw fit to adopt Trajan as his son. This adoption would become for the period of adoptive emperors a paradigmatic event, deemed worthy of praise by the authors of encomia, including Pliny the Younger.

Like Galba's speech in Tacitus, Pliny's *Panegyric* to Trajan examines adoption as a mode of imperial succession, but it surpasses the former speech by its universal claims and its rhetorical force. More importantly, while the scholar must constantly wrestle with Tacitus to distinguish his views from those of his historical subjects, Pliny's *Panegyric* likely arose from a direct and intimate connection to the imperial ideology of Trajan himself.[174] Pliny's personal connections to Trajan are well known, but this oration bears importance beyond that amicable relationship. As Fears explains, "Pliny's *Panegyric to Trajan* is a public oration spoken before the emperor and court by Pliny in his official capacity as consul. Like the coinage, public panegyrical orations of this form can be regarded as publicity notices of a reign. . . . His composition was free, but he was aware of the policies and the image of himself which the emperor wished to project."[175] To some degree, this official panegyric discloses the emperor's own conception of the principate.

This speech is the preeminent expression of adoptive imperial ideology, and Pliny front-loads the bulk of his statements on the topic (5–8). Although he knows well the Galba-Piso adoption, he has clearly dismissed it as unsuccessful because he acclaims Trajan's adoption as, "O new and unheard of path to the principate!" (7.1).[176] He defends this new path by several devices. Adoption offers a peaceful means of transmitting imperial power: the *princeps* "was not created for us by civil wars and a country racked by the arms of battle, but in peace, through adoption" (5.1). Piso also tried to make this point (*Hist.* 1.29). Pliny opines about the unpredictability of nature. "Such are the vicissitudes of our mortal lot: misfortune is born of prosperity and prosperity of misfortune" (5.9). Galba too enunciated this idea as a reason for adoption (*Hist.* 1.16). Moreover, it was Trajan's merits that warranted his selection as emperor: "your merits did indeed call for your adoption as successor long ago" (6.3). Pliny plainly employs the language of meritocracy.

The next section alludes strongly to Galba's speech, either drawing on a similar source or, more likely, a *topos* among ancient political theorists.[177] Pliny speaks even more boldly in favor of meritocratic adoptive ideology. He lauds the fact that no *cognatio* bound adopter and adopted, except the bond of excellence (*optimus*, 7.4). "This is the only fitting way to adopt a son, if the adopter is an emperor" (7.5). Thus Pliny advocates choosing from outside the family line: "would you look for a wife to provide him, or seek no further than the four walls of your own home? . . . If he is destined to rule all the people, he must be chosen from all the people" (7.5–6). He also makes evident the comparison to kingship that Galba only implied, declaring that "*not* to adopt the one man, who in the eyes of all could have proved himself an emperor even without adoption, would be tyrannical and kingly!" (*superbus* and *regius*, 7.6). If an excellent man is available for adoption, only a tyrant or king would neglect that option.

Then, after narrating the divine blessings concomitant with Trajan's adoption, Pliny contrasts it with the adoption of Piso. "It is not so long since there was an adoption which failed to check an outbreak of rebellion, and indeed was its occasion" (8.5). Pliny even delineates why this adoption succeeded when the other failed—because of the charismatic authority of the adopted. "Can it be doubted that if an emperor who had forfeited men's regard was able to bestow the imperial power, it could only be because of the *auctoritas* of the recipient?" (8.6). This main section on the adoption ends with a memorable phrase to sum up Pliny's archetypal vision of imperial succession. After a peaceful adoption of a person with charismatic authority, the adopted son becomes "*simul filius, simul Caesar*" (8.6). There should be no doubt that the adopted son, as *Caesar*, is the next emperor; but the adopted son should also honor his role, as *filius*, until his adoptive father dies. This is the Trajanic model of imperial succession.

Pliny returns to these themes at the end of the *Panegyric*. He repeatedly invokes Trajan's merits as the source of his greatness (88–89). His imperial power was not the result of biological chance; he earned it. Pliny even tackles the problem of Trajan's two fathers in a finely crafted and diplomatic paragraph, lubricated with compliments. Although he honors *divus Nerva* (adoptive father) as being above *Trajan pater* (natural father) in the celestial realm, he tries to mitigate their difference in status. "You also, *Trajan pater*, must know such delight . . . when you enter into most friendly rivalry (*amicissime contendis*) with his adopter [Nerva] so as to determine where the greater glory must be assigned—to his begetter or to the one who made him his choice" (89.2). This playful image attempts to smooth over an unusual situation, when an important man had two fathers of high status. We saw above (with Augustus and Agrippa) how such a conundrum was negotiated with the art of sculpture; we see here how it is done with the art of rhetoric.

In the years from Augustus to Trajan, then, the *Panegyric* of Pliny stands out as the most developed exposition of the meritocratic adoptive ideology. But one must read it all the way to the end. The very last sentence of the body of the speech—the last word on the subject—subverts the audience's expectation. Pliny addresses the gods to end his speech:

> I make this my earnest prayer: If he rules the *res publica* well, and in the interests of all, first preserve him for our grandsons and great-grandsons; *then grant him one day a successor born of him and formed by him in the image of the adopted son he is*; or if fate denies him this, guide and direct his choice to someone worthy to be adopted in your temple on the Capitol. (94.5)[178]

So after all that, after composing the most persuasive exposition of meritocratic imperial ideology in Roman history, does Pliny's last word on the subject undermine the whole enterprise? His first prayer is for Trajan's long life, but his second prayer is for a *natural* son to be his successor—someone that he will "beget" and "form." He combines this smoothly with the fact of Trajan's own adoption, but the prioritization of dynastic ideology is unmistakable. Pliny only prays in the third place for Trajan to find a worthy successor by adoption—and only if fate denies him a natural son. Was Pliny merely offering a standard invocation at the end of the speech, one directed as much at Trajan's wife as the emperor himself? Or was he stepping back from the meritocratic adoptive ideology of succession, so sumptuously argued earlier in the speech? The spirit of Roman dynasty hovers over even this masterful defense of adoption.

In Roman culture, where political, economic, and social powers were governed by father-son relations, natural family lines were undoubtedly important. Family ideology was *so* important, in fact, that any successor to great paternal power ought to be construed as the son of that father. If the most powerful fathers in the cosmos—paradigmatic emperors such as Augustus and Trajan—did not have eligible natural sons, the adoption of sons would therefore be necessary and appropriate to the propagation of Roman power and ideology. In the second, third, and even fourth century, the practice of adoption was often hailed as the best mode of familial and political succession.[179] In sum, when Roman adoption is properly understood and anachronistic comparisons to the modern West are avoided, we can more precisely interpret Roman father-son relationships and, in particular, the transmission of imperial power. Whenever a man in the Roman world is the son of a powerful father, whether through decree or narrative characterization, his sonship can be interpreted anew in the pervasive light of Roman family ideology, which was concentrated in the imperial household. And the more powerful a father is—even all-powerful, as a god—the more relevant adoption becomes to understand that father's relationship to his son.

4 Rethinking Divine Sonship in the Gospel of Mark

In the preface to this book, through a short thought experiment, I tried to imagine the real options and significant challenges Mark faced when beginning to narrate the life of Jesus. He had received the central Christian kerygma that Jesus of Nazareth was the son of God. But how could he put this proclamation into narrative form, especially if the God of Israel had no partner? Where would one begin? It is extremely difficult to imagine his situation as an author, writing before there existed other narratives of Jesus' life. Especially if one is a Christian or a scholar of early Christianity, this requires some disciplined forgetting. Think of everything that must be left behind: Chalcedonian christological orthodoxy, the philosophical foundations of Nicea, the emanations of neo-Platonism, the procreative cosmologies of the Gnostics, the logos Christologies of Justin or John, and the virgin birth narratives of Matthew and Luke. But then what remains? The resources available to Mark: his Jewish traditions and his Greco-Roman world. With these resources, how could Mark best narrate the kerygma about the divine sonship of Jesus Christ?

In her study of the transfiguration in the Gospel of Mark, Candida R. Moss demonstrates how Mark utilized the conventions of Hellenistic epiphany stories in addition to the motifs of the Jewish Scriptures.[1] She argues that interpreters of Mark have often worked with the incorrect assumption that "New Testament authors, such as Mark, were unaware of the diversity of their intellectual climate."[2] By showing the multiple connections between the transfiguration and Hellenistic epiphany stories, Moss does not, however, reject the commonly proposed allusions to the Hebrew Bible. Rather, she takes seriously the diversity of the audience and recognizes the probability that Mark intended the narration of this one event to have multiple functions: "This practice of accommodation conveyed the gospel message to a variegated audience with varying degrees of familiarity with Jewish and non-Jewish Hellenistic traditions."[3]

I maintain that this foundational concept of "Markan accommodation" can be fruitfully applied to the rest of the Gospel of Mark. This chapter will deal with aspects of the baptism of Jesus and its repercussions in the rest of the gospel. Readers of Mark have long noted the allusions to Jewish Scriptures in the baptism account, and those will not be rejected—though they will be held up to scrutiny. But how would a listener more attuned to Roman culture than the Jewish Scriptures have understood this short narrative?[4] What connections and conclusions might that listener have made concerning the identity of Jesus? This chapter will analyze the account of Jesus' baptism in light of contemporaneous Roman culture, specifically the burgeoning ideology of the Roman emperor. Reading the baptism of Jesus through the lens of this ideology encourages one to see the baptismal voice as an adoption, the beginning of Jesus' accession as a counter-emperor.[5] The dove will be interpreted as an omen and counter-symbol to the Roman eagle, which was a public portent of divine favor and ascension to imperial power. Concomitantly this reading eradicates the supposedly "low" christological connotations of such an adoption. Finally, the adoptive relationship, which can be traced later in the gospel, also relates to the divine sonship offered by God to all people through the Spirit.

■ MARK AND ROME

Author-Text Relationship: Connecting Mark to Rome

Among the four canonical Gospels, probably none is more consistently associated with a particular place than Mark is with Rome. From the earliest *testimonia* to modern commentaries, most historians of early Christianity favor the connection. For patristic writers, the connection between Mark and Rome was mediated by the figure of Peter. Mark was thought to have helped Peter in Rome, perhaps as an interpreter or scribe, and written down some of Peter's accounts after his martyrdom. As C. Clifton Black notes, "Nowhere in patristic testimony . . . is a link between Mark and Rome ever wrought in the absence of a coincident coupling of Mark and Peter."[6] Yet modern scholars are suspicious of the Mark-Peter-Rome connection, corresponding to their general mistrust of patristic *testimonia*. Wouldn't a connection to the apostle Peter be exactly what one would fabricate—so goes the hermeneutic of suspicion—if one wanted to authenticate an anonymous, non-apostolic gospel? Perhaps so, but Black rightfully adds, "The figure of Peter played a significant role in Syrian Christianity, but none of the early fathers—even those from Syria themselves—located the composition of the Second Gospel there."[7] If the tradition of Mark's provenance was flimsy in the minds of the patristic authors, wouldn't some of them—so goes a different hermeneutic of suspicion— have tried to claim the Gospel of Mark for themselves and *their* locales? Furthermore, Mark was hardly a popular text among Christians in the patristic era, neither was its content the most Petrine: why would it (and not Matthew) have been universally connected to Peter and Rome? Yet the mistrust of the patristic *testimonia* lingers among most modern scholars.

Therefore, most arguments about the provenance of Mark focus instead on internal evidence, among which the most important aspects are (in a descending order of specificity): Latinisms, errors of Palestinian geography, the explanation of Jewish customs, connections to Paul's Epistle to the Romans, and motifs of persecution and martyrdom.[8] The so-called Latinisms provide significant support for the Mark-Rome connection. Most obvious are the occasions where Mark uses specific Latin terms to explain Greek words (12:42; 15:16). But there are many other individual Latin words and also awkward Greek phrases that can be explained by linguistic interference from Latin.[9] The term "Syro-Phoenician" has also caused debate, since this geographical designation is only evidenced from the West at the time of Mark's composition. The infelicities in describing Palestinian geography (especially at 5:1 and 7:31) would not necessarily favor a Roman context, except that when scholars reject that context, it is usually in favor of a Syrian or Palestinian one (where geographical errors would be less likely). Mark's occasional explanation of Jewish customs also suggests an audience unfamiliar with typical Jewish practices (e.g., 7:3–4), which would make more sense at some distance from Palestine. Some scholars find ample resonances of Markan terminology, theology, and community concerns in Paul's Epistle to the Romans, not to mention the tantalizing "Rufus" greeted there by Paul (Rom 16:13; cf. Mark 15:21).[10] Finally, almost all scholars who take up the issue address the correlation between the evident motif of persecution in Mark and the known persecution of Christians by Nero, which possibly involved the martyrdom of Peter. Based on the content of Mark's Gospel and the context of the early Christians in Rome, Black summarizes the defense of Roman provenance in this way: "Given our present state of knowledge, we can nevertheless acknowledge *an appreciable social, religious, and theological congruence* between the Second Gospel and first-century Roman Christianity."[11]

As I have already mentioned, when scholars reject a Roman provenance for Mark, it is in favor of Palestine or Syria. Though a theory of Galilean provenance was once popular among some prominent scholars, Syria is now a more prevalent choice.[12] Joel Marcus has argued for Syria, claiming that Mark makes the most sense when read in the immediate geographical context of the Jewish War: "Mark 13 and the gospel in general seem to many scholars to mirror more closely [than the Neronian persecution] the events of the revolt of Palestinian Jews against the Romans in 66–73 c.e. . . . And the course of events in chapter 13 matches the general course of events in the Jewish War."[13] Marcus reads the apocalyptic vision of Jesus in Mark 13 as a detailed prophecy *ex eventu*; once this linchpin is established, "other elements of the Markan Gospel fall neatly into place," some of which are fleshed out in the course of his commentary.[14] As for the motif of persecution, he argues that Mark reflects the Eusebian report of early Christians' flight from Jerusalem to Pella (*Hist. eccl.* 3.5); once they had moved farther north, Christians "may have become targets" when the Jewish War "spilled over" from Palestine into Syria.[15] Moloney replicates this argument, arguing that "the recalcitrant states of Syria and Palestine" were places where "the might of Rome" was felt more poignantly.[16]

Each of these arguments can be matched by an argument in favor of Rome. The interpretation of Mark 13 as *ex eventu* prophecy is the strongest of the points, but it does not necessitate geographical proximity to the site of battle. The movements, successes, and failures of the Roman military were among the most trafficked bits of information available in the Empire, through oral reports and official propaganda (cf. military processions and the famous *Judaea capta* coins).[17] And if Mark was not relying on eyewitness experience of the war, what would be the difference between a location in Syria or Rome? Both were some distance from Jerusalem;

both would have received reports of the events there. In any case, many citizens of the Empire would have *seen* the events of the Jewish War—realistically depicted on multistory panels—as Titus led his processions through their cities on the way back to Rome.[18] Yet even the *ex eventu* argument is still stronger than the vague argument about persecution. In fact, we know nothing about early Christian experience of persecution in Syria (even though we know as much about Antioch as just about anywhere else). However, a specific persecution of Christians in Rome was documented by Tacitus, a non-Christian source.

In my assessment, the internal evidence, though sparse, slightly favors Rome. The geographical "absurdities"—called such by a defender of Syrian provenance—surely count against Syria or Palestine.[19] The arguments about Mark 13 and persecution are similarly strong for Rome or Syria; perhaps geographical proximity explains the *ex eventu* prophecies better, but the documentation of a temporally proximate Roman persecution mitigates that argument. Finally, the Latinisms suggest a Roman context in tangible ways that the other internal evidence cannot. The detractors of the Roman hypothesis unsuccessfully dismiss their extent and specificity.

But even if the arguments over internal evidence were called as a stalemate, all the external evidence would lead to Rome. As stated above, the patristic *testimonia* connecting the authorship of the Gospel of Mark to Rome are strong but viewed suspiciously by most modern scholars. Mark was believed to have been in Rome with Peter, derived his material from the teachings of Peter, and authored the work while still in Rome or elsewhere in Italy.[20] The *testimonia* to these basic facts have been compiled and analyzed elsewhere;[21] in short, the list extends from the ancient report of the "elder" *via* Papias *via* Eusebius (*Hist. eccl.* 3.39), to Irenaeus, Clement of Alexandria, Tertullian, Origen, Ephrem, Epiphanius, and Jerome.[22]

In the search for provenance, though, we should keep this fact in mind: if we know nothing else about early Christian leaders, we know that they traveled. The author of the Gospel of Mark might have been born in Jerusalem, traveled often to nearby major cities like Antioch, and ended up later in Rome. In fact, these are the places with which the biblical "John Mark" (a traditional option for matching up the author "Mark") is associated: first found in Jerusalem (Acts 12:12), then traveling with Barnabas and Paul (Acts 13:5, 13; 15:36–41), then living in Rome (Phlm 24; cf. Col 4:10) with Peter (1 Pet 5:13; patristic *testimonia*). This traditional "Mark" was a Judean-Syrian-Roman—that is, he was exactly what a composite of modern scholarship says he was.

Among all the *testimonia*, there is one that deserves special mention for the purposes of this chapter. Clement of Alexandria provides second-century attestation of Mark's connection with Peter and Rome, but only three of his four comments usually figure into scholarly analysis. Those are his two explanations of Mark's activity in Rome (*apud* Eusebius, *Hist. eccl.* 2.15 and 6.14), which cohere with the general picture summarized above, along with Morton Smith's controversial discovery of his comments on the so-called "secret Gospel of Mark."[23] The fourth comment comes from Clement's *Adumbrationes*, which were short expansions on lines of scripture.[24] His expansion on 1 Pet 5:13 is unsung in the study of Mark's origin, but it contains a peculiar detail. It was preserved only in Latin, passed on by Cassiodorus, the sixth-century founder of a monastery and library at Vivarium, Italy:

> When Peter was openly preaching the Gospel in Rome, in front of certain imperial *equites*, and furnishing for them many testimonies of Christ, Mark, a follower of Peter, having been petitioned by these men (so that they might be able to commit to memory what had been said), wrote the Gospel called "According to Mark" from the things which were spoken by Peter.[25]

This does not contradict Clement's other reports nor the general patristic narrative. However, it does make the audience of Peter's preaching, upon which Mark based his text, much more specific. In the other *testimonia*, Peter's listeners are imagined, if they are mentioned at all, as a generic crowd who eventually persuades Mark to write things down for posterity. But here, Peter speaks "in front of certain imperial *equites*" (*coram quibusdam Caesareanis equitibus*), men of the equestrian order in close proximity to the imperial household. In the early Empire, the majority of these *equites* had political roles "as senior local magistrates and councillors or as high priests of the imperial cult"—and it was precisely *at their request* that Mark decided to put stylus to papyrus.[26] According to Clement, the fact that such imperial men heard and requested more of "the good news" had some explanatory power for understanding the Gospel of Mark. This testimony encourages us to read Mark not only in light of Roman provenance, but even in light of Roman imperial ideology.

The connection of Mark and Rome has been often defended by German scholars,[27] and by way of conclusion to this survey, Martin Hengel offers a curt and forceful representation of their position:

> The constantly repeated assertion that the [Gospel of Mark] was written in Syria-Palestine—most recently, Antioch has also been mentioned—has no really serious basis. . . . In the case of the earliest Gospel we are in the happy position of being able to define a historical point of origin with more accuracy than in the case of the later Gospels. It was written in a time of severe affliction in Rome after the persecution of Nero and before the destruction of Jerusalem, probably during AD 69, the "year of revolution."[28]

Though I am not as confident as Hengel about such a positive identification as the "Year of Four Emperors," I find the general connection between Mark and Rome persuasive.[29] More importantly, there is great value in spinning out some interpretations on the loom of this or that theory. Theories about the distant past are not so much proven or disproven as they are employed. They allow us to see certain things, even if they do not let us know anything with certainty. In the words of John Ashton, "Nevertheless a 'may be,' even one masquerading as an 'is,' often promotes understanding and when it does is to be preferred to a prudent 'don't know.'"[30]

Text-Reader Relationship: Mark's Ancient Readers and Roman Culture

According to Adela Yarbro Collins, "the evidence is not strong enough to point definitively to either Rome or Antioch," the two favored options for Markan provenance, "but it is compatible with both locations (and others)."[31] And despite my assessment of Rome as the most probable location of Mark's Gospel, the argument of this chapter does not depend on it alone. This chapter will interpret the divine sonship portrayed by Mark in the light of Roman imperial ideology, and that ideology, though concentrated in Rome, pervaded the Empire. Rome's projection of power was not bounded by the *pomerium* of the city; it was similarly propagated— and just as vital—at the Empire's distant frontier. Recent scholarship on the mechanisms of Roman imperial ideology has specifically analyzed its spread to the eastern provinces of Asia, Syria, and even Judea. Through an analysis of material evidence, Roman historian Werner Eck even demonstrates that Judea was in many ways "a normal province" of the Roman Empire.[32] Whether or not Mark was written in the city of Rome, it was written in the context of empire.

The extent and distribution of Roman imperial ideology can be traced through its diverse means of transmission, such as imperial coinage, portraiture, and official texts. Coins were by far the most abundant, reliable, and portable means of imperial news and values. Through their images and legends, emperors communicated military victories, largesse to the provinces, the securing of heirs to the throne, and the virtues with which they wanted to be affiliated.[33] Furthermore, coins were uniquely effective at controlling a message—it was quite against the interest of their recipients to deface their texts and images.

Imperial portraits were less abundant but no less significant than coins. In truth, they were rather *more* abundant and significant than is usually acknowledged. According to Fronto, images of the emperor were literally "anywhere and everywhere."[34] Modern scholars estimate that between 25,000 and 50,000 portraits of Augustus existed in the Roman Empire—about one portrait for every 1,000– 2,000 people.[35] Those numbers become more understandable by considering an analogy to the contemporary United States: there were as many portraits of Augustus *per capita* then as there are Christian churches *per capita* now in the United States.[36] To get a sense of how widespread the *imago* of Augustus was, we might imagine seeing him in the place of every church in an American neighborhood or city; and all those churches would be strikingly similar to each other in their art and architecture, each designed to reinforce the same features and values.[37] With this analogy in mind, it does not seem an exaggeration to call the emperor—especially Augustus—the only Empire-wide god in the Roman pantheon.[38] Furthermore, these portraits did not only establish a visual connection between the emperor and his subjects; they also brought the *presence* of the emperor to places he would never actually be. This presence was thought necessary to conduct all manner of official business, from judicial procedures to birthday celebrations. As noted in chapter 3, portraits were also manufactured to legitimate the processes of imperial succession—to explain who was related to whom, by blood or adoption, and to whom obeisance should be paid.

Imperial values, events, and movements were also broadcast through texts, both documentary and monumental. The most pertinent text for our topic is the famous inscription from Priene, which proclaims a redating of the Asian calendar. The proconsul Paullus Fabius Maximus had reconfigured the year (effective c. 9 B.C.E.) to begin with the birthday of Augustus. Then "the Greeks of Asia" made a formal decree in praise of the decision. In the decree, they praise Augustus, among other things, as the "savior" and describe "the birthday of the god" Augustus as that which "began for the world the good news that happened because of him."[39] The connections between this text and the opening of Mark's Gospel are well known.[40] Mark introduces Jesus' status of "son of God" as the "beginning" of his "good news."[41] Augustus, at that time the only universal god of the Roman Empire, was imagined also as a "god" and a "son of god" who "began" the "good news" for the world. Also relevant to the argument of this chapter is the "good news" reported of Vespasian's accession to the principate. When the channels of communication spread the news that the chaotic "Year of the Four Emperors" was over and Vespasian would be the new emperor, "every city celebrated the good news [εὐαγγέλια]."[42] As I will argue later, the baptism of Jesus can be fruitfully compared to such a Roman imperial accession.

In addition to this general picture of Roman imperial ideology, historians have also assessed the specific role of emperor worship throughout the Empire. Chapter 2 grew out of the seminal work of Simon Price (regarding the province of Asia) and Duncan Fishwick (the Latin West) and the recent research of Ittai Gradel (Italy) and Maria Kantiréa (Achaia), among others. Less well known is the work of Monika Bernett, who has challenged standard views about emperor worship in Judea, Samaria, and Galilee.[43] Scholars have long noted the presence of imperial temples in first-century Palestine, even if they have often downplayed their significance. A generation before the birth of Jesus, Herod the Great had already established three:[44] a temple of Augustus at the new city Sebaste in Samaria (27 B.C.E.);[45] a temple of Roma and Augustus and correlated imperial games at the new Caesarea Maritima (23 B.C.E.);[46] and another temple of Augustus near Banias (20 B.C.E.), placed at the erstwhile sanctuary of Pan, above what later became Caesarea Philippi.[47] (A fourth temple, whose date and function is still being debated, is currently being excavated at Khirbet Omrit, a few kilometers southwest of Banias.)[48] These temples are spread throughout the Herodian territory, and each is prominently situated—Samaria's on the summit of a hill, with the sea visible many kilometers to the west; Caesarea's on a manufactured hill, facing the harbor port and visible from far out at sea, and Banias's either directly in front of the ancient grotto of Pan or on a cliff summit adjacent to the grotto. (The Omrit temple is also on a summit east of the Hula valley, adjacent to and above where the Roman road to Damascus passed by.) Indeed, a strong argument could be made that these imperial temples were *more* prominent in Palestine than elsewhere because of their sharp contrast to the surrounding religious environment. An imperial temple in Herodian Palestine was not just one among many temples to various gods, as in a city such as Ephesus. These monuments to the emperor—each almost as large as a football field and towering over its surroundings—would not have escaped the attention of local residents and passersby.[49]

Bernett demonstrates that scholars have made two mistaken assumptions about emperor worship in Roman Palestine. First, they considered the Jews to have been exempt from participation in emperor worship. She argues instead that a legal exemption for the Jews never existed because "no law requiring veneration of the Roman emperor in cultic forms existed, and therefore nobody could be exempted from it."[50] The burgeoning worship of the emperor presented unique problems for the Jews, but they could not avoid it by a legal pronouncement. Throughout the first century, "emperor worship was steadily becoming an established form by which someone in the Roman Empire . . . expressed his connection to the Roman imperial household."[51] Second, scholars have interpreted the appearance of imperial temples in Palestine as examples of Romanization which encroached upon the otherwise purely Jewish land and culture. But Bernett questions the simplicity of that dichotomy. Jews did not just accept or resist a dominant Roman ideology; as she demonstrates, the Jews understood emperor worship as a "huge, acknowledged symbolic communication system" and used it to negotiate their new identities as residents of the Empire.[52] There were many points on the spectrum of identity between Herod the Great's acceptance and Judas the Galilean's resistance.[53]

To read Mark as having some general connection to Rome is not a novel idea, but new and surprising interpretations do emerge when specific aspects of Roman culture and ideology are emphasized. Whether located in Rome or elsewhere in the Empire, Mark's narrative characterization of Jesus can be justifiably construed in the light of Roman imperial ideology. Regardless of exactly where Mark began to narrate the Son of God, he was doing so in the Empire governed by the other "god" and "son of god," the emperor who had begun to be worshipped in Palestine itself.

■ BAPTISM AS ADOPTION

> Calling him "son," Galba led Piso into the praetorian camp, and before
> the assembly, he adopted him.
>
> —SUETONIUS, Galba 17

"σὺ εἶ ὁ υἱός μου ὁ ἀγαπητός, ἐν σοὶ εὐδόκησα."[54] This divine voice at Jesus' baptism has usually been regarded by commentators as a composite allusion to Jewish Scriptures. The argument goes: a listener attuned to Jewish Scriptures probably had a category in his or her mind into which to assimilate the voice as a characterization of Jesus; this new "anointed one" was construed in terms of messianic expectations which perhaps combined Davidic kingship with Isaianic restoration. My argument does not flatly reject such suggested allusions. On the contrary, this chapter will ultimately offer a different reading of the voice from heaven, an interpretation that imagines how the voice might have resonated in its Roman imperial context. What category would a listener attuned to Roman culture have had in his or her mind? And what might Mark have had in his mind, when he attempted to depict Jesus' divine sonship in a Roman milieu?

It will now come as no surprise to the reader that my argument will refer to the ancient practice of adoption. But when this chapter suggests that the baptismal scene would have been interpreted as an adoption, the implications of adoption should be understood much differently than they have been by previous scholarship.[55] The very mention of the word "adoption" in the same sentence as "Jesus" can stymie a conversation and kindle the ire of typically placid scholars. Furthermore, since Adolph von Harnack's *History of Dogma* popularized the term, "adoptionism" has become one of heresiology's black holes, a center of gravity which collects into itself multifarious constellations of "low" Christology, obscuring any nuanced perspective on them.[56]

But adoption has been misconstrued, and an analogy might help to explain how. Not long ago, most biblical scholars thought they had an adequate understanding of slavery in the Roman Empire. They maintained an unstated assumption that slaves were destitute, without hope, at the bottom of the social system. But research has shown that this picture of Roman slavery looks more like the popular American visualization of slavery—gleaned unconsciously from *Uncle Tom's Cabin* or Civil War movies—than the ancient Roman economy of status. In his book *Slavery as Salvation*, Dale Martin demonstrated that most biblical scholars carried around an image of ancient Roman slavery that ignored a key aspect—the use of slavery as upward mobility in the Roman Empire.[57] Through an examination of the classical sources and material culture, Martin illuminated a new way of understanding the motifs of slavery, manumission, and freedom in Pauline soteriology.

I contend that there is an analogous misconception among biblical scholars about adoption in Roman culture. The crucial unstated modern assumption is that adopted sons carried a lower status than biological sons in the Roman conception of the family (see argument from chapter 3). In some cases this was true. But the creation of fictive kinship was common in the Roman world, and it was binding. Far from carrying a stigma, adoption could be a vehicle for prestige.[58] What is more, the most important and visible Roman family in the first century, the imperial family, executed many high-profile adoptions which contributed to a burgeoning imperial ideology. By applying our understanding of how adopted sons were viewed in Roman culture and the imperial family, we can better understand how Mark and others depicted the relationship of Jesus and God as son and father.

This is not to say that Mark was "adoptionist" in the usual sense of the term, which tends to be an imprecise catch-all for "low" Christologies, as noted above. Mark's Christology was neither connected to the second- and third-century

Roman "adoptionists" (Theodotus and followers) nor somehow related to the so-called adoptionism of eighth-century Spain.[59] But Mark's Christology can be interpreted as "adoptionist," if by that term one means that Mark narratively characterizes Jesus in comparison with the adopted Roman emperor, the most powerful man-god in the universe. If readers of Mark consider the resonance of the concept of adoption in the Roman ideology of Mark's era, it does not appear to be a "low" Christology at all. To the contrary, adoption is how the most powerful man in the world gained his power.

■ . . . IN THE LIGHT OF JEWISH PRACTICE
AND IDEOLOGY

Traditional Interpretations of the Voice

Earlier I wrote that this chapter does not "flatly reject" suggested allusions to the Old Testament in the divine voice at Jesus' baptism. However, these suggested allusions merit a bit more scrutiny than they typically receive. Here let us first examine how commentators have traditionally understood the divine voice and then review the evidence for adoption in ancient Judaism.

Critical scholarship about the divine voice at Jesus' baptism is bifurcated. On the one hand, there is almost universal agreement about the set of biblical texts to which the divine voice is thought to allude. On the other hand, there is a panoply of judgments about what these allusions might mean for the overall interpretation of the episode. Most commentators suggest allusions to Ps 2, the royal psalm of coronation, and Isaiah 42, one of the so-called Servant Songs. Some commentators also point to Genesis 22, where Abraham binds and almost offers up his "beloved son" Isaac. Taking these allusions together, the reader supposedly understands Jesus to endow the Messianic role with a composite character: as a Davidic royal Son of God (Ps 2:7), a Spirit-possessed servant of God (Isa 42:1), and perhaps an obedient suffering son (Gen 22:2).[60] But do these allusions hold up under scrutiny?

The latter portion of Ps 2 is paramount among the suggested allusions made by "you are my son" (σὺ εἶ ὁ υἱός μου). The fact that this psalm addresses the coronation of an "anointed one" as king of Israel anchors the interpretation of this allusion. In the Gospel of Mark, Jesus has already been introduced as the anointed one (1:1). The divine voice, according to the standard interpretation, then ratifies this ascription with reference to the royal psalm of coronation. An influential commentary calls it a "near-exact quotation" of the psalm,[61] but we should not forget that the correspondence ("you are my son") includes some of the most common words in Greek—or any language, for that matter—and Mark does not include the rest of Ps 2:7.

For the second phrase, usually rendered "with you I am well pleased" (ἐν σοὶ εὐδόκησα)—but see the section on this translation below—an allusion to Isaiah 42 is frequently adduced but also not without problems. In fact, the relevant portion of Isaiah 42:1 LXX (προσεδέξατο αὐτὸν ἡ ψυχή μου) shares exactly *zero* verbal correspondences with the divine voice in Mark.[62] The correspondence is made rather through other means: (1) the subsequent line of Isaiah 42 states "I gave my spirit upon him," which correlates to the overall scene in Mark, though not the exact voice; (2) an alternate Greek translation of Isaiah 42:1–4, preserved in Matt 12:18–21, *does* exhibit verbal correspondences with the divine voice in Mark; (3) the Hebrew verb רצה (of Isa 42:1 MT) can exhibit a similar semantic range to the Greek εὐδοκέω. What is missed by most commentators in this morass is the fact that the verbs involved in the suggested allusions (Isa 42:1 and Matt 12:18) connote something like "election" or even "adoption." The words from Isa 42:1 LXX (προσδέχομαι) and from Matt 12:18 (αἱρετίζω and εὐδοκέω) normally suggest the performance of a choice. What is more, if Matt 12:18 is the hermeneutical key to this allusion, then the first line of it must be accounted for, "Here is my servant, whom I have *chosen*." The verb αἱρετίζω ("chosen") is used twice in the LXX to mean precisely the act of adoption, the choosing of a son (1 Chr 28:6, 29:1; Mal 3:17), just as it is used by Plutarch when discussing the Emperor Galba's adoption of a son.[63] On the whole, the allusions to Ps 2 and Isa 42 are not as unshakable as commentators make them out to be, and the connotations of those biblical texts are not always spelled out in full.

According to the standard interpretations, then, what was the point of the divine voice at Jesus' baptism? Commentators do not agree exactly on that, but most do agree on what the voice did *not* do. Just as they are sure that Jesus' baptism was *not* for repentance and forgiveness of sins (even though that is exactly what Mark tells us John was doing out there in the wilderness), so also are they sure that the divine voice did not announce anything new or change Jesus. Apparently, at this profound inaugural event in the life of Jesus and the Gospel of Mark, nothing really happened. Certitude about this fact comes packaged in many forms. According to Cranfield, "The voice does not proclaim Jesus' newly established status of sonship . . . rather it confirms his already existing filial consciousness."[64] According to Lane (italics original), "Jesus did not *become* the Son of God, at baptism or at the transfiguration; he *is* the Son of God"—it is "an eternal and essential relationship."[65] R. T. France is most emphatic, asserting:

> The divine declaration, and the whole experience of which it forms a part, is not phrased in such a way as to suggest that Jesus at this point becomes something which he was not before. The pericope has sometimes been spoken of as marking Jesus' *adoption* as Son of God. Such a view cannot be derived from Mark's wording, but must be based on dogmatic considerations drawn from elsewhere.[66]

France's accusations of dogmatism are poorly chosen. Certainly dogma is on the side of *his* position, which attempts to harmonize Mark's narrative depiction of Jesus with those of the other Gospels and with later christological orthodoxy. Indeed, Bart Ehrman has thoroughly charted how "dogmatic considerations" *à la* France contributed continuously to "anti-adoptionistic" modifications of biblical manuscripts in antiquity.[67]

Throughout commentaries on Jesus' baptism according to Mark, actual arguments about divine sonship are found wanting. Scholars that are otherwise critical simply assert that the adoptive interpretation is false. The voice was not declaring anything new, but was simply a confirmation of an already existing state. Taylor summarizes, "The words are best understood as an assurance, or confirmation, of this relationship, rather than a disclosure or revelation."[68] But if the voice is directed privately to Jesus, and Jesus already was the son of God, and already knew that he was, then why did the scene happen at all? Perhaps the episode took place for the sake of the reader. However, later readers know what it looks like for an author to portray Jesus' already-existing status as son of God (see Matthew, Luke, John). If Mark was trying to depict Jesus as already God's Son, he did not do a very good job. Maybe that was not his intention.

Despite the chorus of scholars that forcefully disavow the adoptive reading—protesting too much, like the queen in *Hamlet*—there are some commentators that do acknowledge its plausibility. Yarbro Collins argues against interpreting Ps 2:7 as an adoption in its original Israelite context, but she also states, "it may be that this language evoked ideas of adoption in at least some of the early social contexts in which Mark was read and heard."[69] Donahue and Harrington go further, using the language of adoption to interpret the meaning of Jesus' baptism. Mark "narrates simply the baptism of Jesus in preparation for the opening of the heavens and the divine adoption and commissioning of Jesus."[70] Their exegesis then opens up to imagine the early Christian experience of the text: Jesus' baptismal scene "contains resonances with the experiences of Mark's first readers . . . [who] received a spirit of adoption at their baptisms."[71] They suggest that the divine sonship of Jesus was more similar to the adoptive divine sonship of early Christians than it was different.[72] Christians saw in Jesus' sonship a resonance with their own baptisms.[73]

In the analysis of Eduard Schweizer, the allusion to Ps 2 "indicates that the baptism of Jesus was considered to be his induction into the eschatological office of the Son of God, corresponding to the enthronement of an Israelite king."[74] To be "inducted" into a new "office" as a "son" sounds quite like an adoption; sensing this fact, Schweizer nominally disavows an adoptive reading, saying that Mark is *not* expressing "the concept of some kind of adoption as the Son of God." But without resolving the tension between how he describes the sonship and what name he gives it, he moves on by asserting that sonship "is not the real issue" in this episode. "Who Jesus might have been before his baptism or even before his birth is a question which might be asked in modern times, but is not being asked here. . . . What is important to Mark is the beginning of Jesus' sonship in the world, i.e., the point in time when he began to exercise his sonship."

Later in his commentary, Schweizer analyzes Jesus' divine sonship in ways compatible with my argument from chapter 2.

In Old Testament terminology "son" was purely a statement of function and described the authority of the one who reigned on behalf of God over his people. A contemporary of Jesus who was instructed in the Old Testament would be more concerned about a person's action or a thing's function than about its nature. He would not be interested in the question of whether a person was God's Son "in and of himself"; in fact, he would not have been able to understand such a question. He considered a person's actions to be important because they really indicated that this person encountered him as one who demanded obedience, exercised authority over him, protected and guided him. It was in this sense that the church confessed it had experienced Jesus' authority since Easter, i.e., his divine Sonship, and had proclaimed this to the whole world. But if the one who arose on Easter was the same person who lived on earth as Jesus of Nazareth, his baptism must be regarded as the actual beginning of his reign as God's representative.[75]

Though Schweizer ultimately avoids the cultural practice of adoption as the master-metaphor by which to understand Jesus' divine sonship in Mark, his interpretations share affinity with those offered in this chapter. Contemporaries of Jesus were not concerned with the "nature" of God's Son, but with his "status" and "authority." With respect to his status and authority, Jesus had not always functioned as God's Son. Rather, he was "inducted" into a new office as son, which inaugurated "the actual beginning of his reign" as God's representative.

According to some scholars, something really happened that day in the Jordan River. Perhaps adoption is the best way to understand it. But when one is open to the suggestion that, according to Mark, Jesus' divine sonship is adoptive, it still remains to be asked: what is the best cultural matrix in which to understand the episode? To what kind of adoption can this sonship be compared? This chapter will ultimately offer a reading informed by the Roman cultural context, but could the adoptive reading also be maintained in light of Jewish thought and practice?

Jewish Adoptions in Antiquity?

This line of inquiry leads us to a fundamental question: were there Jewish adoptions in antiquity? The short answer is "not exactly"—not in the sense that we normally think of adoption.[76] Then can we, in light of Jewish practice and ideology, interpret Jesus' baptism as an adoption? That question requires a longer answer. Though there is no certain evidence of adoption law or adoption ceremonies in the canonical literature of ancient Judaism, there are episodes resembling what we call adoption and there are examples of parent-child relationships developed through nonbiological means. Specifically, ancient Jews encountered identity questions about foundlings, fosterage, and the practice of surrogate motherhood. To whom does a foundling belong? Should it be considered a child of its foster parent on a par with that parent's biological children? Whom should a child call "mother"— the one who bore him or the (different) one who reared him? In the rabbinic period, the question was raised: whom should a child call "father"—the one who begat him or the (different) one who instructed him? Furthermore, ancient Jews often found themselves in foreign legal contexts that had codified adoption. To explore these questions, we will examine biblical narratives, rabbinic exegesis, and the sparse nonliterary evidence.[77]

Though biblical law provides no prescriptions for adoption, several biblical narratives present scenarios relevant to the study of adoption.[78] Only the strongest cases will be summarized here. The most famous foundling and fosterage candidate in ancient Judaism is, of course, Moses (Exod 2:5–10). After his abandonment by his mother and sister, Moses was found by Pharaoh's daughter at the river. Serendipitously, he was nursed and reared to adulthood by his own mother. But when he had grown up, he was brought back to Pharaoh's daughter, and "he became her son" (ויהי־לה לבן, Exod 2:10). The interpretation of this event as an adoption is corroborated by Philo (*Mos.* 1.19–33), Josephus (*A.J.* 2.232), and New Testament authors (Acts 7:21; Heb 11:24). Another famous case of fosterage is that of Esther, whom Mordecai "reared" (אמן) and "took as his daughter" (לקחה מרדכי לו לבת) after her mother and father died (Esth 2:7).[79] Finally, the reaction of Naomi after the birth of Ruth's child appears to instigate a scene of adoption: Naomi "took the child [of Ruth and Boaz] and laid him in her bosom, and became his nurse (אמנת). The women of the neighborhood gave him a name, saying, 'A son has been born to Naomi (ילד־בן לנעמי)'" (Ruth 4:16–17). However, this declaration does not affiliate the child to Naomi as a son but rather as a grandson. From a legal viewpoint, the purpose of Ruth's marriage to Boaz was "to engender a son who would be accounted to Ruth's dead husband," and thus "the child is legally Naomi's grandson."[80] These three examples are clear cases of fosterage and/or nursing; in addition, the first two examples resemble the cultural practice we would call adoption. However, their relevance for our understanding of common Jewish practices is diminished by their extraordinary circumstances and their occurrence in some foreign context (under Egyptian rule, under Persian rule, and with a Moabite, respectively).

Different perspectives on these and other biblical narratives are provided by rabbinic interpretations. The *locus classicus* for examining nonbiological parent-child relationships in rabbinic literature is one *sugya* from the Babylonian Talmud (*b. Sanh.* 19b) and its parallels in the Tosefta (*t. Sotah* 11:17–20). The situation discussed is too complex for a complete analysis here, but in short, the Tosefta and Talmud deal with a perceived problem in the biblical record of David's wives and children. On the one hand, several texts from 1 Samuel and 2 Samuel coalesce to express an unproblematic narrative about David and two of Saul's daughters, Merab and Michal (cf. 1 Sam 18:17–27; 25:44; 2 Sam 3:14–16; 6:23). Merab, daughter of Saul, was promised to David, but actually Saul had already given her to Adriel. Instead Saul gave another daughter, Michal, to David in marriage. But then Saul took Michal from David and gave her to a certain Palti, who was ultimately left without her when David demanded her back. Through it all, Michal remained childless. On the other hand, there is one verse (2 Sam 21:8) which clearly witnesses to Michal's bearing children—five of them, to Adriel! What is going on here?[81] To whom do these children belong?

Both the Tosefta and the Talmud treat the specific exegetical and halakhic problems of the narrative, trying to understand how all the texts can be telling the truth. But while the Tosefta is mostly interested in resolving specific problems, the Talmud includes some generalizing principles about fosterage and nonbiological parent-child relationships. In order to address the contradiction between Michal's fertility in one text and her childlessness in another, the Tosefta affirms that her childlessness was true in the plain sense (she did not conceive and bear them), but that she did have five sons in another sense. Merab actually gave birth to them but Michal *reared* them (ילדה מירב וגידלה אותן מיכל, 11:20). In order to justify their being called Michal's sons, even though she did not bear them, the author marshals two prooftexts. The first is the aforementioned situation of Ruth and Naomi. The second prooftext simply records a discrepancy at the beginning of Aaron's lineage (Num 3:1–2); this text introduces the lineage of Moses but never actually provides the list of his offspring. If the Tosefta's author wants the reader to interpret this text by analogy to Ruth and Naomi, then one would conclude that Aaron begat the sons and Moses reared them.

Thus the Tosefta makes specific points about fosterage and child-rearing, but both prooftexts are expanded by the Talmud. The first expansion comes after a repetition of the Tosefta's conclusion that Merab bore the sons but Michal reared them. Then the Talmud states, "This teaches you that whoever brings up an orphan in his home, Scripture ascribes it to him as though he had begotten him" (כאילו ילדו).[82] This generalizing principle of fosterage is as close as one comes in ancient Judaism to a principle of adoption—the relationship of foster-parent to foster-child is "as though he had begotten him."

This generalizing doctrine is only the first of the Talmud's expansions on *t. Sotah* 11:20. The Talmud includes both previous prooftexts from the Tosefta (about Naomi and Moses), but it expands on these examples and adds two more. Whereas the Tosefta marshals the examples of Naomi and Moses to corroborate the specific instance of Merab and Michal, the Talmud proffers three examples from which the general principle could have been derived. First, it could be derived from the infancy of Moses. The example hinges on a comparison between different accounts of Moses's ancestry: 1 Chronicles 6:3 calls Moses, Aaron, and Miriam the children of Amram. Numbers 26:59 calls these three the children of Amram *by Jochebed*. But 1 Chronicles 4:17–18 records Miriam to be the child of Bithiah (the daughter of Pharaoh), whom Mered married. Furthermore, Mered's "Judean wife"—presumed by R. Yohanan to be the same person as Bithiah—also "bore Jered father of Gedor, Heber father of Soco, and Jekuthiel father of Zanoah." The rabbis had to account for these different sets of data. A full explanation is offered by R. Yohanan elsewhere, in *b. Megillah* 13a. There, R. Yohanan first demonstrates why Bithiah, the daughter of Pharaoh, is the same person as Mered's "Judean wife"—because she repudiated idolatry by bathing in the river (Exod 2:5). Once he has connected these two names, he then shows through etymologies that the six names born by Mered's Judean wife were all references to Moses.[83] That argument is presumed knowledge here in *b. Sanhedrin*. Bithiah is the same person as the Judean wife, and the children of this Judean wife are all encoded names for Moses. From all of these premises, R. Yohanan can draw his conclusion and relate it back to the general principle in question: "But was he [Moses] indeed born of Bithia and not rather of Jochebed? But Jochebed bore and Bithia brought him up. Therefore he was called after her." Again, the nonbiological parent-child relationship occurs through a situation of fosterage.[84]

The next example, brought by R. Eleazar, involves Jacob and Joseph. He defends the general principle through an interpretation of Ps 77(76):15, "With your strong arm you redeemed your people, the descendants of Jacob and Joseph." He asks, "Did then Joseph beget them; surely it was rather Jacob? But Jacob begot and Joseph sustained (כילכל) them; therefore they are called by his name." R. Eleazar does not elaborate on how Joseph "sustained" them, but he probably refers to Joseph's actions during the famine in Egypt (Gen 47:11–12). Even so, this explanation does not exhaust the meaning of R. Eleazar's argument. There were other possible examples of nonbiological parenthood concerning Jacob and Joseph. That is, they are also implicated in what some scholars consider an overt "adoption ceremony" in the Bible—the adoption of Joseph's sons (Ephraim and Manasseh) by their grandfather Jacob (Gen 48:1–12).[85] When Joseph and his sons visited Jacob on his deathbed, Jacob said, "Your two sons, who were born to you in the land of Egypt before I came to you in Egypt, are now mine; Ephraim and Manasseh shall be mine, just as Reuben and Simeon are. As for the offspring born to you after them, they shall be yours" (Gen 48:5–6). After this speech, but before Jacob delivered his blessing, "Joseph removed them from his father's knees,[86] and he bowed himself with his face to the earth" (Gen 48:12). Then Jacob blessed both of them with words that omit Joseph from the lineage (Gen 48:15–16). Even granting that this episode serves an etiological function, explaining the place of Joseph's sons instead of Joseph in the twelve tribes, that fact does not preclude understanding it as an adoption. Therefore when R. Eleazar offers the example of Jacob and Joseph to defend the general principle of nonbiological parenthood, he draws on a polysemic tradition. The biological children of Joseph were also sons of Jacob through an adoption ceremony (biblical text), and the biological children of Jacob were also sons of Joseph through his *sustenance* (R. Eleazar's argument).

The final example, offered by R. Samuel b. Nahmani in R. Jonathan's name, involves Moses and Aaron. This example is not brought as proof for the general principle about raising another's child; rather it introduces a different principle: "Anyone who teaches the son of his neighbor the Torah, Scripture ascribes it to him as though he had begotten him" (המלמד בן חבירו תורה מעלה עליו הכתוב כאילו ילדו כל). The earlier principle encompassed examples of *caring for* someone else's child; this principle explicitly denotes the *teaching of Torah* to someone else's child. Here the Talmud draws on the second of the two Tosefta prooftexts (11:20). "'Now these are the generations of Aaron and Moses's' (Num 3:1); while further on it is written, 'These are the names of the sons of Aaron:' thus teaching thee that Aaron begot

(ילד) and Moses taught them (לימד); hence they are called by his name." The prooftext left bare in the Tosefta is expanded in the Talmud. Moses deserved to be called their father in so far as he taught them the Torah.

The Talmud therefore encapsulates various teachings under two generalizing principles. Scripture ascribes the parent-child relationship not only to biological processes, but also to two other circumstances—"whoever brings up an orphan in his home" and "whoever teaches the son of his neighbor the Torah." We can further notice how the Talmud arranges the examples of nonbiological parentage in a kind of ascending order. There are five examples given and four different types of parentage: Merab/Michal head the list with an example from fosterage; then follow Ruth/Naomi (nursing/fosterage); Jochebed/Bithia (fosterage); Jacob/Joseph (sustenance); and Aaron/Moses (teaching of Torah). The series from Naomi to Moses is shaped by the Talmud to represent the stages of human growth: Naomi nurses an infant; Bithia raises a child to adulthood; Joseph sustains the bodily health of his people; and ultimately, Moses teaches the Torah. For the Talmud, the teaching of Torah is the ultimate way to gain the status of parent to another's child.[87]

In addition to these examples from the Bible and rabbinic literature, there are intriguing (though sparse) documentary and epigraphic examples to corroborate relationships of adoption or fosterage in ancient Judaism. One of the Aramaic papyri from Elephantine is documentary evidence of manumission and adoption among the Jews in that place and time (papyrus dated 416 B.C.E.). A certain Uriah has an adoption contract written to secure the manumission and transfer of a certain Yedoniah. In addition to manumitting him, Uriah also adopts him in plain language: the text uses the adoption formula, "My son he shall be" (ברי יהוה) three separate times in the course of the declaration.[88] Finally, evidence of adoption (or at least fosterage that uses parent-child language) also exists in the Jewish inscriptions of ancient Rome. At least four of the inscriptions reveal an intimate relationship between a foster-parent and foster-child.[89]

In sum, we do not have evidence of a codified or widespread system of adoption in ancient Judaism, as we do for the Roman world. However, biblical accounts of some key figures (Moses, Joseph, Ruth, David) do portray parent-child relationships enacted not through biological reproduction but through nursing and fosterage. By the Tannaitic period, some of these examples were deployed to resolve exegetical problems of biblical genealogy. By the Amoraic period, these examples had been developed into generalized principles promoting the parentage of foster-parents and teachers. Such principles offer a glimpse into one of the interstices of rabbinic law: while the lack of adoption law in Tannaitic or Amoraic literature does demonstrate its diminished importance vis-à-vis Roman law, the rabbinic support of fosterage shows concern for the actual conditions of a society brimming with orphans. Finally, evidence from ancient Egypt and Rome suggests some practice of fosterage or adoption by Jews in those locales. This evidence notwithstanding, one may still wonder to what degree these examples should be understood as indicators of actual social practices. Since we have scant evidence of legal adoption in ancient Judaism (save the Elephantine papyrus), should we not regard the available evidence in the metaphorical way? Indeed, adoption was employed as a metaphor in ancient Judaism, a phenomenon to which we now turn.

Adoptive Divine Sonship in Ancient Judaism

In ancient Judaism, God was understood to have offered adoptive divine sonship to specific communities and individuals, in addition to the well-known portrayal of God's parent-child relationship with all Israel in the Hebrew Bible (e.g., Exod 4:22–23; Jer 3:19; 31:9, 20; Hos 11:1–4) and New Testament (Rom 9:4).[90] The early Christians—especially the communities founded by Paul—are the most famous group from antiquity that thought God had established a special adoptive relationship with them.[91] Early Christian family relations have been explored in some detail by scholars, and it is clear that Christians' understanding of themselves in kinship, family and household metaphors was one of the most widespread features of the nascent movement.[92] For now, we will put this part of the argument on hold and examine a different group of Jews who can be seen as a large family under God: the Essenes.

According to Josephus, the Essenes imagined their social relations to be as one large family "like brothers" (B.J. 2.123), although "among them, marriage is looked down upon" (B.J. 2.120). Pliny the Elder expresses amazement at their continuous existence as a kinship group (gens) amid such conjugal restrictions: "Thus for thousands of ages—unbelievable to say—there exists an eternal gens, in which no one is born!" (Nat. 5.73).[93] How then did they perpetuate this large family, if they did not customarily procreate with each other? Josephus describes it: "having received the children of others, while they are still impressionable enough to be instructed, they consider them to be family members and form them in their customs" (B.J. 2.120). He does not say that the Essenes adopt these young members as their own children, but rather that they consider them to be family members (συγγενεῖς). Did new members also receive a parent along with their new siblings? Was there an overall head of the Essene family?

While the interpretation that the Essenes imagined this large family to be under God as adoptive parent is not certain, there is at least one text from Qumran that offers strong support of it.[94] One of the Hodayot contains a discrete section of prayer, in which the speaker[95] reflects on the different parent-child relationships he experiences as a member of this community. Speaking directly to God, he writes:

> For you have known me since my father,
> from the womb [. . .,. . . of] my mother you have rendered good to me,
> from the breasts of her who conceived me your compassion has been upon me,
> and on the lap of my wet-nurse [. . .]
> From my youth you have shown yourself to me,
> in the intelligence of your judgment,

and with certain truth you have supported me.
You have delighted me with your holy spirit, and until this day [. . .].
Your just rebuke is with my [. . .],
your complete watchfulness has saved my soul,
with my steps there is an abundance of forgiveness,
and a multitude of compassion when you judge me,
and until old age you will sustain me.
   For my father did not know me,
and my mother abandoned me to you,
because you are father to all the [son]s of your truth.
You will rejoice in them, like her who loves her child,
and like a wet-nurse you will sustain in your lap all your creatures.

—1QH[a] XVII.29–36[96]

In this remarkable text, the speaker first traces God's guidance over time, from his father's seed and mother's womb, to the nursing of his mother and wet-nurse, through his maturity and learning, his blessings and missteps. He concludes with assurance that God will continue to sustain him until old age. Through the first section, it seems that the speaker holds a rather unproblematic view of how God's sustenance has corresponded to that provided by his biological parents. However, the second section takes a sharp turn, like a Petrarchan sonnet, and recounts a rejection and abandonment by his biological parents. The key line is: "For my father did not know me, and my mother abandoned me to you, because you are father to all the [son]s of truth" (line 35). In one stanza, the author believes that God has sustained him since his mother's womb, but in the next, he recounts a specific moment of transfer from the care of his biological mother to that of God as adoptive parent. The author then depicts God providing the same services—nursing/rearing (אמן) and sustaining (כלכל)—which typified foster-parents or adoptive parents in the narratives of the Hebrew Bible (see above).

His biological father did not know him, and his (unmarried?) mother abandoned (עזב) him to God—does this line recall the procedure by which he entered the covenant community at Qumran?[97] It coheres with Josephus's explanation of how children came to enroll in the Essene community; the mother did not abandon her child in some vague manner, but she handed her child over specifically "to you," acknowledging God also as parent to her child. After she hands him over to God, God the father also replaces the role of the mother (to love) and the wet-nurse (to sustain/nurse). While the first stanza portrays God's sovereign guidance of the mother's and wet-nurse's sustenance up to the point of maturity, the second stanza portrays the author—though clearly an adult—as an infant again, in need of God's sustenance as father, mother, and nurse. What is more, after being handed over and adopted by God, the child is no longer alone but lives in a family under God. Though he was at risk of becoming an orphan, he now lives with "all the [son]s of truth," God rejoices in "them," and God sustains in his lap "all his creatures." In short, though a certain conclusion cannot be drawn from the sparse evidence, these texts from Josephus and the Dead Sea Scrolls suggest an image of the Essenes as a large family, linked to one another by their adoptive relationship to God.

Ancient Jews also used metaphors of adoption to express the divine sonship of individuals—especially the Israelite king.[98] Through biblical and other ancient texts, scholars have traced a royal ideology of adoptive sonship between the Davidic king and the God of Israel. John J. Collins has analyzed the relevant materials, building on a solid line of previous research.[99] The foundational event for the royal ideology is Nathan's oracle to David (2 Sam 7:5–17), during which God declares about David: "I will be a father to him, and he shall be a son to me." The oracle was spoken both to glorify David's earthly royal lineage and to promote the status of his son in an adoptive relationship to God.[100] As Collins writes, "The king becomes the son of God by adoption but the paternity of the human father is also essential to the ideology."[101] The related Psalms demonstrate how the trope of divine sonship formed a key aspect of the overall royal ideology. The Davidic king's status as son of God was what assured his "perdurable dynasty," which God makes clear he will not destroy in the "ultimate statement" of Ps 89:19–27:[102]

> I have set the crown on one who is mighty,
> I have exalted one chosen from the people.
> I have found my servant David;
> with my holy oil I have anointed him;
> my hand shall always remain with him;
> my arm also shall strengthen him. . . .
> He shall cry to me, "You are my Father,
> my God, and the Rock of my salvation!"
> I will make him the firstborn,
> the highest of the kings of the earth.
>
> (Ps 89:19–21, 26–27)

This text corroborates several points made about divine sonship in chapter 2. Divine sonship was thought of as a status that a human being could acquire through election, as God says, "I have exalted one chosen from the people." Nevertheless, this new adopted status can be depicted in the mixed metaphor of "making" someone "begotten," as in "I will make him the firstborn." To be "the firstborn" and "the highest" was not a feature natural to the king; rather, a "servant" was "chosen" and "exalted" to that status.

The crucial text of Ps 2—often quoted by early Christian authors—also portrays the royal ideology of divine sonship. The central proclamation, "You are my son; today I have begotten you" (Ps 2:7), is thought to have been the apex of a Jerusalem enthronement ceremony for an Israelite king. Mowinckel encapsulates this view:

> In spite of all the mythological metaphors about the birth of a king, we never find in Israel any expression of a "metaphysical" conception of the king's divinity and his relation to Yahweh. It is clear that the king is regarded as Yahweh's son by adoption. When, in Ps. ii, 7, Yahweh says to the king on the day of his anointing and installation, "You are My son; I have begotten you today," He is using the ordinary formula of adoption, indicating that the sonship rests on Yahweh's adoption of the king.[103]

Though the text uses the language of "begetting," it does not suggest a preexistent divine sonship for the king.[104] Indeed, it makes precisely the opposite point, by declaring that the king becomes a son of God "today." The psalm thus had a performative function: it enacted a new status for the king, but said nothing about his former status. Collins finds this point essential for understanding the overall relationship between the ideas of messiah and son of God: "The designation 'Son of God' reflects the status rather than the nature of the messiah. He is the son of God in the same sense that the king of Israel was begotten by God according to Ps 2. There is no implication of virgin birth and no metaphysical speculation is presupposed. He may still be regarded as a human being, born of human beings, but one who stands in a special relationship to God."[105]

On the whole, can the baptism of Jesus be interpreted as an adoption in the light of Jewish practice and ideology? The evidence for Jewish adoptions in antiquity does not, in general, resemble the kind of adoptive sonship imagined by Mark. But many scholars are correct to see the adoptive sonship of Israelite kings as a background to understand the narrative characterization of Jesus' divine sonship. The textual allusions are not as strong as they are normally made out to be, but there is some continuity of imagery and concepts with royal divine sonship in the Jewish Scriptures. On the other hand, Mark writes to a diverse audience, and a fresh interpretation of his gospel arises when the Roman practice and ideology of adoption is spelled out. What does this new comparison allow us to see?

▣ . . . IN THE LIGHT OF ROMAN PRACTICE AND IDEOLOGY

Chapter 3 laid out a historical argument about the social practice and conceptual understanding of adoption in the Roman world. That argument will be presumed here in our rethinking of Mark's Gospel. In addition to that cumulative presentation, there is one specific linguistic argument that supports my interpretation of the baptism as an adoption. A detailed word study of the verb used by God's voice reveals that its customary English translation has been misleading to generations of scholars, dating back to 1611.

The Greek Root ευδοκ-

In Mark's version of the baptism, the divine voice declares two things to Jesus: (1) "you are my beloved son" and (2) ἐν σοὶ εὐδόκησα, often translated "with you

I am well pleased." But many philological questions surround the second declaration. What is the force of the verb εὐδοκέω? Why is it in the aorist tense (as opposed to the perfect or the present)? How does it function with the preposition ἐν? Does the verb confirm something previously known about its object or, rather, does it declare something new about its object? In other words, does this verb have a performative function? This section addresses these questions by summarizing the usage of the Greek root ευδοκ- and analyzing some key examples.[106]

The verb εὐδοκέω occurs frequently in the LXX and NT. Its semantic field encompasses meanings such as: to choose, to select, to take pleasure, to have delight, to agree, to consent, etc. Yet all of the major English translations of Mark 1:11 (except one[107]) translate the verb in the same way, as "to be well pleased," based undoubtedly on the precedence of the King James Version.[108] While "to be well pleased" is a legitimate translation for some of the LXX and NT texts, so too are many of those texts translated by other verbs—verbs which shade toward the "to choose" or "to select" side of the semantic field. And for scholars not as influenced by the King James, the translations vary more widely: a foundational German commentary translates the relevant phrase as "*dich habe ich erwählt*" (I have chosen you); and an important French translation of the Bible also emphasizes the choice, "*il m' a plu de te choisir*" (I was pleased to choose you).[109] If we were looking for one English translation that fits the most examples, the translation "pleased to choose" would better express the usual force of the Greek verb.

In texts from the Septuagint, the verb can connote a collective decision made by a group of people. When Jonathan and the Jews are debating whether to support King Demetrius or Alexander Epiphanes, the text states that "they did not believe or accept" the words of Demetrius, but εὐδόκησαν ἐν Ἀλεξάνδρῳ (1 Macc 10:47). The context indicates that the verb connotes more than pleasurable feelings toward Alexander; it manifests a choice of Alexander from the two available options.[110] Later, after the death of Jonathan, the people select Simon as their new leader and high priest with the following words: "The Jews and their priests εὐδόκησαν τοῦ εἶναι αὐτῶν Σίμωνα ἡγούμενον καὶ ἀρχιερέα forever, until a trustworthy prophet should arise" (1 Macc 14:41; cf. 14:46–47). The verb here takes an accusative object and a genitive articular infinitive, which could be translated as "[they] were pleased to choose Simon to be their leader and high priest." Again the text and the context indicate that the verb connotes a choice—a selection based indeed on positive feelings toward Simon, but a selection nonetheless.

The use of the verb to describe choosing or selecting is not limited to the human domain. For example, the LXX records God's choice of a dwelling place by means of it. Psalm 68(67) provides a liturgical commemoration of God's dwelling on the temple mount, and it mocks other mountains for looking upon Mount Zion, τὸ ὄρος, ὃ εὐδόκησεν ὁ θεὸς κατοικεῖν ἐν αὐτῷ (Ps 67:17 LXX). The juxtaposition of this one mountain vis-à-vis the other mountains highlights the connotation of choice in the verb. From among the available options, God chose to dwell on this one.[111]

Most importantly for our purposes, the LXX uses the verb to record God's election of a particular person. The most relevant example comes from Ps 151 (= 11QPs^a XXVIII 3–12), which records the election and anointing of David, purportedly from his own point of view. The relevant portion (Ps 151:4–5) from the LXX reads:

> It was [the Lord] who sent his messenger
> and took me from my father's sheep
> and anointed [ἔχρισεν] me with his anointing oil.
> My brothers were handsome and tall,
> but the Lord οὐκ εὐδόκησεν ἐν αὐτοῖς.

The psalm reports how, though David was the youngest in the house of his earthly father and the tender of his sheep, God chose him instead of his older brothers to be the leader of the people. The Lord "was not pleased to choose them," but anointed David instead.[112] The connotation of choice in this text is corroborated by the Hebrew version of the psalm, which was discovered at Qumran. That version offers a fuller narrative than the Greek, and the order of the verses flows more logically. The parallel portion (lines 9–12) reads:

> My brothers went out to meet him,
> handsome of figure and handsome of appearance.
> Though they were tall of stature, handsome by their hair,
> the Lord God did not choose [בחר] them,
> but sent to fetch me from behind the flock
> and anointed me [וימשחני] with holy oil,
> and made me leader of his people
> and ruler over the sons of his covenant.

The Hebrew version makes clear the connotation suggested by the Greek, since the Hebrew verb בחר ("to choose") functions equivalently to εὐδοκέω + ἐν. God surveyed the available options, did not choose any of the brothers, did decide to select David, and anointed him as leader of the people. In these examples from the LXX, one can see that the verb εὐδοκέω, even in its different grammatical formulations, readily functions as a verb of choosing or selecting.

In other Greek texts from the Greco-Roman world, the verb functions in similar ways, although two other connotations are also prominent: "to be satisfied" and "to consent." Examples abound in authors like Polybius and Diodorus Siculus.[113] In addition, Greek papyri from the Roman era offer plentiful examples of the meanings "to approve" or "to consent." The verb can be used in the body of a document to approve or disapprove of a state of affairs or course of action. For example, when a certain Tabetheus was explaining how her son, Tiberianus, had encountered some unfortunate circumstances, she expressed her disapproval of his actions in this way: οὐκ εὐδόκηκα αὐτὸν τὸν υἱόν μου α[ὐ]τὸν πιστεῦσαι Μηνᾷ ("I did not approve that he, my son, should trust Menas").[114] The verb is also used by authors of documentary papyri (in the body or conclusion of a document) to indicate a party's consent to the terms of a contract. For example, a certain Tabesammon was left without a male guardian and needed to choose someone to act as her κύριος. In the document, she recorded that Amoïtas, her new guardian, was παρόντα καὶ εὐδοκοῦντα ("present and consenting") to the new relationship.[115]

One tantalizing example for our purposes comes from a Roman adoption contract. When a certain Teeus drafted a contract to adopt her grandson Paësis as her own son, she added the following subscription to the papyrus in her own handwriting: Αὐρη[λ]ί[α Τ]εεὺς Παήσι[ο]ς ἡ προκειμένη ἐθέμην τὴν υἱοθεσί[α]ν καὶ εὐδοκῶ καὶ πί[θ]ομαι π[ᾶ]σι τοῖς ἐγγ[εγρα]μμέγ[ο]ις ὡς πρόκειται ("Aurelia Teeus Paesios, mentioned above, established this adoption and I consent and I comply with everything as it is written above").[116] In this text, the best preserved adoption papyrus from Roman antiquity, Teeus uses the verb εὐδοκέω as her personal ratification of the adoption. While it is certainly true that the verb had a formulaic function in various papyrus contracts, it is nonetheless noteworthy that the verb is linked here to the act of adoption. Furthermore, it is crucial to examine the rhetorical force of the verb in these documentary instances. My translation of εὐδοκέω as "I consent" should not be understood as only a confirmation of a pre-existing state of affairs. On the contrary, the verb εὐδοκέω has a performative function in this and other papyrus contracts; that is to say, the adoption was really enacted through the adopter's declaration of "εὐδοκέω," just as the English declaration "I do" really enacts a marriage in contemporary American society. One could say quite properly that, in the case of this adoption contract, the verb εὐδοκέω completes the act of adoption and formally inaugurates the new adoptive relationship between parent and child.

It remains to consider the usage of the verb in the New Testament. In general, the semantic field of the verb in the NT is narrower than elsewhere. It only rarely connotes "to be well pleased," "to be satisfied," or "to consent," as it sometimes does in the LXX and Greco-Roman texts. Rather, most of the NT examples would best be construed as "to choose," "to elect," or "to decree." The subject of the verb is most frequently God, and Schrenk interprets it on almost all occasions as election, choice, or decree—regardless of the grammatical formulation (εὐδοκέω + ἐν, + εἰς, + accusative, + dative, or + infinitive).[117] He deals directly with the divine voice at the baptism and transfiguration (Mark 1:11 and parr.):

What is meant [by εὐδοκέω + ἐν] is God's decree of election, namely the election of the Son, which includes His mission and His appointment to the kingly office of Messiah.... Of all the terms for election (αἱρετίζειν, ἐκλέγεσθαι, προσδέχεσθαι, θέλειν), εὐδοκεῖν brings out most strongly the emotional side of the love of Him who elects. The question whether the election of Jesus as Son comes only at baptism or is already present before is not answered by the term in spite of the aor. εὐδόκησα.... In view of the total presentation in Mt. and Luke. we can hardly read into the baptism an adoptionist deduction from Is. 42:1.[118]

From a philological perspective, Schrenk concludes that the verb functions in the baptismal voice as "God's decree of election" with a strongly "emotional" connotation. Realizing, however, that this philological conclusion may lead toward a Christology he would rather avoid, he quickly qualifies it. He states that the question of *when* the election to divine sonship happened is "not answered" by the philological analysis, "in spite of" the aorist tense. Schrenk thus admits ("in spite of") that the aorist tense indicates the punctiliar aspect of the action, whereas a perfect tense would have indicated an action completed in the past and carried into the present. (For instance, the divine voice in Luke's version of the transfiguration uses the perfect tense: οὗτός ἐστιν ὁ υἱός μου ὁ ἐκλελεγμένος, Luke 9:35.) Yet to avoid presenting an "adoptionist" Christology for Mark, he must move beyond the philological analysis and interpret the baptismal voice "in view of the total presentation in Matt. and Luke." Schrenk's analysis, while philologically astute, exemplifies the difficulty scholars have in reading Mark's version of the baptism on its own terms. Having reached a philological conclusion about the baptismal voice, first attested in the Gospel of Mark, he nonetheless abandons that conclusion in light of the "total presentation" of Jesus' identity in the other Gospels.

Later in his article, Schrenk takes up the temporal question again, asking "Does εὐδοκεῖν imply an eternal decree of pre-temporal resolution or an intervention of God in the course of temporal affairs?"[119] Having already decided that, in the case of Jesus' baptism, the question is not answered by the verb alone, he turns to different cases from the epistles. Based on two Pauline texts (Gal 1:15 and 1 Cor 1:21), he argues that the verb does not indicate an eternal decree but rather "the divine resolve which is contemporary with the historical revelation."[120] In these two texts, the verb indicates a new event that God elected to perform in the world: the choice to reveal God's son to Paul (Gal 1:15) and the choice to save believers through Christ crucified (1 Cor 1:21).[121] Schrenk concludes that some uses of the verb indicate divine intervention in the normal course of events, but he leaves open the possibility that the verb can indicate an eternal decree. The philological analysis of "the temporal question" is ultimately difficult to extricate from a philosophical analysis of God's transcendence vs. God's immanence in the act of electing (an analysis that Schrenk does not attempt, nor will I).

The text that provides the best analogy to the use of εὐδοκέω in Mark 1:11 is Colossians 1:19—ὅτι ἐν αὐτῷ εὐδόκησεν πᾶν τὸ πλήρωμα κατοικῆσαι. Schrenk treats this text only briefly, taking "God" as the subject of the verb, and interpreting it as God "resolving" that the whole pleroma should dwell in Christ. With regard to the temporal question, he does not think the context fixes any particular time when God did this "resolving." On the contrary, Gerhard Münderlein has argued that Colossians 1:19 does identify a particular point in time: it is a specific allusion to the baptism of Jesus.[122] Münderlein first provides his own survey of the verb εὐδοκέω in the NT. He echoes the general conclusions of Schrenk, but with regard to the baptismal voice, he does not attempt to avoid the christological implications of his philological analysis:

It is clear, therefore, that in the New Testament, we are dealing with the citation from Isaiah 42 in almost all instances. It evidently occurs in contrast to the Old Testament usage, as a narrowing of its field of application and also of its meaning. God testifies his *Wohlgefallen* [εὐδοκία] clearly to his son and with that brings him out from the crowd of other human beings, indeed thereby making him properly and actually to be his son (= adoption formula). Therefore, the sense of εὐδοκεῖν ἐν can clearly be defined as "to choose."[123]

Applying this narrower understanding of the verb's meaning to the text of Colossians, he adduces that "God chooses for himself his firstborn, his image, and makes him to be head and lord over all people and things."[124] Moreover, he highlights the punctiliar aspect of the verb: "It remains still to emphasize that εὐδόκησεν should be understood as an aorist in the strict sense, which indicates the one-time performance of an event."[125] But Münderlein goes further than drawing an *analogy* between the texts of Mark and Colossians:

> But if one goes ahead and takes the word group ἐν αὐτῷ εὐδόκησεν, in its meaning 'to choose,' as the crucial point, then one must earnestly raise the question of *whether Col. 1:19 must then be understood as an allusion to the baptism (and respectively the transfiguration) of Jesus.* . . . Our interpretation of Col. 1:19 as a statement about the election of Christ—more specifically as a comment on the baptism—moves this term [πλήρωμα] to a certain sphere and suggests that we should understand it *as a peculiar circumlocution for the Holy Spirit.*[126]

In the most relevant examples from the LXX and the NT, both Schrenk and Münderlein thus interpret the verb εὐδοκέω and the clause ἐν αὐτῷ εὐδόκησεν with the force of to "choose," "select," or "elect." With regard to the baptismal voice specifically, Münderlein further argues for the interpretation of the punctiliar aspect of the aorist verb, going so far as to call the voice an "adoption formula." He finds in Colossians 1:19 a direct allusion to the baptismal voice and the descent of the Holy Spirit. In short, our study of the Greek verb εὐδοκέω does not inveigh against interpreting this scene as an adoption; on the contrary, a philological analysis supports it.

The Greek noun εὐδοκία is not as widely used as the verb εὐδοκέω. It is first attested in the LXX and used mostly there and in the NT; it is not well attested outside of biblical literature and correlated patristic comments on biblical citations. A preponderance of examples occur in Sirach (twenty-three times), where the word usually signifies God's "will," "grace," or "favor" and translates the Hebrew רצון.[127] The examples from the NT mostly signify God's "will" similarly to the LXX. It is important to note that the noun does not usually signify God's feeling of "good pleasure" at a previously existing state of affairs, as most English translations imply; rather, it connotes "the strongest expression" of "all the descriptions of the divine will."[128] The word εὐδοκία expresses God's sovereign will to elect and to save.

An important usage for our purposes comes from the opening exordium of Ephesians (1:3–14). In praising God's saving work among the Ephesians, the author recounts how God "destined us for υἱοθεσία through Jesus Christ to him, according to the εὐδοκία of his will, to the praise of his glorious grace, which he freely granted us in the beloved one" (1:5).[129] In this sentence, God's εὐδοκία is clearly linked to adoption (υἱοθεσία)—indeed, it is the specific feature of God's will that has established the adoption of those in Christ. By the title of "the beloved one"—in some manuscripts "his beloved son"[130]—the author also alludes to the baptismal voice, which designated God's primary son through whose grace (χάρις) God's other children could be adopted. The rest of the benediction continues the other chief metaphors of the divine family (God's οἰκονομία, also established according to εὐδοκία, 1:10; and κληρονομία, 1:14), which has been inaugurated through baptism in the Holy Spirit (1:13). Therefore, God's εὐδοκία is understood by the author of Ephesians as the aspect of God's will that inaugurated the new adoptive divine family through baptism. This usage is corroborated by Luke's use of the word, when he has Jesus encourage his disciples, "do not be afraid, for your Father εὐδόκησεν [was pleased to choose] to give the kingdom to you" (Luke 12:32). The disciples' membership in the divine family and subsequent inheritance of the divine kingdom is granted by God's εὐδοκία.

In sum, a philological analysis of the LXX, the NT, and other Greco-Roman texts demonstrates that both the verb and the noun from the root ευδοκ- support an interpretation of Jesus' baptism as a scene of adoption. The verb frequently signifies choice, selection, or election in different grammatical formulations and in diverse contexts. Even when the verb signifies consent, it often has a performative function, as in the papyri. Therefore, the popular English translation of "well pleased," which implies static approval of a pre-existing condition, does not adequately portray the verb's dynamic agency. Moreover, both the verb and the noun were used in allusion to the act of baptism and in connection with the act of adoption, examples which constitute small but vital parts of the cumulative argument of this chapter.

The Spirit of the Divine Family

Like the traditional interpretations of the divine voice at Jesus' baptism, the traditional interpretations of the Spirit are usually based on perceived allusions to the Jewish Scriptures. Stated most simply, the "Spirit" or "Holy Spirit" or "Spirit of the Lord/God" in the Hebrew Bible seems to be a property of God that can be bestowed upon a human and which confers some kind of power. Those endowed with it play many different roles: for example, it enables prophecy (Mic 3:8), physical strength (Judg 14:6), charismatic authority (1 Sam 16:13), or the mantle of kingship (Isa 11:2). At a future time, it is even promised to all humankind (Joel 2:28–29).[131] The Spirit is, in short, a chief manifestation of God's power. The text of Isaiah 61:1–2 enjoys particular favor as a background for the descent of the Spirit, because Mark's opening chapter characterizes Jesus in Isaianic terms: "The Spirit of the Lord" is what "anoints" Isaiah and sends him to "proclaim the good news," among other noble deeds.

Some of these meanings of "Spirit" are congruent with the Spirit in Mark. According to Mark, the Spirit certainly comes from God (1:10) and confers power (1:21–28; 3:28–30), and the Isaianic echoes are compelling. However, among all the options for interpreting the Spirit by means of the Jewish Scriptures, none mention divine sonship, which is a precise feature of Jesus' baptism. The divine voice reveals that the Spirit is the identifying characteristic of the divine family, of which Jesus is the beloved son. He receives the Spirit of sonship, just as others will receive it later. Though we do not *see* the disciples receive it in Mark, we are told that Jesus would baptize with it (1:8), and later it is clear that they possess it (13:11). Moreover, the Spirit is not some inert attribute that just identifies them like an iconographic halo would; rather, it is the active expression of the will of the Father through the children. In Jesus, the Spirit enables his power of healing, such that when his powers are questioned, he understands this questioning as blasphemy against the Spirit (3:28–30). In the disciples, the Spirit will speak the proper words in future times of trial (13:11) and ensure that they do God's will as members of the family (3:35). Yet even these same disciples can be hindered: though the Spirit dwells in them and is "eager" to act, their "flesh" does not cooperate (14:38). The parallels to Paul's understanding of the Spirit and divine sonship (Rom 1:4; 8:9–30) will be treated in the next chapter.

If the suggested biblical allusions do not help us interpret Mark's connection between the Spirit and divine sonship, perhaps a different set of *comparanda* can illuminate the scene. Here I contend that the Spirit-sonship connection can be fruitfully understood by reference to the Roman concepts of the *genius* and *numen*, especially as they were combined in the emperor.[132] In the general Roman worldview, a *genius* is an unseen spiritual power, often personified as an object of worship, which unifies the members of a family (*gens*).[133] Though each member of a family has a share in the family *genius*, it is manifested uniquely by the head of the family, the *paterfamilias*. Overall, the *genius* has two chief functions: it is a life-force that enables the continuation of a family (passed on by both procreation and adoption) and also a tutelary spirit that guards over its members while they are alive.

In modern scholarship on the history of religions, the Roman concept of *numen* has often been thought of as an impersonal superhuman power; however, recent scholarship on primary sources, especially material artifacts, demonstrates that a *numen* is attached to a specific being and is best defined as "the expressed will of a divine being."[134] Ancient and modern grammarians interpret the noun as developed from the verb *nuere* (to "nod")—a gesture which expresses the internal will of an agent.[135] Though often appearing along with *genius* in votive inscriptions, it is a distinct property of divine beings, separable from the *genius* and somewhat distinguishable from the divine being itself. In terms of the phenomenology of religion, the *numen* of a divine being expresses its immanence; it is "the functional property of a god" in the world.[136]

According to my interpretations of Mark (and Paul in the next chapter), the Spirit represents the functions which Romans ascribed to the *genius* and the *numen*. I am drawing a functional—not a linguistic or etymological—connection.[137] Like the *genius*, the Spirit is the unifying life-force of a family, the divine family inaugurated by God's election of Jesus as Son. The Spirit is possessed by Father, Son, and all the new members of the family. Like the *genius*, it must be honored by members of the family; indeed, dishonoring it is unforgivable (Mark 3:29). The tutelary aspect of the Roman *genius* can be compared to how the Spirit guards the members of the divine family, attempting to preserve them when their lives are in danger (Mark 13:11). Like the *numen*, the Spirit expresses the will of God in the world. It has endowed Jesus with God's power, and others who possess it also do God's will (Mark 3:35).

The Roman concepts of *genius* and *numen* gained specifically imperial resonances in the first century of the Empire, as they were brought together in new ways during the principate of Augustus (see above chaps. 2 and 3). The *genius* and *numen* of the emperor were honored primarily during an emperor's life—after all, they were the life-force and manifest power. One crucial instance from 18 c.e. invites the *genii* of the living Augustus and his adopted son Tiberius, on their respective birthdays, to dine at an altar dedicated to the Augustan *numen*.[138] The development of a cult to the *genius Augusti* makes sense, once the emperor was thought of as the *paterfamilias*; but the surprising boom in the cult of the *numen Augusti* suggests attention to the emperor that can properly be described as worship. In the words of Fishwick, the effect of the cult of the *numen Augusti* "can only have been to focus attention more sharply on the person of the living emperor and to enhance the charisma of Augustus and his successors. Freely used by the poets, the concept might even conjure up the idea of Augustus as a deity on the same level as the gods."[139]

While the functional concept of Spirit in Mark (and Paul) resembles the general concepts of the *genius* and *numen*, it also mimics their imperial versions. Like the imperial *genius* and *numen*, the Spirit is a divine agent that must be honored and not blasphemed. Romans honor and participate in "the *genius* of the Lord Emperor" even as Christians honor the "Spirit of the Lord God." The Spirit is concentrated in the "*paterfamilias*" (God) and his chosen son (Jesus)—just like in the imperial family—while it watches over the other members of the family and empowers them to do the will of the *pater*.[140]

During the second and third centuries, there developed some tension for early Christians compelled to honor the spirits of two different divine fathers, a fact brought out by early Christian martyrdom accounts. It is well documented that swearing by or sacrificing to the *genius* of the emperor was a test by which imperial subjects could avoid persecution.[141] If someone would "swear by the *genius* of our Lord the emperor," he or she would be left alone. But Christians, having been adopted by God as Father and honoring Christ as Lord, preferred not to honor the emperor as *paterfamilias*. Having been united by the Spirit into the family of the

Father and the Son, they would not honor the guardian spirit of the imperial family. Their imperial *pater* unfortunately did not regard their supposed adoption into a different divine family, so he had them killed. For Christians in the Empire, divine sonship confers not status but suffering.

The Dove as Omen

> Διατί δὲ ἐν εἴδει περιστερᾶς; Ἥμερον τὸ ζῶον καὶ καθαρόν.
> But why in the form of a dove? Gentle is that animal, and pure.
> —JOHN CHRYSOSTOM, Hom. in Matt. *12.3*

> ... neque imbellem feroces progenerant aquilae columbam. ...
> and courageous eagles do not beget unwarlike doves.
> —HORACE, Odes *4.4.32*

The long history of New Testament exegesis never fails to provide abundant interpretations—from the skeptical to the whimsical to the brilliant—of the smallest words and phrases. The words used by Mark to describe the spirit that descended on Jesus at his baptism, "as a dove" (ὡς περιστεράν), certainly do not disappoint in this respect. The poet Wallace Stevens penned "Thirteen Ways of Looking at a Blackbird," but one New Testament commentary offers *sixteen* ways of interpreting the dove.[142] Other studies describe even more interpretations, many of which stretch the boundaries of plausibility.[143] Despite these many options, there seems to be a consensus view, namely that the spirit which descends as a dove alludes to the spirit that hovered over the face of the waters at creation (Gen 1:2).[144] The allusion rests on the connection between water and spirit in the two images. This consensus view is far from perfect, since the spirit in Genesis is only linked to a bird through an interpretation of the verb (מרחפת / ἐπεφέρετο). Was the spirit "hovering" over the waters *like a bird*? Genesis is not explicit.[145] R. T. France adopts the consensus view but chooses not to speculate about the dove *per se*: "we are not aware of any ready-made dove symbolism at the time of Mark, and it seems futile to try to provide one. More probably the species of bird is not at issue, any more than it was in Gen 1:2; the dove is mentioned simply as one of the commonest and most familiar birds."[146] Notice how, even as he affirms the connection with Genesis 1:2, this author reveals its tenuousness. He proposes that "the species of bird is not at issue, any more than it was in Gen 1:2," which would be a fine argument, except that there is no bird in Gen 1:2!

This chapter cannot address most of the options for interpreting the dove. Some of the proposed allusions are tenable, but many of them are fanciful and most are only attested from sources much later than Mark. Furthermore, this chapter tries to imagine how a listener attuned to Roman culture might understand the dove, but most of the interpretations offered in commentaries are based squarely in the Palestinian or Babylonian Jewish traditions. The few exceptions are suggested allusions to Persian or other Near Eastern motifs. Again, let me reiterate that the connections to Jewish motifs are not rejected by this chapter; rather, it presumes that Mark was written to a diverse audience.

Bird Omens in Roman Culture

In many ancient Mediterranean cultures, the flight of birds was pregnant with meaning. Individual birds helped seafarers navigate, while flocks of birds marked the seasons. Birds were "messengers" of other meanings in diverse ways throughout the Near East.[147] Romans took special concern for augury, a precise practice that observed the flight of birds in the quadrants of the sky. But they were also attuned to the omens borne by individual birds in flight, omens which were not authorized by a college of augurs but rather by common opinion. One could say that *Romans used omens* to interpret and explain their experience of the world in analogous ways to how *Jews used Scriptures* to interpret and explain their experience of the world. If scholars have had trouble interpreting the baptismal dove, perhaps that is because they have been using too limited a set of cultural symbols. So what might the alighting of a bird on a person have meant in a Roman context?

Suetonius, the Roman historian and collector of tales, reports many bird omens from the lives of the emperors. For instance, he describes how an eagle was an omen of Domitian's victory over Lucius Antonius. "Even before news of this success arrived, Domitian had wind of it from portents: on the very day of battle, a huge eagle embraced his statue at Rome with its wings, screeching triumphantly."[148] In all his accounts, Suetonius is a rich source of common Roman assessment of omens such as birds, weather, dreams, oracles, soothsayers, and unusual spectacles. Unlike other Roman historians, he prefers to record these kinds of omens instead of the official public portents and divinations common since republican Rome. Andrew Wallace-Hadrill notes that "Suetonius' signs are of the types that best reveal the destinies of individuals."[149] Furthermore, he argues that "all Suetonius' lists of signs revolve round two issues, and two only: the rise to imperial power and the fall from it."[150]

For example, the accession of Claudius was predicted by a bird omen as he began public life: "Claudius entered on his belated public career as Gaius's colleague in a two-months' consulship; and when he first entered the Forum with the consular rods, an eagle swooped down and perched on his shoulder."[151] Augustus had personal eagle omens early[152] and late[153] in life but also at a key moment in his rise to power: "At Bononia, where the army of the Triumvirs Augustus, Antony, and Lepidus was stationed, an eagle perched on Augustus's tent and defended itself vigorously against the converging attack of two ravens, bringing both of them down. This augury was noted and understood by the troops as portending a rupture between their three leaders, which later took place."[154]

Signs illuminating the rise to imperial power are especially important to this chapter because, in the years preceding the Gospel of Mark, imperial power was transmitted through adoption. The most crucial imperial adoption in this period was Augustus's adoption of Tiberius, primarily because it was the first peaceful transfer of imperial power. If Augustus had ruled because of his personal or "charismatic authority," then it could not have been clear whether or how such rule could be passed on.[155] The final omens that Suetonius records before the accession of Tiberius are revealing for our purposes: "Finally, a few days before the letter arrived recalling him from Rhodes [where he was exiled], an eagle—a bird never previously seen in the island—perched upon the roof of his house; and on the very eve of this welcome news the tunic into which he was changing seemed to be ablaze."[156] The two final omens indicating the ensuing accession of Tiberius are a bird, as at the baptism of Jesus, and a transfiguration of his tunic, as happened to Jesus in Caesarea Philippi.

Suetonius's references to eagles in the life of Vespasian bear more than analogical relevance to our topic, since Vespasian's quelling of the incipient Jewish revolt catalyzed his accession to imperial power. Suetonius recounts the conditions of Vespasian's accession in the following way:

> An ancient superstition was current in the East, that out of Judaea at this time would come the rulers of the world. This prediction, as the event later proved, referred to a Roman emperor, but the rebellious Jews, who read it as referring to themselves, murdered their Governor, routed the Governor of Syria when he came down to restore order, and captured an Eagle. To crush this uprising the Romans needed a strong army under an energetic commander, who could be trusted not to abuse his considerable powers. The choice fell on Vespasian.[157]

The fact that the Judeans "captured an Eagle" (*rapta aquila*) was the last straw in Suetonius's account.[158] This symbolic action indicated the magnitude of the revolt and the necessity for a sweeping Roman military response. Later, when Otho, Vitellius, and Vespasian were "disputing the purple," an omen appeared just before the battle of Betriacum between the armies of Otho and Vitellius (69 C.E.): "two eagles fought in full view of both armies, but a third appeared from the rising sun and drove off the victor."[159] This final bird omen indicated that the military leader from the East would eventually accede to imperial power over both Otho and Vitellius.

All these bird omens involve the rise to power, but Suetonius provides one omen associated explicitly with adoption—the adoption of Octavian by Caesar.

> As Julius Caesar was felling a wood near Munda in Spain to clear a site for his camp, he noticed a palm-tree and ordered it to be spared, as a presage of victory. The tree then suddenly put out a new shoot which, a few days later, had grown so tall as to over-shadow it. What was more, a flock of doves began to nest in the fronds, although doves notoriously dislike hard, spiny foliage. This prodigy was the immediate reason, they say, for Caesar's desire that his grand-nephew, and no one else, should succeed him.[160]

This omen does not accompany the exact moment of adoption, a procedure scarcely attested in Roman historical sources, but it does relate to the moment when Caesar *knew* he would adopt Octavian. What about this omen inspired Caesar's choice? Suetonius does not interpret it. It seems clear that the "new shoot" that sprouted from and outgrew Caesar's victory tree was understood to represent Octavian's succession of Caesar, since sprouting shoots are common in Roman folklore as symbols of successful children.[161] The flock of doves is open to multiple interpretations—Suetonius does not cite doves as symbols anywhere else. One likely option is that the doves, often symbolic of peacefulness in ancient Mediterranean culture (see next section), portend the *pax Romana* inaugurated with the victory of Octavian at the battle of Actium. The "hard, spiny foliage" of the civil wars would soon be occupied by the "doves" of imperial peace. According to the scholar of Roman omens and divination, Annie Vigourt, the doves might also have called to mind Caesar's special relationship to Venus Genetrix.[162]

As tempting as this final omen is for the argument of this chapter, its bird imagery is ambiguous, and it seems that the sprouting tree constitutes the primary symbol. The doves add a sort of bonus to the omen. On the other hand, the frequent eagle omens exemplified above do depict a common Roman point of view: they thought that birds, especially eagles, indicated providential favor for the accession to power of the person on or near whom they alighted.[163]

Eagles and Doves

Roman authors refer to doves often enough that one can get a sense of their usual symbolism. First, Roman authors occasionally associate doves with the geographical region of Syria-Palestine. For example, the Roman elegist Tibullus (c. 55 B.C.E.–c. 19 B.C.E.), when describing the peaceful aftermath of a military victory, writes: "Why should I tell how the white dove, sacred in Syria-Palestine, flies safely through the crowded cities?"[164] In addition to the sense that the dove was sacred to those in Syria-Palestine—a fact seemingly corroborated by Lucian—there may also have been knowledge of the dove and pigeon industry in the area, which provided many birds for sacrificial offerings (e.g., Mark 11:15).[165] Coins minted in Ashkelon during the Roman era also frequently display doves, corroborating Tibullus's notion that they were "sacred in Syria-Palestine."[166]

But the most prevalent employment of the dove as a symbol occurs in relation to that most famous bird, the eagle. These two comprise a contrasting pair of birds, a recognizable juxtaposition of natural enemies (like the wolf and the lamb), in which one is the mighty predator and the other the timorous victim. Ovid portrays the pair in his *Metamorphoses*: "O nymph, I beg, daughter of Peneus, stay! I who pursue you am not an enemy. O nymph, stay! So lambs flee the wolf, so deer flee the lion, so doves with trembling wings flee the eagle, all things flee their enemies: but the cause of my pursuit is love."[167] Another example of the traditional contrast between eagle and dove occurs in Horace's *Odes*. He devotes *Ode*

4.4 to praise of Drusus's military might on the northern frontier (c. 13 B.C.E.). After noting how the Claudians were nurtured in youth by the "fatherly disposition of Augustus" (*Augusti paternus animus*), he continues by describing how strength begets strength in the animal kingdom. "Strong men are created (only) by strong and good men; in both steers and horses appears the *virtus* of their fathers, and courageous eagles do not beget unwarlike doves."[168] The fatherly Augustus is thus imagined as an eagle that produced a succession of warlike eagles in the Julio-Claudian "dynasty." The final two lines of the stanza epitomize Horace's style of antithetic juxtaposition: the qualities of the two birds are set side-by-side (*imbellem feroces*) to prepare for the juxtaposition of the two nouns to complete the stanza (*aquilae columbam*).[169] Other examples could be brought to confirm the contrast of eagle and dove in the Roman worldview.[170] But we have enough here to establish that the bellicose eagle was the primary symbol of Roman military might and concomitantly of the Roman imperial ideology, while the dove was a contrasting symbol of nonviolence or fear.

Several examples of extra-biblical Jewish literature also utilize these symbolic roles of eagles and doves. Josephus expresses a Jewish attitude toward the Roman eagle in the build-up to the Jewish War. For example, he recounts the famous tearing down of the golden eagle, which constituted the apex of disgust with Herod, especially his collaboration with Rome. After outlining the pay-offs that Herod had made to various members of the imperial family and his own kin (*A.J.* 17.146–8), Josephus narrates how Judas and Matthias, two men "well beloved by the people," instigated many young men "to pull down all those works which the king had erected contrary to the law of their fathers" (*A.J.* 17.149). He provides the example that Herod had erected a large golden eagle over the great gate of the Temple; although Herod claimed this eagle was dedicated to God, it was a not-so-subtle honoring of Rome that overlooked the Jerusalem Temple. Monuments such as these were common among all the client kingdoms of the Roman Empire, but the Judeans would not endure it because of their stance against idolatry. Therefore, "in the very middle of the day, they got upon the place, they pulled down the eagle, and cut it into pieces with axes, while a great number of the people were in the temple" (*A.J.* 17.155).

Josephus also provides a clear analysis of the military symbolism which the legionary eagle bore for the Romans and their enemies. As mentioned above, the Judeans had stolen a legionary eagle from the *XII Fulminata* legion in 66 C.E.. Josephus portrays the position of such an eagle in the military procession of Vespasian's army in Galilee:

> After these came the commanders of the cohorts and tribunes, having around them selected soldiers. Then came the standards surrounding the eagle, which is at the head of every Roman legion, both the king and the most warlike of all birds, which seems to them a sure sign of empire, and an omen that they shall conquer all against whom they march. These sacred things are followed by the trumpeters.[171]

The eagle leads every Roman legion; it is the "king" (βασιλεύς) and "most warlike" (ἀλκιμώτατος) of all birds, a "sure sign of empire" (τῆς ἡγεμονίας τεκμήριον), and an "omen" of victory (κληδών). From the Roman perspective, the eagle was the legion's "very own *numen*," or divine power.[172] With this symbolism, it is not surprising that the *XII Fulminata* was terrified after having its legionary eagle stolen or that the golden eagle over the Temple incited a minor sedition.

The apocalypse called 4 Ezra employs the symbol of an eagle in the seer's fifth vision (4 Ezra 11–12). "I saw rising from the sea an eagle that had twelve feathered wings and three heads . . . it reigned over the earth and over those who inhabit it. And I saw how all things under heaven were subjected to it, and no one spoke against it" (11:1, 5–6). The eagle is "the fourth kingdom that appeared in a vision to your brother Daniel. But it was not explained to him as I now explain to you or have explained it" (12:11–12). The author explicitly interacts with the four kingdoms vision of Dan 7 and reinterprets the fourth kingdom as Rome (whereas it originally symbolized the Greek or Macedonian Empire in Daniel). The vision concludes with a lion, which chastises the eagle for unrighteousness and represents "the Messiah whom the Most High has kept until the end of days" (12:32). Although 4 Ezra chooses to symbolize Rome as a bellicose eagle, it does not symbolize Israel's salvation with a contrasting bird of peace. Rather, the author chooses the king of the land (a lion) to overpower the king of the air (an eagle). But elsewhere the author acknowledges that, among the species of birds, God has selected the dove for Israel: in the second vision, Ezra says, "O sovereign Lord, . . . from all the birds that have been created you have named for yourself one dove, and from all the flocks that have been made you have provided for yourself one sheep" (5:26).[173]

Two other extra-biblical works provide a Jewish perspective on the dove that illuminate the argument of this chapter.[174] Like Josephus and 4 Ezra, the *Liber antiquitatum biblicarum* of Pseudo-Philo probably emerged from Palestinian Judaism in the first century C.E. Among several different uses of the dove as a symbol in this work, one scene imagines the dove as a long-suffering or even forgiving bird. In his targumic interpretation of the Jephthah story, the author expands at length on Judg 11:7. Jephthah protests to the elders of Gilead because they had previously rejected him but now they begged his help in their time of distress; in short, he sternly rebukes them as hypocrites. But they respond thus: "Let the dove to which Israel has been compared teach you, because when her young are taken from her, still she does not depart from her place, but she puts away the injury done her and forgets it as if it were in the depth of the abyss" (*L.A.B.* 39:5).[175] As opposed to the aggressive eagle, the dove here depicts clemency and a spirit of forgiveness.

The *Letter of Aristeas* contains an ethical interpretation of doves in terms of Jewish halakha. The text is well known for its allegorical and ethical interpretations of various commandments and prohibitions of the Torah. The author desires to demonstrate that the laws are not primitive or arbitrary but "in each particular everything has a profound reason for it, both the things from which we abstain in use and those of which we partake" (*Let. Aris.* 143).[176] As one example of this rational basis, Aristeas explains why some birds are permitted and others forbidden.

> The birds which we use are all gentle and of exceptional cleanliness, their food consisting of wheat and pulse—such birds as doves (περιστεραί), turtledoves, [etc.] . . . As to the birds which are forbidden, you will find wild and carnivorous kinds, and the rest which dominate by their own strength, and who find their food at the expense of the aforementioned domesticated birds—which is an injustice. . . . By calling them impure, he has thereby indicated that it is the solemn binding duty of those for whom the legislation has been established to practice righteousness and not to lord it over anyone in reliance upon their own strength, . . . in the manner of the gentle creatures among the aforementioned birds . . . . By means of creatures like this the legislator has handed down (the lesson) to be noted by men of wisdom, that they should be righteous, and not achieve anything by brute force, nor lord it over others in reliance upon their own strength.[177]

For Aristeas, the salient feature of these permitted birds is gentleness, which is also construed as righteousness. The vocabulary corresponds exactly to the quotation from John Chrysostom that preceded this section of the chapter: the dove is ἥμερος and καθαρός. On the contrary, the forbidden birds "dominate by their own strength" and prey on other birds—this domination is plainly called injustice (ἀδικία). We should not forget that the first bird listed among the forbidden birds in the Levitical law is the eagle. "And these you shall regard as abominable among the birds, and they shall not be eaten, it is an abomination—the eagle and the vulture and [etc.]" (Lev 11:13 LXX).[178] In the Torah, the eagle further symbolizes how a foreign nation can quickly and powerfully overtake Israel, such as Rome had done in the first century: "The Lord will bring a nation from far away, from the end of the earth, to swoop down on you like an eagle, a nation whose language you do not understand" (Deut 28:49). Aristeas envisions the dove as the primary symbol of gentleness, purity, and even righteousness among the birds of the air, as opposed to the eagle, which is the abomination among birds in the Torah. Israelites are called to "practice righteousness," like the dove, and not "achieve anything by brute force," like the eagle.

Other Bird Omens in Early Christianity

In terms of modern scholarship on the Bible, I am offering a new reading of the baptism of Jesus in Mark. Therefore, a fair question to ask is whether any *ancient* readers interpreted Mark in this way. That question is almost impossible to answer because so few interpretations of Mark have come down from late antiquity. The consensus view is that Mark was the earliest gospel of the canonical four, but it was eventually trumped by Matthew and John in the teaching and preaching of the major Christian commentators.[179] The Gospel of Mark—especially chapters 1–9—was scarcely quoted and barely interpreted in writing, although many authors clearly knew its content. It is possible that understanding the baptism in Mark as an adoption helps account for the diminished reception of Mark in early Christian communities.

We lack extant homilies or commentaries on the Gospel of Mark from antiquity that could corroborate my interpretation of his baptismal narrative, and the ancient interpretations of the baptism in Matthew, Luke, and John are usually overshadowed by the pre-baptismal narratives of those gospels. Nevertheless there are a few examples from early Christianity that presume a cultural context in which my reading of Mark would have been plausible or even likely. Two texts use dove omens as indicators of divine election. Eusebius's *Ecclesiastical History* records the accession of Fabian to the episcopal seat of Rome (236 C.E.) in the following way:

> They say that Fabianus having come, after the death of Anteros, with others from the country, was staying at Rome, and that while there he was chosen to the office through a most wonderful manifestation of divine and heavenly grace. For when all the brethren had assembled to select by vote him who should succeed to the episcopate of the church, several renowned and honorable men were in the minds of many, but Fabianus, although present, was in the mind of none. But they relate that suddenly a dove flying down lighted on his head, resembling the descent of the Holy Spirit on the Savior in the form of a dove. Thereupon all the people, as if moved by one Divine Spirit, with all eagerness and unanimity cried out that he was worthy, and without delay they took him and placed him upon the episcopal seat.[180]

The connection to the baptism of Jesus is made explicit, and at least a few elements of his interpretation are clear. He interpreted the dove at Jesus' baptism in connection with this actual bird that landed on Fabian. The spirit was not like a dove only in so far as both things "descend" or "hover"; rather, the bodily form of the dove constituted the descent of the spirit. Here in the case of Fabian, it was a real dove that flew down and alighted on his head. In place of the general verb, καταβαίνω ("to descend"), Eusebius uses the specific verb for birds, καταπέτομαι ("to fly down"). For everyone present, the flight of this bird was an omen of divine election. Note also that it indicated an accession to power—not of a Roman emperor, but of a Roman bishop. This is not a case of adoption, to be sure, but it does enact a Roman rise to power, which is at the same time a divine election through a descending dove.[181]

Second, the *Protoevangelium of James* utilizes a dove omen in connection to the sonship of Jesus. Amid the "garland of legends" that comprises the pre-history of Jesus' family in this text, the author relates a story of Joseph's betrothal to Mary (*Prot. Jas.* 8.1–9.1).[182] Mary spent her childhood in the temple, being "nurtured like a dove" (ὡσεὶ περιστερὰ νεμομένη), but when she turned twelve, the priests did not know what to do with her. An angel commanded that all the widowers should each bring a rod—a clear allusion to the election of Aaron in Numbers 17—and "to whomsoever the Lord shall give a sign, his wife she shall be." But whereas the sign in Numbers 17 was the sprouting of the rod, here the sign is different:

And when they were gathered together, they took the rods and went to the high priest. The priest took the rods from them and entered the Temple and prayed. When he had finished the prayer he took the rods, and went out and gave them to them: but there was no sign on them. Joseph received the last rod, and behold, a dove came out of the rod and flew on to Joseph's head.[183]

Like the previous example, this story uses a dove as an omen indicating divine election. But what is more, the dove here marks a critical moment in the sonship of Jesus. Whereas the dove in Mark's baptism account signifies the adoption of Jesus by his divine father, the dove in the *Protoevangelium* signifies the earthly (though non-biological) father of Jesus—an earthly succession of human sonship. In the virgin-birth Christology of the *Protoevangelium*, the divine sonship of Jesus is never questioned, but the earthly sonship must be established and vindicated through stories.

The eagle-dove trope can even be found centuries later, in a Christian discourse about baptism. During his oration, *In sanctum baptisma*, before baptismal candidates, Gregory of Nazianzus encourages them to protect themselves from the temptations of the urban life: "As much as possible, flee also from the marketplace along with the good company, putting on yourself the wings of an eagle—or, to speak more appropriately, of a dove. For what do you have to do with Caesar or the things of Caesar?"[184] It is a playful turn of phrase, of which there are many in Gregory's corpus, but as such it attests to the recognizable symbolism of the eagle-dove pair in the Roman world. The imagery was stable enough that the imperial eagle and the baptismal dove could be conjured in a quick, almost parenthetical remark. At this feast-day sermon *on baptism* in fourth-century Constantinople, Gregory knew he could play on his audience's "common sense" interpretation of doves—a Christian counterpoint to the eagle omens and imagery of imperial lore. Through these small examples, we can imagine one more way in which the flight of a dove had meaning in the Roman world.

Divorum Filii

This foray into Roman, Jewish, and early Christian literature has often wandered from the target text for our exegesis, the baptism of Jesus in Mark. With this analysis of the dove and the eagle, we can now step back to assess our original topic: when Mark depicts the voice and the dove at Jesus' baptism, what is he up to? And how might this affect a listener attuned to Roman culture? This chapter has tried to show that, with the baptism, Mark begins a narrative characterization of Jesus as a counter-emperor. This Jesus of Nazareth is an adopted heir to power. The dove is a bird omen of the transmission of power from father to son. But this counter-emperor will rule not in the spirit of the bellicose eagle, but in the spirit of the pure, gentle, peaceful, and even sacrificial dove.

Furthermore, this characterization of Jesus can be construed in terms of colonial mimicry.[185] In postcolonial theory, the concept of mimicry has been described as "a reinscription or duplication of colonial ideology by the colonized."[186] It describes instances in which the colonized produces discourse that simultaneously and necessarily mimics the domination of the colonizer even as it differentiates itself and disavows the other. In the theory of Homi Bhabha, "colonial mimicry is the desire for a reformed, recognizable Other, *as a subject of a difference that is almost the same, but not quite* . . . . mimicry emerges as the representation of a difference that is itself a process of disavowal" (italics original).[187] Therefore, the colonized subject is not an autonomous agent that cleanly and in its own terms renounces the colonizer. The very process and signification of disavowal is necessarily intertwined with the powerful discourse of the authoritative other. Stated another way, the act of disavowing the colonizer depends on the forms through which the colonizer enacted its domination. Bhabha again: "It is as if the very emergence of the 'colonial' is dependent for its representation upon some strategic limitation or prohibition *within* the authoritative discourse itself."[188]

Hence the eagle and the dove: a bird descends and absolute power comes upon a son of God—almost the same, but not quite. Read in the light of Roman imperial ideology, the narrative characterization of Jesus' baptism mimics the accession of imperial power even as it disavows the authority and methods of imperial power. It mimics Roman imperial adoption but disavows the militaristic type of power transmitted through adoption. It mimics the bird omens of Roman warfare and imperial lore but disavows the dominating war-symbol of the Roman eagle. The bird omen of the dove instead portends the accession of a different son of God, whose rise to power, though it would be mocked and suspended by the colonial authority, would ultimately be vindicated by his adoptive father.

■ TRACING THE ADOPTIVE RELATIONSHIP THROUGHOUT MARK

The benefits of understanding the inaugural baptism as an adoption scene do not stop the moment Jesus leaves the Jordan River. One can trace the adoptive relationship throughout Mark's Gospel, from the baptism to the passion, and it helps explain some subsequent features of the text. Regarding the early chapters of the gospel, our new understanding clarifies why Mark did not provide details about the genealogy or childhood of Jesus, as Matthew and Luke would do later. Whatever former stance Jesus had as a son under a former father, it was no longer relevant under the *patria potestas* of his new father. His former ancestors and familial status were abrogated. He had no claim on the inheritance of his previous father or forefathers. In the Roman conception, he was now a true son of the new father, and he accrued all the status associated with true sonship in this new family.

Mark's narrative clearly portrays the baptism of Jesus as the inaugural event that authorizes Jesus to do works of power. Much later in the gospel, when asked about the origin of his authority to do such things, Jesus himself points to that inaugural event—the baptism offered by John. Though his authority was a source of wonderment and confusion from the beginning of his ministry (1:22–27), Jesus is only directly asked about it near the end: the chief priests, scribes and elders asked him, "By what authority (ἐξουσία / potestas) are you doing these things? Who gave you this authority to do them?" (11:28). Jesus responds with a question, referring them back to the baptism of John: "Did the baptism of John come from heaven, or was it from human origin?" (11:30). The questioners had been trying to entrap Jesus, trying to get him to say that his authority came from God. But Jesus' response springs their own trap back on them, according to Mark's narration (11:31–32), because they do not want to publicly dismiss the popular John the Baptist, but neither can they explain why they did not believe in his baptism if it was divine in origin.[189] Thus Jesus forces them either to admit that Jesus' own authority came from heaven at his baptism—which the reader of Mark knows from the outset—or to deny the divine sanctioning of John's baptism, which had been well received among the people. It is true that Jesus does not explicitly say that he himself received his authority at the baptismal event, but then again, he does not explicitly answer most questions in this string of controversies in Mark. Nevertheless, the beginning of Mark's Gospel, coupled with this elliptical reference to baptism in the dialogue, encourages such an interpretation.

Furthermore, the entire debate takes on a different tone when imagined from a Roman worldview. As Mary Rose D'Angelo has argued, the uses of "father" and his accompanying potestas in the Roman imperial context have received too little attention in interpretations of the fatherhood of God in Jewish and Christian texts. According to Cassius Dio, the title pater for the emperor "acknowledges that the emperor has the same authority (ἐξουσία [= potestas]) over his subjects as the father once had over children . . . that of patria potestas."[190] When Jesus is asked about his potestas, he refers to the sonship he received at baptism from his pater.

The adoptive sonship of Mark's Jesus is also upheld when Jesus rejects the ideology of dynastic sonship by which some Jewish followers try to understand him. Though he was hailed as "son of David" by Bartimaeus (10:47–48) and as the harbinger of David's kingdom by the Jerusalem crowds (11:10), Davidic descent is neither confirmed by Jesus nor emphasized by Mark, as it is in Matthew's portrayal.[191] According to Benjamin Bacon, Mark only reports "a bare trace or two of the early (perhaps authentic) belief in Jesus' Davidic descent. But so little value attaches to it that the reader remains wholly in the dark as to whether Jesus is, or is not, actually descended from David."[192] Mark is fixed not on Davidic but on divine sonship, and a reading of Jesus' baptism as an adoption helps explain this curious feature. As a contrast to Matthew's emphasis on Davidic descent, Mark has an "ἀγενεαλόγητος" (genealogy-less) Christology, in Bacon's words, which is "almost defiantly independent of what the scribes say" in 12:35–37.[193] In this controversy, they say the Christ is the son of David, but Jesus questions that dynastic ideology: David himself calls the Christ "Lord," so how can the Christ be David's son? According to Mark, Jesus is indeed related to God as a son to a father, but he is not concerned with any lineage of Jesus before his baptism.

The new familial ties depicted at the baptism are sustained throughout the Gospel of Mark, in which a previous father never appears. Indeed, in the places where one expects to find a reference to an earthly father in Mark, one finds every other kind of family member *except* a father. It seems that Mark knew not Joseph. For example, when Jesus' "family" comes to round him up early in the gospel (3:21–35), an earthly father never appears looking for him—it is only "his mother and his brothers" from his former family. His mother and brothers think "he has gone out of his mind" because of his controversial teachings and miracles. Jesus only confirms their fears—from their point of view—when he disavows any familial ties to them. He does not even admit them entry inside to speak with him, but rather he rejects their familial claims on him. Furthermore, Jesus affirms his membership in a new family and explains how one joins it, when he says, "Whoever does the will of God—that one is my brother and sister and mother" (3:35).

An earthly father is also absent later in Mark's version of the "rejection" at Nazareth, when the onlookers ask, "Is not this the carpenter, the son of Mary and brother of James and Joses and Judas and Simon, and are not his sisters here with us?" (6:3). Only in Mark's version is Jesus called "the carpenter, the *son of Mary*" by the synagogue crowd.[194] Matthew labels him "the son of the carpenter" (Matt 13:55), while Luke (4:22) and John (6:42) call him "the son of Joseph." It makes sense for Matthew and Luke to use patronymics, since they have already established the royal lineage of Joseph and taken pains to connect Jesus to this lineage.[195] But why does Mark have the crowd call Jesus by his mother's name? One may conjecture that the crowd's appellation for Jesus casts doubt on the legitimacy of his birth, that calling him by his metronymic effectively labeled him fatherless. However, Tal Ilan, an expert in ancient Jewish onomastics, has made "a strong case against the assumption that the metronymic, as used in Mark 6:3 and studiously avoided in the synoptic parallels, conferred an air of odium on the man so designated."[196] Neither Mark nor the synagogue crowd slandered Jesus through the metronymic. Either they did not know the identity of Jesus' earthly father or they chose to de-emphasize it. In any case, the title "son of Mary" and the absence of "Joseph" in Mark 6 corroborate the new father-son relationship begun in chapter 1 and continued in chapter 3.[197]

The absence of the earthly father is confirmed a third time in Jesus' teachings after the second passion prediction, when he goes beyond the Jordan, on his way to Jerusalem (10:1–31).[198] There he encounters the rich man who asks how to inherit eternal life (10:17), a question which provokes Jesus' difficult teachings on wealth to the rich man (10:21) and to Jesus' own disciples (10:23–27). After hearing the challenge, Peter responds affirmatively: "Look, we *have* left everything and followed you" (10:28). Jesus acknowledges the accuracy of Peter's statement and explains the rewards the disciples should expect for their renunciation: "Truly I tell you, there is no one who has left house or brothers or sisters or mother or father or children or fields, for my sake and for the sake of the good news, who will not receive a hundredfold now in this age—houses and brothers and sisters and mothers and children and fields, with persecutions—and in the age to come eternal life" (10:29–30). Although all the Synoptics (Mark 10:29; Matt 19:29; Luke 18:29) have some form of the first list in this saying (the list of things left behind), only Mark contains the second list (the list of things received "a hundredfold now in this age").[199] A closer inspection of the two lists in Mark reveals the function of the second list:

house	house**s**
brothers	brothers
sisters	sisters
mother	mother**s**
father	
children	children
fields	fields
	with persecutions

The first list delineates a realistic description of what a disciple must leave behind. The list is framed by the *material property* left behind (the central "house" and the surrounding "fields") and filled in by the *family relationships* left behind (brothers, sisters, mother, father, children). In return for this extreme renunciation, all the Synoptics portray an inheritance of "eternal life." But Mark's version promises a second list, comprised of particular rewards in *this* age: before you had one house and some fields, now you will have many houses and fields; before you had brothers and sisters and children, now you will have them a hundredfold; before you had a mother, now you will have many mothers. This is beginning to sound like the "prosperity gospel" so prevalent in American Christianity, in which discipleship leads to riches. But Mark's Gospel cannot be championing that, given the previous teachings on the perils of wealth. So what is Mark saying? For example, how can one receive new mothers in this age?

The contents of the second list can be fruitfully interpreted in the context of early Christian social relations. From the earliest Christian texts, Paul's Epistles, we know that Christians addressed each other in kinship language. "Brother" and "sister" are most commonly known, but Paul also calls Onesimus his "child" (Phlm 10) and the mother of Rufus his own "mother" (Rom 16:13).[200] Therefore, the new household members gained in this age would be the new family gained through the network of hospitality for itinerant Christians. Depending on age, one would relate to the new kin as to mothers, siblings, or children. These people were the new family, and one would relate to them and their property—their houses and fields—as to the previous biological family. As the movement grew in the cities around the Mediterranean, a disciple could literally receive new family relationships and material possessions "a hundredfold." For every biological brother or sister left behind, there were hundreds of new "brothers" and "sisters" to be had. For every biological mother left behind, there were hundreds of new "mothers." But the same is not true for the "father" left behind. In the first list, the biological father is present, but in the second list, he is not replaced by the plural "fathers." Rather, there is a gap in the list, one that cannot be easily explained by recourse to scribal error or intentional textual corruption. As we have seen, Mark has previously omitted references to a father where we might have expected it. Again in this case, something more is going on in Mark's omission.

Reading this text in its surrounding literary context helps us interpret Mark's curious omission. The block of teaching from Mark 10:1–31 is grouped in part by various associations to familial teachings and metaphors (marriage, children, household members, inheritance). The omission of "father" or "fathers" in the second list (Mark 10:30) coheres with the previous texts. That is to say, Mark 10:17–31 should be read as one continuous encounter, so that the lists of 10:29–30 are Jesus' ultimate response to the rich man's question posed in 10:17, "What must I do to inherit eternal life?" One must leave behind everything in the first list, and one will inherit everything in the second list now and eternal life in the age to come. Not only is the textual unit grouped by teachings on wealth and poverty, but more specifically it is unified by the familial metaphor of inheritance.

From whom does one inherit? In the ancient context, one inherits most frequently from a father. Just previously, Jesus had established that the kingdom of God belongs to ones like the little children, and "whoever does not receive the kingdom of God as a little child will never enter it" (10:14–15).[201] How does the omission of the "father" or "fathers" fit in with this message? When a disciple leaves behind an earthly father for the sake of the good news—which is, we must not forget, the good news of *the kingdom of God* (1:14–15)—he or she has accepted the invitation of the heavenly Father. The disciple has become "like a little child" in relation to God, has been adopted by God, and thus cannot relate to anyone else as to a father. When entering the new family of God by relating to God as Father, the disciple cannot *ipso facto* receive new "fathers" in the same way that other new family members would be received. There is only one new Father to receive, and the disciple has already received him, a reception which is the precondition for all the other benefits in the second list.[202]

The inheritance from the Father in the age to come is perfectly clear: through membership in the new family of God, the household of the divine *paterfamilias*, the disciple will inherit eternal life. Thus the rich man's question is answered. But in the Gospel of Mark, relating to God as Father does not only entail a hundredfold benefits and eternal life. Just as something was omitted from the second list above, so also was something added. When a disciple leaves behind an earthly father to do the will of the heavenly Father, that person receives, in this age, "persecutions." The sign of one's new identity as son or daughter of God is not only a new network of familial hospitality; unfortunately the sign is also persecution. This corresponds to the motif of suffering in Mark. Earlier in the gospel, suffering has already been linked to *discipleship* (8:34); here we learn that suffering is also necessary for divine *sonship* and inheritance of the kingdom of God. One might say that in the Gospel of Mark, this is the "bad news."

If the text just analyzed has only intimated the connection between suffering and sonship, the connection is confirmed by the accounts of Jesus in Gethsemane and his death on the cross. The Gethsemane account has many functions in the Gospel of Mark, one of which is to clarify the divine sonship of Jesus. In Jesus' crucial prayer to God, he says, "Abba, Father, for you all things are possible; remove this cup from me; yet, not what I want, but what you want" (14:36). Several features of this brief prayer support the image of divine sonship laid out in the previous pages. First, this is the only time Jesus directly addresses God as "Father" in Mark and the only time Jesus addresses God as "Abba" in any of the Gospels. If that seems unremarkable to most readers, it is likely because of the prevalence of Jesus' addresses to God as Father in the other Gospels, especially John. However, interpreting Mark on its own terms, with its own distinctive view of divine sonship, Jesus' prayer is important because it recalls when Jesus first introduced the stipulations for membership in the divine family. In Mark 3, Jesus rejected his biological family and claimed that the new divine family consisted of "Whoever does the will of God" (3:35). Here at Gethsemane, Jesus enacts this obedience, a fact obscured a bit by English translations but clear in the Greek. In his prayer, he commits to doing not what I *will* (θέλω), but what you will, drawing on the same Greek root as the *will* (θέλημα) of God in chapter 3.

Second, when Jesus acknowledges that for the Father "all things are possible" (πάντα δυνατά), this is not the first time he has made this claim. In the passage analyzed above (Mark 10:17–31), Jesus taught that, although it is very difficult for "children" to "enter the kingdom of God" and receive a new "Father," the disciples should not despair because for God "all things are possible" (πάντα δυνατά, 10:27). These are the two times in Mark where Jesus aphorizes about the Father's omnipotent sovereignty. But Jesus' request in Gethsemane is ironic: whereas earlier he had declared the Father's omnipotence to welcome whomever he wanted into the divine family, here he wants to avoid the suffering obedience which is the very identifier of membership in the divine family. The absolute sovereignty of the Father has two sides: on one side is sonship, on the other side is suffering. Just as the Father exercises sovereignty by adopting "whoever does the will of God" into the divine family, so does the Father exercise sovereignty by requiring the "persecutions" which lead ultimately to Gethsemane and the cross. Such power over life and death resonates poignantly with that of the *paterfamilias* in the law and ideology of the Roman family.[203] The two sides of paternal sovereignty are two sides of the same coin. Just as the Roman *paterfamilias* holds the power of benefactions to his household, so does he hold the notorious *ius vitae necisque*—the legal power of life and death—over everyone in his *familia*. From Gethsemane to the cross, God exercises that power available to every *paterfamilias*. For a father, "all things are possible" indeed.

It remains in this section to examine the two other times in Mark where Jesus' divine sonship is identified: the divine voice at the transfiguration and the centurion at the crucifixion. Both of these scenes can be reasonably interpreted in the light of Roman imperial ideology. First, scholars have noted the specific and peculiar location of the transfiguration in Mark: Jesus was with his disciples in "the villages of Caesarea Philippi" (8:27) from where he led Peter, James, and John up to a high mountain and was transfigured before them (9:2–8). Why does Mark place Jesus specifically there, the remote northern tip of Israel, to declare him as Christ (8:29) and Son of God (9:7)?[204] As noted above, this was one of the sites of emperor worship in the first century. Herod's son Philip had refounded Paneion as Caesarea and erected a temple to Augustus there. To declare Jesus as "son of God" at Caesarea Philippi was therefore to challenge the "son of God" already being worshipped in the immediate vicinity—the emperor. Furthermore, God's declaration of Jesus as "my son" to Peter, James, and John provides witnesses to Jesus' status, a key point because the earlier voice was given only privately to Jesus. This gathering would then resemble the *comitia curiata*, or "representative assembly," necessary to confirm Roman adoptions. Though a father could adopt a son in private at any time, that transaction must eventually be made public, either through a *comitia* or a final testament. At the site of another adopted *divi filius*, God makes his election of Jesus known.

At the crucifixion, Jesus is finally announced publicly as God's son (15:39), but the unexpected identity of the announcer has become—pardon the pun—a *crux interpretum*. To the question of "Why a Roman centurion?" there have been many scholarly responses.[205] Viewed in the light of Roman imperial ideology, a new one arises. Let us recall that the charismatic authority of the Roman emperor was derived in part from military achievement and concomitant military acclamation. Before an emperor could be *divi filius*, he must first be regarded as a "commander" (or *imperator*, the source of the English word "emperor"). Even adopted imperial heirs needed to prove themselves in battle and gain the approval of (enough of) the army. An emperor could simply not accede to the principate without it.

Returning to Mark's characterization of Jesus, we can see some events with new eyes. Jesus' "battles" are mostly with unclean spirits, the exorcisms of which have been interpreted fruitfully through postcolonial criticism—the Roman colonizers being symbolized as the "spirits" convulsing the people of Palestine. Mark cues the reader toward this interpretation in the exorcism of the Gerasene demoniac, in which Jesus purges and fantastically destroys the violent and indomitable "legion."[206] After his battles are completed, and after his status is announced above the site of imperial worship in Caesarea Philippi, Jesus marches into Jerusalem in a mock triumphal entry (11:1–11).[207] While there, he himself initiates a direct comparison between his father, the God of Israel, and the father-son gods imaged on Roman coins (12:15–17). He declares himself to be the son of the God of Israel (14:61–62), but is mockingly clad in imperial purple by Roman soldiers of the *praetorium* (15:16–20).

The first and final public declaration of Jesus' divine sonship—the statement of the centurion, "Indeed, this man was God's son"—is perhaps explained best by colonial mimicry. Roman power, concentrated in the figure of its military, is at once both the challenge to and the legitimation of Jesus' divine sonship. Up to this point, Mark had narratively characterized Jesus as a counter-emperor, a "son of God" whose rise to power in the cosmos had mimicked imperial power on a kind of parallel *cursus* and *triumphus*. Now the course ends with a mockery and subversion of the triumph. But with the Roman centurion's cry, the parallel tracks of analogy and reality converge and intersect, like a cross: the acclamation of the army was in reality a necessary element of imperial power, and the death of an emperor was in fact the time when his exalted status was finally evaluated.

The public declaration of Jesus as God's son also confirmed his status as God's rightful heir. For that heavenly inheritance to function as an earthly one would, Jesus' divine father would need to have died—and such an audacious claim is not made. God did not die, but God's inheritable goods were certainly perishing during the time of Jesus' life and Mark's writing: God's land and people, name and glory, temple and cult, had all been or were about to be usurped by the Roman legions, under the authority of *their* imperial divine father. As for Jesus, he felt like his own divine father had "abandoned" him—"disinheriting" him as God's son by "exposing" him to death on a Roman cross. His father gave him a sign, however, that the inheritance was about to be transferred. God did not die, but with the tear of the temple curtain, God was beginning to let go of his inheritable goods. In one sense, they were being usurped by the Romans. In another sense—despite appearances—the Son of God was about to inherit the Empire of his Father.

The centurion therefore got it right: *vere hic homo divi filius erat*. Almost the same, but not quite. In the end, Mark's view of divine sonship, which had been refracted throughout the gospel in the light of the Roman emperor, now shines through unmediated. It is Jesus who is the Roman world's "son of God"— sorrowful as a Roman criminal, and powerful as a Roman emperor.

Reading Mark from the perspective of Roman adoption and imperial ideology allows us to see the ingenuity of Mark's theological mind. Faced with an unprecedented challenge—narrating the divine sonship of a human being in relation to a God that did not procreate—Mark articulated a model of sonship that was theologically coherent and also resonated in his cultural context. Later authors chose incarnational moments or virgin birth vignettes to characterize the divine sonship of Jesus. Therefore, compared with these narrative developments, Mark's Christology is usually labeled "low." And that label certainly fits in the terms of later christological debates, heavily influenced by philosophical categories. But viewed in the political ideology of its time period—a view of the cosmos more widely held than that of Platonist philosophy—Mark's Christology was as high as humanly possible. The Roman emperor, the most powerful person in the world, gained his sonship by adoption. If Mark was crafting a narrative that presents Jesus to Roman listeners as a counter-emperor, the authoritative son of God, then adoption was the most effective method of portraying his divine sonship.

5 Begotten and Adopted Sons of God—Before and After Nicea

The same thing happens regarding us also, for whom the Lord has
become an exemplar: being baptized, we are illuminated; being
illuminated, we are adopted as sons; being adopted as sons, we are
perfected; being perfected, we become immortal. "I said, 'You are
gods,'" he said, "'and all sons of the Most High.'"

—CLEMENT OF ALEXANDRIA

No one among the sons of God can be likened to the Son of God.
He himself is called "Son" of God, but we are called "sons" of
God. . . . He is unique, we are many; he is one, we are one in him;
he was born, we were adopted; he was begotten as Son through nature
in eternity, we were made sons through grace in time.

—AUGUSTINE

The close examination of Roman fathers and sons allows us to hear new resonances
of divine sonship in early Christianity, as I hope to have just demonstrated with the
Gospel of Mark. This final chapter will analyze how those resonances changed over
time—the shifting relationship between begotten and adoptive metaphors in early
Christianity. My framework is roughly chronological, and therefore different genres
have been interspersed. But the diachronic presentation enables a clearer view of
the interweaving themes on the road to Nicea: begotten and adopted, the sonship of
Christ and the sonship of Christians, Christ as unique and Christ as exemplar,
philosophy and narrative, theological doctrine and liturgical practice.[1]

In the first two centuries, and especially in areas more influenced by Roman
culture, the high view of adopted sons was well established, and I contend that it
influenced the metaphors used to portray divine sonship. At that time, "begotten"
natural sonship and "made" adoptive sonship were metaphors based on actual
human practices. And contrary to popular belief, *both* metaphors were used to refer
to the divine sonship of Jesus Christ *and also* to the divine sonship afforded to all
Christians. This will be demonstrated through some major New Testament and
second-century authors on divine sonship. For them the metaphors were mixed.

But by the fourth century, the metaphors no longer referred to actual practices;
stated another way, the metaphors were no longer metaphors. In Roman culture,
adoption had ceased to be a crucial, visible component of imperial ideology.
Moreover, with the rise of philosophical, especially Platonist, speculation
among Christian leaders, the terms "begotten" and "made" changed in meaning.
They became increasingly abstract concepts, until the watershed debates of the
Nicene era established them finally as the property of theologians alone. Jesus was

the begotten one, and everything else was made—and "made" now meant "created," in addition to "adopted." This Nicene orthodoxy struggled, however, to line up with the way the terms were still being used by Christians "on the ground." It is true that *adoption* metaphors were no longer common to describe Jesus, but *begotten* metaphors were still extremely common to describe Christians. The final section of the chapter maps one liturgical trajectory in which these metaphors were brought under control.

■ A D O P T E D A N D B E G O T T E N I N T H E N E W T E S T A M E N T

The "Backwards Development" of Christology and the Synthesis of Luke

Among the most influential ideas in Raymond Brown's *The Birth of the Messiah*, his classic study of the infancy narratives in Matthew and Luke, is his opening sketch of the "backwards development" of Christology in the New Testament.[2] He argues that, in the period before the Gospels were written, the chief moment encapsulating Jesus' divine power as God's son was his resurrection. Brown finds this primitive Christology in sections of Paul's letters and older strata of Acts.[3] He suggests that even this might not be the oldest understanding of the "christological moment," proposing that the earliest disciples of Jesus might have focused on the second coming (*parousia*)—"when Jesus would return in glory, then God would fully reveal him."[4] Either way, the Gospel of Mark decisively moved the moment backward into Jesus' lifetime, emphasizing his baptism, transfiguration, and crucifixion. Matthew and Luke went further still, back to his conception and birth: in Brown's careful words, "Matthew and Luke saw christological implications in stories that were in circulation about Jesus' birth; or, at least, they saw the possibility of weaving such stories into a narrative of their own composition which could be made the vehicle of the message that Jesus was the Son of God acting for the salvation of mankind."[5] Finally, the Gospel of John championed the idea of Jesus' preexistence before all creation.[6] The key moment of Jesus' relationship to the Father thus moved from the end of time—in so far as his resurrection was understood to have inaugurated the last days—all the way back to before the beginning of time.

Brown's sketch was filled out a few years later by James Dunn's *Christology in the Making*, whose treatment of divine sonship was analyzed and praised earlier in this volume in chapter 1. Dunn traces the term "son of God" as a "concept in transition," from the primitive resurrection Christologies retained by Paul and Acts to the pre-existence Christology of John. Though he relies on Brown's synthesis, Dunn thinks it would be "unwise" to chart "a straight line of development" as Brown's explication had implied, "if only because we cannot be sufficiently certain of dates of documents or of interrelationships of the communities, individuals, traditions, and ideas which lie behind them."[7] Brown's big picture was the right outline for historical-critical scholars, but filling in the contours and shading has not proved easy.

What is more, early Christians like Luke "saw no difficulty in affirming *several* christologically decisive moments in Jesus' life and ministry."[8] The picture painted of Jesus' divine sonship in the New Testament should be more cubist than realist.[9] One reader might try to unearth the primitive Christology preserved in the speeches of Acts, in which the resurrection was the moment where God "made" Jesus "Lord and Messiah" (2:36) and "begat" him as "son" (13:32–33), in the words of Ps 2. Perhaps this begotten-made Christology is older than the begotten-born Christology of the infancy narrative. Another might emphasize the "Lukan variant" at the baptism of Jesus (3:22), a fuller citation of Ps 2:7 that locates divine sonship at baptism instead of at conception and birth (the latter being stories which would have been added, according to this reading, at a still later stage of redaction).[10] Nevertheless the final composite text of Luke-Acts remains before us: Jesus is God's son at conception, baptism, and resurrection.[11] What we find to be mutually exclusive—because of our Nicene emphasis on the *when* of divine sonship—Luke seems to have found mutually reinforcing.[12]

In this way, Luke was similar to many other Christians of the first and second centuries: regarding the concept of divine sonship, they mixed metaphors. Begetting, making, genealogical chronicling, bearing, or adopting were all reasonable ways of portraying the mystery of how God might have human children. (Through the influence of Platonism, many Christians would also add emanating and proceeding to this list.) A textual reason for metaphor-mixing in the New Testament was that Ps 2, the Israelite royal psalm of coronation in which so many early Christians found christological import, encouraged the mixing of metaphors in the first place.[13] In Ps 2:7, the king is "begotten" as God's "son," but the begetting happens "today." The fact that it happens "today" implies that the recipient of the voice was not God's son yesterday, and so the metaphor would seem to be that of "adopting." But the verb itself is clearly "begetting," and the metaphor remains mixed.[14]

In the famous *catena* that begins the Epistle to the Hebrews, its author also quotes Ps 2 to bolster the status of Jesus Christ—and there too, interpreters have had difficulty assessing precisely which status that quotation is intended to bolster. Does the quotation imply a preexistent begotten sonship or an eschatological adoptive sonship? "The tradition of citing Ps. 2:7 in connection with Christ's exaltation points in one direction," writes Harold Attridge, but "the cosmic perspective of the prologue of Hebrews points in another direction."[15] Several attempts have been made to reconcile these seemingly conflicting presentations of sonship.[16] But it is crucial to remember that the exegetical conflict primarily concerns the *origins* of sonship—the *when* question—which has preoccupied christological interpretations of the New Testament since the Nicene era. Regarding the *final* status of Jesus' divine sonship, Hebrews does present a coherent message: he is the super-exalted Son of God, at the highest status possibly imaginable for a human being to possess. The proclamation of this super-status is the purpose of the *catena*. The author's overall goal is "to establish the significance of Christ for the present and future of his addressees by indicating the superiority of the Son to any other agent of God's purposes."[17]

Returning now to Luke, perhaps he had a different rhetorical reason for his mixed images of divine sonship: namely, his concern for, and masterful skill with, presenting the history of nascent Christianity to a broad audience with diverse social practices and cultural ideologies.[18] *Adoptive divine sonship* is suggested by the resurrection (Acts 13:33) and the baptism (Luke 3:22), a proximate *divine begetting* is secured in the infancy narrative (Luke 1:35), while a distant *divine genealogy* is also delineated (Luke 3:23–38). That "genealogy" is not as simple as it appears, however: Jesus is a *non*-biological son of Joseph,[19] whose ancestry passed through the Davidic royal line—those kings who themselves were *begotten-adopted* sons of God (2 Sam 7:14; Ps 2:7; Ps 89:19–37)—and primordially originated with Adam, the *created-made* son of God (Luke 3:38; Gen 1:26–27). The more sources of legitimacy that Luke could articulate for Jesus, the better. Such an approach is similar to how the divine sonship of the Roman emperors in the Julio-Claudian era was legitimated, as explained in chapter 2. Augustus was son of the divine Apollo by begetting and son of the divine Julius by adoption; he traced ancestry to the divine Mars and styled himself as a new Romulus. In the Julio-Claudian dynasty—and again later in the second-century imperial successions—the adoptive relations turned out to be the most important. But like the supporters of Roman divine sons, Luke might have thought, why not claim all the different sources of legitimation, to reach the widest possible audience?

Among New Testament authors, Paul and John represent the closest we have to ideal types of portraying divine sonship, with one preferring adoptive imagery and the other begotten imagery.[20] They do not mix their metaphors—or mix them the least. The following sections argue that, despite their different choices of metaphor, their visions of divine sonship have key similarities. In crafting their metaphors, neither is primarily concerned with the precise temporal origins of Christ's divine sonship. More importantly, for both authors divine sonship unites Christ with Christians more than it divides them.

Paul on Adoptive Divine Sonship

There are several excellent explications of Paul's arguments on adoptive sonship in Galatians and Romans.[21] Here I will primarily emphasize that the imagery is perfectly in line with our knowledge about adoption in Roman society.[22] James Walters is right to argue that Paul's adoption metaphor functions well in the cultural context of Greco-Roman household practices, and especially laws of inheritance.[23] In the two places where Paul explains adoption as the means of Christian divine sonship, he has already introduced inheritance as the chief concern.[24] In both contexts "there was controversy regarding the status of Gentile believers vis-à-vis Jewish believers. So adoption functions for Paul as a metaphor that gives nuance to what he wishes to communicate about inheritance."[25]

In Gal 3:23–4:7, Paul establishes adoption as his master-metaphor for Christian divine sonship, and he returns to it again in Rom 8:12–25. In the first example, Paul envisions a realistic household of both "slaves" and children (νήπιοι or "minors"), in which the children are afforded a παιδαγωγός or "tutor" throughout their youth. In this household, the "sons" of the father—and thus his rightful heirs—are not empowered until adulthood, and they can be drawn from either the slaves or the children. That is to say, the adoption of an adult slave (or any other man) as a son should not place that adopted son in a lower status than the biological children. Until maturity, the children are kept under "guardians" and "trustees" anyway (ἐπιτρόπους καὶ οἰκονόμους). The ultimate factor determining who counts as a son is the father's judgment, regardless of whether a son has just completed a yoke of slavery or the lighter burden of the παιδαγωγός.

Whoever is granted sonship by adoption also gains inheritance. As I argued in chapter 3, adoption in the Roman world was enacted for far different reasons than it is in the modern Western world; the securing of an heir was the chief impetus. That inheritance included not only land and other wealth, but also the family name, the family glory, and a share of the family spirit. These are high stakes, and Paul no doubt knew that there were often disputes between biological and adopted sons, or between adopted sons and biological nephews or grandsons. His argument thus relies on a crucial feature of the social context—the *certainty* of an adopted son's right to inherit from his adoptive father. Roman laws and cultural mores clearly held that the inheritance claims of adopted sons were valid. For example, the high-profile adoptions of Octavian by Julius Caesar and of Tiberius by Augustus were legally bound to be honored in the distribution of inheritances. Or, as Paul says to the Galatians, whether Jew or Gentile: "if a son, then an heir."

In his letter to the Romans, the imagery is quite similar and rather cleaner in its exposition (as are the other tropes revised from Galatians into Romans). But here Paul further emphasizes the adult-age, even eschatological-age, time frame of adoption into God's family. The divine family spirit has been given already—"the spirit of adoption" (Rom 8:15)—but the ultimate adoption has not yet occurred.[26] Adoptive sonship is both already and not yet, a fact which Paul expresses through two images familiar to other ancient apocalypticists: the birth pangs of labor and the first-fruits of harvest. "For the yearning of creation is awaiting the revelation of the sons of God," he writes, and "all of creation has been joined in groans and labor pains until now. Not only that, but we ourselves, who have the first-fruits of the spirit, we also groan while we wait for adoption, the redemption of our body" (Rom 8:19, 22–23). He returns the imagery at the end to that of the household; the transition from slave to son is enacted by the "redemption" of the slave's price and a subsequent "adoption." Divine sonship for Paul did not look primarily backward to origins, but forward to inheritance—just as it did in Roman society.

Paul's understanding of Christian divine sonship is continued by other writings in the Pauline tradition. The eloquent *exordium* of Ephesians (1:3–14) echoes the "household" ideas of Galatians 3–4 but somewhat collapses the time line of adoptive sonship articulated in Romans 8.[27] The Father "chose" those whom he wanted as sons "before the foundation of the world" and "predestined" them for "adoptive sonship" (1:4–5). But the *already* aspect of this redemptive adoption is emphasized, since the time when the "household plan" takes effect—"gathering up all things" under God as Father and Jesus Christ as Lord—seems to be now (1:10). God's adoptive sons have already "been made heirs" (ἐκληρώθημεν, 1:11). There is a gesture, however, toward the *not yet* aspect of adoptive divine sonship in the portrayal of the Spirit: it is the "pledge" or "down payment" of the "inheritance" (1:14).

The apocryphal Pauline letter known as *3 Corinthians* also uses the metaphor of adoptive sonship at a crucial juncture—when the author is summarizing his version of Christian doctrine.[28] Straightaway in the letter "Paul" encapsulates the kerygma that he "received from the apostles" who came before him, which includes the birth of Christ from Mary, Christ's "liberation of all flesh through his own flesh," and his resurrection that typified the future resurrection of all (4–6). The next of the doctrines to be passed on is "that the human being was fashioned by his Father; and thus he was sought while he was lost, so that he might be made alive through adoptive sonship" (7–8).[29] This teaching is intended to refute a doctrine that the "Corinthians" claimed they were being taught by others, that the human being was *not* created by God.[30] But it also serves to combine different Pauline images into one moment: the eschatological "adoption" foretold in Romans is united with the "making alive" of the dead Adamic body described in 1 Corinthians (15:22).

Through these texts from Paul and the Pauline tradition, the adoptive metaphor of Christian divine sonship is relatively easy to parse, especially using details of the Greco-Roman social context. As for the divine sonship of Jesus Christ himself, the details are more difficult to discern. Paul proclaimed the *kerygma* of Jesus Christ's divine sonship often enough,[31] but he never tried to narrate its *mythos*, as did the evangelists. He did not chart the origin and development of Jesus' relationship to God the Father.[32] Scholars have only a few distinct moments through which to interpret Paul's take on Jesus as "Son of God"—why, when, and how?

The question *why* is the easiest to answer: First, Paul makes clear that Jesus' divine sonship is constitutive of his being the eschatological Messiah (e.g., 1 Cor 15:20–28). "Son of God" is a royal title. But Paul also explains that, in the interim, Jesus is God's Son for the purpose of making other sons of God, of gathering up the rest of humanity into a divine family under the paternal God. Paul understands Jesus' divine sonship as primarily soteriological and eschatological. He expresses it eloquently in Gal 4:4–5:

> When the fullness of time had come,
> God sent his son,
>> born of woman
>> born under the law,
> so that he might redeem those under the law,
> so that we might receive adoptive sonship.[33]

The purpose of God's sending Jesus his son was so that others might receive sonship. But what about this verb "sent"? Doesn't it answer the question *when*?

Interpreted in the framework of post-Nicene orthodoxy, God's "sending" of his son implies the preexistence of Jesus Christ as God's son. It is possible that Paul meant that, but it is not very likely. As Dunn and others have argued, God's sending of Jesus is eschatological, not protological.[34] Throughout his writings, Paul is not concerned with proclaiming that God sent Jesus to be incarnated and born, but rather to be crucified and resurrected. God sent him to Golgotha—not Bethlehem.

Paul's emphasis on death and resurrection does, in fact, lead us to an answer of the question *when*, which turns out to be inextricable from the question *how*. In the very first sentence of his most influential letter, Paul tells us the *when* and *how* of Christ's divine sonship: Jesus Christ, a son of David by natural lineage, was "appointed God's son in power, by the Spirit of holiness at the resurrection of the dead" (Rom 1:4).[35] The resurrection of Jesus was the key event in Jesus' relationship to God, as Paul expresses elsewhere (1 Cor 15:20–28), just as in Luke's portrayal of Paul's missionary speech (Acts 13:30–37). But from late antiquity to the present, some translators and commentators have attempted to diffuse this interpretation of Rom 1:4, which locates Christ's divine sonship as adoptive at the resurrection.[36] For example, the extant Latin translations of this verse rendered the participle "appointed" (ὁρισθέντος) as *praedestinatus* ("appointed beforehand" or "predestined") instead of the expected *destinatus*. Those translators apparently understood the Greek word as I have and by changing it were attempting to bring it in line with later christological orthodoxy.[37] Ironically, these careful scribes overlooked the fact that calling Jesus "predestined" for divine sonship at resurrection would not go very far in solving their christological conundrum—doing so would say no more about Jesus' sonship than Paul also says about the divine sonship of *all Christians*. Paul is clear that all Christians, who will receive adoptive sonship at the resurrection, have also been "predestined" for it (Rom 8:29).[38]

Paul's portrayal of a powerful father granting adoptive sonship would have had particular resonance in Rome itself, which was—lest we forget—the intended destination of the text in question. Not only would it have appealed to common social practices, but it would also have invoked the transmission of power in the imperial family. The Julio-Claudian "dynasty" was a mix of begotten and adoptive relationships (though I have argued the adoptive were more influential), with a correlated tension between dynastic and meritocratic ideologies of political succession. Through his opening proclamation of the sonship of Jesus as both dynastic (through David) and adoptive (through God), Paul—like Luke—would have appealed to both kinds of father-son relationships, which were the central loci of power in Roman society.

That being said, Paul does *not* use the begotten metaphor to describe the divine sonship of Christians or Christ himself. The dynastic image comes only through Abraham (especially for Christians) and David (especially for Christ), not directly through God. Nonetheless, there are Pauline texts that have been thought to make his presentation of adoptive sonship less clear. For example, Paul also uses the adoption metaphor to refer to the filial relationship maintained by the *Israelites* with God: "to them belong the adoption, the glory, the covenants, the giving of the law, the worship, and the promises" (Rom 9:4). If this "adoption" is neither messianic (as for Christ) nor eschatological (as for Christians), then what does Paul mean by it? Dunn has argued that the assigning of "the adoption" and "the glory" to the Israelites at the head of the list draws a link between their status and the status of the new community in Christ, whose adoption (8:15, 23) and glory (8:18, 21, 30) had just been discussed.[39] Hebrew biblical texts suggest that God's adoption of Israel as son was understood chiefly to have occurred at the Exodus (Exod 4:22; Hos 11:1).[40] Therefore, just as that adoption was effected by passing through the water, with a period of waiting before ultimately entering the promised land, so will the adoption of all in the messianic age occur through water (Gal 3:26–28; 1 Cor 10:1–2) and a period of waiting before final consummation (Rom 8:18–39). The adoption of Israel was a type of the eschatological adoption.

A final text where one might see a begotten metaphor in Paul's Epistles comes just earlier: "Those whom [God] foreknew, he also predestined to be conformed to the image of his son, so that he might be the firstborn (πρωτότοκον) of many brothers" (Rom 8:29).[41] But despite the English translation "first-*born*," the Greek πρωτότοκος does not necessarily designate a begotten sonship.[42] It is true that the word derives etymologically from the verb for birth (τίκτω), but it had come to signify sonship in different ways. Most importantly for our purposes, the term is quite clearly denotative of *adoptive* sonship in the text of the royal Ps 89, in which God says: "I have set a crown on one who is mighty, I have exalted one chosen from the people. I have found my servant David; with my holy oil I have anointed him. . . . He shall cry to me, 'You are my Father, my God, and the Rock of my salvation!' I will make him the firstborn (πρωτότοκον θήσομαι αὐτόν), the highest of the kings of the earth" (Ps 89[88]:19–20, 26–27, NRSV). God finds his servant, his anointed one, his son, and then *makes* him the *firstborn*, with the LXX Greek using one of the common verbs for adoption (τίθημι). As a signifier of divine sonship, then, the metaphor was already being mixed centuries before Paul would employ it.[43] The term is also used for adoptive sonship in the best extant Greek adoption contract from antiquity, *P. Lips.* 28.[44] The contract stipulates that the adopted son will "be your legitimate and firstborn son, as if begotten to you from your own blood" (τὸ εἶναι σοῦυἱὸν γνήσιον καὶ πρωτότοκον ὡς ἐξ ἰδίου αἵματος γεννηθέντα σοι).[45] Nowhere is it clearer than here—in an official adoption contract—that "firstborn" in Greek often connotes "privilege more than primogeniture."[46] The evidence that the term πρωτότοκος was used for adoptive sonship thus comes from both an everyday papyrus transaction and the highest messianic language in the Jewish Scriptures.

The context of the verse in Romans suggests that, in any case, Paul is not trying to *separate* the divine sonship of Christ from the divine sonship of Christians. On the contrary, he draws them together as closely as he can. "Conformed to the image of his son" and "firstborn of many brothers" are meant to unify all those who share in the spirit of the resurrection, the family spirit which binds them under one father.[47] A Nicene reading would take "firstborn" to distinguish Christ as begotten from Christians as adopted, but a less anachronistic interpretation takes "firstborn" to designate Christ as the preeminent son among a large and growing group of siblings. Scott's summary of adoptive sonship in Paul hits the mark:

> It seems that πρωτότοκος in 8:29c expresses the same adoption of the Son according to the Davidic promise at the resurrection as ὁρισθέντος υἱοῦ θεοῦ in 1:4, except that in 8:29c πρωτότοκος is used to draw in the relationship of the Son to the sons, that the sons follow the destiny of the Son at the resurrection. Actually, however, Rom. 1:4 already hints at this relationship between the Son and the sons, since ἀνάστασις νεκρῶν implies that the Son's resurrection is proleptic to the future resurrection of the dead. At the resurrection of the dead, the elect will be conformed to the image of the Son (v. 29b), which expresses the redemption of the body associated with υἱοθεσία (v. 23). Since the purpose for which the elect will be conformed to the image of the Son at the resurrection is that the Son might be the Firstborn among many brothers (v. 29c), the adoption of the sons (v. 23) is directly related to the adoption of the Firstborn. In fact, it can be said that the sons who share in the messianic inheritance and reign with the Son (vv. 17b, 32b) are adopted on the basis of the same Davidic promise as the Son, because they participate in the sonship of the Son.[48]

The adoptive divine sonship imagined by Paul, though it can be effectively interpreted in the Greco-Roman context of adoption and inheritance, was not simply an allegory of or transfer from social practices into soteriology. For example, the abundance of Christian women in Pauline communities, who presumably were considered to have filial relationships with God (2 Cor 6:18), would not have mapped on to the all-male social practice of Roman adoption. Furthermore, while Paul's vision of an ever-expanding family under one father does fit well with the Roman family's well-documented "readiness to extend relationships," his soteriology is built on a crucial discontinuity with the sociopolitical context. In law and literature about Roman adoption, the rivalry of sons over inheritances constituted a central *topos*. In Paul's cosmic vision, the privileged son of the father—the πρωτότοκος—is instead engaged in the process of making more children for the father, of increasing the size of the family. This son is paradoxically eager to share and thus dilute his inheritance; such behavior is decidedly "foolish" by worldly standards, but for Paul, it shows the power of Christ through his mercy. A century later Irenaeus would also come to read Paul in this way, such that Christ demonstrates his "power made perfect in weakness" in part through his communal sharing of sonship.[49] Christ is willing to share his rightful inheritance and glory with countless siblings, and this disconnection with social reality is for Paul a chief manifestation of his abundant grace (χάρις).

John on Begotten Divine Sonship

For the metaphor of begotten divine sonship, one turns undoubtedly to Johannine literature. There the metaphor of begottenness is used to describe both Christians and Christ himself. Because of the prominence of Jesus' dialogue with Nicodemus in Christian popular consciousness (John 3:1–21, especially vv. 1–10), the fact that Christians are begotten or "born" from above is widely known. Being "born again" has caught on as shorthand for being Christian in a way that being "adopted" never has. But the proclamation of Christ himself as "begotten" or "born" of God is actually *not* found in John's Gospel.[50] Nowhere in the Johannine prologue (1:1–18) is Jesus called God's "begotten" son, despite the important role the prologue would later play in the shoring up of Nicene christological orthodoxy. There is someone "sent from God" according to the prologue, but it is *John*, not Jesus (1:6); and God does do some "begetting," but it is *Christians* who are begotten, not the Christ (1:12–13). To find a reference to Jesus Christ as God's "begotten" son, one has to read to the very end of John's first Epistle—and even there, one finds substantial disagreement among the manuscripts (see below).

Let us not get ahead of ourselves, though, but work first from John's Gospel. In the famous dialogue already mentioned, Christians are clearly portrayed as "begotten" or "born" in a metaphorical way (John 3:3–8). The begetting happens "from above" and/or "again" (ἄνωθεν, 3:3) and is enacted by "water and spirit" (3:5), or simply "the spirit" (3:6, 8). The double-meaning of the spatial-temporal word ἄνωθεν combines with the twin-agency of water and spirit in order to generate an image of divine begetting that is both sacramental and sapiential. The sacrament of baptism is implied by the temporal "again"[51] and the substance of "water," while the spatial imagery of a "spirit" birth "from above" perhaps suggests a wisdom tradition.[52] The result of the begetting is the ability to "see the kingdom of God" and "enter into" it, the former of which is distinct from other New Testament authors' concepts of "inheriting" and "entering" the kingdom of God. For John, the begetting assures not only an eschatological inheritance of a father's goods, as does divine sonship for Paul, but a currently accessible *revelation* of God as father—his glory, truth, grace, light, and life. This revelation can only happen through his son, Jesus Christ, who has already claimed possession of the kingdom (John 18:36).

The begotten relationship between Christians and God is further solidified in the rest of the Gospel and especially the first Epistle. In John 8:39–47, Jesus draws a kind of "dichotomous key" for the human race, dividing people ultimately into children of God and children of the devil.[53] The question-and-answer of this dialogue format is then clarified in 1 John by the author's plain and repeated declarations about the "children of God" (3:1–2, 10; 5:2), who have been "begotten" (2:29; 3:9; 4:7; 5:1, 4, 18). The metaphors of divine and diabolical lineage are made even more concrete when the author emphasizes how "everyone who commits sin is (a child) of the devil," but "everyone who has been begotten by God does not sin because God's seed (σπέρμα) abides in each of them" (1 John 3:8–9). The image could hardly be more tangible. While other proto-orthodox authors (especially Paul and Matthew) were concerned with Jesus' lineal descent from the "seed" of David or Gentile-Christians' relationship to the "seed" of Abraham, for John it is *God's own* σπέρμα that issues forth. The seed of David is mentioned in John only by a crowd questioning Jesus' origins (John 7:42), and descent from Abraham is never claimed as positive during the debate over lineage (John 8:31–59). For John, as for many proto-heterodox Christians in the second century, earthly lineage was trumped by divine begetting.[54]

The two remaining texts about begetting are crucial—yet both have variants in ancient manuscripts or citations. In the Johannine prologue, after explaining that the Word/Light was rejected by "his own," John 1:12–13 states that, "as many as received him, to them he gave authority to become children of God, to those who believe in his name: they were begotten not by blood, nor by the desire of the flesh, nor by the desire of man, but by God." This rendering interprets v. 13 as an elaboration of v. 12. *How* did they become children of God? They were begotten by God. A text-critical question has arisen, however, regarding whether v. 13 has a plural verb ("they were begotten") resuming the noun "children" or a singular ("he was begotten") resuming "him," namely the Word. Despite the fact that not one Greek manuscript supports the singular reading, several scholars have argued for it, based on a few early Latin sources.[55] Tertullian cited the singular version in order to defend his proto-orthodox Christology, and perhaps he knew of Greek manuscripts that contained it.[56] But he seems also to have known that his version was not the only one, since he accused others of altering the text to a plural. With the impressive manuscript evidence and a reasonable interpretation, the plural reading is compelling.

One must go to 1 John, then, to find the references to Jesus Christ as a "begotten" son of God. When the author is exhorting Christians to the sinless life proper to the children of God, he writes, "We know that *everyone who has been begotten* by God does not sin, but rather, *he who was begotten* by God protects him (ὁ γεννηθεὶς ἐκ τοῦ θεοῦ τηρεῖ αὐτόν) and the evil one does not touch him" (5:18). There are textual variants of ἡ γέννησις for ὁ γεννηθείς and ἑαυτόν for αὐτόν, and the resulting clause would mean "the begetting by God protects him(self)." But Vellanickal explains well how these variants might have arisen in the manuscript tradition, and I concur that the majority readings cause less difficulty than the variants.[57] The idea that Christ offers protection for the Christian against the devil fits well the immediate context (5:19–20) and also recapitulates an earlier theme (3:7–10). In this text, then, the author links the divine sonship of Christ and Christians in their begottenness, but he distinguishes the two with the tense of the participles: a Christian "*has been* begotten" (perfect tense, ὁ γεγεννημένος) while Christ "*was* begotten" (aorist tense, γεννηθείς). This corresponds to the other reference to Christ as begotten, which is also a bit elliptical (1 John 5:1).

Unfortunately for our purposes, the author does not specify in either verse of 1 John the point at which Christ was begotten—whether baptism, birth, conception, or earlier.[58] He does not answer the question *when*. Most scholars think that John does support a preexistent view of the divine sonship of Jesus Christ. Some kind of personal preexistence is expressed by texts about the descent from above (6:38; 8:23; 16:28) or the previous apprenticeship with the Father (5:19; 8:38), but especially the claim of existence "before Abraham" (8:58) and "before the world existed" (17:5, 24). I would still stress, however, that John is never explicit about a divine begetting that occurred before the earthly life of Jesus. He might presume it in the passages just cited, but he does not articulate it, especially in the prologue where one might expect it (see below). Regarding divine sonship, John is actually quite restrained in his mythologizing; he could have extrapolated much more narrative from the sonship metaphor.[59] But for John, the divine father-son relationship is more *logos* than *mythos*: the *logos* connects the son to the siblings, whereas a *mythos* would have divided them. So regardless of when the divine begetting occurred, the parallel use of begotten metaphors in 1 John "underlines the solidarity" between the divine sonship of God's son and God's children.[60] According to John, Jesus Christ is absolutely unique—but his uniqueness is *not* his begottenness.

This leads us back to the Johannine prologue and two interrelated questions. First, why do most readers think the prologue proclaims the begottenness of Jesus? For sixteen centuries, readers have been led to believe that John 1:14–18 presents the Word as the "only-begotten Son" of God, even though the word "begotten" is nowhere to be found in the Greek text of the prologue (and the word "son" appears only in a contested variant, about which see below). The Greek term behind the translations "only begotten" (1:14; kjv), "only begotten son" (1:18; kjv), and "only son" (1:14, 18; nrsv) is μονογενής, an adjective that is best translated as "unique," "only," or "one of a kind."[61] It *can* refer to an only *son*, but that is because an *only* son fits into the category of unique; it can also refer to a unique son that is *not* an only-begotten son.[62] The word further describes unique non-human things, of which two relevant examples are: the "unique spirit" (πνεῦμα μονογενές) that subsists in God's "wisdom" (σοφία; Wisd 7:22); and according to one summary of Plato's cosmology, the cosmos we inhabit is "unique and beloved to God" (μονογενῆ τῷ θεῷ καὶ ἀγαπητόν).[63] The trajectory that led to today's mistranslation of μονογενής seems to have begun in the second century, when Justin Martyr interpreted the word in connection with the notion of preexistent begottenness in his Logos Christology.[64] The trend took off primarily in the fourth and fifth centuries, however, with the switch from Greek to Latin. The oldest Latin manuscript of the Gospels, dated to the mid-fourth century, uses *unicus* ("unique") as the translation.[65] But instead of the suitable *unicus*, Jerome's *Vulgate* (c. 383 c.e.) offered the christologically charged term *unigenitus* ("only-begotten") for μονογενής.[66] He was following a pattern established by Hilary of Poitiers, who also used *unigenitus* to translate μονογενής in the Nicene Creed.[67] These translations were solidified through the influence of the Creed and eventually the King James Version, which used "only begotten."

The second question is: what constitutes Jesus' unique-ness or only-ness, if not begotten-ness? In John 1:14–18, the uniqueness of Jesus Christ is imagined through his functioning as the Word/Light, which is unique in its glory, its closeness to the Father, and its power to reveal. John proclaims that, after the incarnation of the

Word, "we beheld its glory—glory as of a unique [one/kind] from a father—full of grace and truth" (1:14). The phrase, δόξαν ὡς μονογενοῦς παρὰ πατρός, is difficult to translate without supplying a noun for μονογενής, which is the reason why the word "son" has been added to translations so often. Yet the main point is not about sonship or begetting, neither of which is present in the verse. On my reading, the main point is that the Word/Light revealed the glory of the Father in a unique way through the incarnation.[68] This was the turning point in cosmic history, as John then explains: "As for God, no one has ever *seen* him. But the only God (the Word/Light), who was in the bosom of the Father, that one *revealed* him" (1:18). Again the translation is challenging, not least because of the text-critical problem with the noun modified by μονογενής.[69] I contend that this verse is also not about sonship or begetting, neither of which is present in the text (according to Nestle-Aland and most text critics). It is primarily about the combined transcendence and immanence of God in the Incarnate Word/Light. The Word is the only God and is thus one with God, as in 1:1, but it also reveals the previously unseen God, as Light that shines in darkness (1:5) and Word that becomes flesh (1:14).

I grant that this verse—like v. 14—would be much easier to construe and translate with the addition of the word "son," just as many manuscripts have it.[70] But the addition of "son" to each would not, in any case, undercut my main point: there is no divine begetting expressed in the prologue, except that of Christians in v. 13. Even if one admits that the word "son" must be supplied in vv. 14 and 18, the process of that sonship is not a focus for the author. The Word is uniquely *close* to the Father—in his very bosom—a relational bond between God and the Incarnate Word portrayed in various ways throughout the rest of John's Gospel.[71] And the Word uniquely *reveals* the Father, mediating between the unseen God and the world. But begotten sonship is not an issue.

The Word's revelation of God is inextricable from Jesus' mission of salvation as God's unique son on earth.[72] In the one pericope where the μονογενὴς υἱός does actually appear as a title, during the teaching to Nicodemus, the unique son's mission is that everyone might believe in him and have eternal life (3:16–18). This mission continues throughout the gospel, according to John Ashton, a scholar who interprets Father-Son unity with great dexterity and appropriate tentativeness.[73] He finds a paradox at the heart of the Father-Son relationship in John. In one sense, the sender is greater than the one sent; in another sense, the one sent—as emissary—possesses the full agency of the sender. These statements cannot be isolated from one another without distorting John's image of Jesus. The Johannine conceptions of Jesus are best understood, in Ashton's estimation, within the context of Jewish juridical conventions: the functional "son" executing a father's will may be the natural son, but the natural son is not necessarily the functional "son." For John, Jesus' moment of mission (sending) is conceived primarily as a commission (the bestowal of authority of plenipotentiary powers). As son, Jesus has been given full control over the household of God. Therefore, Ashton finds a strikingly similar meaning of divine sonship in John as others have found in the Synoptics and Paul—an eschatological, functional sonship, which consists primarily in a mission to make other sons and daughters for God. In John's own words, Jesus' divine sonship was "to gather into one the dispersed children of God" (11:52).

In the end, divine sonship is an image that unites Christ with Christians more than it separates them—another similarity John has with Paul on this topic. Each point that might be advanced to separate off the sonship of Christ can be countered or tempered. First, the terminological argument that the word "son" separates Christ from Christians, who are called the "children" of God, cannot bear much weight. As I said in chapter 1, υἱός is different from τέκνα in gender and number, not nature.[74] Whether "son" or "child," all are "begotten" of God in John's understanding—and he would not want to exclude from divine filiation the women central to his gospel (especially Mary, the Samaritan Woman, Martha, and Mary Magdalene). Second, some have proposed a distinction based on the *when* of divine begetting. In 1 John 5:1 and 5:18, the begetting of Christians is denoted by the perfect tense, while Christ was begotten in the aorist. Perhaps this does refer to the incarnation of the Word in the person of Jesus.[75] But a simpler explanation for this would be that Christ was dead and resurrected at the time 1 John was composed; while Jesus was alive he himself spoke of his begetting in the perfect tense (John 18:37).[76] Furthermore, the immediate contexts of these passages in 1 John concern the relationship that Christians share with Christ as children of God. In Judith Lieu's expert analysis, the use of the begotten metaphor for both Christ and Christians "acknowledges some degree of consanguinity between them." Regarding the function of Christ's relationship with the Father,

> 1 John is neither interested in the nature or the occasion of this begetting, nor concerned with the inner being of God. . . . On the contrary, it is the relationship that the Son shares with them as born from God that enables them to share in the benefits that he has achieved. Without this connection, the imagery of believers as having been born of God could suggest that they possess in their own right all the benefits this brings, leaving no meaningful role for the Son of God, whose importance the author has been at such pains to assert.[77]

The third proposed marker to distinguish Christ's divine sonship has the most merit—his portrayal as the μονογενής son (John 3:16, 18; 1 John 4:9). But for John, his unique-ness or only-ness was not due to his means of acquiring sonship. John's use of μονογενής is therefore analogous to Paul's use of πρωτότοκος. In John's portrayal, Jesus Christ was uniquely close to God the Father, uniquely revelatory of God's glory, and uniquely able to empower others to become God's sons and daughters. But, with apologies to King James, he was not the only begotten son.

Mixed Metaphors

The kinds of divine sonship attributed to Christ and Christians were not uniformly portrayed by the earliest authors. Divine sonship followed something like the "backwards movement" of Christology delineated by Brown and filled out by Dunn, but the texts do not always fit the neat historical model. Early Christians widely agreed that Jesus Christ was God's son, and God was their father too—the head of a new extended family for the eschatological age. But these proclamations were not precisely located temporally, nor were these family metaphors easily explainable without further metaphors. Still more onerous was the task of *narrating* how these things were true. Paul and John are the closest examples we have to ideal types of understanding divine sonship in earliest Christianity, but dogmatic theologians they were not. Their metaphorical sketches of the divine-human relationship often leave us without conclusive interpretations of divine sonship.

What we can say for sure about the New Testament authors that deal with divine sonship is that baptism was crucial to their understanding of it. The way for Christians to become God's sons and daughters, according to John, is to be begotten from above by water and spirit—that is, to be baptized, just as Jesus himself was. On the centrality of baptism, John and Paul agree, but they choose different metaphors to portray what happens. Through his description of Jesus' own baptism, John draws a ritual connection between the sonship of Christ (1:32–34) and Christians (3:3–8). Jesus says Christians must be begotten of "water and spirit"; John describes Jesus' baptism in exactly those terms. Jesus says Christians must be begotten "from above"; John recounts the descent of the Spirit from heaven. The baptism of Jesus took place "so that he might be revealed to Israel" (1:31), and the content of that revelation is then stated by John: "This is the Son of God" (1:34).

The narration of the divine sonship of Jesus may have moved backward over time, from resurrection to death to baptism to birth, but in Paul's understanding of Christian initiation, the ritual of baptism could simultaneously enact all four of these events in the life of Christ. During the early centuries of Christianity—and already present *in nuce* in Paul's letters—baptism epitomized the divine sonship of begetting/birth, of adoption, of death, and of resurrection.[78] This surplus of meaning was eventually brought under control in later centuries, but here in the nascent Christian movement, the living-dying-rising of one's filial relationship to God in Christ was richly imagined. In early Christianity the begotten and adoptive metaphors of divine sonship were mixed. Perhaps they were mixed in the font.

■ ADOPTIVE DIVINE SONSHIP IN THE SECOND CENTURY

> There is none other called "God" by the Scriptures except the Father of all, and the Son, and those who possess the adoption.
>
> —IRENAEUS

If asked to discuss adoptionistic kinds of Christology in early Christianity, most scholars would likely mention the Ebionites right away. Indeed, Bart Ehrman leads off his popular New Testament introductory textbook with this "group of second-century Jewish Christians known to be living in Palestine, east of the Jordan River," who "maintained that Jesus was a remarkable man . . . chosen by God to be his son . . . 'adopted' at his baptism."[79] But we really know very little about the so-called Ebionites, and from what we do know, they did *not* use adoptive imagery *per se* to describe the divine sonship of Jesus or themselves.[80] The description of Jesus' baptism in the "Gospel of the Ebionites"—in so far as it can be reconstructed from quotations in Epiphanius—does little more than harmonize the two attested baptismal voices, claiming that both resounded from heaven.[81] But if their focus on Jesus' baptism and their full citation of Ps 2:7 makes them "adoptionist," then many other early Christians are also.[82] Or if their lack of biographical material about Jesus' first thirty years makes them "adoptionist," then Paul, Mark, and John will also be subject to the same criticism. Therefore some scholars have wisely rejected the term "adoptionist" with regard to the Ebionites.[83] The truth is, we do not know enough about the Ebionites to assess their imagery and metaphors of divine sonship.

Rather, if adoptive imagery were to have successfully portrayed the divine sonship of Christ or Christians in the first centuries of Christianity, I have argued it would have been more at home in definitively Roman cultural contexts. In fact, besides the Ebionites, the other famous handbook "adoptionists" *were* located in Rome: Theodotus and his followers, who were active in the late second century.[84] Unfortunately, we do not know much about them either. The group is traced to a certain Theodotus, a σκυτεύς (leather-worker, shoemaker, cobbler), who was active in Rome under Bishop Victor (c. 189–99 C.E.) and was succeeded by followers during the time of Bishop Zephyrinus (c. 199–217 C.E.). They were said to have been well educated and scientifically inclined, and they were accused of manipulating texts of Scripture.[85] As to their teachings, the anonymous source quoted by Eusebius claims that Theodotus, the "founder" and "father" of the "God-denying apostasy," was the "first" to teach that the Christ was a "mere man."[86] According to the source, it was primarily for this doctrine that Victor excommunicated Theodotus (though the group lingered for some time). Hippolytus records that Theodotus's teachings focused on the baptism of Jesus. It was through the water and the dove that Jesus was empowered by the Spirit of Christ from above, although there seems to have been disagreement within the group about whether Jesus became divine at that time, later at his resurrection, or not at all.[87] Beyond these glimpses, we are not able to see much more of this group of early Christians. But we can say that the adoptive imagery of the Theodotians would have been especially resonant in urban areas of the second-century Roman Empire because of the established adoptive imperial ideology. The long chain of "good and adoptive emperors" (96–180 C.E.) led to a concomitant political ideology of meritocratic succession that praised adoptive father-son relations. This worldview provides a reasonable basis for explaining why adoptionistic Christologies were, in the words of one scholar, "mostly a Roman affair."[88]

We have scant evidence about the handbook "adoptionists," the Ebionites and the Theodotians, but there are some well-attested Christian theologians that can be fruitfully interpreted in the sociopolitical context of the second century.[89] One is usually associated with "adoptionist" Christology (Hermas). The other two are famous for denouncing proto-heterodox Christologies (Irenaeus and Clement)—while actually being quite innovative themselves. What they all have in common is familiarity with Roman family ideology, a fact which situates their theological metaphors in a particular sociopolitical context.[90] For these early Christians, adoption was far from a low concept. It was a powerful, eschatological expression of divine sonship.

The Shepherd of Hermas

The second-century Christian named "Hermas" was a freed slave from "central Italy and probably Rome," who became "a moderately wealthy freedman and householder" and eventually wrote one of the most popular early Christian texts that is not in the canon—*The Shepherd of Hermas*, or simply, *The Shepherd*.[91] The Christology of *The Shepherd* has been often discussed by modern scholars, despite the fact that the words "Jesus" and "Christ" are never used in the text.[92] Rather, christological analysis focuses on the "son / Son of God" in the text and especially his relationship to the "highest angel" and the "spirit / Holy Spirit," both of whom are profoundly important in the revelations of *The Shepherd*. Though many have attempted to decipher an underlying cosmology in *The Shepherd* that might explain these different heavenly figures and their relationships,[93] I agree with Carolyn Osiek that "speculative or systematic christology is not the author's goal. All attempts to reconstruct a systematic christology in *Hermas* falter." It is "only by letting each passage and each image stand on its own" that we can "come to some glimpse of the whole."[94]

The most influential stand-alone passage for scholarly assessment of the author's Christology is undoubtedly *Similitude* 5—the "Parable of the Son, Slave, and Vineyard" and its accompanying explanations.[95] In the course of teaching Hermas about the best kind of fasting, the Shepherd tells him the following parable (here paraphrased): *A wealthy householder chose a slave and gave him charge of his vineyard while he was away. He promised the slave his freedom if he would build an enclosure around it. The slave did so and also decided to remove its weeds, so that the vineyard flourished. When the householder returned, he was very pleased and decided to make the slave co-heir with his son, who had been summoned to the scene as an advisor along with the householder's friends. The householder then sent much food to the slave to celebrate his new status, and the slave distributed most of it to his fellow slaves. Again, the father, son, and friends were overjoyed at the behavior of the slave, who was now co-heir.* The different explanations of the parable in the subsequent text can be outlined as follows:[96]

The Shepherd describes how to fast (5.1)
The Shepherd tells the parable (5.2)

1st explanation: an ethical exhortation about fasting (5.3)

Hermas requests further explanation (5.4–5.5.1)

2nd explanation: a doctrinal-allegorical interpretation about Christian cosmology (5.5.2–3)

Hermas asks a clarifying *christological* question (5.5.4–5)

The Shepherd answers (5.6.1–4a)

3rd explanation: the relationship between the "son" and the "slave" (5.6.4b–7a)

Paraenetic application of the 3rd explanation (5.6.7b–5.7.2)

Hermas asks a clarifying *soteriological* question (5.7.3a)

The Shepherd answers and concludes (5.7.3b–4)

There are three explanations of the parable, which I will summarize briefly before going into detail about the second and third of them. The first is an ethical exhortation about fasting, in which Hermas is encouraged to keep the commandments of the Lord and even to go beyond them in generosity during his fasts. The second is a doctrinal-allegorical interpretation with point-by-point correspondences between the story world and the real world. Of the ten correspondences revealed by the Shepherd, the relevant ones for our topic are these: the "master of the field" is the one who created everything [= God]; the "son" is the Holy Spirit; and the "slave" is the Son of God (5.5.3).[97] The third explanation is an expansion of the second, spelling out in more detail the relationship between the "son" and the "slave" in the parable—that is to say, the relationship between the Holy Spirit and the Son of God. This explanation leads into paraenesis for Hermas about his own relationship to the Holy Spirit; Hermas must keep his flesh pure and undefiled because the Holy Spirit dwells in it. After each of the second and third explanations, there is a question-answer session that elaborates on the Shepherd's previous comment.

Franz Overbeck has rightly quipped, "There is no interpreter from whom one can expect the solution to every riddle of the Shepherd."[98] But the understanding of adoptive sonship laid out in this book can help to unlock at least the riddle of *this* parable and its explanations. The challenge begins with the second explanation, which comprises ten point-by-point correspondences between the story world and the real world (5.5.2–3).

"field" = this world

"master of the field" = the one who created everything (God)

"son" = the Holy Spirit

"slave" = the Son of God

"vines" = this people

"fences" = angels

"weeds" = lawless deeds of God's servants

"food" = commandments given through the Son of God

"friends and advisors" = angels that were created first

"absence of the master" = time remaining until his arrival

Such allegorical readings are familiar enough to readers of early Christian texts. Hermas is perplexed, though, by the equation of the "slave" with the Son of God, and he asks, "Why, sir, in the parable is the Son of God placed in the guise of a 'slave?'" (εἰς δούλου τρόπον κεῖται, 5.5.5). Modern scholars have wondered the same thing. But the Shepherd's answer has not always been helpful. He says, "Listen, the Son of God is *not* 'placed in the guise of a slave,' but rather he is placed in great authority and dominion" (εἰς ἐξουσίαν μεγάλην κεῖται καὶ κυριότητα, 5.6.1). By denying that the Son of God was placed in the guise of a "slave," the Shepherd's answer seems to contradict his own allegorical interpretation. Confusion about this led one ancient scribe to omit the word "not" (οὐ) from this sentence, and Osiek avers that "the interpretation is easier without it."[99] But emphasizing the unique understanding of sonship in the Roman worldview can provide the social context for making sense of it. Hermas's question was motivated by concern about the *origin* of the figure that symbolized the Son of God: why was he "placed" in the guise of a slave? The Shepherd, on the other hand, emphasizes the *final status* of the figure that symbolized the Son of God: regardless of where he was "placed" at the beginning of the parable, look at where he ends up! He is ultimately "placed" in great authority and dominion. The "not" of the Shepherd's answer is thus crucial to his overall point, an idea stated often in this book: sonship did not primarily point backward to origins but forward to inheritance.

The remainder of the Shepherd's answer fills out his correction of Hermas's misunderstanding. The Son of God is placed in great authority and dominion

> because God "planted the vineyard," that is, created the people, and gave them over to his Son. And the Son appointed the angels over them to protect them. But the Son himself cleansed their sins, laboring much and undergoing much toil. For no "vineyard" can be "dug" without toil or labor. Then, when he had cleansed the sins of the people, he showed them the ways of life, giving them the law which he received from his Father. You see, therefore, that he is lord of the people, having received full authority from his Father.[100]

Thus ends the christological question-and-answer—and with it the main section used to deduce the Father-Son relationship in the Shepherd's cosmology. (The Son-Holy Spirit relationship is yet to come.) This Christology has often been called "adoptionist," but it is not definitively so.[101] In the parable, the "slave" is never explicitly adopted as "son"; and in the answer to Hermas's question, the Son of God is designated as such from the beginning.[102] But in the parable, the "slave" does change status, being granted "freedom" and made an "heir," which are pronounced, dramatic movements upward in the household; likewise, in the allegorical interpretation, the Son of God does gain authority from his Father, so that he himself is lord of the people with full authority in the end. This upward mobility from slave to heir with full paternal authority might have been enacted through a presumed adoption, but it would more properly be called an "exaltationist" Christology.

Commentators have had difficulty interpreting the text immediately following the Shepherd's answer to Hermas's christological question.[103] In Osiek's words, "the correspondence of characters suddenly shifts with brutal abruptness. We are back to the parable . . . ."[104] It is true that a shift in allegorical correspondences occurs, but the Shepherd indicates the beginning of a new explanation with the rhetorical cue, "Listen" (ἄκουε). He uses it to introduce four parts of this *Similitude*: the original parable, the second explanation, the answer to the christological question, and here to begin the third explanation.[105] He now addresses the relationship between the Holy Spirit and the Son of God, or the "son" and the "slave" in the parable. And his explanation is tricky to interpret, just as above, because he blends figures from the story world and the real world:

> But now listen to why the "master" took his "son" as an "advisor"—along with the glorious angels—concerning the "inheritance" of the "slave." The Holy Spirit, the preexistent one that created all of creation, God caused to dwell in flesh which he (or it) preferred. Then this flesh, in which the Holy Spirit dwelled, "served" the Spirit nobly, living in sanctity and purity, not defiling the Spirit in any way. Then when the flesh had lived nobly and purely, having both labored with the Spirit and cooperated with it in every deed, behaving with strength and bravery, God chose it as a partner with the Holy Spirit. For the behavior of this flesh pleased God, namely that it was not defiled while possessing the Holy Spirit on earth. Therefore, God took the "son" as an "advisor"—along with the glorious angels—so that this flesh, which had "served" the Spirit blamelessly, might have a certain resting place and not seem to have lost the "reward" for its "service."[106]

In this explanation, the exaltationist Christology is continued, but the role of the Holy Spirit (or "son") in the exaltation of the Son of God (or "slave") is delineated. In the original parable, the "advising" role of the "son" was limited only to observing the productive work of the "slave" and agreeing with the decision of the "master" to make the "slave" his "co-heir." But the Shepherd predicts the confusion of one who hears this parable: why would the "son" have been involved in this decision at all, which was the father's alone to make? Furthermore, any ancient listener to this parable would have been shocked by the willingness of a son and sole heir to share his inheritance, if he were actually to have been summoned as an "advisor" on the decision. As with the parables of Jesus, the moment of shock is likely the best place to pursue this parable's meaning. So here the Shepherd is attempting to justify the surprising graciousness of the "son."

In his interpretation, the Holy Spirit (or "son") was involved from the beginning in the selection and advancement of the Son of God (or "slave"). The explanation of in what sense the "son" was an "advisor" comes through a verbal correspondence between the noun "advisor" (σύμβουλον, 5.6.4b) and the verb in the phrase, "flesh which he (or it) preferred" (ἠβούλετο, 5.6.5). It is grammatically likely that God did the "preferring" of which flesh the Holy Spirit would inhabit because "God" is the noun closest to the verb, but it is possible that the Spirit is the subject of the verb.[107] The latter option would make more sense of the Shepherd's argument—the Spirit was an advisor (σύμβουλον) in that the Spirit chose (ἠβούλετο) which flesh to inhabit. The matter remains obscure, though, and one must be satisfied only with the conclusion that God and the Holy Spirit are closely united in their counsel from the beginning. Therefore, though not reported in the parable, the "sonship" of the "son" was proleptically present in the "slave" from the moment he was chosen by the "father." From the time of his selection until he is made "heir" and partner with the "son," the "slave" is serving the "son" and "father" together as a tandem. He is able to do so successfully because he already possesses a share of "sonship." In theological terms, the Father chose that the Holy Spirit should dwell in the particular flesh of the Son, and because the Son lived perfectly while the Spirit dwelt in him, the Son was exalted to be the partner of the Holy Spirit, sharing the inheritance of the Father in his final resting place.[108]

Despite this cosmological interpretation, the Shepherd's ultimate focus in the fifth *Similitude* is not the relationships among heavenly beings. The immanent Trinity may be a concern of Hermas, as it will be for later Christian theologians, but the Shepherd wants to emphasize the economic Trinity.[109] In other words, what do the relationships between heavenly beings mean for human flourishing and salvation?[110] According to the Shepherd, the Holy Spirit has a clear soteriological purpose because it enables *all Christians* to gain *their* status as heirs of the Father's inheritance—the reward for their service. He concludes the third explanation thus: "For *all flesh* in which the Holy Spirit has dwelt, if it be found undefiled and spot-less, shall receive a reward."[111] We might then call the Christology of this *Similitude* "exemplarist," in addition to "exaltationist." The course of action that "this flesh" (αὔτη ἡ σάρξ, i.e., the "slave" or Son of God, 5.6.5) has experienced and achieved through the Holy Spirit is precisely the model that the Shepherd wants "all flesh" (πᾶσα σάρξ, 5.6.7) to follow under the Spirit's direction. This conclusion hearkens back to the original allegorical explanation, in which the Son of God was one "slave" serving among the other "slaves of God" (δοῦλοι τοῦ θεοῦ, 5.5.3).

Hermas, as a former slave himself, knew well the trials experienced by human flesh in the pursuit of a life according to God's Spirit. When he tried to imagine what the human Son of God did to deserve his exalted status, as joint heir with God's own Spirit, he turned to his own social context—where upward mobility toward the inheritance of a divine family spirit was enacted through manumis-sions and adoptions.[112] The Son of God was the exemplar of how Christians might gain their share of God's inheritance through the Holy Spirit. In the second century, this was modeled at the top by the divine imperial family and presented by *The Shepherd* as a model of the divine Christian family. So when Norbert Brox won-ders how the author of *The Shepherd* got away with publishing such a Christology *in Rome*, I respond, how could he have published it anywhere else?[113]

Clement of Alexandria

Clement of Alexandria's articulation of Christian identity in the terms of procre-ation and kinship has been well documented and deftly analyzed by Denise Kimber Buell.[114] She demonstrates how procreative metaphors serve to naturalize a set of socially constructed relations, in order to empower one kinship group over another. Procreation and kinship thus constitute a "rhetoric of legitimacy." Though such natural, begotten metaphors do predominate in Clement's corpus, he also uses the adoption metaphor to great rhetorical effect.[115] It enables him to portray the divine sonship of Christians, but he does not shy away from using it with reference to the divine sonship of Christ himself. By the time of the fourth-century controversies, adoption will have become the christological metaphor that dare not speak its name. But here in the second century, it could still be put to good rhetorical use.

Let us begin by looking at how Clement used the metaphor for Christians. In the New Testament, the Johannine corpus prefers "begotten" language, while the Pauline corpus prefers "adoption" language. As an heir of both apostolic traditions, Clement mixes the metaphors. For example, in book 1 of the *Paedagogus*, when explaining the ways in which Christians are children of God, he writes: "The Father of all accepts those who have taken refuge in him, and having begotten them again by the Spirit into adoption, he knows them as gentle, he loves them alone, he fights on their behalf, and therefore names them 'child.'"[116] Christians are *begotten again* into *adoption*—John and Paul are both appeased. In the *Stromata*, he mixes the metaphors again, this time with respect to a Christian's status as legitimate heir: when speaking about a human being's highest attainable level of relationship to God, Clement promises the revelation of the holiest things to "those who are legitimately and not illegitimately heirs of the lordly adoptive sonship."[117] Here the crafty rhetorical move is not as clear in translation as it is in the original: in Greek, the categories of "legitimate / genuine" (γνήσιος) and "illegitimate / spurious" (νόθος) are used most fundamentally to distinguish certifiably natural children from those who are not; metaphorically the terms can also be used to distinguish all kinds of true and false lineages.[118] But here—for one of the only times in ancient Greek literature—Clement combines the concept of "legitimate/genuine" with *adoptive* sonship.[119] This is a singularly Roman perspective, in which adopted heirs could be regarded as γνήσιος, a term normally reserved for begotten children.[120] The metaphors of both begetting and adopting were thus found by Clement to be useful for articulating the divine-human relationship.[121]

These initial formulations do not give us any sense of a chronology of divine sonship, of any time that might elapse between begetting again, receiving the Spirit, and adoption into inheritance. One might guess that they are rolled into one event at baptism. But Clement's usage implies that adoption is a metaphor for an adult, while begetting is a metaphor for an infant. When explaining how Jesus, our παιδαγωγός, established for us the model of the true life, Clement imagines Jesus to have had a role in every stage of a Christian's maturation: "It seems to me that [Jesus] himself formed the human being from the dust, begat him again in water, reared him in Spirit, and instructed him in word into adoption and salvation, leading him by holy commandments."[122] Adoption comes late in this process, and it is linked with salvation itself.[123] This vision of maturation lines up perfectly with the Roman social practice of Clement's day, in which the vast majority of adopted sons were adult males—the most prominent of them being the so-called adoptive emperors of the second century. Clement probably knew of many other adult adopted sons from his upbringing among elites.

Elsewhere, Clement demonstrates how, in the household image, adoption is the highest advancement. He describes the upward progression from first being God's "slave" (δοῦλος), then God's "trustworthy attendant" (πιστὸς θεράπων), until finally, if one ascends higher, "he is enrolled among the sons" and "integrated into the chosen adoptive sonship which is called 'beloved of God.'"[124] Adoptive sonship is "the highest advancement" (ἡ μεγίστη προκοπή), and also carries with it a certain "authority" (ἐξουσία) that can be difficult to bear.[125] In short, adoption for Clement is a metaphor of perfect maturation—adoptive sonship is τέλειος.[126]

Yet even though adoption comes later in life, making an adult male into a son, it can be conceived much earlier in the mind of the father. Alluding to Pauline language, Clement states that "before the foundation of the world," God "predestined the friend of God"—that is, the true Gnostic or perfect Christian—"to be enrolled in the highest adoption."[127] This is compatible with Roman social practice, as Paul also knew. Roman fathers often decided which men they wanted as sons well in advance of the actual adoptions, as was the case with the most famous adoption in Roman history: the posthumous testamentary adoption of Octavian by Julius Caesar.

Clement also uses the adoption metaphor to depict Christ himself. In an early portion of the *Paedagogus*, Clement expounds what it means for Christians to be children of God, but in this text he makes specific comparisons with the divine sonship of Jesus Christ. He portrays Christ as an exemplar of Christian life, beginning with his baptism: "At the moment when the Lord was being baptized, a voice sounded from heaven as a witness for the beloved: 'You are my beloved son, today I have begotten you.' Then let us ask the wise ones, 'Is Christ, having been begotten again today, already perfect?'"[128] Clement goes on to debate this issue in a long diatribe, which I will not analyze here. At the end, he concludes that

> [Christ] was perfected by the washing alone and sanctified by the descent of the Spirit. Such is the case, and the same thing happens regarding us also, for whom the Lord has become an exemplar: being baptized, we are illuminated; being illuminated, we are adopted as sons; being adopted as sons, we are perfected; being perfected, we become immortal. "I said, 'You are gods,'" he said, "'and all sons of the Most High.'"[129]

The presentation of Christ here as the "exemplar" (ὑπογραφή) of adoptive divine sonship is as clear as any in early Christian literature.[130] The striking text has received full treatment by Antonio Orbe, who concludes that the exemplarist Christology, even with its adoptive imagery, is unmistakable. Jesus was the model of progress, and "the baptism of Jesus was the exemplar for all baptisms. . . . In his humanity, Jesus passed through various stages to attain exemplary perfection: cleansing, illumination, proclamation of sonship, infusion of the Holy Spirit."[131]

Despite Orbe's expert analysis, he nonetheless flinches when translating Clement's text about sonship: the Greek verb used for Christians is the same as that for Christ, but Orbe calls the former "*adopción*" and the latter "*filiación*." The text of Clement is quite clear, though, in its parallelism: adoption is a crucial step for Christians on the path from baptism to immortal divinization, a step taken first by Christ himself.[132] Psalm 82 is understood to predict both divinity and divine sonship.[133] As I have argued, adoptive sonship was not a "low" concept in Clement's world-view, based as it was on the actual social practices of contemporary Roman culture. Adoption was how the most powerful men in the world gained their power; and he quotes the psalmist to that effect—to be an adopted son of God is to be a god, a sentiment quite in line with Roman imperial theology.

Let us not forget, though, that Christ is the exemplar of *begotten* divine sonship too. While Clement undoubtedly presupposes and preserves a unique divine son-ship for Jesus Christ—none of what is quoted and analyzed above challenges that, in Clement's view—Christ's uniqueness was not primarily constituted by begot-tenness. Christ's baptism was his "being begotten again" (ἀναγεννηθείς), though this word is translated without the "again" prefix in the most-widely available English translation of the text.[134] And this begetting again was a model for Christian baptismal rebirth. Christ was begotten again *and* adopted as son, just as Christians were foreordained to be. Christ was the unique exemplar that Christians followed.[135]

Irenaeus

That one might eventually look to Irenaeus of Lyons, the great heresiographer, during a discussion of adoptionistic Christology in the second century should not come as a surprise. His chief publication included all the heresies fit to print. But I turn now to Irenaeus not to examine his opponents, whom he so excellently dis-sects and whose Christologies come down to us sometimes only through his descriptions, but rather to consider Irenaeus himself. He was certainly a theological innovator, even as he styled himself a chronicler and protector. Several of his texts use adoptive metaphors in scintillating, even shocking, ways. Some of his formula-tions are so receptive to adoptionistic interpretations that it took Antonio Orbe, the peerless scholar of Irenaeus, almost fifty pages to answer the question, "*¿San Ireneo adopcionista?*"[136] Why did it take Orbe so long? How did Irenaeus use the metaphor of adoptive divine sonship?

In the words of Walter Kasper, "the depth and breadth of Irenaeus's Christological ideas have never really been equalled."[137] Irenaeus thought and wrote expansively about how the fact of Jesus Christ reconstituted everything, and accordingly, his Christology is deserving of the large-scale treatments it has received.[138] But here, I must limit my own analysis to his deployment of adoptive metaphors. Like others before him, Irenaeus found the adoption metaphor particularly useful in the overall context of household imagery. More specifically, it was a necessary part of the argument for how Christians might receive inheritance from God the Father. The question of who rightfully possessed the inheritance of Abraham was crucial, just as it was for Paul and John. Irenaeus defends the Christian possession of the inheritance against Marcion and his followers (who disregarded the covenant with Abraham), claiming that Abraham's "seed" is the "church," to whom is bestowed "the adoption and the inheritance promised to Abraham."[139] When defending the incarnation against opponents such as the Ebionites, Irenaeus claims that there would be no divine inheritance for Christians, unless it came through Abraham. For if Christ had been begotten by Joseph, he argues, Christ himself would not have had the inheritance allotted by the God of Israel, since Joseph's ancestors had been disinherited (3.21.9). In general, whenever covenants and inheritances are at issue in the arguments of Irenaeus, "those who have received adoption" becomes a shorthand designation for Christians.[140]

The shorthand can also be elaborated through an image of upward mobility in a household. During one of Irenaeus's sweeping summaries of salvation history, he describes the ascent of humanity through God's household ranks: God (or the Logos) was "at one time conversing with his creature, at another time giving the law, one time reproaching, another time exhorting, then subsequently liberating him from being a slave and adopting him as a son, and at the proper time, furnishing an incorruptible inheritance for the perfection of humanity."[141] The human race, figured as usual for Irenaeus in the body of Adam, ascends through the probationary childhood and servitude before being liberated, adopted, and made heir of God's household.[142] In other texts, he conflates this longer trajectory into a concise slave-son trope, with its correlated culminations of liberation and adoption.[143]

Sometimes Irenaeus mixes begotten and adoptive metaphors when portraying the divine sonship of Christians. For example, writing again against the Ebionites, Irenaeus asks: "How can a human pass into God, unless God has passed into a human? And how can [humanity] leave behind the *generatio* of death, unless they are begotten again by faith into a new *generatio*, wonderfully and unexpectedly granted by God as a sign of salvation, which is from the Virgin? Or how can they receive *adoptio* from God, if they remain in this *genesis*, which is according to humanity in this world?"[144] The normal human mode of begetting (called by the Latin *generatio* and Greek *genesis*) is only a begetting unto "death," but a "new begetting" (*novam generationem*) has been introduced "from the Virgin" as a "sign of salvation."[145] And yet this new begetting is either a preparation for or tantamount to "receiving adoption from God" (*adoptionem accipient*).[146] Elsewhere, Irenaeus seems to equate "adoption" with "begetting" more explicitly. When arguing for the unity of God, even amid God's different manners of relating to the world, he makes the following distinction: God's Logos gives the Spirit to some as *a spirit of creation, which is made, on account of their createdness,* but to others as *a spirit from God, which is begotten, on account of their adoptedness.*[147] The text is difficult to understand and translate, but it is clear that begottenness and adoptedness are one side and createdness and madeness are on the other. It is possible that, just as for Clement of Alexandria, the mixing of metaphors can be attributed to Irenaeus's reliance on both Paul and John in developing his soteriological vocabulary. What is important to see now, though, is that divine sonship by adoption had not yet been linked with "createdness" or "madeness." To the contrary, adoption was connected closely to begottenness and distinguished from madeness.

That being said, Irenaeus does seem to prefer the adoptive metaphor to portray the divine sonship of Christians.[148] The first key text occurs during his scriptural arguments against Valentinian theology. Irenaeus argues against the proliferation of divine beings in the Valentinian system by attempting to demonstrate from Scripture that only the Father and the Son are properly called "God" and "Lord." But in doing so, he must deal with texts that complicate that thesis, such as those mentioning other "gods." Chief among them is Ps 82 (81), a vision of a divine council where God judges the other gods, whose sixth verse reads: "I have said you are gods and all sons of the Most High."[149] Irenaeus interprets the "gods" of this psalm to be a prediction of the exalted status afforded to Christians through adoptive divine sonship. When the psalm says, "God stood in the congregation of the gods" (82:1), Irenaeus argues that the Spirit "spoke about the Father and the Son and those who have received adoption; then these are the church, that is the 'congregation' of God, which God, that is the Son, has gathered himself."[150] Irenaeus de-emphasizes the "gods" *per se* and focuses instead on the "gathering" function of the Son to constitute a "congregation" of divine "sons." He later clarifies that this interpretation is derived primarily from Pauline teaching about divine sonship. Irenaeus again: "Of which 'gods,' then, did the Spirit speak? Of those to whom it said, 'I have said you are gods and all sons of the Most High,' undoubtedly of those who have obtained the gift of adoption, through which we cry, 'Abba, Father.'"[151] Therefore, Ps 82 becomes for Irenaeus not a justification of multiple primordial divine beings but a prophetic foreshadowing of eschatological adoptive sonship of Christians.[152] He later summarizes this teaching in the preface to the next book: "There is none other called 'God' by the Scriptures except the Father of all, and the Son, and those who possess the adoption."[153]

Irenaeus further tries to explicate the relationship between the divine sonship of Christ and that of Christians. How was the sonship of the sons connected to the sonship of the Son? According to the Irenaean script, God's unique Son played the pivotal role in the dramatic plot through which the lost children of God gained sonship in the immortal, divine family. In a reframing of the Pauline sonship soteriology of Gal 4:4–5, Irenaeus teaches, "the Son of God was made a son of a human, that through him we might receive adoption—humanity bearing and receiving and embracing the Son of God."[154] But this soteriology is also expanded through Johannine theology to include the incarnation of the Word, which Irenaeus depicts as a necessary event in the process leading to divine sonship for all. "For by what method could we become partakers of [God's] adoption of sons, unless we had received from [God] through the Son that communion which is with Godself—unless [God's] Word had communed with us by being made flesh?"[155] This synthesis of Pauline and Johannine ideas in Irenaeus is often called the "exchange formula," since it presents a parallel descent and ascent that implies an exchange of humanity and divinity between the Son and the sons.[156] Such an understanding is adequate, as long as one does not press it into a static Christological dogma. In Kasper's words, for Irenaeus, "the larger theological context of the Christological problem is apparent: the unity of Godhead and humanity in Christ also involves the question of the unity of creation and redemption, of God and world. Jesus Christ is not understood simply as a great exception, but rather as the new beginning. Consequently Irenaeus treats the Christological problem particularly from the soteriological point of view."[157] Irenaeus undoubtedly portrays Christ as the uniquely incarnate Son of God (the "great exception"), but when he speaks about divine sonship, he is more concerned with Christ as "the new beginning," the key to the eschatological adoption of Christians. Divine sonship unites Christ with Christians more than it divides them—indeed, it is their "*communio*."[158]

The fullest expression of the "exchange formula" comes further on in book 3. When defending the unique birth of Jesus Christ, that he was not a "mere man, begotten by Joseph," Irenaeus writes:

> For this reason the Word of God became human, and he who was the Son of God became a son of a human: so that a human, having been joined with the Word of God and receiving adoption, might become a son of God. For by no other means could we have attained to incorruptibility and immortality, unless we had been united to incorruptibility and immortality. But how could we be joined to incorruptibility and immortality, unless, first, incorruptibility and immortality had become that which we also are, so that the corruptible might be swallowed up by incorruptibility, and the mortal by immortality, so that we might receive the adoption of sons?[159]

The Pauline sonship formula of Gal 4, which had already been reframed and expanded with Johannine Logos theology, has now been bolstered further by Pauline resurrection language (1 Cor 15:50–57). Humanity will share not only the sonship of the Son, but also the "immortality" (ἀθανασία) and "incorruptibility" (ἀφθαρσία) proper to divine beings. In the end, then, will the Son and the sons be indistinguishable?[160]

That is a difficult question to answer, but Irenaeus does begin to answer a different question about divine sonship—the main question that has driven this whole chapter. Namely, how did the divide between the begottenness of Jesus Christ and the adoptedness of Christians come to be articulated in early Christianity? It perhaps began *in nuce* with Paul, but it becomes explicit here with one of Paul's great interpreters. Just before the large quotation above, Irenaeus describes his opponents who deny the incarnation with these words: they are "those who *have not received the gift of adoption*, but rather, they dishonor the incarnation of *the pure begetting of the Word of God* and defraud humanity of its ascent to God."[161] This is the most clear distinction yet between the begottenness of Jesus Christ, "the pure γεννήσις," and the "adoption" of Christians. The language is unmistakable.

Elsewhere Irenaeus supports the begotten divine sonship of Jesus Christ, even as he encourages his readers not to speculate about it. In book 2, he is plainly frustrated with the ever-multiplying begettings and emanations within the theological systems of his opponents, and he counsels for apophaticism about the *how* and the *when* of the Son of God's begetting:

> If anyone says to us, "How then was the Son produced by the Father?" we reply to him, that no one understands that production or begetting or calling or revelation, or by whatever name one may describe his generation, which is in fact altogether indescribable—neither Valentinus, nor Marcion, nor Saturninus, nor Basilides, nor angels, nor archangels, nor principalities, nor powers—but only the Father who begat, and the Son who was born. Since therefore his begetting is unspeakable, those who strive to set forth generations and productions cannot be in their right mind, inasmuch as they undertake to describe things which are indescribable.[162]

Despite his commitment to the begotten, incarnate Son of God, Irenaeus is still not at pains to make the distinction between the Son and the sons in the way later authors would be. On the whole, he views divine sonship as the *communio* that unites Christ with Christians (3.18.7; cf. 3.20.2). In the words of Richard Norris, "Irenaeus is eager to maintain the analogy—indeed the commonality of nature— between the Christ and believers that is presupposed by his understanding of the adoption of sons."[163] Because of this emphasis on *communio*, he actually leaves several other texts open to adoptionistic interpretations. For example, when arguing again against the Ebionites and other incarnation-deniers, Irenaeus describes how the Spirit announced through the apostles that "the fullness of the time of adoption had arrived"—and that this was made known to those who acknowledge the virginal birth of Jesus Christ (3.21.4). Knowing his whole system of exchange, one can figure out what Irenaeus must have meant: the same Spirit which begat Jesus Christ in the virginal womb of Mary also adopts Christians later. But a fourth-century author with primarily Nicene concerns would never voluntarily put adoption language so close to a discussion of Jesus' divine sonship. That would be too close for comfort.[164]

In summary, Irenaeus provides a synthesis of the images of divine sonship that came before him (at least among proto-orthodox authors). He mixes the begotten and adoptive metaphors, but he is beginning to separate them apart through the influence of Johannine Christological language.[165] The begottenness of Jesus Christ has begun to separate from the adoptedness of Christians, a great unmixing that will take two more centuries to effect. He was still influenced, though, by the positive connotations of adoption in the sociopolitical context of the second century. For Irenaeus, the adoption metaphor performs the dramatization of upward mobility, just as it did for previous authors. And a grandiose ascent it is— described as an ascent of the human to God, the greatest glory of promotion. Finally, the adoption metaphor helps Irenaeus in his overarching project of defending the unity of God against the various cosmologies of the "Gnostics falsely so-called."[166] The imagery of divine begottenness had engendered vast cosmic lineages among proto-heterodox Christians in the second century, like divine stemmata fractured across the heavens. Irenaeus loathed such complex cosmologies, whether from Valentinians or other Christian groups, and adoptive imagery was well suited to his monarchian tendency. That is to say, a large adoptive household is unified under the *paterfamilias*. The father passes on the divine family spirit through his son, and if he wants more sons, he does not have to find a new partner. All by himself, he can adopt them into the family as heirs—this is the glory of promotion, "to receive adoption and become a son of God."

■ UNMIXING METAPHORS

Regarding the divine sonship of Christians, the metaphors of begetting and adoption were interwoven through the first four centuries, and especially the first two centuries. In the mid- to late-fourth century, however, the emphasis of Christian divine sonship shifted markedly toward adoption. A broad historical perspective allows us to see why: during the fourth-century's christological controversies, the divine sonship of Jesus Christ came to be authoritatively defined as "begotten, not made." In order to shore up this definition thereafter, the divine sonship of Christians should not be portrayed as "begotten," lest their filial relationship to God be confused with that belonging to Jesus Christ alone. Instead, the divine sonship of Christians would be portrayed as adoptive. By the end of the fourth century, several Christian leaders were preaching the same message: Jesus is God's begotten son, by nature; you are all God's adopted sons, by grace.

Since the christological developments of the third and fourth centuries are among the most well-known paths of Christian theology, I will not attempt here to blaze a new trail. I would like only to pass quickly along the road from the second to the fourth century and highlight a few signposts.[167] Through the texts of third-century theologians such as Origen; the Nicene-era disputes of Alexander, Arius, and Athanasius; and then the post-Nicene Latin formulations of Augustine, the unmixing of metaphors can be plainly observed to the end of the fourth century.

Origen

Origen, writing about 150 years after Mark, is the first major theologian to distinguish starkly the begotten and adoptive metaphors for the divine sonship of Christ. According to Peter Widdicombe, "the contrast and the similarity between the two types of sonship are central to Origen's thinking" about how humans come to know God as Father.[168] For example, in his major theological work, *On First Principles*, Origen treats the issue of the Son of God's origin in some detail.[169] He endorses the begotten metaphor for the relationship of Father and Son, but he is not comfortable with the modes of begetting—sexual relations and birth—that this metaphor calls to mind from the human and animal world. He seeks out instead "some exceptional process, worthy of God," in order to "apprehend how the unbegotten God becomes Father of the only-begotten Son."[170] Origen suggests the now-classic image of "light from light": the generation of Father to Son "is an eternal and everlasting begetting, as brightness is begotten from light."[171] He also relies on the figure of Wisdom as an explanation of the Son, although this figure gets him into a bit of trouble: Origen is clear that the Son is "begotten," but if the Son is Wisdom, then he is also a "created thing" (κτίσμα) according to Scripture.[172] That is, the Son is both "begotten" and "made," a tension that would be precisely forbidden later by Nicene orthodoxy. Nevertheless, whatever image one chooses, Origen is clear to exclude the adoptive metaphor entirely: "He does not become Son in an external way through the adoption of the Spirit, but he is Son by nature."[173]

Since John himself does not narrate or locate the divine begetting of the Son of God, Origen is also wary to mythologize it. He emphasizes the naturalness of the sonship as opposed to adoption, but he does not want to elaborate the *how* or the *when* of it much further. In his words, nowhere does John "set forth the noble birth of the Son. But when 'You are my son, today I have begotten you' is said to him by God, it is always 'today' for God. . . . [Any] day for God is 'today,' in which the Son has been begotten. Therefore the origin of his beginning is not found [in the Gospel of John], nor is the day [of that beginning found there]."[174] Even though the quotation of Ps 2:7 does not occur in John's Gospel, Origen claims it to mark the divine sonship of Jesus, and he offers an interpretation of the troubling "today" that would influence subsequent theologians.[175] The begotten metaphor is certain for Origen, but the "origin of his beginning" (ἀρχῆς γενέσεως) is not determinable because for God every day is "today."

As for the divine sonship of Christians, Origen still mixes the metaphors of begetting and adoption. In his treatise on Passover, he quotes the plural reading of John 1:13 as applying to Christians, who are "*begotten* of God," but then explains the reading with the adoptive metaphor: "*For adoption in Christ has given us the authority of such a salvation*, we who came to be not from the blood and desire of man and woman, and whom [Christ] confesses to be his brothers when he says, 'I will proclaim your name to my brothers'" (Ps 22[21]:23; Heb 2:13).[176] Similarly, he describes Christian divine sonship as both begotten and adopted in his exposition of Proverbs—even endorsing a begetting from Wisdom: "Let Christ be a friend to you in every season, and if the sons are of Christ, they are friends to each other. The angels and the righteous human beings are brothers to each other, since they are begotten by the spirit of adoption. It was for this purpose that they are begotten by wisdom: so that they might guide people from wickedness to virtue and from ignorance to knowledge of God."[177]

The begotten metaphor is unavoidable when interpreting Johannine literature, but when Origen interprets Paul, he makes the division between the begottenness of Christ and the adoptedness of Christians with a force not yet seen. And the text that allows him to make the distinction is one flagged earlier, when discussing

Paul's views on divine sonship—the use of the word ἴδιος, "God's *own* son," in Rom 8:32. Origen interprets it thus: Paul "had said above that even we who have received the Spirit of adoption are sons of God. But lest it should be thought that he handed over one of these who appeared to be adopted among his own sons, by the general sense of 'sons,' he has added, 'his own Son,' in order to point to him who alone is begotten by an ineffable generation from God himself."[178] The distinction of the Son from the sons that Paul had left *in nuce* has now grown and sprouted in early Christian theology.[179]

Like Irenaeus, Origen was shaped by Paul's imagery of adoption and John's metaphor of rebirth. At times he seems to prefer the adoptive metaphor for Christians because it connoted a progression to exalted status.[180] At other times, however, he uses the begotten metaphor for Christians to portray their unity with Christ: "If the Savior is continuously begotten by the Father, so also, if you possess the spirit of adoption, God continuously generates you in him [the Savior] according to each of your works, each of your thoughts. And being begotten, you thereby become a continuously begotten son of God, in Christ Jesus."[181] In this concluding peroration of a homily, the hortatory power of unifying Christians with Christ seems more important than the finer distinctions of dogma. Participation in the sonship of Christ may be through a "spirit of adoption," but it also allows a Christian to be a "continuously begotten son of God" (ἀεὶ γεννώμενος υἱὸς θεοῦ). After the Nicene era, to which we now turn, that kind of description of Christian divine sonship would no longer be casually uttered.

The Nicene Era

The distinction of the Son from the sons had its watershed moment in the Arian controversy of the Nicene era. This complex period of theological, ecclesiological, and political strife has been treated with great dexterity by many scholars,[182] so I will here only include the points crucial for my history of begotten and adoptive metaphors. Before Arius and Nicea, the begottenness of Christ was quite well established, but the question of when that divine begetting had occurred was still not emphasized. Christian theology had been using ideas from (Middle and Neo-) Platonism for at least 200 years already, especially the doctrine of the Logos as a mediating agent between the transcendent God and the created world. But a new question was now being pressed: what was the *temporal* relationship between the Father-God and the Son-Logos? Did the Son-Logos belong to the transcendent realm of Being or to the lower realm of Becoming? In the words of the Nicene era, was there a time, at the beginning of time, when the Son was not? Here in the fourth century, the "backwards movement" of Christology, which had begun in the New Testament era, was finally approaching its *terminus*—or rather, its *principium.*

As far as the texts allow us to see, Arius himself did not prefer the adoptive metaphor to describe the divine sonship of Jesus Christ; as I said, the begottenness of

Christ was now being used as the master-metaphor about which all debate revolved.[183] But adoption remained a relevant image for *opponents' descriptions* of Arianism because of the dual valence of the term "made" in the Nicene era. On the one hand, "made" (ποι-) meant "created" (κτισ-), and so the Nicene formulation "begotten not made" (γεννηθέντα οὐ ποιηθέντα) defined Jesus Christ as not a created thing (κτίσμα). On the other hand, "made" also meant "adopted" when used in the context of sonship, as many ancient sources attest,[184] and so the divine sonship of Christ was also officially pronounced as *not* adoptive.

The "Letter of Alexander of Alexandria," a key document of the early Arian controversy, illuminates the role of the adoption metaphor for the opponents of Arius.[185] After explaining all the Scriptures that proclaim the eternality of the Son—that there was never a time when the Son was not—Alexander then offers the following distinctions between the "son-ness" of the Son and the sons:

> The son-ness of our savior has nothing in common with the son-ness of the rest [of the sons]. For just as it has been shown that the nature of his existence cannot be expressed by language, and infinitely surpasses in excellence all things to which he himself has granted existence, so also *his son-ness, naturally partaking of the paternal divinity, is unspeakably different from those who have been adopted as sons by adoption through him.* He is by nature immutable, perfect, and all-sufficient, whereas they are liable to change and need his help.[186]

The crucial Platonic distinction of Being and Becoming is here shown to undergird the debate on divine sonship. Jesus Christ is "immutable" (ἄτρεπτος) and "perfect" (τέλειος) in the realm of pure Being, while Christians are "liable to change" in the realm of Becoming. To mark the static sonship of the Son, fourth-century authors coined and propagated the term "son-ness" (υἱότης).[187] This unchanging son-ness had "nothing in common" (οὐδεμία κοινωνία) with the sonship of the sons, those who were "adopted as sons by adoption" (θέσει υἱοθετηθέντων). Natural sonship is "unspeakably different" from adoptive sonship.

A lot had changed since the second-century writings of Clement and Irenaeus. For Clement, *adoptive* sonship was described as "the highest advancement" and "perfect," and immutability was not a point of emphasis for him, Platonist though he was.[188] Perhaps it is better, then, to speak of two different inflections of Platonic metaphysics: if the Nicene orthodox theologians are Platonists of the "divided line," where the realms of Being and Becoming are clearly demarcated and bounded, Clement would instead be a Platonist of the "myth of the cave," where in fact the divided line can be breached through the cave's mouth—individual souls progressing and ascending into the realm of pure Good.[189] For Irenaeus, sonship was a characteristic that united Christ with Christians; it was precisely their *communio*. But in Alexander's perspective, the Son of God has no κοινωνία with the sons of God.

Like Origen before him, Alexander uses Paul's language in Romans 8 to provide his best scriptural defense of how the Son differed from the sons. Commenting again about natural vs. adopted sons, he writes:

[O]ur Lord, being the Father's natural Son, is worshipped by all. But whoever casts off the spirit of slavery, and by brave deeds and progress receives the spirit of adoption, receives benefaction through the natural Son, and they themselves become sons by adoption. As for *his legitimate, individual, natural, and exceptional son-ness,* Paul declared it in the following way: speaking about God, he said, "who did not spare his own Son, but on behalf of us"—who are clearly not sons by nature—"he handed him over." For it was to distinguish him from those who are not his own that he said "his own son."[190]

Alexander piles up the adjectives that set Jesus' sonship apart and then champions the separation of sonships through the little word ἴδιος. That word was introduced by Paul, he argues, precisely to "distinguish" (πρὸς ἀντιδιαστολήν) the Son over against the sons. Viewed in a longer historical trajectory, John's μονογενής may have begun the separation of sonships in Christian theology, but Paul's ἴδιος closed the deal.

A further point about adoptive sonship in the Nicene era is that its connotation of upward mobility, of progress, was no longer viewed positively. For Clement and Irenaeus, adoption had been the "highest advancement" and the "greatest promotion," the ascent to perfection with God. Alexander acknowledges the connotation of progress in adoption, but he makes sure that progress is not attributed to Christ: "[The] natural son-ness and paternal birth [of the Son] is his not by diligence of conduct or exercise in moral progress but by individuality of nature. Hence it follows that the son-ness of the unique Son of the Father is incapable of falling. The adoptive sonship of reasonable beings, however, because it does not belong to them naturally but by a certain fitness of character and a gift of God, may fall away."[191] The static/dynamic distinction between "son-ness" (υἱότης) and "adoptive sonship" (υἱοθεσία) is here emphasized. Alexander's chief concern is: if one could progress, one could also regress.[192] In other words, progress means change, and change means becoming, and the realm of Becoming is not where the Son eternally Is. Existing in the realm of pure Being, the Son does not go up or go down. He just Is.

The debate over progress has catalyzed an important scholarly analysis of Arianism that preceded my own work on adoptive metaphors. Typically, the Arian controversy has been considered as a theological debate about the relationship between the Son and the Father, the Christological controversy *par excellence,* and it can be fruitfully interpreted as such. But Robert Gregg and Dennis Groh have offered an alternative view of the controversy that merits serious attention, even if it shall remain the so-called minority interpretation of the era.[193] Gregg and Groh contend that early Arianism was less about Son-Father relations than it was about the relationship between the Son and the sons; that is, it was a soteriological controversy. In short, they argue that Alexander and Athanasius were driven by the idea that everything predicated of the Father must be predicated of the Son; salvation relied on the Son's essential identity with the Father. But Arius thought that salvation relied on the Son's identity with the sons—a communion of will. The Son does not descend to their level; rather, they ascend to his level of divine sonship and divinity.

Believers' identification of themselves with the pioneer and perfecter of their faith, as proclaimed by Arianism, Athanasius hoped to combat with a sharp line of demarcation: "But if [Christ] wishes us to call his very own Father 'our Father,' it is not necessary, on account of this, to equate ourselves with the Son according to nature." The entire campaign of the Arians is waged, however, in order to win just this. . . . The Arians proclaim no demotion of the Son but a promotion of believers to full and equal status as sons—that is, υἱοί, understood to mean θεοί.[194]

Through a worldview that maintains a high view of adoption, so that adopted sons are not second-class sons but really and truly sons just like natural sons, the Arian argument makes sense.[195] But through a worldview that props up natural sonship above adoptive sonship, identity of essence over communion of will, Being over Becoming, then Nicene orthodoxy will triumph.

As is well known, Athanasius did more than anyone to establish the orthodox position on divine sonship. His writings were "the first time in the Christian tradition [that] the concept of divine fatherhood and the relation of Father and Son are made the subjects of systematic analysis. Confronted with the challenge that he believed Arian theology posed to the church's largely unreflective acceptance of fatherhood language to refer to God, Athanasius attempted to clarify and to determine specifically what that tradition of usage meant for a coherent theology of the divine nature and a coherent theology of salvation."[196] Regarding the issue of begotten and adoptive imagery, Athanasius continued Origen's division of the two and rooted it more deeply in scriptural exegesis. For example, he strongly preferred adoptive language for Christian divine sonship: according to Widdicombe, "the begetting language of Scripture is reserved for the Son; there is to be no blurring of the sonship of the Son and that of man."[197] Therefore Athanasius had to deal gingerly with the begotten imagery in John 1. Because John says that people can "become" children of God (1:12), Athanasius argues that this means they "are not sons by nature but by adoption."[198] Why then did John use the word "begotten" (1:13) to describe Christians? Because "they too had received, in any case, the name 'son,'" and Athanasius apparently presumes that only begotten sons deserve properly to be called "sons."[199] The idea that natural sonship is the only real sonship thus served as a crucial, unstated premise of his scriptural argument.

He also takes up the issue of the key terms μονογενής and πρωτότοκος, which I argued above served rather similar functions in the biblical formulations of John and Paul. Athanasius ascribes distinct meaning to the two terms, however: μονογενής seems to denote the unique, eternal relationship between the Father and the Son, while πρωτότοκος refers to the role of the incarnate Son as the preeminent, but not necessarily unique, exemplar of Christian divine sonship.[200] In other words, Athanasius deftly uses the two terms to straddle the sides of the Arian controversy: in his reading, Scripture portrays the Son as unique, only-begotten, and essentially unified with the Father (μονογενής) and also as a model of the adoptive divine sonship that all Christians can share (πρωτότοκος). For Athanasius the distinction between sonships must not be blurred because, in the words of Virginia Burrus, "therein lies the fertile tension from which man emerges not as a divine but yet as a divinized subject, for whom transcendence (having begun as a gift) must become second nature, founded on the suppression of another nature that came first."[201]

There remain moments, nonetheless, when Athanasius seems to cross one of his own boundaries and blur the lines between the sonship of Christ and that of Christians. One of these times occurs—perhaps unsurprisingly—when he discusses baptism, the fundamental enactment of divine sonship that unites Christ with Christians. When Christians are baptized, Athanasius says, "we also are truly made sons" (υἱοποιούμεθα καὶ ἡμεῖς ἀληθῶς).[202] He does make sure to clarify that Christian sonship is not "natural" like Christ's, but it is still surprising that he would use the word "truly" (ἀληθῶς) because "true" sonship is one of the attributes he elsewhere ascribes to Christ alone.[203] "True" (ἀληθινός) sonship is supposed to be *opposed* to sonship "by adoption" (θέσει) in Athanasius's system.[204] The text about baptism, then, is "an index of how important it was for [Athanasius] to be able to affirm the reality of that sonship, even if it is an adoptive sonship."[205] As we saw above and will see below, Athanasius is not the only one to have blurred the lines between sonships when discussing the effects of baptism.

The debate that peaked with Arius and Athanasius would rage for decades and linger for centuries—in a sense, it is never over. We have enough now for the purposes of my christological narrative, but I would like to conclude this section by recalling the importance of political ideology for theology. The nexus of religion and politics in the Nicene era has been given careful study by Roman historian T. D. Barnes,[206] but most theologians or religious historians have avoided the political undertones of the theological discourse.[207] As one small but shocking example of that nexus, when Athanasius needs an analogy to explain the divine unity of Father and Son, he appeals to the imperial statues ubiquitous around the Empire: just as Christ said "I and the Father are one," so "the statue would say [if it could speak], 'I and the Emperor are one.' . . . Whoever worships the image, in it worships the Emperor also."[208] More pronounced is the case of Eusebius, who overtly champions a monarchic political ideology of dynastic succession in the exact era when theologians articulate an analogous vision of God.[209] The opening lines of Eusebius's *Life of Constantine* envision the immortal Constantine in heaven, a great monarchical sovereign dwelling with the Great Monarchical Sovereign. But what is more revealing is the way in which the adoptive mode of political succession, a quasi-meritocratic succession of adopted adult sons—which had secured a flourishing empire in a previous era—was now viewed as superseded by Constantine and his begotten sons. Eusebius showers praise on Constantine's provision of natural sons, through whose rule on earth one may still perceive "the Blessed One, present with his own sovereignty" and "powerfully alive."[210] The emperor's natural sons are "like new lamps filling the whole with his radiance"—indeed, their father-son relationship is "light from light."[211]

Eusebius is content to praise natural succession, but Constantine, in his own letter to Arius and his followers, brings adoption into the discussion. Pausing to beseech his "monarchic" God during a lengthy invective, the emperor says:

> O master, who has supreme dominion over all things, O Father of singular power, because of this unholy man [Arius] your church receives both reproaches and bruises, indeed both wounds and pains. Presently, Arius furnishes a place for you and—this is quite clever—establishes there, it seems to me, a "synod" for himself; or rather, he establishes your Christ as a son. He procures and retains for himself the one born from you, the source of our assistance, by the law of adoption.[212]

The mockery runs thick. The Father has sole rule (μονήρης), in contrast to the two gods which Arius's opponents accuse him of supporting. But instead of chastizing Arius for holding an adoptionist Christology between Christ and God, Constantine imagines Arius convening an episcopal "synod" for himself and there taking Christ, the natural Son of God, as a child *for himself* by adoption.

Through the efforts of many, the begotten sonship of Christ carried the day. Eusebius could conclude his magisterial history of Christianity with reference to the divine tandem of Father and begotten Son in heaven that guided the divine tandem of father and begotten son on earth. After achieving supreme power, the *sovereign* Constantine "went forth with his son Crispus, a most beneficent *sovereign*, and extended the *saving* right hand to all who were perishing," they being together a "father and son, having God, the *sovereign* of all, and the Son of God, the *savior* of all, as their leader and ally . . . ."[213] The father-sovereign and son-savior on earth are the image of the father-sovereign and son-savior in heaven. Or perhaps it is the other way around.[214]

By the end of the pivotal fourth century, it had become completely normal for Christian theologians to segregate begotten sonship from adopted. Among the many great post-Nicene defenders of orthodoxy, Augustine stands out as eloquent and precise.[215] For example, commenting on Ps 89, a christological crux, he preached: "He is unique, we are many; he is one, we are one in him; he was born, we were adopted; he was begotten as Son through nature in eternity, we were made sons through grace in time."[216] All the questions of the previous centuries can be resolved in one pithy quote—the issues of uniqueness, individuality, origin, and temporality. Augustine even connected the issue directly to the Arian controversy, which he perceived as the pivotal battle in the fight against the adoptive metaphor. Again from one of his sermons: "What do you say, Mr. Arian? . . . You say [the Word] was made. If you say it was made, you are denying he is the Son. You see, we are looking for a Son by nature, not by grace, a Son who is unique, only-begotten, not adopted. That's the kind of Son we are looking for—a legitimate Son."[217] In Augustine's formulation of divine sonship, the concepts of adopted, created, and made are equated without a blink. And those categories have nothing to do with a *legitimate* son—a *verus* son, like the *verus* Caesar some longed for in the early Empire. Here at the end of the fourth century, the divided line is sharp, the metaphors are unmixed, and the Son is distilled. Unique means only-begotten. Legitimate means natural. That's the kind of Son they were looking for.

BAPTISM AND DIVINE SONSHIP IN THE FOURTH CENTURY

The unmixing of metaphors was not happening only in the papyri sent back and forth between theologians and bishops of the third and fourth centuries. Christians were still becoming God's children all the time through baptism—even at a higher rate than before—and they needed metaphors, of course, to enact their divine sonship. This final section of the chapter will demonstrate how the begotten and adoptive metaphors of sonship, separated out by the highest authorities of hierarchy and monarchy, came also to be distinguished in the context of Christian ritual practices common throughout the Empire. The extant texts describing baptismal liturgy from Eastern Christianity—we do not have as much evidence from the West—offer us a unique view of the shift in metaphors during the fourth century.[218] We will examine the two primary sources from Syria: the *Didascalia Apostolorum* (DA) and the *Apostolic Constitutions* (AC), which redacts the DA as part of its compilation. Chronologically in between these church orders are two sources for understanding baptismal liturgy in the Jerusalem church—a letter of Macarius, bishop of Jerusalem, and the catechetical writings of Cyril of Jerusalem, bishop a short time later. Looking at these four sources chronologically allows us to recapitulate a *leitmotif* of the chapter. In the Nicene era, one can watch the divine sonship of Christians change.

The DA, considered to have been composed in North Syria during the first half of the third century, is a chief source for our knowledge of early Christian liturgy. Of interest for our topic are the description of baptism and its concomitant effect of divine sonship. In the course of exhorting Christians to honor their bishop, the DA highlights his role in their baptism and rebirth: he is the one "through whom the Lord in baptism, by the laying on of the hand of the bishop, bore witness to each one of you and caused his holy voice to be heard that said: 'You are my son: today I have begotten you.' On this account, O human, you should acknowledge your bishops, those through whom you became a son of God, and the right hand, your mother."[219] Liturgical historians are tentative about whether Ps 2 was actually invoked by the bishop at baptism.[220] Yet the quotation from Ps 2 was undoubtedly meant to signify the divine sonship of Christians, and not just Christ himself. The Ethiopic version of the *Didascalia* corroborates this fact, when it renders the quotation with a plural predicate: "You are my *sons*."[221] The metaphor of the psalm's verb is certainly one of begetting, as it was in the Hebrew and still is in the Syriac. The metaphor is then elaborated in the subsequent exhortation, in which the fatherhood of God is unified with the spiritual parentage of the bishop. One becomes a son of God through the parentage of the bishop, the spiritual father-mother. What is more, the begotten metaphor is not only used when quoting Ps 2, but it is also linked with baptism two other times in the text.[222]

Chronologically the next piece of evidence comes from Macarius, bishop of Jerusalem in the early fourth century (314–333). In his *Letter to the Armenians* of

335 C.E., which survives only in Armenian and has recently been published by Abraham Terian, Macarius responds to a written petition delivered by Armenian priests about discrepancies between the performance of baptism and Eucharist in the two locations.[223] The relevant excerpt occurs when Macarius explains and defends the three particular days when baptisms were performed in Jerusalem: the feast of Nativity/Epiphany (a combined feast), Easter, and Pentecost. Macarius spells out the symbolism: baptism unifies Christians with Christ's birth/baptism, with his death/resurrection, and with the descent of the Spirit. The connection between baptism and birth can be seen through the celebration of Christ's own birth and baptism on the same feast day—Nativity and Epiphany were both cele-brated on January 6.[224] Christians are called to identify with not only his baptism, but also his birth: as Macarius says, "For on that same salutary day, with the luminous Nativity of Christ, our expiatory birth of the holy font is realized; for on that same day he himself was baptized, condescending to be among us." He later quotes from John's Gospel, "Unless one is born of water and the Spirit, he cannot enter into the kingdom of God," and then concludes, "In the same fashion as we are born with him, we are baptized with him, on the same holy day of the Nativity of Christ." The Jerusalem church of the early fourth century thus drew from the "begotten" and "born" images of John's Gospel and used them to articulate the divine sonship available to all Christians through baptism.[225] Christians were born and baptized with Christ.[226]

If Macarius's letter offers us a quick glimpse into the interpretation of baptism in the Jerusalem church, the teachings of Cyril present a sweeping panorama. He was bishop from 350–386, but his most important extant writings, the pre-baptismal *Catechetical Lectures*, were begun early in his episcopate or even while he was still a presbyter.[227] Several times in these lectures, Cyril provides catechesis about divine sonship, no doubt a hot topic of the fourth century. But contrary to the letter of Macarius, Cyril draws a sharp distinction between the sonship of Christ and the sonship of Christians. The most emphatic statement comes in Lecture 3, "On Baptism." After explaining the descent of the Holy Spirit and the sounding of the Father's voice at the baptism of Jesus, Cyril says to the catechumens:

> If you yourself also have genuine reverence, the Holy Spirit comes down upon you too, and a Fatherly voice sounds over you from above—not "This one *is* my son," but "This one *has now become* my son." For the "is" comes upon him [that is, Christ], since "in the beginning was the Word, and the Word was with God, and the Word was God." The "is" comes upon him, since he is always God's son. But upon you comes the "now has become," since you do not possess it by nature; rather, by adoption, you receive adoptive sonship. He is eternal, but you receive the grace of advancement. Therefore, prepare the vessel of your soul, so that you might become God's son—an heir of God and co-heir with Christ.[228]

Recall that for Bishop Macarius, the union of a Christian with Christ's birth was a chief function of baptism. But in this pithy teaching, Cyril tries to *prevent* several ways by which Christian baptism could be unified with the sonship of Christ himself. It is true that they both receive the Spirit, they both hear Ps 2 overhead, and they both are called God's son. But not so fast. Before the text quoted above, Cyril had already explained that Jesus didn't need the Spirit the way Christians do; it was sent upon him for the benefit of John's testimony.[229] The voice was different too: Jesus heard the voice, in what we now have as Matthew's version, saying, "This *is* my son," but a Christian hears, "This *has now become* my son." It is unclear whether those modified words were actually uttered over the baptized in the Jerusalem church of Cyril's day or they were merely supposed to be imagined. (We already saw how the Ethiopic *Didascalia* modified the psalm to fit a liturgical situation; there is no reason why Cyril's church could not have done the same.) In any case, Cyril completely avoids the "begotten" metaphor that follows in the psalm; either he is more familiar with a version of the baptismal voice that ends differently, or he cuts the quotation short on purpose.

That is to say, instead of dealing with the troublesome verb of the second clause ("begotten"), he focuses on the verb of the first clause ("is")—and he does so in a way that resonates with the Platonism of the Nicene era. Jesus *is* God's son, existing as such in the realm of pure Being; there is no change in Jesus' divine sonship. Elsewhere in the *Lectures*, Cyril uses the newly coined term to describe Jesus' unique divine sonship: υἱότης, or "son-ness," which ensured there was no slippage between Jesus' son-ness (υἱότης) and υἱοθεσία, the adoptive sonship that Christians possessed.[230] Returning to Platonist terms, Christians *become* God's sons, dwelling in the lower realm of Becoming, and their sonship is an advancement from one state to another. Here Cyril explains the advancement with the metaphor of adoption into inheritance; later he will elaborate the household image further—the advancement is from slavery to adoptive sonship and an unmerited inheritance alongside Christ, the true son and heir.[231]

Our fourth text, the late-fourth-century (c. 380) compilation called the *Apostolic Constitutions* (AC), returns us to Syria. Its first six books redact the text of the *Didascalia* (DA), revealing how the portrayal of divine sonship in Syrian Christian liturgy had changed in 150 years—and after Nicea. The AC retains the "begotten" metaphor of Ps 2 but makes several key changes in the elaboration of the quotation: "You are my son: today I have begotten you," but then it adds, "Through your bishop, God adopts you, O human."[232] From begotten to adopted—why this change of metaphors at baptism? I argue that the redactor of AC knew well the many ways Ps 2 was applied to Jesus in early Christianity; it was a hotly contested scriptural citation already, but it was made more contentious if it applied to all Christians as well as Jesus. By the late fourth century, Christians should no longer be begotten of God; they were adopted, even if that meant that the metaphors—which had become mutually exclusive—were clumsily left side-by-side. The unusual juxtaposition can perhaps be attributed to the conservatism of liturgical redactors, who are much more likely to add than subtract from their received texts. The AC keeps the quotation of Ps 2, either out of conservatism or knowledge of its actual liturgical usage, but makes sure to elaborate its meaning in a way congruent with late-fourth-century theological language. The redactor did the same thing in a previous section of the text, adding an adoption metaphor without deleting the begotten metaphor from the DA.[233] But redactors do sometimes delete things from their received texts. Later in this section, he omits one use of the begotten metaphor by reordering his received text.[234] Much later in the AC, when he is no longer redacting the DA, he uses exclusively the adoption metaphor when discussing Christian baptism.[235] For our purposes, the chief example of deletion occurs when the redactor removes the phrase "son of God" from the DA's description of Christian baptism and replaces it simply with "son."[236] Presumably he finds the title "son of God" for a Christian to be too close for comfort; if Christians are called "son of God," well, someone might get the wrong idea. The begotten sonship of Christ must be protected as unique.

In a sense, that last line is a summary of what many Christian theologians spent the late fourth century trying to do: defining and protecting the unique sonship of Jesus Christ.[237] Earlier, in the first two centuries, adoptive sonship could be used to symbolize both Christ and Christians, based as it was on the exalted status of well-known adopted sons in Roman society. But by the late fourth and into the fifth century, theologians like Cyril and Augustine would hammer home a different point: *stop mixing metaphors*. Jesus is God's begotten son by nature; you are all God's adopted children by grace. Orthodoxy is nothing if not tidy.

And yet, something ancient and crucial was lost in their drawing of the sharp dichotomy—namely, the sense of Christ's divine sonship as an exemplar. In the earlier texts, Christ is imagined *alongside* the Christian being baptized. Christ was the "firstborn" of a large family, to use Pauline language; and the Christian follows his lead. But in the later texts, Christ becomes distanced.[238] He is not the "firstborn" older brother, standing in the Jordan with the one being baptized; he is the "only-begotten," in the sky above. He was naturally begotten, the rest are adopted—and since that split, the ideology of the Christian family has never been the same.

One Sunday morning in the late-fourth century, a congregation gathers to pray to God and celebrate their Lord Jesus Christ, who by now had become the dominant Son of God in the Roman world. As a bonus, they get to listen to the greatest preacher in the history of Christianity—just like they do every week. John, also called "Chrysostom" or "golden mouth," is set to preach on the baptism of Jesus.[1] It's not seen as a tough text for preaching nowadays, but in the fourth century, it posed significant doctrinal challenges. If we listen in, Chrysostom's homily can offer an opportunity to review several main themes of this book. In early Christianity, attentive listeners might have wondered: Why did Jesus need to be baptized? Did he possess the Holy Spirit before the dove descended? Most importantly, what did Jesus' baptism signify about his divine sonship, and their own? The congregation perks up their ears. Thankfully, someone is taking notes.

Chrysostom answers the doctrinal questions swiftly, effortlessly, elegantly. Jesus Christ was God made human and μονογενής. But knowing that this incarnational Christology does not flow obviously from the baptismal narrative, he defends against some common (mis)interpretations of it. Jesus was not in *need* of anything that day in the Jordan; rather, he went to the water for the sake of the plan of human salvation—for *you*. And yes, it may seem that Jesus was portrayed as *just like you*, one of many coming to the waters of baptism, but the miraculous signs surely identify him as unique. And no, the dove did not deliver the Spirit to Jesus, as if he didn't have it before; rather, the descending bird was like the finger of God pointing out to whom the voice was directed. It's *this* one (the baptized), not that one (the baptizer). Chrysostom is carefully tending his flock and protecting them from error. So far, so good.

But a great preacher is never content with doctrinal clarifications alone. Once Chrysostom has gotten those out of the way, he shifts his direction to the lives of the people in front of him. Specifically, he relates the baptism of Jesus to their own baptismal experience. The baptism of Jesus indeed symbolizes the close connection of divine sonship shared by Christ and Christians. Why were the heavens opened? Because the same thing happens to you at your baptism. Why the dove? To teach you that the Spirit comes also upon you. Even the voice speaks to you: God calls you heavenward because *you* are "sons of God" and "beloved," Chrysostom says.

And just like that, Christological doctrine is no longer at issue. The divine sonship of Jesus Christ, unique though Chrysostom declares it to be, has begun to be shared with the Christians participating in the homily. Jesus is not the only "son of God," and "beloved" sonship is not his distinctive feature. In fact, the baptism of Jesus has opened up divine sonship to the entire world, and *that* is the grander reason for the dove's descent. Chrysostom recalls the end of the flood, when the world had been washed and saved from its sin by drowning and rising again. But now a greater gift is brought by the dove: "For it does not lead just one person out of an ark, but when it appears it leads the whole world to heaven. And instead of an olive branch, it brings adoptive sonship to the universal human race."[2] For the gift of adoption, Christians must remain thankful, Chrysostom warns. "Don't become ungrateful to your benefactor," for "wherever the status of adoptive sonship is granted, there is the removal of bad things and the giving of every good thing."[3]

Chrysostom has now hit his homiletical stride, bringing the baptism of Jesus backward to the world-changing flood and forward into the daily practices of Christian gratitude to God. But one now wonders whether the baptism of *Jesus* is still being preached. If the dove offers adoptive sonship to the world, what did the dove offer Jesus? Chrysostom, if given a pop-quiz of theological dogma, would no doubt provide the orthodox answers—that the dove did nothing to Jesus, added nothing to the μονογενής Son of God. But as every preacher knows, homiletics is not dogmatic theology. And here Chrysostom gives us a glimpse of how the different metaphors of divine sonship, the one afforded to Christ and the other to Christians, could be difficult to keep separate in practice.[4]

He calls on Christians to "keep watch of their noble lineage (εὐγένεια), which [they] received from the beginning," a lineage which they acquired legitimately through adoption and whose beginning was at baptism, not birth.[5] They should focus not on earthly things but on their imperial courts (*basileia*) above, which they will inherit.[6] Sensing a good rhetorical flourish—and now seemingly unconcerned with the danger of preaching about adoption during a homily on the baptism of Jesus—Chrysostom then makes this analogy:

> For if a *basileus*, one of the earthly ones, were to find you as a poor beggar and suddenly adopt you as a son, you would never stop to think about your little hut and its meager conveniences, even though in that case the difference [between former life and new life] is not very much. So here, in this case, do not take account of the former things, for you are called to something far greater. The one who calls you is the master of the angels, and the good things that are given surpass every thought and accounting. For this one does not take you from one piece of land to another, as the *basileus*, but rather from earth to heaven, and from mortal nature to immortal, and to an unspeakable glory, which can only be manifested at that time when we will profit from it.[7]

To exhort Christians to appreciate and honor their adoptive divine sonship, Chrysostom describes the highest kind of sonship on earth—an adoption into a ruling family. He does not necessarily refer to the imperial family in his example, although βασιλεύς is a Greek word typically used for the emperor.[8] Certainly for him and his congregation, the imperial family has the highest status imaginable. Even in the late-fourth century, well after the main era of adoptive political ideology, he still finds it useful to compare divine sonship to the adoptive sonship offered by powerful rulers to exalt those below them.[9] In short, it is exceedingly good to be adopted as a son by an emperor or other sovereign, and thus to be granted a noble lineage through adoption; but it is unspeakably, unimaginably good to be adopted as God's son and await an inheritance in the heavenly courts.

Such an exalted sonship comes with a caveat, however. A Christian, if he or she should falter and displease the Father, is not punished as a human but as *a son of God*, warns Chrysostom. And the Christian will not be spared on account of the sonship; Chrysostom claims that masters punish slaves and sons just the same, especially if they have received a great benefaction. In fact, the punishment of a son of God will be worse than that inflicted upon the primordial Adam: "For if he who had paradise for his portion, but after his honor, underwent such dreadful things because of his one disobedience; then as for us, who have received heaven and become joint heirs with the μονογενής, what excuse shall we have if, after the dove, we run to the serpent?"[10]

Chrysostom's homily eventually ends on a positive note, but we will stop listening in at this point. The portion narrated and explained provides a fitting conclusion to this book's examination of divine sonship in early Christianity. Through the homily, several themes can be recapitulated. The imagery of the Roman household, and especially the ruling imperial household, comprised a pervasive cultural ideology within which early Christian authors lived, thought, and wrote. A key aspect of this family ideology was the upward mobility of adoption. Adoptive metaphors were used for diverse rhetorical purposes, especially in the first two centuries of Christianity, but even here in the late-fourth century. The doctrines about divine sonship had taken several centuries to be distilled, codified, and disseminated; and even when that had been accomplished, those ideas did not always translate into other forms of speech. That is to say, theological doctrines about divine sonship were not easily transferrable into other genres, such as narratives, homilies, and liturgies. Finally, the idea of Christ as exemplar of divine sonship demonstrated surprising staying power, even when it had become difficult to uphold doctrinally. In the end, through these intersecting themes, I hope to have demonstrated that the social and political practices of adoption during the Roman Empire, especially those of the ruling imperial families, can indeed help us to re-imagine divine sonship and resurrect the "son of God" metaphor.

EPILOGUE: THE SON OF GOD IN THE CHRISTIAN WORLD

One Sunday morning in Boston—sixteen centuries later—I was in a Roman Catholic parish, listening to a different homily about the Son of God. While looking up to the front of the church, I had a stark realization about the abiding presence of the Roman son of God in my Christian world. Recall that earlier in this book, I encapsulated my criticism of biblical scholarship on my topic by claiming that its field of vision has a blind spot the size of the Roman emperor. At that point, I meant that we should not interpret the "son of God" in the Roman world without consideration of what it meant also to call the emperor by that title. But more might be done with the image I chose. A blind spot is that singular place that one cannot see, although the surrounding periphery can be seen just fine. When it occurs in the center of the eye—the relatively common condition called "macular degeneration"—a person is prevented from seeing precisely the location at which he or she is looking. Have we overlooked the emperor's significance for interpreting early Christianity, even though he was right in front of our eyes?

Here at St. Cecilia parish in Boston's Back Bay neighborhood, I discovered one of my own blind spots. Indeed, the emperor *has* been right in front of our eyes. Looking at the photo of the church's apse (Fig. 7.1), what do you see? What don't you see? What I did *not* see, for the first time that day, was a colossal statue of Jesus Christ in the center niche, at the focal point of the architecture and the liturgy. There are statues to the right and left; there is a statue in the wall above; there are certainly more statues around the church that I do not recall. But there in the center, the colossal Christ whom Christians worship is absent.

Compare this to the architecture of imperial temples and shrines throughout the Roman Empire: for example, a shrine of similar design is currently being excavated at Hippos-Sussita, a Roman city of the Decapolis. It is adjacent to the western gate of the city, which is on a hill high above the eastern shore of the Sea of Galilee. It stands above the kind of precipitous slope down which Jesus cast the *legion* into the sea. The excavators have identified this imperial shrine as a "*kalybe* structure," a term derived from that Greek word (meaning something like "hut" or "cabin"), which happened to be found in an inscription at one of the seven known structures of this type in the Roman East. In the reconstructions of these shrines (Fig. 7.2), one will find in the central of three niches the towering figure of the emperor, a marble colossus glistening against the surrounding basalt walls.[1]

I am certainly not the first to notice connections between Greco-Roman and Christian architecture. For example, it is well known that Christians, after the conversion of the Empire, adapted Roman basilicas to be used as churches, and

Fig. 1 Photo by Raymond Ward. Used by permission.

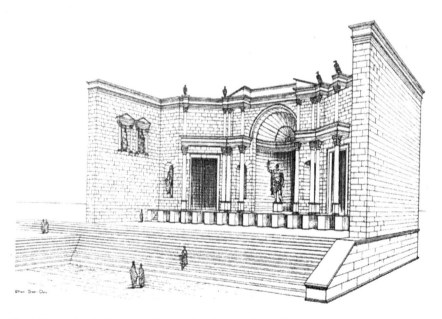

Fig. 2 Illustration by Eran Ben-Dov and Arthur Segal. Used by permission.

that even the positioning of clergy and other authority figures in those basilicas-*cum*-churches perhaps resembled the previous placement of Roman political officials. However, there is more than architectural borrowing happening—or rather, *not* happening—in the central niche of St. Cecilia's. That is to say, the adaptation of the form is almost the same, but not quite: it can be interpreted fruitfully, as I have done with other images, in the terms of colonial mimicry. This Roman Catholic church is a suggestive adaptation of a Roman imperial shrine, but at its precise focal point—where the emperor should be—the niche is empty. There is no statue of Christ, the triumphant "son of God" more powerful than Caesar. The Son of God is not there.

Or so I thought, at first glance. Walking closer, one can see that the niche is indeed empty of a statue, but it does contain two images. Just below where the colossus would be, there stands a small crucifix, dwarfed by the statues to its right and left and rendered virtually invisible from the pews by the scope of the entire scene. Where the Roman emperor should be, there stands a miniature of the most famous Roman criminal, crucified for sedition against imperial power. The second image is a replica of Da Vinci's *Last Supper* within the niche itself. This celebration of the death of Christ combines with the crucifix image—and the funerary meal celebrated just below it. Together the images make the "empty" niche into a compelling postcolonial enactment, a performance still re-enacted centuries after the conversion of the Empire.

The power of the Roman emperor, a son of god, came down with brutal authority upon Jesus Christ, the crucified Son of God. But for Christians, this power and authority unto death provided a generative grammar to articulate the way in which the crucified one had triumphed. Just as the eagle—the power of Roman conquest—had been mimicked by the Christian dove, so also do Christians mimic the statue-*cum*-cross—the power to punish the conquered. The Roman centurion, at the foot of this cross, proclaimed Christ as *divi filius*. Roman power both challenged and legitimated Jesus' divine sonship. Still today, Christians honor the crucified one in the niche of the emperor—almost the same, but not quite. It is Jesus, the dove on the cross, who became the Roman world's Son of God. What else might the resurrection of this metaphor allow us to see?

ABBREVIATIONS

ABD	*Anchor Bible Dictionary*
ANF	*Ante-Nicene Fathers*
ANRW	*Aufstieg und Niedergang der römischen Welt*
BASOR	*Bulletin of the American Schools of Oriental Research*
BDAG	*A Greek-English Lexicon of the New Testament and Early Christian Literature*
BTB	*Biblical Theology Bulletin*
CBQ	*Catholic Biblical Quarterly*
CCSG	Corpus Christianorum Series Graeca
CIL	*Corpus Inscriptionum Latinarum*
FRLANT	Forschungen zur Religion und Literatur des AT und NT
GCS	Griechischen Christlichen Schriftsteller
HTR	*Harvard Theological Review*
IEJ	*Israel Exploration Journal*
IG	*Inscriptiones Graecae*
IGRR	*Inscriptiones Graecae ad Res Romanas Pertinentes*
JBL	*Journal of Biblical Literature*
JECS	*Journal of Early Christian Studies*
JHS	*Journal of Hellenic Studies*
JRA	*Journal of Roman Archaeology*
JRASup	Journal of Roman Archaeology Supplements
JRS	*Journal of Roman Studies*
JSJSup	Journal for the Study of Judaism Supplements
JSNT	*Journal for the Study of the New Testament*
JTS	*Journal of Theological Studies*
LCL	Loeb Classical Library
NHMS	Nag Hammadi and Manichaean Studies
NIGTC	New International Greek Testament Commentary
NovT	*Novum Testamentum*
NovTSup	Novum Testamentum Supplements
NPNF	*Nicene and Post-Nicene Fathers*
NTS	*New Testament Studies*
OGIS	*Orientis Graecae Inscriptiones Selectae*
OTP	*The Old Testament Pseudepigrapha*
RIC	*Roman Imperial Coinage*
RPC	*Roman Provincial Coinage*

SHA	*Scriptores Historiae Augustae*
SNTSMS	Society of New Testament Studies Monograph eries
TDNT	*Theological Dictionary of the New Testament*
WUNT	Wissenschaftliche Untersuchungen zum Neuen Testament
ZAW	*Zeitschrift für Alttestamentliche Wissenschaft*
ZNW	*Zeitschrift für Neutestamentliche Wissenschaft*
ZPE	*Zeitschrift für Papyrologie und Epigraphik*

Abbreviations for papyri are according to: John F. Oates, Roger S. Bagnall, Sarah J. Clackson, Alexandra A. O'Brien, Joshua D. Sosin, Terry G. Wilfong, and Klaas A. Worp. *Checklist of Greek, Latin, Demotic and Coptic Papyri, Ostraca and* Tablets. Online: http://scriptorium.lib.duke.edu/papyrus/texts/clist.html.

■ NOTES

▨ Introduction

1. Raymond E. Brown, *The Birth of the Messiah* (New York: Doubleday, 1977), 134 n. 6; cf. 29–32.

2. Pope Pius XII, *Divino Afflante Spiritu* 19, official English version reproduced in *The Scripture Documents: An Anthology of Official Catholic Teachings* (ed. Dean P. Béchard, S.J.; Collegeville, Minn.: Liturgical Press, 2002), 128.

3. The Latin "*natum non factum*" is the original translation done by Hilary of Poitiers between 356 and 361. The Western recension of the Niceno-Constantinopolitan Creed (381), confirmed by the Council of Trent and still present in the Roman Missal, uses *genitum* instead of *natum* in this phrase, though the *natum* a few lines earlier is left alone. The Athanasian Creed also prefers *genitum* over *natum*. Cf. Jaroslav Pelikan and Valerie Hotchkiss, eds., *Creeds and Confessions of Faith in the Christian Tradition* (4 vols.; New Haven and London: Yale University Press, 2003), 1:158, 1:672, 1:675.

▨ Chapter 1

1. Throughout I use the shorthand of "Nicea" or "Nicene" to refer to the Niceno-Constantinopolitan Creed, the combination which emerged from the Councils of Nicea (325) and Constantinople (381). There are many translations, of which the most common in English is the 1975 version from the International Consultation on English Texts. The following survey is limited to biblical scholarship on earliest Christianity, but divine sonship is a key concept in the study of later Christian theology, especially from the Nicene era. Important treatments of that era include: Frances M. Young, *From Nicaea to Chalcedon* (Philadelphia: Fortress Press, 1983); Rowan Williams, *Arius: Heresy and Tradition* (London: SCM Press, 1987); R. P. C. Hanson, *The Search for the Christian Doctrine of God: The Arian Controversy 318–381* (Edinburgh: T. & T. Clark, 1988); Lewis Ayres, *Nicaea and Its Legacy: An Approach to Fourth-Century Trinitarian Theology* (Oxford: Oxford University Press, 2004). For an influential challenge to standard interpretations of the controversy, see Robert C. Gregg and Dennis E. Groh, *Early Arianism—A View of Salvation* (Philadelphia: Fortress Press, 1981). For the discussion throughout later theology, see the relevant sections of Adolph Harnack, *History of Dogma* (7 vols.; trans. of 3rd German edition by Neil Buchanan; Gloucester, Mass.: Peter Smith, 1976); Aloys Grillmeier, *Christ in Christian Tradition* (2 vols.; 2d ed.; trans. John Bowden; London: Mowbrays, 1975); cf. Roger Haight, *Jesus, Symbol of God* (Maryknoll, N.Y.: Orbis, 1999), for engagement with the postmodern context of pluralism.

2. There are notable exceptions to this statement, such as Eberhard Jüngel, who used "Son of God" as the guiding example of metaphorical speech in theology. Eberhard Jüngel, "Metaphorische Wahrheit: Erwägungen zur theologischen Relevanz der Metapher als Beitrag zur Hermeneutik einer Narrativen Theologie," in Paul Ricoeur and Eberhard Jüngel, with an introduction by Pierre Gisel, *Metapher: Zur Hermeneutik religiöser Sprache* (Munich: Chr. Kaiser Verlag, 1974), 71–122. Cf. John Dominic Crossan and Jonathan L. Reed,

Excavating Jesus: Beneath the Stones, Behind the Texts (San Francisco: HarperSanFrancisco, 2001), 85–88; and idem, *In Search of Paul: How Jesus' Apostle Opposed Rome's Empire with God's Kingdom* (San Francisco: HarperSanFrancisco, 2004), passim. Crossan and Reed rightly emphasize comparisons between the many titles of Jesus and the Roman emperor, and my work extends one aspect of this comparison, examining the "son of God" connection in more detail.

3. William L. Lane, *The Gospel According to Mark* (Grand Rapids: Eerdmans, 1974), 58. Italics original.

4. Frances M. Young, *The Making of the Creeds* (London: SCM Press; Philadelphia: Trinity Press International, 1981), 65, describes the chief issue of Nicea as how to put the Son/Logos on the side of "radical transcendence."

5. Simon J. Gathercole, *The Preexistent Son: Recovering the Christologies of Matthew, Mark, and Luke* (Grand Rapids: Eerdmans, 2006), 1. For a strong critique of Gathercole's exegesis, see Adela Yarbro Collins and John J. Collins, *King and Messiah as Son of God* (Grand Rapids: Eerdmans, 2008), 123–26.

6. Gathercole, *Preexistent Son*, 274.

7. Ibid., 276.

8. For another example of concern about Jesus' "unique metaphysical" sonship, see I. Howard Marshall, "The Divine Sonship of Jesus," *Interpretation* 21 (1967): 87–103. His exegesis of the Gospels seems to begin from the "one-in-being" part of the Creed.

9. Gathercole, *Preexistent Son*, 79.

10. Richard Bauckham, "The Sonship of the Historical Jesus in Christology," *Scottish Journal of Theology* 31 (1978): 249. He relies on the earlier argument of Jeremias, that "In Jesus' eyes, being a child of God is not a gift of creation, but an eschatological gift of salvation." (Joachim Jeremias, *New Testament Theology* [New York: Scribner, 1971], 181).

11. Bauckham, "Sonship," 257–58. Similar arguments are found in William R. G. Loader, "The Apocalyptic Model of Sonship: Its Origin and Development in New Testament Tradition," *JBL* 97 (1978): 525–54; James D. G. Dunn, *Christology in the Making: A New Testament Inquiry into the Origins of the Doctrine of the Incarnation* (2nd ed.; Grand Rapids: Eerdmans, 1989), 12–64. Regarding Paul's view of divine sonship, a similar point is argued by Karl-Josef Kuschel, *Born Before All Time? The Dispute Over Christ's Origin* (trans. John Bowden; London: SCM Press, 1992), 305–08.

12. On the method of narrative criticism, see Mark Alan Powell, *What Is Narrative Criticism?* (Minneapolis: Fortress, 1990); this method's challenge to historical criticism is deftly laid out in Stephen D. Moore, *Literary Criticism and the Gospels* (New Haven: Yale University Press, 1989).

13. Jack Dean Kingsbury, *Matthew as Story* (2nd ed.; Minneapolis: Fortress, 1988), 38; cited in Powell, *Narrative*, 20.

14. Donald J. Verseput, "The Role and Meaning of the 'Son of God' Title in Matthew's Gospel," *NTS* 33 (1987): 532. Italics original.

15. Verseput, "Role and Meaning," 532. This argument is demonstrated more fully by John Nolland, "No Son-of-God Christology in Matthew 1.18–25," *JSNT* 62 (1996): 3–12.

16. Verseput, "Role and Meaning," 539–40.

17. Ibid., 541.

18. Matthew's use of "son of God" language has been problematic for dogmatic Christology because he uses the term explicitly for Jesus' followers (e.g., the "peacemakers" are called "sons of God" in Mt 5:9).

19. On the use of the same Greek word (γένεσις) in Matt 1:1 and 1:18, see John Nolland, *The Gospel of Matthew: A Commentary on the Greek Text* (NIGTC; Grand Rapids: Eerdmans; Bletchley: Paternoster Press, 2005), 71; and Raymond E. Brown, *The Birth of the Messiah* (New York: Doubleday, 1977), 58 and 123.

20. Verseput, "Role and Meaning," 533.

21. Cf. Yigal Levin, "Jesus, 'Son of God' and 'Son of David': The 'Adoption' of Jesus into the Davidic Line," *JSNT* 28 (2006): 415–42.

22. Verseput, "Role and Meaning," 536. For a full defense, see Brian M. Nolan, *The Royal Son of God: The Christology of Matthew 1–2 in the Setting of the Gospel* (Fribourg: Éditions universitaires; Göttingen: Vandenhoeck & Ruprecht, 1979).

23. Jack Dean Kingsbury, *The Christology of Mark's Gospel* (Philadelphia: Fortress, 1983).

24. Ibid., 66.

25. The secrecy motif was identified and coined by Wilhelm Wrede, *Das Messiasgeheimnis in den Evangelien: Zugleich ein Beitrag zum Verständnis des Markusevangeliums* (Göttingen: Vandenhoeck & Ruprecht, 1901); *The Messianic Secret* (trans. J. C. G. Greig; Cambridge: James Clarke, 1971).

26. Kingsbury, *Christology*, 141.

27. Charles G. Dennison, "How Is Jesus the Son of God? Luke's Baptism Narrative and Christology," *Calvin Theological Journal* 17 (1982): 6–25. A related treatment of Luke is Malcolm Wren, "Sonship in Luke: The Advantage of a Literary Approach," *Scottish Journal of Theology* 37 (1984): 301–11.

28. Dennison, "How Is Jesus the Son of God?," 22. Italics original.

29. Dennison, "How Is Jesus the Son of God?," 24–25.

30. Cf. quotation of Athanasius at the end of this chapter.

31. Wren's essay on Luke argues a similar point: "Luke seems to be confusing the issue [of Jesus' divine sonship] deliberately in order to underline the impossibility of making total sense of Jesus. The principal literary effect of chapter 3 is that, in demonstrating the impossibility of defining the term 'son of God' in a rational sense, it leads us to expect of the remainder of the text a solution to the question 'What is the Son of God?' in terms of the role and activity of the person. Luke's is a narrative where meanings come from the portrayal of a life, rather than a discourse where meanings are presented in definitions." Wren, "Sonship in Luke," 309–10.

32. Dennison, "How is Jesus the Son of God?," 11.

33. The *religionsgeschichtliche Schule* had concentric circles, at the center of which was Wilhelm Bousset. Others near the center included Albert Eichhorn, Hermann Gunkel, Wilhelm Heitmüller, and Johannes Weiss. Franz Cumont and Richard Reitzenstein provided much of the data on Hellenistic religion that catalyzed the school's research on the New Testament and early Christianity. Cf. William Baird, *History of New Testament Research*, Vol. 2 (Minneapolis: Fortress, 2003), 221–53, and literature cited there.

34. This presupposition—or rather, its extravagant use—was decried in the middle of the century on the largest stage for biblical scholars, during Samuel Sandmel's SBL Presidential Address; cf. Samuel Sandmel, "Parallelomania," *JBL* 81 (1962): 1–13. He criticizes "that extravagance among scholars which first overdoes the supposed similarity in passages and then proceeds to describe source and derivation as if implying literary connection flowing in an inevitable or predetermined direction" (p. 1). The tendency is especially heightened when new data arrives on the scene, as it did for the *religionsgeschichtliche Schule* in the form of Hellenistic religious texts and for mid-century scholars in the form of the Dead Sea Scrolls (about which Sandmel speaks at some length) and the Nag Hammadi hoard.

35. This presupposition was made explicit by Bousset, who traced the progressive evolution of religion up to its apex with Jesus and Paul in the first century; cf. Wilhelm Bousset, *Das Wesen der Religion: Dargestellt an ihrer Geschichte* (3d ed.; Halle: Gebauer-Schwetschke, 1906); *What Is Religion?* (trans. F. B. Low; New York: G.B. Putnam, 1907).

36. As has been often noted, the "s" in *religion-s-geschichte* is not plural but genitival—the history of one religion is at issue. The river metaphor is more evident in German, where notions of "influence" (*Einfluß, beeinflußen*) are etymologically connected to the word for river (*Fluß*).

37. Baird, *History*, 243.

38. Wilhelm Bousset, *Kyrios Christos: Geschichte des Christusglaubens von den Anfängen des Christentums bis Irenaeus* (4th ed.; Göttingen: Vandenhoeck & Ruprecht, 1935); quotations from *Kyrios Christos* (trans. John E. Steely; Nashville: Abingdon, 1970). The titular approach to Christology on display in Bousset's analysis was later delineated and brought into scholarship through a similar work by Ferdinand Hahn, *Christologische Hoheitstitel* (Göttingen: Vandenhoeck & Ruprecht, 1963); *The Titles of Jesus in Christology* (trans. Harold Knight and George Ogg; London: Lutterworth, 1969).

39. Bousset, *Kyrios*, 93.

40. Ibid., 93–96.

41. Ibid., 97.

42. For confirmation of this, see the wide semantic range on display in Adela Yarbro Collins, "Mark and His Readers: The Son of God among Jews," *HTR* 92 (1999): 393–408; and eadem, "Mark and His Readers: The Son of God among Greeks and Romans," *HTR* 93 (2000): 85–100; both discussed below.

43. Bousset, *Kyrios*, 206–07.

44. Ibid., 207. German of first quotation: "ein überweltliches, in engster metaphysischer Beziehung zu Gott stehendes Wesen."

45. Ibid., 208–09. German: "die göttliche vorweltliche Wesenheit."

46. The German words are "Wirklichkeit" and "Wesenheit."

47. Ibid., 207.

48. Ibid., 207 n. 142.

49. Ibid., 209.

50. Ibid., 213.

51. I grant that his book is primarily about the κύριος title, which is not important for John. This gap left an opening for the work of Matthew Vellanickal, *The Divine Sonship of Christians in the Johannine Writings* (Analecta Biblica 72; Rome: Biblical Institute Press, 1977).

52. Bousset, *Kyrios*, 213.

53. Ibid., 215, 227–242. Contra Bousset, see chap. 5 on John Ashton's interpretation of Father-Son unity in John.

54. Bousset, *Kyrios*, 235.

55. This interpretation seems to rely on the Gnostic "redeemer myth" that had just begun to enter the dogma of the *religionsgeschichtliche Schule*, mostly through the work of Richard Reitzenstein on the *Corpus Hermeticum*. Defending the relevance of this myth were Richard Reitzenstein, *Die hellenistichen Mysterienreligionen: Nach ihren Grundgedanken und Wirkungen*, (3d ed., 1927; repr. Stuttgart: B.G. Teubner, 1956); ET: *Hellenistic Mystery-Religions: Their Basic Ideas and Significance* (trans. John E. Steely; Pittsburgh: Pickwick Press, 1987) and Rudolf Bultmann, "Die Bedeutung der neuerschlossenen mandäischen und manichäischen

Quellen für das Verständnis des Johannesevangeliums," in *Exegetica: Aufsätze zur Erforschung des Neuen Testaments* (ed. Erich Dinkler; Tübingen: J. C. B. Mohr [Paul Siebeck], 1967), 10–35, while later scholars like Carsten Colpe, *Die religionsgeschichtliche Schule: Darstellung und Kritik ihres Bildes vom gnostichen Erlösermythus* (FRLANT 78; Göttingen: Vandenhoeck & Ruprecht, 1961), and Edwin M. Yamauchi, *Pre-Christian Gnosticism: A Survey of the Proposed Evidences* (Grand Rapids, Mich.: Eerdmans, 1973), offered sharp criticisms. The interpretation of Christology according to a purported pre-Christian Gnosticism, though important for understanding twentieth-century biblical scholarship, will not be treated here.

56. Bousset, *Kyrios*, 215.

57. Ibid., 210.

58. With respect to divine sonship, the division of the Synoptics from Paul and John is widespread in the work of this group of scholars. For another example, see Eduard Schweizer, "Variety and Unity in the New Testament Proclamation of Jesus as the Son of God," *Australian Biblical Review* 15 (1967): 1–12.

59. Bousset, *Kyrios*, 342.

60. Ibid., 344. German: "eine volkstümliche Vergröberung der Idee des überweltlichen Gottessohnes."

61. Bousset, *Kyrios*, 344. German: "Man wird sich deshalb auch der Folgerung nicht entziehen können, daß auf diese Vulgärtheologie des jungen Christentums Einflüsse des umgebenden hellenistichen Milieus eingewirkt haben."

62. A shorter work on the topic was completed just earlier by Petr Pokorný, *Der Gottessohn: Literarische Übersicht und Fragestellung* (Zürich: Theologischer Verlag, 1971), which was a summary of ancient sources with some ramifications for theology.

63. Martin Hengel, *Der Sohn Gottes, Die Entstehung der Christologie und die jüdisch-hellenistische Religionsgeschichte* (Tübingen: J.C.B. Mohr [Paul Siebeck], 1975); *The Son of God* (trans. John Bowden; London: SCM; Philadelphia: Fortress, 1977). Page numbers from English version.

64. Hengel, *Son of God*, 8.

65. The German "*Duktus*" or "duct" behind the English translation "trend" fits nicely our previous comparison to a river. If the *Schule* tried to chart the flow of the Christian river, this "son of God" question is a key component in the flow. Hengel, *Son of God*, 18.

66. Hengel, *Son of God*, 40.

67. Ibid., 30.

68. Ibid., 30. German: "Die offiziell-profane Staatsreligion war bestenfalls negativer Anstoß, nicht Vorbild."

69. E.g., Helmut Koester, *Ancient Christian Gospels: Their History and Development* (Philadelphia: Trinity Press; London: SCM, 1990), 1–4; quoted in Adela Yarbro Collins, *Mark: A Commentary* (ed. Harold W. Attridge; Hermeneia; Philadelphia: Fortress Press, 2007), 130 n. 2. See also chap. 4, on connections between Mark and Rome.

70. Graham N. Stanton, *Jesus and Gospel* (Cambridge: Cambridge University Press, 2004), 2; quoted in Yarbro Collins, *Mark*, 130 n. 2. Italics original.

71. As critical theory has demonstrated, there are more than two options (appropriation or rejection) when cultures and their symbols encounter one another. Postcolonial theory proves especially useful, as in chapter 4 below, to illuminate how early Christians understood Jesus' exaltation vis-à-vis the Roman imperial ideology.

72. The German "*Anstoß*" behind the English translation "stimulus" can mean "initiative, impetus, nudge, etc.," but it often has a negative connotation of "offense," as with the adjective

"*anstößig*" or "offensive." The noun is also used for the "kickoff" of a soccer/*Fußball* match: did the imperial usage of the title "kick off" a culture/counterculture competition for who was the preeminent son of God in the Roman world?

73. Hengel, *Son of God*, 42.

74. Ibid., 57.

75. Ibid., 58.

76. Ibid., 66.

77. Ibid., 67–71.

78. Dunn, *Christology*, 12–64.

79. Ibid., xiv. Cf. idem, "In Defence of a Methdology," *ExpT* 95 (1983–84): 295–99.

80. Ibid., xvi.

81. On one important detail, Hengel is more precise than Dunn. Dunn conflates the various sons of named gods in the Greco-Roman world ("son of Hercules," etc.) with the much less common "son of God" title. The bare title "son of God" for an individual was less common than Dunn's summary implies. Dunn, *Christology*, 14–16.

82. Dunn, *Christology*, 22.

83. Ibid., 32.

84. Ibid., 36.

85. Ibid., 36–46.

86. Ibid., 46–50.

87. Cf. below, chap. 5, on this topic. Liturgical commemorations of Jesus Christ also moved backwards in his own life as the Church moved forward in time. Early liturgies primarily celebrated his death and resurrection. Furthermore, the feast of his Baptism/Epiphany was more prominent than the feast of Nativity (which did not gain prominence until the late-fourth century and was still joined to or overshadowed by Epiphany in the East after that). Cf. Hermann Usener, *Religionsgeschichtliche Untersuchungen. Erster Theil: Das Weihnachtsfest* (Bonn, 1889).

88. Dunn, *Christology*, 54.

89. Ibid., 59.

90. Ibid., 64.

91. Ibid., 62.

92. I am here alluding to descriptions of low Christologies by ancient heresiologists: *nudus homo* (e.g., Irenaeus, *Haer.* 3.19; Tertullian, *Carn. Christ.* 14.5) or ψιλὸς ἄνθρωπος (e.g., Eusebius, *Hist. eccl.* 5.28; 6.17; *Eccl. theol.* 1.45.)

93. Larry W. Hurtado, *Lord Jesus Christ: Devotion to Jesus in Earliest Christianity* (Grand Rapids: Eerdmans, 2003), 11–12. Though he apparently did not invent the label, attributing it to Hengel, Hurtado "think[s] there is reason to describe this more recent body of work as constituting a 'new history-of-religions' effort that can be linked with and likened to the classic efforts of the Göttingen circle."

94. Besides the reviews cited below, see that of Stephen E. Fowl in *Modern Theology* 22 (2006): 152–54; Luke Timothy Johnson in *Scottish Journal of Theology* 59 (2006): 358–62; and the long review by Maurice Casey, "Lord Jesus Christ: A Reponse to Professor Hurtado," *JSNT* 27 (2004): 83–96, and Hurtado's response (97–104).

95. Hurtado, *Lord Jesus Christ*, 2. By "extraneous," I take Hurtado to mean its etymological but lesser-used sense of "external" or "foreign." If he means "extraneous" in its more frequently used sense of "irrelevant," then he is arguing against a straw man.

96. Hurtado, *Lord Jesus Christ*, 653.

97. Ibid., 2–3.

98. Ibid., 3.

99. Ibid., 22.

100. Ibid., 22. Italics original.

101. Larry W. Hurtado, "Son of God," *Dictionary of Paul and His Letters* (ed. G. F. Hawthorne et al.; Downers Grove, Ill.: InterVarsity, 1997), 900; cf. Hurtado, *Lord Jesus Christ*, 101–8.

102. Hurtado, *Lord Jesus Christ*, 171.

103. Hurtado, "Son of God," 900.

104. Hurtado, *Lord Jesus Christ*, 253.

105. The "Johannine thunderbolt" is Luke 10:22–23//Matthew 11:25–27.

106. Hurtado, *Lord Jesus Christ*, 287, 306.

107. Ibid., 306.

108. Ibid., 358–63.

109. Ibid., 362.

110. On this key aspect of Johannine thought, see chap. 5 below and also the excellent analysis in Vellanickal, *Divine Sonship*, 89–351. It is distinguished in metaphorical imagery (though not necessarily in functional meaning) from the adoptive sonship of Christians in the Pauline writings.

111. Cf. 1 John 2:29–3:10; 4:7–8; 5:1–4. The similarity is most explicit in 1 John 5:18.

112. William Horbury, review of Larry W. Hurtado, *Lord Jesus Christ: Devotion to Jesus in Earliest Christianity*, *JTS* 56 (2005): 537–38.

113. Horbury, review of Hurtado, 536.

114. After using "scrupulous" early in the book (34–38), Hurtado settles on the term "devout" (passim).

115. Larry W. Hurtado, "First-Century Jewish Monotheism," *JSNT* 71 (1998): 3–26; repr. as chap. 5 of *How on Earth Did Jesus Become a God?* (Grand Rapids: Eerdmans, 2005), 111–33; see esp. 117, 121, 127–28. Here too we find one instance of Jews both "scrupulous" *and* "devout"—a super group able to avoid syncretism (125).

116. Cf. the first four chapters of *How on Earth Did Jesus Become a God?* in which "devout Jews" is predominant.

117. Paula Fredriksen, review of Larry W. Hurtado, *Lord Jesus Christ: Devotion to Jesus in Earliest Christianity*, *JECS* 12 (2004): 539.

118. Fredriksen, review of Hurtado, 541.

119. A helpful balance to this view, concerning Galilee in particular, is Mark A. Chancey, *The Myth of a Gentile Galilee* (SNTSMS 118; Cambridge: Cambridge University Press, 2002).

120. Clement of Alexandria, *Strom.* 1.5.29.

121. The most poetic use of the metaphor comes in Grillmeier's depiction of how Christology diffused in the second century before coming together again: "In the second century, the Christian tradition is like a young stream, coming down from the mountains, which can now for the first time spread itself on a broad landscape and extend into a lake. The landscape becomes wider and more varied, but at the same time less noble. The lake threatens to lose itself at the edges and to form stagnant water. But then at last the river again re-forms, to go on its way more strongly and more swiftly than before." The broad lake comprises the pseudonymous and apocryphal works of the second century, while the re-formed river includes the proto-orthodox witnesses of that era. Grillmeier, *Christ in Christian Tradition*, 1:53–54.

122. Hurtado, *Lord Jesus Christ*, chapter 8, "The Second Century—Importance and Tributaries," and chapter 9, "Radical Diversity."

123. Hurtado, *Lord Jesus Christ*, 2.

124. Walter Bauer, *Orthodoxy and Heresy in Earliest Christianity* (trans. by a team from the Philadelphia Seminar on Christian Origins; ed. Robert A. Kraft and Gerhard Krodel; Philadelphia: Fortress Press, 1971); original ed.: *Rechtgläubigkeit und Ketzerei im ältesten Christentum* (Tübingen: Mohr, 1934).

125. Hurtado's avoidance of ruler cults in his argument has also been noted by Adela Yarbro Collins, "'How on Earth Did Jesus Become a God?' A Reply," in *Israel's God and Rebecca's Children: Christology and Community in Early Judaism and Christianity* (ed. David B. Capes, April D. DeConick, Helen K. Bond, and Troy A. Miller; Waco: Baylor University Press, 2007), 55–66.

126. The challenge, which will not be taken up here, is from Crispin H. T. Fletcher-Louis, "The Worship of Divine Humanity as God's Image and the Worship of Jesus," in *The Jewish Roots of Christological Monotheism* (ed. Carey C. Newman, James R. Davila, and Gladys S. Lewis; JSJSup 63; Leiden: Brill, 1999), 112–28. Fletcher-Louis's work on angels and other intermediary beings shows another possible accounting for the development of Christology. Cf. Crispin H. T. Fletcher-Louis, *Luke-Acts: Angels, Christology, and Soteriology* (WUNT II 94; Tübingen: Mohr Siebeck, 1997).

127. Quotations in this paragraph are from Hurtado, *Lord Jesus Christ*, 38.

128. This is a truism of social-scientific studies, philosophically elaborated by Pierre Bourdieu, *The Logic of Practice* (trans. Richard Nice; Cambridge: Polity, 1990).

129. Hurtado, *Lord Jesus Christ*, 75–76. See his other assessments of language used for the emperor at 21, 92, 102, 108–9, and 516–17. Throughout the book, when the emperor or other "foreign" influences are mentioned, they are often positioned with a false dichotomy: Christianity either rejects or appropriates the foreign elements. But theorists of religion and identity present more complex and nuanced descriptions of cultural interaction, some of which will be used later in my argument. Hurtado seems to know the dichotomy is false, admitting it at least once (75), but he does not incorporate theories of cultural interaction in his analysis. Cf. also his interpretation of Ignatius vis-à-vis emperor worship (638), and idem, "Christ-Devotion in the First Two Centuries: Reflections and a Proposal," *Toronto Journal of Theology* 12 (1996): 17–33.

130. Notably Lily Ross Taylor, *The Divinity of the Roman Emperor* (Middletown, Conn.: American Philological Association, 1931).

131. Here I allude to the playful and often illuminating work, Keith Hopkins, *A World Full of Gods* (New York: Free Press, 2000).

132. Adolf Deissmann, *Licht vom Osten: das Neue Testament und die neuentdeckten Texte der hellenistisch-römischen Welt* (2d and 3d ed.; Tübingen: Mohr, 1909); Crossan and Reed, *In Search of Paul*.

133. Yarbro Collins, "The Son of God among Jews," and "The Son of God among Greeks and Romans." The subsequent quotations are from her methodological outline in eadem, "Among Jews," 393. Though I am calling this the method of a fourth "group," one which can be traced back to Adolf Deissmann, I treat only Yarbro Collins's work here because hers is the only example I know of that applies the method uniquely to divine sonship. The other giant figure in this group is John Dominic Crossan, whose work with Jonathan L. Reed on Jesus and Paul in their Roman imperial contexts is among the most impressive examples of this burgeoning field. His research is primarily synthetic, however—and excels in that

vein—so that he does not offer a sustained "thick" description and analysis of the sonship motif in Roman imperial society and early Christian theology. That I have benefited much from Crossan and Reed should be evident from the thrust of my book.

134. For example, her interpretation of the blasphemy encounter with the high priest, Yarbro Collins, "Among Jews," 404–5.

135. An example of this phrasing is from Yarbro Collins, "Among Jews," 400.

136. Yarbro Collins, "Among Jews," 394. The history and interpretation of "Son of God" as a royal and messianic title among ancient Jews and early Christians is given a longer treatment in Collins and Collins, *King and Messiah*.

137. Yarbro Collins, "Among Jews," 408.

138. Yarbro Collins, "Among Greeks and Romans," 86.

139. Ibid., 98. I would add Egyptian usage as well, due to their regard for divine succession among their rulers. Augustus's situating himself as *divi filius* would have resonated with the native Egyptian ideology of divine rulers. Cf. Günther Hölbl, *Altägypten im römischen Reich: der römische Pharao und seine Tempel* (3 vols.; Mainz: Philipp von Zabern, 2000–05), 1:22–46.

140. My method is thus related to New Historicism, and connections to Foucauldian interpretation will be unavoidable, since my specific subject involves power relations—between fathers and sons, emperor and subjects, the Roman gods and the God of Jesus Christ.

141. Mark Antony even claimed descent from the obscure (and too-conveniently named) "Anton," a son of Hercules. A statue of Hercules as Antony's ancestor was probably set up in Rome (cf. Taylor, *Divinity*, 107). On the Antony-Hercules connection, cf. Appian, *Civil Wars* 3.16–19.

142. Clifford Geertz, "Thick Description: Toward an Interpretive Theory of Culture," in *The Interpretation of Cultures: Selected Essays* (New York: Basic Books, 1973), 3–30.

143. Clifford Ando, *Imperial Ideology and Provincial Loyalty in the Roman Empire* (Berkeley: University of California Press, 2000), 392. The emperor held this role alone for four centuries, until the universalizing of Christianity by Theodosius I (380 C.E.).

144. A noteworthy exception is the work of Mary Rose D'Angelo, who has studied Roman family relationships in order to understand early Christian family language, e.g., "Abba and 'Father': Imperial Theology and the Jesus Traditions," *JBL* 111 (1992): 611–30. See also Halvor Moxnes, ed., *Constructing Early Christian Families: Family as Social Reality and Metaphor* (London; New York: Routledge, 1997).

145. I call this a "presupposition" of my work primarily to indicate the unfortunate fact that I will not labor to defend it in this book. Although the "religion and politics" nexus is a foundation of my thinking about early Christianity, it will have to remain—for now—a presupposition that I do not have the space to explore and defend. For excellent essays on this interface in general, see Peter Scott and William T. Cavanaugh, eds., *The Blackwell Companion to Political Theology* (Malden, Mass.: Blackwell, 2004). In the Roman context, Jörg Rüpke notes the connection between theology and political ideology. Of the burgeoning imperial ideology, he writes: "A slowly developing absolute monarchy and a monistic world view . . . are snug bed-fellows. Chicken-and-egg-like, they exercise a mutual influence upon one another—sometimes, through failure to be flexible, for the worse." Jörg Rüpke, *Religion of the Romans* (trans. Richard Gordon; Cambridge: Polity, 2007), 78, 84. Original ed.: *Die Religion der Römer* (Munich: Beck, 2001).

146. Hurtado, *Lord Jesus Christ*, 653.

147. Some exceptions to this sweeping criticism will be noted in the next chapter.

■ Chapter 2

1. Cf. S. R. F. Price, *Rituals and Power: The Roman Imperial Cult in Asia Minor* (Cambridge: Cambridge University Press, 1984), 5–7.

2. Discussion in Willem den Boer, ed., *Le Culte des Souverains dans l'Empire Romain* (Entretiens sur l'antiquitè classique 19; Vandœuvres-Genève: Fondation Hardt, 1973), 37. In the same conference volume (p. 12), Bickerman similarly wanted to understand Roman religion "not according to our ideas of religion, or on authority of Roman intellectuals" but with regard to "rites, auspices, and the interpretation of omens."

3. John Scheid, *An Introduction to Roman Religion* (trans. Janet Lloyd; Bloomington: Indiana University Press, 2003), 183; trans. of *La Religion des Romans* (Paris: Armand Colin/Masson, 1998). Elsewhere he comments, "The speculations on the ultimate nature of the divine in which philosophers of antiquity sometimes indulged have nothing to do with the Roman religion of ritual and sanctuaries and amount rather to an attempt to reduce polytheism to monotheism" (158). Jörg Rüpke foregrounds philosophical systems in his presentation of Roman divinity, but only in order to demonstrate their limited usefulness—to leave them behind for the rest of the study. Jörg Rüpke, *Religion of the Romans* (trans. Richard Gordon; Cambridge: Polity, 2007), 65–68; trans. of *Die Religion der Römer* (München: Beck, 2001).

4. Cicero, *Acad.* 1.9. Cited also by Arnaldo Momigliano, "The Theological Efforts of the Roman Upper Classes in the First Century BC," *CP* 79 (1984): 199–211.

5. Ittai Gradel, *Emperor Worship and Roman Religion* (Oxford: Clarendon Press, 2002), 3.

6. Many of the shifts in the field have been helpfully delineated by James B. Rives, "Roman Religion Revived," *Phoenix* 52 (1998): 345–65.

7. These assumptions are tilted toward the priorities typically associated with Protestant Christianity. Price, *Rituals*, esp. 10–15. On these points, Price uses as a foil the work of J. H. W. G. Liebeschuetz, *Continuity and Change in Roman Religion* (Oxford: Oxford University Press, 1979).

8. Some of the data were not actually "new" but were buried in old volumes of the antiquarian approach to ancient religion—lists of priesthoods, inscriptions, altars, etc. E.g., Georg Wissowa, *Religion und Kultus der Römer* (2nd ed.; München: C.H. Beck, 1912).

9. See below for Alföldy's assessment of the broad appeal of emperor worship.

10. E.g., Price, *Rituals*, 241–42. Mary Beard, John North, and Simon Price, *Religions of Rome, Volume I: A History* (Cambridge: Cambridge University Press, 1998), 43, note the impossibility of extricating religion from other aspects of Roman society. For a critical analysis of using the category "religion" in the study of the Roman Empire, see Brent Nongbri, "Dislodging 'Embedded' Religion: A Brief Note on a Scholarly Trope," *Numen* 55 (2008): 440–60.

11. E.g., Price, *Rituals*, 248.

12. Clifford Ando, "Idols and Their Critics," in *The Matter of the Gods: Religion and the Roman Empire* (Berkeley: University of California Press, 2008), 21–42.

13. Rüpke, *Religion*, 69–74, and James B. Rives, *Religion in the Roman Empire* (Malden, Mass.: Blackwell, 2007), 32–37, also treat this issue.

14. Otto Weinreich, "Antikes Gottmenschentum," *Neue Jahrbücher für Wissenschaft und Jugendbildung* 2 (1926): 633; repr. in *Römischer Kaiserkult* (ed. Antonie Wlosok; Wege der Forschung 372; Darmstadt: Wissenschaftliche Buchgesellschaft, 1978), 55. Trans. my own. I offer this quotation as a concise statement of a perspective and not as a criticism of the

remainder of Weinreich's article. The position is still defended by Peter Herz, "Der römische Kaiser und der Kaiserkult: Gott oder primus inter pares?", in *Menschwerdung Gottes— Vergöttlichung von Menschen* (ed. Dieter Zeller; Novum Testamentum et Orbis Antiquus 7; Freiburg: Universitätsverlag; Göttingen: Vandenhoeck & Ruprecht, 1988), esp. 135–40.

15. Rudolf Otto, *The Idea of the Holy* (trans. John W. Harvey; London: Humphrey Milford, Oxford University Press, 1925), 25—a phrase used also by Kierkegaard and Barth.

16. On this topic, see Paula Fredriksen, "Mandatory Retirement: Ideas in the Study of Christian Origins Whose Time Has Come to Go," *Studies in Religion / Sciences Religieuses* 35/2 (2006): esp. 241–43. A wide-ranging critique of constructions of monotheism is found in Henry Corbin, *Le Paradoxe du Monotheisme* (Paris: Éditions de l'Herne, 1981).

17. Neither were pagan thinkers as polytheistic as the dichotomy suggests. The main philosophical trajectory from Plato through late antiquity and into the Islamic era was trending toward monotheism (a trend in which Christianity came to fit nicely, after a few centuries of conceptual tinkering). Cf. Robert M. Grant, *Gods and the One God* (Philadelphia: Westminster Press, 1986); and the excellent set of essays, *Pagan Monotheism in Late Antiquity* (ed. Polymnia Athanassiadi and Michael Frede; Oxford: Clarendon, 1999), esp. the summary of the issue in Polymnia Athanassiadi and Michael Frede, "Introduction," 1–20.

18. On the inclusion of Jews in this argument, see Paula Fredriksen, "What 'Parting of the Ways'?," in *The Ways that Never Parted* (ed. Adam Becker and Annette Yoshiko Reed; Tübingen: Mohr Siebeck, 2003), 35–63.

19. On the martyrs, see now Candida R. Moss, *The Other Christs: Imitating Jesus in Ancient Christian Ideologies of Martyrdom* (New York: Oxford University Press, 2010), esp. chap. 5, "Martyr as Divine Heir."

20. Fredriksen's call for the "mandatory retirement" of the category "monotheism" in the study of ancient religion is perhaps too strong, but her argument generally hits the mark. Scholars have used the term anachronistically when describing ancient phenomena. Fredriksen, "Mandatory Retirement," 231.

21. Arthur Darby Nock, "Notes on Ruler Cult I-IV," *JHS* 48 (1928): 31; repr. in *Essays on Religion and the Ancient World* (2 vols.; ed. Zeph Stewart; Cambridge, Mass.: Harvard University Press, 1972), 1:145. Nock is often cited as promoting a distinction between "homage" and "worship" with regard to ruler cults, but he warns, "our distinction between worship and homage, *Kultus* and *Ehrung*, did not exist with anything like comparable sharpness in antiquity." Arthur Darby Nock, "ΣΥΝΝΑΟΣ ΘΕΟΣ," *HSCP* 41 (1930): 52; repr. in *Essays*, 1:241.

22. Hans-Josef Klauck, *Die religiöse Umwelt des Urchristentums II: Herrscher- und Kaiserkult, Philosophie, Gnosis* (Kohlhammer-Studienbücher Theologie 9.2; Stuttgart: Kohlhammer, 1996), 72.

23. Many different metaphors are used to express the notion: gradient, spectrum, sliding scale, etc. Cf. Duncan Fishwick, *The Imperial Cult in the Latin West* (2 vols.; Leiden: Brill, 1987–92), 1:33, "divine and human honours differed in degree but not in kind; both belong at different intervals on essentially the same scale." In her book on the divine qualities or abstractions in Republican Rome, Gillian Clark notes the "fluid boundaries" between deities and divine qualities. Gillian Clark, *Divine Qualities: Cult and Community in Republican Rome* (Oxford: Oxford University Press, 2007), 25. Cf. the discussion of "the nature of the divine" in Rives, *Religion*, 15–21.

24. J. M. C. Toynbee, "Ruler-apotheosis in ancient Rome," *Numismatic Chronicle* 7 (1947): 126–27. Cf. her similar remarks in the review of H. P. L'Orange, *Apotheosis in Ancient*

Portraiture, JRS 38 (1948): 160–63. It should be noted that, as an art historian, she was immersed in the images and rituals of antiquity and thus less prone to construing it through philosophical models alone.

25. J. Rufus Fears, *Princeps a diis electus: the Divine Election of the Emperor as a Political Concept at Rome* (Rome: American Academy in Rome, 1977), 131.

26. Gradel, *Emperor Worship*, 25–26.

27. Others seeing emperor worship as a coherent aspect of Roman religion are Manfred Clauss, *Kaiser und Gott: Herrscherkult im römischen Reich* (Stuttgart; Leipzig: Tuebner, 1999); and Rüpke, *Religion*, 85.

28. *IGRR* 4.39, col. b, lines 12–18; cited also in Paul Zanker, *The Power of Images in the Age of Augustus* (trans. Alan Shapiro; Ann Arbor: University of Michigan Press, 1988), 304, and Price, *Rituals*, 243 no. 31. Greek: εἰ δέ τι τούτων ἐπικυδέστερον τοῖς μετέπειτα χρόνοις εὑρεθήσεται, πρὸς μη[δὲν] τῶν θεοποιεῖν αὐτὸν ἐπὶ [πλέ]ον δυνησομένων ἐλλείψει[ν] τὴν τῆς πόλεως προθυμίαν καὶ εὐσέβειαν. Although the word [πλέ]ον is partially damaged, its reconstruction is in line with other inscriptions that increase honors to various gods, e.g., *OGIS* 1.56A.9: τὰς τιμὰς τῶν θεῶν ἐπὶ πλέον αὔξοντες.

29. I prefer the term "emperor worship" to "imperial cult," as has probably become clear by now, for reasons explained later (cf. Gradel, *Emperor Worship*, 7). In this section, I cannot treat the larger subject of "ruler cult" in antiquity, which can be surveyed with the help of: Arthur Darby Nock, "ΣΥΝΝΑΟΣ ΘΕΟΣ"; Christian Habicht, *Gottmenschentum und Griechische Städte* (2nd ed.; München: Book, 1970); Simon R. F. Price, "Hellenistic Cities and Their Rulers," in *Rituals*, 23–52; Frank W. Walbank, "Könige als Götter: Überlegungen zum Herrscherkult von Alexander bis Augustus," *Chiron* 17 (1987): 365–82; R. R. R. Smith, *Hellenistic Royal Portraits* (Oxford: Clarendon, 1988); Frank Kolb, *Herrscherideologie in der Spätantike* (Berlin: Akademie Verlag, 2001); and Angelos Chaniotis, "The Divinity of the Hellenistic Rulers," in *A Companion to the Hellenistic World* (ed. Andrew Erskine; Malden, Mass.; Oxford: Blackwell, 2003), 431–45.

30. Lily Ross Taylor, *The Divinity of the Roman Emperor* (Middletown, Conn.: American Philological Association), 237–38. At the time, an important dissenting voice to this view was Mason Hammond, *The Augustan Principate in Theory and Practice During the Julio-Claudian Period* (Cambridge, Mass.: Harvard University Press, 1933), 107–08: "There is no evidence that [Augustus] deliberately or artificially sought to set himself up as a god for any political reasons. But there is plenty of proof that the world to which he had brought peace and prosperity, from the most polished court poets to the humble artisans, felt that his achievements were more than human."

31. J. S. Reid, "Roman Ideas of Deity," *JRS* 6 (1916): 174.

32. E.g., Kurt Latte, *Römische Religionsgeschichte* (München: C.H. Beck, 1960), 308, 312–26. Cf. Martin Nilsson, *Geschichte der griechischen Religion* (2 vols.; 2nd ed.; München: C.H. Beck, 1961), 2:384–95. Latte was so incredulous concerning the worship of the emperor that he privately told Robert Étienne that he thought it was an invention of Christian apologists! Cited from a personal letter in Robert Étienne, "Du nouveau sur les débuts du culte impérial municipal dans la péninsule ibérique," in *Subject and Ruler: The Cult of the Ruling Power in Classical Antiquity* (ed. Alistair Small; Journal of Roman Archaeology Supplements 17; Ann Arbor: University of Michigan Press, 1996), 153.

33. The "Greek intellectuals" covered by Bowersock include Plutarch, Marcus Aurelius, Dio Chrysostom, Aelius Aristides, Lucian, and Pliny. The string of quotes comes from G.W. Bowersock, "Greek Intellectuals and the Imperial Cult in the Second Century A.D.," in

den Boer, *Culte*, 183, 187, 180, 185, 206, 187. For a different analysis of similar data, see Harold W. Attridge, "The Philosophical Critique of Religion under the Early Empire," *ANRW* 2.16.1 (1978): 45–78.

34. Millar, "The Imperial Cult and the Persecutions," in den Boer, *Culte*, 164. Another of the early studies focused on the temples for Julius Caesar and Augustus: Heidi Hänlein-Schäfer, *Veneratio Augusti: Eine Studie zu den Tempeln des ersten römischen Kaisers* (Archaeologica 39; Rome: Giorgio Bretschneider, 1985).

35. H. W. Pleket, "An Aspect of the Emperor Cult: Imperial Mysteries," *HTR* 58 (1965): 331–47.

36. Cf. also C. R. Phillips, "The Sociology of Religious Knowledge in the Roman Empire to A.D. 284," *ANRW* 2.16.2 (1986): 2697–2711; and on Roman "knowledge" as counterpart to Christian "belief," see Ando, *Matter of the Gods*, esp. 1–18. In fact, the entire notion of belief as a universally applicable category has been deftly challenged by Rodney Needham, *Belief, Language, and Experience* (Chicago: University of Chicago Press, 1972).

37. E.g., the fresh interpretation of Seneca's *Apocolocyntosis* in Gradel, *Emperor Worship*, 325–30.

38. Keith Hopkins, "Divine Emperors or the Symbolic Unity of the Roman Empire," in idem, *Conquerors and Slaves: Sociological Studies in Roman History* (Cambridge: Cambridge University Press, 1978), 242. Cf. similar remarks by Paul Zanker about the material artifacts of Augustan ideology: "In his images, Augustus was thus manifest as both god and man." Zanker, *Power*, 300. Rives, *Religion*, 153, describes how "the emperor's status flickered back and forth between divine and human."

39. Géza Alföldy, "Subject and Ruler, Subjects and Methods: An Attempt at a Conclusion," in Small, *Subject and Ruler*, 255.

40. On Gaius, e.g. Suetonius, *Cal.* 22, 52; and Philo, *Legat.* 78–113. On Domitian, e.g., Suetonius, *Dom.* 13; and Pliny, *Pan.* 2, 52. See brief discussion at Beard, North, and Price, *Religions*, 209–10. C. J. Simpson argues that even the divinity of Caligula should be taken more seriously than it has been, C. J. Simpson, "Caligula's Cult: Immolation, Immortality, Intent," in Small, *Subject and Ruler*, 63–71.

41. Robert Étienne, *Le Culte Impérial dans le péninsule ibérique d'Auguste à Dioclétien* (Paris, E. de Boccard, 1958); Price, *Rituals*; Fishwick, *Imperial Cult*; Uta-Maria Liertz, *Studien zu Kaiserkult und Kaiserverehrung in den germanischen Provinzen und in Gallia Belgica zur römischen Kaiserzeit* (Rome: Institutum Romanum Finlandiae, 1998); Gradel, *Emperor Worship*; Monika Bernett, *Der Kaiserkult in Judäa unter den Herodiern und Römern: Untersuchungen zur politischen und religiösen Geschichte Judäas von 30 v. bis 66 n. Chr.* (Tübingen: Mohr Siebeck, 2007); Maria Kantiréa, *Les dieux et les dieux augustes: Le culte impérial en Grèce sous les Julio-claudiens et les Flaviens: Etudes épigraphiques et archéologiques* (ΜΕΛΕΤΗΜΑΤΑ 50; Athens: Κέντρον Ἑλληνικῆς καὶ Ρωμαϊκῆς Ἀρχαιότητος τοῦ Ἐθνικοῦ Ἱδρύματος Ἐρευνῶν; Paris: Diffusion de Boccard, 2007). To this one might add a study of Egypt: Eleanor G. Huzar, "Emperor Worship in Julio-Claudian Egypt," *ANRW* 2.18.5 (1995): 3092–3143.

42. Translation: "The *princeps* did not make himself worshipped; he allowed it." Kantiréa, *Les dieux et les dieux augustes*, 197.

43. In addition to the previous citations, see Ronald Mellor, "The Goddess Roma," *ANRW* 2.17.2 (1981): 950–1030, esp. 1004.

44. Cf. his (mis?)interpretation of Lucian, *Apol.* 13 at Bowersock, "Intellectuals," 202. Lucian alludes to the emperor being "paid" with honor and worship, but it is not at all clear

he is mocking that fact. In any case, his use of this example as an *a fortiori* argument attests to widespread acknowledgment of the honors-for-benefactions structure of Greco-Roman society. Whether satire or not—and in this case, it would be self-satire, since he is defending his own position as a paid member in an imperial administrative post—Lucian was here appealing to a generally accepted view of emperor worship.

45. At Sinai, the first words of God to Moses refer to the destruction of the Egyptians and the liberation of the Israelites (Exod 19:4).

46. Kantiréa, *Les dieux et les dieux augustes*, 198–99.

47. The term "soteriology" is introduced by Kantiréa, *Les dieux et les dieux augustes*, 14.

48. Price, *Rituals*, 9. Cf. 235–48. Jörg Rüpke also uses Bourdieu to defend his focus on practices, which are "not of course unnecessary codes for something that could be expressed more easily in words." Rüpke, *Religion*, 68.

49. Clifford Ando, *Imperial Ideology and Provincial Loyalty in the Roman Empire* (Berkeley: University of California Press, 2000), xiii. This is the argument of his whole book, but for some passages relevant to our topic, cf. 19–48 and 385–98.

50. Ando, *Imperial Ideology*, 6–7.

51. In addition to this basic reconceptualization of power, many scholars have found the most useful concept from postcolonial theory to be that of "mimicry," famously encapsulated in Homi K. Bhabha, "Of Mimicry and Man: The Ambivalence of Colonial Discourse," in *The Location of Culture* (London: Routledge, 1994), 85–92. Some historians of Roman provincial material culture have hinted at this view without using the critical jargon: commenting on the Sebasteion at Aphrodisias, one scholar suggested, "we should bear in mind the possibility that Aphrodisians, on occasion, looked to Roman colonists in Asia for evidence of what a Roman community, and of what they as *syngeneis*, relatives, of Rome through Aphrodite, should be doing." Joyce M. Reynolds, "Ruler-cult at Aphrodisias in the late Republic and under the Julio-Claudian emperors," in Small, *Subject and Ruler*, 49–50. There was also an indigenous development of emperor worship in rural Spain, among the Celtic Iberians, who had received no physical colonization, and yet responded to imperial power with worship. Leonard A. Curchin, "Cult and Celt: Indigenous Participation in Emperor Worship," in Small, *Subject and Ruler*, 143–52. The question remains whether provincial mimicry served to challenge the authority of the colonizer or not. In the study of early Christianity, the assumption is usually that it did.

52. Varro, *Ling. Lat.* fr. 2 (*apud* Servius, *Ad Aen.* 12.139) and Varro fr. 424 (*apud* Servius, *Ad Aen.* 5.45), *Grammaticae Romanae fragmenta* (ed. Hyginus Funaioli; Stuttgart: Tuebner, 1969); cited in Gradel, *Emperor Worship*, 65 no. 23, 66 no. 24. On distinguishing the terms in modern scholarship, see W. Schwering, "*Deus* und *divus*. Eine semasiologische Studie als Ergänzung zum Artikel *divus* in Thesaurus linguae latinae," *Indogermanische Forschungen* 34 (1914–15): 1–44. Cf. Stefan Weinstock, *Divus Julius* (Oxford: Clarendon, 1971), 391–92.

53. Gradel, *Emperor Worship*, 66–67.

54. Fears, *Princeps*, 98.

55. E.g., Horace, *Carm.* 4.5.32, Ovid, *Ep. ex Pont.*, 4.9.117; for inscriptions, see citations and discussion in Fishwick, *Imperial Cult*, 2:436–54. It is surprising to find that Lucretius increasingly presents Epicurus as a god over the course of *De Rerum Natura*, a trend which culminates in the proem of Book 5 (cf. 5.8).

56. Cf. the interpretations of Dio in Gradel, *Emperor Worship*, 61–65.

57. The original is אלם עונכסט. Cf. Hänlein-Schäfer, *Veneratio*, A53, lines 8–10, p. 227.

58. Cf. the many examples from diverse authors and genres in *BAGD* 451b–452a. For example, the author of a papyrus letter regards his brother "not only as a brother but also as a father, lord, and god" (θεόν, *P.Mich.* III 209.12–13 [II/III]). Even Paul, a "monotheist," refers to "the god of this age/world" (ὁ θεὸς τοῦ αἰῶνος τούτου, 2 Cor 4:4) and admits, perhaps ironically, "there are many gods" (εἰσὶν θεοὶ πολλοί, 1 Cor 8:5, perhaps referring to Ps 136:2).

59. His eloquent case is made in Simon R. F. Price, "Gods and Emperors: The Greek Language of the Roman Imperial Cult," *JHS* 104 (1984): 79–95.

60. Even John Chrysostom used the word when referring to emperor Severus Alexander (*PG* 61:580), though perhaps that was in response to his well-documented affection for Christ? (*SHA, Sev. Alex.* 14, 22, 29, 49, 63). For examples from literature, coins, and inscriptions, see the previously cited bibliography on emperor worship; for papyri, see also Janneke de Jong, "Egyptian Papyri and 'Divinity' of the Roman Emperor," in *The Impact of Imperial Rome on Religions, Ritual, and Religious Life in the Roman Empire: Proceedings of the Fifth International Network, Münster, June 30–July 4, 2004* (ed. Lukas de Blois, Peter Funke, and Johannes Hahn; Leiden: Brill, 2006), 239–52.

61. Price, "Gods and Emperors," 85. This view is endorsed by Kantiréa, *Les dieux et les dieux augustes*, 198.

62. E.g., Christian Habicht, "Die augusteische Zeit und das erste Jahrhundert nach Christi Geburt," in den Boer, *Culte*, 41–88, esp. 76–85.

63. Philo, *Legat.* 154. Trans. LCL.

64. Philo, *Legat.* 162–65.

65. For example, Moses is a θεός (*Mos.* 1.158; *Mut.* 128; *Det.* 161–62; *Prob.* 43–44), a designation Philo takes over from Exod 4:16 and 7:1. Cf. Wayne A. Meeks, "Moses as God and King," in *Religion in Antiquity: Essays in Memory of Erwin Ramsdell Goodenough* (ed. Jacob Neusner; Studies in the History of Religions 14; Leiden: Brill, 1968), 355; John Lierman, *The New Testament Moses: Christian Perceptions of Moses and Israel in the Setting of Jewish Religion* (WUNT II 173; Tübingen: Mohr Siebeck, 2004), 229–46.

66. Published in H. Idris Bell, *Jews and Christians in Egypt* (London: Oxford University Press, 1924) [= *CPJ* 153]. On worship of Claudius in Egypt, see now Huzar, "Emperor Worship," 3136–37.

67. Lines 48–51.

68. Cf. lines 6–9. This paradox will gain more attention, since it has been noted by Beard, North, and Price, *Religions*, 1:313.

69. For the older view, cf. W. Warde Fowler, *Roman Ideas of Deity* (London: Macmillan and Co., 1914), 107–33.

70. Cassius Dio, *Roman History*, 51.20.6–8.

71. Taylor, *Divinity*, 203–04.

72. This argument comprises a large portion of Gradel, *Emperor Worship*. Cf. Ando, *Imperial Ideology*, 385–98. For a helpful critique of Gradel, see John Scheid, "Comprendre le culte dit impérial. Autour de deux livres récents," *L'Antiquité Classique* 73 (2004): 239–49. For a stronger rebuttal, see Peter Herz, "Caesar and God: Recent Publications on Roman Imperial Cult," *JRA* 18 (2005): 638–48.

73. On *genius* and *numen*, see Fishwick, *Imperial Cult*, 2:375–87.

74. E.g., *CIL* 11.3303; 12.4333.

75. Fishwick, *Imperial Cult*, 2:383. On *numen*, see Fishwick, *Imperial Cult*, 2:388–422; Gradel, *Emperor Worship*, 234–50; Walter Pötscher, "'Numen' und 'numen Augusti,'" *ANRW* 2.16.1 (1978): 355–92.

76. For all of this, see the regional works on emperor worship cited above and also J. M. Santero, "The 'Cultores Augusti' and the Private Worship of the Roman Emperor," *Athenaeum* 61 (1983): 111–25.

77. Manfred Clauss, "*Deus praesens*: der römische Kaiser als Gott," *Klio* 78 (1996): 400. Trans. my own. Cf. idem, *Kaiser und Gott*. Clauss is opposed, perhaps balanced, by Peter Herz, "Emperors: Caring for the Empire and Their Successors," in *A Companion to Roman Religion* (ed. Jörg Rüpke; Malden, Mass.: Blackwell, 2007), 304–16.

78. Kantiréa, *Les dieux et les dieux augustes*, 196. Trans. my own.

79. For an example of the emperor's space-transcending presence, consider the scene before a likeness (*effigies*) of Nero (Tacitus, *Ann.* 15.29).

80. Ando, *Matter of the Gods*, 119. This quotation is the Latin translation of Jesus' words to his disciples in Mt 18:20.

81. Frances M. Young, "Prelude," in *The Cambridge History of Christianity* (9 vols.; ed. Margaret M. Mitchell and Frances M. Young; Cambridge: Cambridge University Press, 2006), 1:14.

82. One need only search the word "empire" among the annual conferences of the Society of Biblical Literature, American Academy of Religion, and North American Patristics Society for a sense of the topic's sudden *adventus* into early Christian studies.

83. Richard A. Horsley, *Jesus and Empire: The Kingdom of God and the New World Disorder* (Minneapolis: Fortress Press, 2002); John Dominic Crossan and Jonathan L. Reed, *Excavating Jesus: Beneath the Stones, Behind the Texts* (San Francisco: HarperSanFrancisco, 2001); for a keen assessment of the *status quaestionis*, see Stephen D. Moore, *Empire and Apocalypse: Postcolonialism and the New Testament* (Sheffield: Sheffield Phoenix Press, 2006); for studies specific to Mark, see chap. 4 below.

84. Essays in Richard Horsley, ed., *Paul and Empire: Religion and Power in Roman Imperial Society* (Harrisburg, Penn.: Trinity Press International, 1997); John Dominic Crossan and Jonathan L. Reed, *In Search of Paul: How Jesus's Apostle Opposed Rome's Empire with God's Kingdom* (San Francisco: HarperSanFrancisco, 2004); Adela Yarbro Collins, "Psalms, Phil. 2:6–11, and the Origins of Christology," *Biblical Interpretation* 11 (2003): 361–72; Peter Oakes, "Re-mapping the Universe: Paul and the Emperor in 1 Thessalonians and Philippians," *JSNT* 27 (2005): 301–22; Diana Swancutt, *Pax Christi: Empire, Identity, and Protreptic Rhetoric in Paul's Letter to the Romans* (NovTSup; Leiden: Brill, forthcoming).

85. Steven J. Friesen, *Imperial Cults and the Apocalypse of John: Reading Revelation in the Ruins* (Oxford: Oxford University Press, 2001) is a good gateway into this large bibliography; another cogent analysis is Christopher A. Frilingos, *Spectacles of Empire: Monsters, Martyrs, and the Book of Revelation* (Divinations; Philadelphia: University of Pennsylvania Press, 2004). For a recent analysis with German bibliography, cf. Jörg Frey, "The Relevance of the Roman Imperial Cult for the Book of Revelation: Exegetical and Hermeneutical Reflections on the Relation between the Seven Letters and the Visionary Main Part of the Book," in *The New Testament and Early Christian Literature in Greco-Roman Context: Studies in Honor of David E Aune* (ed. John Fotopoulos; NovTSup 122; Leiden: Brill, 2006), 231–55.

86. This process began in earnest with Adolf Deissmann, *Licht vom Osten: das Neue Testament und die neuentdeckten Texte der hellenistisch-römischen Welt* (2nd and 3rd ed.; Tübingen: Mohr, 1909), 287–328; cf. Dominique Cuss, *Imperial Cult and Honorary Terms in the New Testament* (Fribourg: University Press, 1974); Along with Crossan and Reed, Helmut Koester, *From Jesus to the Gospels*, 204–17, has also recently emphasized the narrative comparisons between Augustus and Jesus, especially the eschatological tenor of Augustus's

principate. The most adventurous of these is Carsten Peter Thiede, *Jesus und Tiberius: Zwei Söhne Gottes* (München: Luchterhand, 2004).

87. Ernst Lohmeyer, *Christuskult und Kaiserkult* (Tübingen: J.C.B. Mohr [Paul Siebeck], 1919); D. L. Jones, "Christianity and the Roman Imperial Cult," *ANRW* 2.23.2 (1980): 1023–54; Adela Yarbro Collins, "The Worship of Jesus and the Imperial Cult," in *The Jewish Roots of Christological Monotheism: Papers from the St. Andrews Conference on the Historical Origins of the Worship of Jesus* (ed. Carey C. Newman, James R. Davila, and Gladys S. Lewis; Leiden: Brill, 1999), 234–57; George Heyman, *The Power of Sacrifice: Roman and Christian Discourses in Conflict* (Washington, D.C.: Catholic University of America Press, 2007).

88. Mary Rose D'Angelo, "Abba and 'Father': Imperial Theology and the Jesus Traditions," *JBL* 111 (1992): 611–30; James S. Jeffers, "The Influence of the Roman Family and Social Structures on Early Christianity in Rome," in *SBLSP 1988* (ed. David J. Lull; Atlanta: Scholars Press, 1988), 370–84; Eva Marie Lassen, "The Use of the Father Image in Imperial Propaganda and 1 Corinthians 4:14–21," *TynBul* 42 (1991): 127–36.

89. Martin Dibelius, *Rom und die Christen im ersten Jahrhundert. Vorgelegt am 10. Januar 1942* (Heidelberg: C. Winter, 1942); Averil Cameron, *Christianity and the Rhetoric of Empire: The Development of Christian Discourse*, (Berkeley: University of California Press, 1991); Allen Brent, *The Imperial Cult and the Development of Church Order: Concepts and Images of Authority in Paganism and Early Christianity before the Age of Cyprian* (Leiden: Brill, 1999); H. A. Drake, *In Praise of Constantine: A Historical Study and New Translation of Eusebius' Tricennial Orations* (Berkeley: University of California Press, 1976); Ando, *Imperial Ideology*, esp. 42–48 and literature cited at 48 no. 148.

90. In addition to the aforementioned work of Crossan, along with Moore's *Empire and Apocalypse*, see Justin Meggitt, "Taking the Emperor's Clothes Seriously: The New Testament and The Roman Emperor," in *The Quest for Wisdom: Essays in Honour of Philip Budd* (ed. C. Joynes; Cambridge: Orchard Academic, 2002), 143–170, available online at <http://www .religion-online.org/showarticle.asp?title=3278>. The direction of these projects has been challenged by Seyoon Kim, *Christ and Caesar: The Gospel and the Roman Empire in the Writings of Paul and Luke* (Grand Rapids: Eerdmans, 2008); and, to a lesser degree, by Christopher Bryan, *Render To Caesar: Jesus, The Early Church, and the Roman Superpower* (New York: Oxford University Press, 2005).

91. See the compilation of evidence by Tae Hun Kim, "The Anarthrous *huios theou* in Mark 15:39 and the Roman Imperial Cult," *Biblica* 79 (1998): 221–41; with corrections and elaborations by Robert Mowery, "Son of God in Roman Imperial Titles and Matthew," *Biblica* 83 (2002): 100–110. But scholars are just beginning to *interpret* the "son of God" connection between the emperor and Jesus Christ, e.g., Adela Yarbro Collins, "Mark and His Readers: The Son of God among Greeks and Romans," *HTR* 93 (2000): 85–100; and eadem, *Mark: A Commentary* (ed. Harold W. Attridge; Hermeneia; Philadelphia: Fortress Press, 2007), 767–68. Thiede's *Jesus und Tiberius*, is an iconoclastic approach to the issue.

92. *P.Oxy.* XII 1453.11. Cited also by Millar, "Imperial Cult," in den Boer, *Culte*, 146. On the precise dating of the papyrus, cf. T. C. Skeat, "The Augustan Era in Egypt," *ZPE* 53 (1983): 241–44. Cf. the same phrase in *BGU* I 16.2594.3; Dittenberger, *OGIS* 655.2. The Egyptian provenance of the language may suggest that it was influenced by Egyptian royal ideas of divine dynastic rulers: for example, on the Rosetta Stone, the Ptolemaic divine dynasty is analogized to Isis, Osiris, and Horus. Ptolemy V is θεὸς ἐκ θεοῦ καὶ θεάς (Dittenberger, *OGIS* 90.10). For other examples invoking Augustus as "son of god" (θεοῦ υἱόν), cf. *BGU* II 543.2–3 and *P.Tebt.* II 382.21.

93. January 1, 42 B.C.E., after which Octavian was *divi filius*. Three expert and distinctive assessments of Caesar's divinity can be found in Taylor, *Divinity*, 58–99; Weinstock, *Divus Julius*; and Gradel, *Emperor Worship*, 54–72. The topic is too large to be treated here, except as it relates to the issue of divine sonship.

94. Cf. Nicolaus of Damascus, *Life* 21, where Antony was thought to have overly exalted Caesar during the Lupercalia in the hopes of being adopted as his son. Text and translation found in *Nicolaus of Damascus' Life of Augustus* (trans. Clayton Morris Hall; Smith College Classical Studies 4; Northampton, Mass., 1923). Cf. Appian, *Bell. civ.* 3.16–19.

95. The adoption of Octavian is described in: Nicolaus of Damascus, *Life* 8, 11, 13, 17–18, 29–30; Livy, *Periochae* 116.5; Appian, *Bell. civ.* 3.11–14; Suetonius, *Jul.* 83.2; *Aug.* 7.2, 94.11. For a compilation and analysis of the candidates available to Caesar for adoption, see Monroe E. Deutsch, "Caesar's Son and Heir," *California Publications in Classical Philology* 9:6 (1928): 149–200.

96. For a study of the testamentary adoption, see Walter Schmitthenner, *Oktavian und das Testament Cäsars* (München: C.H. Beck, 1952). I call it "quasi-legal" because it was not present in the law codes but was enacted through a legally binding document.

97. Nicolaus of Damascus, *Life* 8 and 11.

98. Suetonius, *Aug.* 94.11, discussed in chap. 4.

99. Suetonius, *Aug.* 94.4. Cf. Cassius Dio, *Roman History* 45.2.

100. This is narrated in Appian, *Bell. civ.* 3.11 and Nicolaus of Damascus, *Life* 18.

101. Cf. Nicolaus of Damascus, *Life* 30.

102. Examples abound, but for the beginning of the title, see Taylor, *Divinity*, 106.

103. Otto Kern, *Die Inschriften von Magnesia am Mäander* (Berlin, 1900), no. 157b, housed in the Staatliche Museen, Berlin. Cf. a "son of god" inscription to Drusus the Younger, who was in line to be emperor but never acceded to power (*IG* II² 3257).

104. He took "Caesar" in his official titulature, and "son of god" is found, for example, in a plaque from Achaia (*IG* II² 3281); cf. *RIC* 2, p. 127, note 93. See chap. 3 on adoption and divine election in times of crisis. As for Vespasian's divinity, his deathbed utterance is well known: *Vae, puto deus fio* ("Oh dear, I think I'm becoming a god"), Suet., *Vesp.* 23.

105. On his connection to Aeneas, cf. Cassius Dio, *Roman History* 41.34.1. On the temple of Venus Genetrix, cf. Weinstock, *Divus Julius*, 80–90.

106. On this topic, see T. P. Wiseman, "Domi Nobiles and the Roman Cultural Elite," in *Les «Bourgeoisies» municipales italiennes aux IIe et Ier siècles av. J.-C.* (Cébeillac-Gervasoni; Paris: Éditions du Centre national de la recherche scientifique; Naples: Bibliothèque de l'Institut français de Naples, 1983), 298–306. Cf. the skepticism of Seneca toward such genealogies (*Ben.* 3.28.2).

107. Augustus crowned his new forum with the temple of Mars Ultor, dedicated to Mars in 2 B.C.E. for aid in avenging (hence, *ultor*, "avenger") the murder of Caesar.

108. Taylor, *Divinity*, 138–41.

109. Fishwick, *Imperial Cult*, 2:423–35.

110. Olivier Hekster, "Descendants of Gods: Legendary Genealogies in the Roman Empire," in *The Impact of Imperial Rome on Religions, Ritual, and Religious Life in the Roman Empire: Proceedings of the Fifth International Network, Münster, June 30–July 4, 2004* (ed. Lukas de Blois, Peter Funke, and Johannes Hahn; Leiden: Brill, 2006), 24–35. Cf. idem, "Honouring Ancestors: The Dynamic of Deification," *Ritual Dynamics and Religious Change in the Roman Empire: Proceedings of the Eighth Workshop of the International Network*

Impact of Empire (Heidelberg, July 5–7, 2007) (ed. Olivier Hekster, Sebastian Schmidt-Hofner, and Christian Witschel; Leiden: Brill, 2009), 95–110.

111. Hekster, "Descendants," 35.

112. On the different inflections of "son of God" in Christology, see Adela Yarbro Collins and John J. Collins, *King and Messiah as Son of God* (Grand Rapids: Eerdmans, 2008).

113. During his Nicene-era Christological debate, he was defending the pre-Nicene position of Dionysius of Alexandria. Greek: τῶν ἀγνοουμένων, καὶ προσαγωγῆς εἰς ἐπίγνωσιν δεομένων, οὐ μόνον ἀλλοῖα πολλάκις, ἀλλὰ καὶ ὑπεναντία τεκμήρια γίνεται τῶν ἐπιζητουμένων δηλώματα (Athanasius, *De Sententia Dionysii* 18 [79]; *PG* 25b: 508; critical edition in Hans-Georg Opitz, ed., *Athanasius Werke* 2.1 [Berlin: de Gruyter, 1935], 46–67).

■ Chapter 3

1. For analysis of this issue, see Nicholas D. Kristof, "The Dynastic Question," *New York Times*, January 31, 2008. He does not note the coincidence that a member of the "Julian" household was also among the top candidates for the office—R. Giuliani, former mayor of New York City.

2. Though the actual mechanism of adoption is not relevant in the American political analogy, it did function as a metaphor in the 2008 election. Since Barack Obama was not from a lineage of American "nobility," he was frequently "affiliated" with and sometimes described by pundits as "adopted" by the Kennedys—the only left-wing political dynasty stronger than the Clintons. Cf. Jonah Goldberg, "Myth of Camelot," *National Review Online*, February 1, 2008, available at <http://www.townhall.com/Columnists/JonahGoldberg/2008/02/01/the_myth_of_camelot>.

3. In using the term "ideology," I am relying on the excellent work of Clifford Ando, *Imperial Ideology and Provincial Loyalty in the Roman Empire* (Berkeley: University of California Press, 2000), noted frequently in the following pages. He has used the critical theories of Weber, Habermas, and especially Bourdieu to defend the appropriateness of the term for describing—in Bourdieu's words—the "doxic system" of the Roman Empire. See Pierre Bourdieu, *Outline of a Theory of Practice* (trans. R. Nice; Cambridge: Cambridge University Press, 1977), especially "Structures, habitus, power: basis for a theory of symbolic power," 159–97. Bourdieu's term *doxa* encapsulates those elements of a societal worldview, "social structures and mental structures," which remain "undiscussed" and thus unquestioned by almost all members of a given society. For our purposes, some of these are: the centrality of father-son relationships, the transmission of power from fathers to sons, and the necessity of adoption to fulfill the dynastic grammar through which Roman power was expressed. For Bourdieu (and Ando), ideology denotes the discourses and processes through which power relationships become naturalized and universalized. But ideology is not only, or even primarily, dictated from the powerful at the top of a social pyramid; it permeates the society and is quite like the substrate on which power relationships are activated. Returning to the linguistic metaphor, ideology is the set of grammatical rules according to which power speaks.

4. Alan Watson, *The Law of the Ancient Romans* (Dallas: Southern Methodist University Press, 1970), 37.

5. Gaius, *Inst.* 1.55: *fere enim nulli alii sunt homines, qui talem in filios suos habent potestatem, qualem nos habemus.*

6. Emiel Eyben, "Fathers and Sons," in Rawson, ed., *Marriage*, 106–43; Richard Saller, "*Patria Potestas* and the Stereotype of the Roman Family," *Continuity and Change* 1 (1986):

7–22; idem, "Pietas, obligation, and authority in the Roman family," in *Alte Geschichte und Wissenschaftsgeschichte: Festschrift für Karl Christ zum 65. Geburtstag* (ed. Peter Kneissl and Volker Losemann; Darmstadt: Wissenschaftliche Buchgesellschaft, 1988), 393–410.

7. Cicero refers to the law of adoption as concerning "the inheritance of the name and property and sacred rites of the family," *hereditates nominis pecuniae sacrorum* (*Dom.* 35).

8. The contrast summarized here is discussed in Jack Goody, "Adoption in Cross-Cultural Perspective," *Comparative Studies in Society and History* 11 (1969): 55–78. See also Hugh Lindsay, "Adoption and its Function in Cross-Cultural Contexts," in *Childhood, Class, and Kin in the Roman World* (London: Routledge, 2001), 190–204.

9. On this point, see Halvor Moxnes, "What Is Family?" in *Constructing Early Christian Families* (ed. Halvor Moxnes; London: Routledge, 1997), 19. In the same volume, see also Eva Marie Lassen, "The Roman Family: Ideal and Metaphor," 103–20.

10. Moxnes, "Family," 20–21.

11. *OCD*, 13.

12. Aulus Gellius, *Noct. Att.* 5.19.

13. For a good general treatment of adoption based on the legal codes, see Jane F. Gardner, *Family and* Familia *in Roman Law and Life* (Oxford: Clarendon, 1998), 114–208; and the essays in Rawson, ed., *Marriage, Divorce, and Children in Ancient Rome*. I have found these to be more helpful than Hugh Lindsay, *Adoption in the Roman World* (Cambridge; New York: Cambridge University Press, 2009), which is neither as cogent as Gardner on the legal materials nor as stimulating as Kunst on the nonlegal evidence (see below).

14. The term used is "volksrechtlich" in Marek Kurylowicz, "Adoption on the Evidence of the Papyri," *Journal of Juristic Papyrology* 19 (1983): 61–75.

15. Christiane Kunst, *Römische Adoption: Zur Strategie einer Familienorganisation* (Hennef: Marthe Clauss, 2005).

16. Ibid., *Adoption*, 14. Translations of Kunst are my own.

17. See Martin S. Smith, "Greek Adoptive Formulae," *CQ* 61 (1967): 302–10; and Kunst, *Adoption*, 14 no. 4. Some Greek authors prefer forms of [υἱο]ποιοῦμαι (Polybius, Diodorus Siculus, Dinarchus *apud* Dionysus of Halicarnassus, Cassius Dio, etc.), but others prefer forms of the τίθημι group (Philo and most papyri, though the terminology is not limited to Egypt). Many, such as Appian, prefer the former for a verb (ποιοῦμαι) and the latter for a noun (θέσις). Nicolaus of Damascus varies his terminology when discussing the adoption of Octavian.

18. This argument is further supported by a comparative study of epitaphs for Roman children: Hanne Sigismund Nielsen, "Quasi-Kin, Quasi-Adoption and the Roman Family," in *Adoption et Fosterage* (ed. Mireille Corbier; Paris: De Boccard, 1999), 249–62; and idem, "*Alumnus*: A Term of Relation Denoting Quasi-Adoption," *Classica et Mediaevalia* 38 (1987): 141–88.

19. Kunst, *Adoption*, 31; and Suzanne Dixon, *The Roman Family* (Baltimore: Johns Hopkins University Press, 1992) 162.

20. Watson, *Law*, 39.

21. Cf. Kunst, *Adoption*, 14.

22. See below on Pliny's *Panegyric* of Trajan; cf. Hadrian's speech on adoption of Antoninus Pius (Cassius Dio, *Roman History* 69.20).

23. Cicero, *Leg.* 2.5. *sed necesse est caritate eam praestare*, trans. LCL adapted. In Atticus's response he compares the confluence of a tributary and a main river to "enter[ing] a patrician family" (2.6). The upward mobility of adoption was established enough to be used as an analogy for other phenomena, whether river flow or city citizenship.

24. Kunst, *Adoption*, 294.

25. Mireille Corbier, "Divorce and Adoption as Roman Familial Strategies (*Le Divorce et l'adoption 'en plus'*)," in *Marriage, Divorce, and Children in Ancient Rome*, (ed. Beryl Rawson; Oxford: Clarendon, 1991), 76–77.

26. Marcel-Henri Prévost, *Les Adoptions politiques à Rome sous la République et le Principat* (Paris, 1949), 72. Trans. my own.

27. Trans. my own. Epictetus, *Disc.* 1.3.2: ἀλλ᾽ ἂν μὲν Καῖσαρ εἰσποιήσηταί σε, οὐδείς σου τὴν ὀφρῦν βαστάσει.

28. The phrase "epistemological unconscious" is borrowed from social theorist Pierre Bourdieu (cf. Pierre Bourdieu and Loïs J.D. Wacquant, *An Invitation to Reflexive Sociology* [Chicago, Ill.: University of Chicago Press, 1992], 41).

29. S. F. Bonner, *Roman Declamation in the Late Republic and Early Empire* (Liverpool: University Press of Liverpool, 1949), 40. Suetonius mentions prominent participants and audience members in *Gramm.* 22; cf. *Nero* 10.2.

30. Erik Gunderson, *Declamation, Paternity, and Roman Identity* (Cambridge: Cambridge University Press, 2003), 9. Cf. Mary Beard, "Looking (Harder) for Roman Myth: Dumézil, Declamation and the Problems of Definition," in *Mythos in mythenloser Gesellschaft: Das Paradigma Roms* (ed. Fritz Graf; Stuttgart: Teubner, 1993), 44–64.

31. Gunderson, *Declamation*, 22 and 233.

32. This theme is also examined by Lewis A. Sussman, "Sons and Fathers in the *Major Declamations* Ascribed to Quintilian," *Rhetorica* 13 (1995): 179–92.

33. Gunderson, *Declamation*, 103.

34. The declamations of Calpurnius Flaccus contain three dealing with adoption (nos. 11, 30, and 53, in Lewis A. Sussman, *The Declamations of Calpurnius Flaccus* [Leiden: Brill, 1994]). The major declamations of Quintilian do not address the subject (Lewis A. Sussman, *The Major Declamations Ascribed to Quintilian* [Frankfurt; New York; P. Lang, 1987]). The lesser declamations ascribed to Quintilian contain one instance which treats the rights of a natural father over a son he gave away in adoption (LCL no. 346), but unfortunately the text is cut short.

35. Trans. adapted from LCL. Latin: *si volet ire, quaerat senex ille qui petit quales et quot habeat maiores, quanta bona, an satis magno se possit addicere.*

36. Trans. LCL. Latin: *Fabriciorum imagines Metellis patuerunt; Aemiliorum et Scipionum familias adoptio miscuit; etiam abolita saeculis nomina per successors novos fulgent. Sic illa patriciorum nobilitas <a> fundamentis urbis habet usque in haec tempora constitit: adoptio fortunae remedium est.*

37. Trans. my own. Latin: *cum diceret partem adulescentis Latro et tractaret adoptionis locum, dixit: "iam iste ex imo per adoptionem nobilitati inseritur," et alia in hanc summam.* (The verb *inseritur* is a long-accepted emendation by Nikolai Madvig in an often-corrupt manuscript tradition of the *Controversiae*.) The close connection between adoption and grafting is also employed by Philo in his comments on husbandry (*Agr.* 6), a fact noted already by James M. Scott, *Adoption as Sons of God: An Exegetical Investigation into the Background of ΥΙΟΘΕΣΙΑ in the Pauline Corpus* (WUNT II 48; Tübingen: Mohr Siebeck, 1992), 81, as a *comparandum* for Paul's use of the adoption metaphor. Paul uses images of both adoption (Rom 8–9) and grafting (Rom 11) to symbolize the inclusion of Gentile sons into the inheritance allotted to the sons of Israel. Philo also discusses non-Israelite lineage in terms of plant metaphors at *Praem.* 152. When we add to Philo and Paul this example from Roman declamation—and one other from Pliny the Elder (comparing grafting to

adoption in *Nat. Hist.* 15.41)—we may plausibly suggest that Paul has deftly deployed a commonplace learned in his rhetorical education.

38. The same *controversia* is also extant in the declamations of Calpurnius Flaccus. He speaks against the father, like Latro, but is more positive about the overall benefits of adoption. Speaking on behalf of adoption in general: "Adoption is a sacred process, of course it is, one which duplicates the privileges conferred by birth and statute." Trans. from Sussman, *Calpurnius Flaccus*, no. 30. Latin: *adoptio sancta res est; quidni, quae beneficia naturae et iuris imitatur.*

39. Trans. LCL adapted. Latin: *declamabat illam Caesare Augusto audiente et M. Agrippa, cuius filios, nepotes suos, Caesar adoptaturus diebus illis videbatur.*

40. Trans. LCL adapted. Latin: *erat M. Agrippa inter eos qui non nati sunt nobiles sed facti.* (The phrasing is similar but contrary to the most famous case of *natum non factum*—the Nicene Creed.)

41. Aulus Gellius, *Noct. Att.* 5.19. Trans. LCL adapted. Latin: *Velitis, iubeatis, uti L. Valerius L. Titio tam iure legeque filius siet, quam si ex eo patre matreque familias eius natus esset, utique ei vitae necisque in eum potestas siet, uti patri endo filio est.*

42. Kurylowicz, "Adoption," 72–75; and see the list of papyri cited in Raphael Taubenschlag, *The Law of Greco-Roman Egypt in the Light of the Papyri, 332 B.C. – 640 A.D.* (2nd ed.; Milano: Cisalpino-Goliardico, 1972), 100, especially notes 12–13.

43. Smith, "Formulae," 303–07.

44. Ibid., 302.

45. This event of 59 B.C.E was excoriated by Clodius's political enemy, Cicero, in *Dom.* 34–38: "And so, having thrown the ceremonies of religion into confusion, having polluted both families, both the one which you have abandoned and the one which you have entered, having violated the legitimate practices of the Romans with respect to guardianships and inheritances, you have been made, contrary to all the requirements of religion, the son of that man of whom you were old enough to be the father."

46. Elder Seneca, *Controversiae* 3.3.

47. Philo, *Legat.* 23. ὁ μὲν γὰρ θέσει υἱωνὸς ἦν, ὁ δὲ φύσει Τιβερίου.

48. Philo, *Legat.* 28. Trans. LCL. δέλεαρ γὰρ ἦν ἡ θέσις οὐκ ἐλπιζομένης ἡγεμονίας, ἀλλ᾽ ἀφαιρέσεως ἧς εἶχεν ἤδη . . . ἡ γὰρ υἱοῦ παντελὴς ἐξουσία κατὰ τοὺς τῶν Ῥωμαίων νόμους ἀνάκειται πατρί.

49. Philo's account of this affair is the only detailed one extant: the praetorian guard soldiers dispatched to kill Tiberius Gemellus could not go through with the deed and implored him to kill himself instead. But he was untrained in killing and had to be instructed by the soldiers how to proceed. Cf. Suetonius, *Cal.* 23.3; Cassius Dio, *Roman History* 59.8.1.

50. Philo, *Legat.* 27. Trans. LCL adapted. ἐγὼ δὲ [ἔφη] παιδαγωγοὺς καὶ διδασκάλους καὶ ἐπιτρόπους ὑπερβαλὼν, ἐμαυτὸν μὲν ἤδη γράφω πατέρα, υἱὸν δὲ ἐκεῖνον. Here the verb γράφω is used to enact adoption.

51. Kunst, *Adoption*, 15. Contrast the ritual of placing on the knees in the ancient Near East, presumed by E. A. Speiser, *Genesis* (AB 1; Garden City, N.Y.: Doubleday, 1981), 357, based on B. Stade, "Auf Jemandes Knieen gebären," *ZAW* 6 (1886): 143–56; and Isaac Mendelsohn, "A Ugaritic Parallel to the Adoption of Ephraim and Manasseh," *IEJ* 9 (1959): 180–83.

52. Diodorus Siculus, *Roman History* 4.39.2. Trans. LCL. This text exemplifies the fluidity of Greek terminology for adoption, using the verb υἱοποιοῦμαι, the verbal adjective

θετός, and the noun τέκνωσις—the last of which is used almost always in Greek literature to mean *natural* begetting or bearing of children.

53. Though this is a contrast to the modern West, the focus on inheritance was present in European and some Asian pre-industrial societies. Cf. Goody, "Adoption," and Lindsay, "Adoption."

54. *Res gest. divi Aug.* 35.1; cf. Suetonius, *Aug.* 58.

55. *DNP*, 9:396. Cf. Andreas Alföldi, *Der Vater des Vaterlandes im römischen Denken* (Darmstadt: Wissenschaftliche Buchgesellschaft, 1971).

56. Cassius Dio, *Roman History* 44.4.4; Suetonius, *Jul.* 76.

57. This argument is made persuasively by Ando, *Imperial Ideology*, 400.

58. For example, Harold Mattingly, ed., *Coins of the Roman Empire in the British Museum* (3 vols.; London: British Museum, 1965), Tiberius no. 155 [= plate 26.5]; cf. *RPC* 66–67; 538. Others cited in Charles Brian Rose, *Dynastic Commemoration and Imperial Portraiture in the Julio-Claudian Period* (Cambridge: Cambridge University Press, 1997), 225 no. 15.

59. Included in the formal titulature, abbreviated as *P.P.*, from Augustus to Theodosius.

60. J. Rufus Fears, "Jupiter and Roman Imperial Ideology," *ANRW* 17.1: 20.

61. Ibid., 21.

62. Ibid., 59.

63. After the Julio-Claudian dynasty came to an end, but the Empire continued and expanded, later emperors returned to using Jupiter (and Zeus) as a unifying image to legitimate their rule. According to Fears, there was a conscious attempt after the end of that dynasty, especially under Domitian, Trajan, and Hadrian, to re-establish "the central role of Zeus-Jupiter" as an "ideological foundation for the imperial structure, one which was neither narrowly Roman nor linked to a single dynasty, but which could instead elicit the understanding and loyalty of the empire as a whole." Fears, "Jupiter," 89.

64. Ovid, *Tristia* 2.157: *per patriam, quae te tuta et secura parente est.* Composed c. 9 C.E.

65. Strabo, *Geogr.* 6.4.2. Trans. LCL. χαλεπὸν δὲ ἄλλως διοικεῖν τὴν τηλικαύτην ἡγεμονίαν ἢ ἑνὶ ἐπιτρέψαντας ὡς πατρί.

66. Ovid, *Tristia* 2.181–2. Trans. LCL adapted. *parce, pater patriae, nec nominis inmemor huius / olim placandi spem mihi tolle tui.*

67. Seneca, *Clem.* 1.14.2. Trans. LCL adapted. *Hoc, quod parenti, etiam principi faciendum est, quem appellavimus Patrem Patriae non adulatione vana adducti. Cetera enim cognomina honori data sunt; Magnos et Felices et Augustos diximus et ambitiosae maiestati quicquid potuimus titulorum congessimus illis hoc tribuentes; Patrem quidem Patriae appellavimus, ut sciret datam sibi potestatem patriam, quae est temperantissima liberis consulens suaque post illos reponens.*

68. Cf. Cassius Dio, *Roman History* 53.18.3 on the emperor's function as father.

69. E.g., Taylor does not attend to the family associations of the *genius*, but instead interprets it as a "thin veil for the emperor himself," in Lily Ross Taylor, *The Divinity of the Roman Emperor* (Middletown, Conn.: American Philological Association), 204.

70. Cf. chap. 2 on how the *genius* fits in to the overall picture of emperor worship.

71. John Scheid, *An Introduction to Roman Religion* (trans. Janet Lloyd; Bloomington: Indiana University Press, 2003), 162.

72. Ittai Gradel, *Emperor Worship and Roman Religion* (Oxford: Clarendon Press, 2002), chap. 7, "The Emperor's *Genius* in State Cult," 162–197.

73. Taylor, *Divinity*, 151–54, 182, 220, 227.

74. Gradel, *Emperor Worship*, 187.

75. Ibid., 196.

76. On the compital altars in general, see Michel Hano, "A l'origine du culte impérial: les autels des Lares Augusti. Recherches sur les thèmes iconographiques et leur signification." *ANRW* 16.3: 2333–81; Heidi Hänlein Schäfer, "Die Ikonographie des *Genius Augusti* im Kompital- und Hauskult der frühen Kaiserzeit," in *Subject and Ruler: The Cult of the Ruling Power in Classical Antiquity* (ed. Alistair Small; Journal of Roman Archaeology Supplements 17; Ann Arbor: Journal of Roman Archaeology, 1996), 73–98; Karl Galinsky, *Augustan Culture* (Princeton: Princeton University Press, 1996), 300–12; and Gradel, *Emperor Worship*, 116–28.

77. See J. Bert Lott, *The Neighborhoods of Augustan Rome* (Cambridge: Cambridge University Press, 2004). According to Pliny the Elder, Flavian Rome was "divided into 14 districts and 265 *compita* for the *Lares*" (*Nat. Hist.* 3.66). Suetonius reports these divisions to have originated with Augustus: "He divided the area of the city into regions and neighborhoods (*vicos*), arranging that the former should be under the charge of magistrates selected each year by lot, and the latter under *magistri* elected by the inhabitants of the respective neighborhoods" (*Aug.* 30.1). Some of the names of the neighborhoods and outlines of the compital altars can be seen in the partially preserved "Severan Marble Plan" map of the city; see Lott, *Neighborhoods*, 16–17.

78. *Res gest. divi Aug.* 19–21; Suetonius, *Aug.* 31.4.

79. Ovid, *Fast.* 5.145–46. Trans. my own. *mille Lares Geniumque ducis, qui tradidit illos, / urbs habet, et vici numina trina colunt.*

80. Gradel, *Emperor Worship*, 128.

81. On the relationship of the Roman household to Roman imperial headship, see Moxnes, "Family," 26. Scholars have also emphasized how Augustus did not only enter *others' private houses* as father, but also reshaped the Roman cults to center on *his own house*. Roman religious sensibility was attuned to the proper places for cultic practices, so when Augustus's home on the Palatine became the location of the *pontifex maximus* and the cult of Vesta, it meant that "the public hearth of the state . . . had been fused with the private hearth of Augustus . . . . From 12 B.C. onwards, for the first time, Roman religion had a head." Mary Beard, John North, and Simon Price, *Religions of Rome, Volume I: A History* (Cambridge: Cambridge University Press, 1998), 191–92.

82. Ovid, *Ep. ex Pont.* 4.9.105–12. Trans. LCL adapted. *nec pietas ignota mea est: videt hospita terra / in nostra sacrum Caesaris esse domo. / stant pariter natusque pius coniunxque sacerdos, / numina iam facto non leviora deo. / neu desit pars ulla domus, stat uterque nepotum, / hic aviae lateri proximus, ille patris. / his ego do totiens cum ture precantia verba, / Eoo quotiens surgit ab orbe dies.* Composed c. 16 C.E.

83. Ovid, *Ep. ex Pont.*, 4.9.115–16. Trans. LCL adapted. *Pontica me tellus, quantis hac possumus ara, / natalem libis scit celebrare dei.*

84. Ovid, *Ep. ex Pont.*, 4.9.125–26. Trans. LCL. *et tamen haec tangent aliquando Caesaris aures: / nil illi, toto quod fit in orbe, latet.*

85. Ovid, *Ep. ex Pont.*, 4.9.127, 132. Trans. LCL adapted. *superis ascite . . . caelite novo.* Cf. 4.6.17 on Augustus as a recent *caelitus* after his death and apotheosis, about which Ovid wrote a poem, unfortunately not extant.

86. Ovid, *Ep. ex Pont.*, 4.9.133–34. Trans. LCL adapted. *auguror his igitur flecti tua numina, nec tu / inmerito nomen mite Parentis habes.*

87. Cassius Dio, *Roman History* 51.19.7. Trans. my own. τούς τε ἱερέας καὶ τὰς ἱερείας ἐν ταῖς ὑπέρ τε τοῦ δήμου καὶ τῆς βουλῆς εὐχαῖς καὶ ὑπὲρ ἐκείνου ὁμοίως εὔχεσθαι, καὶ ἐν τοῖς συσσιτίοις οὐχ ὅτι τοῖς κοινοῖς ἀλλὰ καὶ τοῖς ἰδίοις πάντας αὐτῷ σπένδειν ἐκέλευσαν.

88. Petronius, *Satyricon* 60: *Augusto, patri patriae, feliciter!* and *Dii propitii!*

89. Horace, *Carm.* 4.5.31–35: *hinc ad vina redit laetus et alteris / te mensis adhibet deum / te multa prece, te prosequitur mero / defuso pateris et Laribus tuum / miscet numen.*

90. Cf. Horace, *Ep.* 2.1.16, which mentions altars to the *numen* of Augustus.

91. Ovid, *Fast.* 2.633–38: *et libate dapes, ut, grati pignus honoris, / nutriat incinctos missa patella Lares. / iamque ubi suadebit placidos nox humida somnos, / larga precaturi sumite vina manu, / et "bene vos, bene te, patriae pater, optime Caesar" / dicite, suffuso per sacra verba mero.*

92. πατὴρ τῆς πατρίδος καὶ τοῦ σύμπαντος τῶν ἀνθρώπων γένους. E.g., *Ios PE* I² 181.3 (reign of Tiberius). Cf. Ando, *Imperial Ideology*, 403 no. 315, citing inscriptions compiled in W. H. Buckler, "Auguste, Zeus Patroos," *Revue de Philologie* 9 (3ʳᵈ series, 1935): 177–88.

93. Its importance was also emphasized by a contemporary of Hammond: Herbert Nesselhauf, "Die Adoption des römischen Kaisers," *Hermes* 83 (1955): 477–95. The work of Kunst has now superseded that of Nesselhauf, though Hammond's analysis is still the best available in English.

94. Mason Hammond, *The Augustan Principate in Theory and Practice During the Julio-Claudian Period* (Cambridge, Mass.: Harvard University Press, 1933); *The Antonine Monarchy* (Rome: American Academy in Rome, 1959), 1–24; and especially, "The Transmission of Powers of the Roman Emperor from the Death of Nero in A.D. 68 to that of Alexander Severus in A.D. 235," *Memoirs of the American Academy in Rome* 24 (1956): 63–133.

95. Hammond, "Transmission," 65.

96. Cf. Hammond, *Augustan*, esp. 23–24.

97. Hammond, "Transmission," 63.

98. Ibid., 77.

99. Tacitus, *Hist.* 1.4.2: *evulgato imperii arcano posse principem alibi quam Romae fieri.* Trans. LCL.

100. Hammond, "Transmission," 63.

101. Ibid., 67. Italics added.

102. Ando, *Imperial Ideology*, 27.

103. See Max Weber, *Economy and Society* (2 vols.; ed. Guenther Roth and Claus Wittich; Berkeley: University of California Press, 1978), 1:212–301; 2:1111–57.

104. Ando, *Imperial Ideology*, 32.

105. Ibid., 34.

106. This consensus view is still accurate, but it has been tempered by Olivier Hekster, "All in the Family: The Appointment of Emperors Designate in the Second Century AD," in *Administration, Prosopography and Appointment Policies in the Roman Empire* (ed. Lukas de Blois; Amsterdam: J.C. Gieben, 2001), 35–49. He helpfully points out that this was not a clean meritocratic system; there were dynastic considerations even in the period of the so-called adoptive emperors.

107. Ando, *Imperial Ideology*, 39. The connection between second-century adoptive succession and the imperial virtue of *pietas* has been explained well by Brian K. Harvey, "Two Bases of Marcus Aurelius Caesar and the Roman Imperial Succession," *Historia: Zeitschrift für Alte Geschichte* 53 (2004): 46–60.

108. On the general role coins played in legitimating imperial successions, see Christopher Howgego, *Ancient History from Coins* (London: Routledge, 1995), 80–82.

109. E.g., the gold *aurei* and silver *denarii* listed in *RIC* 1, coins 55–56 (= plate IV.207, 209, 211).

110. Hadrian had to respond to skeptical rumors that his adoption by Trajan was not legitimate. One means of response was the issue of silver *denarii* with the legend "ADOPTIO" on the reverse, underneath a scene of Trajan and Hadrian clasping hands (cf. the Galba-Piso adoption, during which Galba "took hold of Piso's hand"; Tacitus, *Hist.* 1.15). Coins are listed in *RIC* 2 under Hadrian as no. 3a (= plate XII.217); cf. no. 22a and 22c.

111. Cf. Rose, *Dynastic Commemoration*, passim. See below on the portraiture of Augustus's adopted sons. See also the adoption relief from the "Great Antonine Altar" at Ephesus, which commemorates Hadrian's adoption of Antoninus Pius (fig. 42, slabs M and N, in Cornelius C. Vermeule, *Roman Imperial Art in Greece and Asia Minor* [Cambridge, Mass.: Harvard University Press, 1968], 111).

112. On the bizarre testamentary adoption of Livia, see Anthony A. Barrett, *Livia: First Lady of Imperial Rome* (New Haven: Yale University Press, 2004), esp. 148–51. Tacitus records how, although the Senate wanted to shower Livia with all kinds of honors after her adoption as "Julia Augusta," Tiberius wanted instead to limit the honors granted to women. Cf. Suetonius, *Tib.* 50.3; Cassius Dio, *Roman History* 57.12. Tacitus states that an "altar of adoption" (*ara adoptionis*) was one of the items Tiberius denied her. This exact term is not used elsewhere, but it corresponds to monuments erected for other major events among ruling families. From the argument of Tacitus, one can plausibly infer that Tiberius himself received some commemoration of his adoption—perhaps an altar—and did not want Livia to receive the same, being "tense with resentment and interpreting her womanly elevation as depreciation of himself" (Tacitus, *Ann.* 1.14; trans. from *The Annals* [trans. A.J. Woodman; Indianapolis: Hackett, 2004]), 11. For comparable altars, cf. Tacitus, *Ann.* 4.74.2; and Suetonius, *Cal.* 8.1. Elsewhere Livia is commemorated as "daughter of Augustus," making her probably unique in world history—as wife (Aug.), daughter (Aug.), and mother (Tib.) of an emperor (e.g., *CIL* 11.1165).

113. This source has been brought into the discussion of emperor worship by Gradel, *Emperor Worship* (see my chap. 2). The *Arvales Fratres* or "Arval brethren" were a *collegium* of 12 priests, known from at least the 4th century B.C.E to the 4th century C.E., who performed periodic sacrificial rituals in a sacred grove west of Rome and at various locations within Rome. Besides their primary devotion to the otherwise unknown goddess Dea Dia, the Arval brethren enacted votives and sacrifices for the emperor and the imperial family. From at least the second century C.E., we know they maintained a Caesareum on their property devoted to the *genius* of the living emperor and also the *divi* and *divae*. The Arval brethren offer unique evidence for Roman imperial religion, since they recorded their *acta* on plaques in the grove, many of which are still extant. The inscriptions are edited in *Acta Fratrum Arvalium* (ed. Guil. Henzen; Berlin, 1874); and John Scheid, *Commentarii Fratrum Arvalium qui supersunt* (Rome: École Française de Rome, 1998). Cf. John Scheid, *Romulus et ses frères: le collège des Frères Arvales, modèle du culte public dans la Rome des empereurs* (Rome: École Française de Rome, 1990).

114. Clearly depicted in the first line of the inscription is the occasion: "*adoptio facta.*" Henzen, p. XCI, lines 24–33 [= Scheid, p. 100, no. 40, lines 24–32].

115. Despite a damaged inscription, we can deduce that, on February 25, 58 C.E., the sacrifices for the adoption of Nero by Claudius (and its anniversary) followed a similar format (Henzen, p. LXVII, lines 28–32 [= Scheid, p. 63, no. 26, lines 28–32]; and Scheid p. 67, no. 27, lines 57–60).

116. Public games for Marcellus and Gaius and Lucius (Suetonius, *Aug.* 43.5); a public adoption of Agrippa Postumus and Tiberius (Suetonius, *Aug.* 65.1); Nerva's adoption of

Trajan at the Capitol (Cassius Dio, *Roman History* 68.3.4). Peter Herz discusses the adoption of Gaius and Lucius Caesar as part of the calendar of festivals at Messene (Achaia): Peter Herz, "Die Adoptivsöhne des Augustus und der Festkalender: Gedanken zu einer Inschrift aus Messene," *Klio* 75 (1993): 272–88.

117. J. Rufus Fears, *Princeps a diis electus: the Divine Election of the Emperor as a Political Concept at Rome* (Rome: American Academy in Rome, 1977), 1.

118. Ibid., 317.

119. Ibid., 68.

120. Ibid., 12.

121. Ibid., 321.

122. On the considerable impact of Hellenistic royal ideology (especially that of Alexander) on Roman imperial ideology, see Fears, *Princeps*, 45–83.

123. The best summary statement is: "And even though he became great through Fortune, he is even greater in that he made good use of his Fortune. And the more we praise his Fortune the more shall we exalt his Virtue by reason of which he became worthy of his Fortune." Plutarch, *Alex. Fort.* 340B. Trans. LCL.

124. Plutarch, *Alex. Fort.* 338F. Trans. my own. "Adoption" is the translation of εἰσποίησις.

125. Plutarch, *Alex.* 703E.

126. Primary publications are in Ernst Kornemann, *Klio* 7 (1907): 278–88; and in *Griechische Papyri im Museum des oberhessischen Geschichtsvereins zu Giessen* (ed. Ernst Kornemann and Otto Eger; Leipzig and Berlin: Teubner, 1910–12), 15–22. Reprinted several times, e.g., no. 29 in P. W. Pestman, ed., *The New Papyrological Primer* (2nd ed.; Leiden: Brill, 1994).

127. This celebration's occurrence in the "Apollopolite" nome is almost certainly the reason why Apollo refers to himself as "not unknown" (= very well known). The nome is named after him.

128. The most relevant phrase, "the *genius* of his father, a god," is a translation of πατρὸς τύχην θεοῦ. The most common Greek rendering of *genius* is τύχη.

129. *RIC* 2, p. 415, coin 589 (= plate XV.304); cf. *RIC* 2, p. 418, coin 602.

130. Fears, *Princeps*, 244; Arthur Darby Nock, "*A DIIS ELECTA*," *HTR* 23 (1930): 268 ; repr. in *Essays on Religion and the Ancient World* (2 vols.; ed. Zeph Stewart; Cambridge, Mass.: Harvard University Press, 1972), 1:265.

131. I await the continued work of Olivier Hekster, which will likely bear some relation to my own. He indicates a research project "eventually to appear as *Emperors and Ancestors: Lineage and Roman Imperial Ideology*" in a footnote to his article, Olivier Hekster, "Descendants of Gods: Legendary Genealogies in the Roman Empire," in *The Impact of Imperial Rome on Religions, Ritual, and Religious Life in the Roman Empire: Proceedings of the Fifth International Network, Münster, June 30–July 4, 2004* (ed. Lukas de Blois, Peter Funke, and Johannes Hahn; Leiden: Brill, 2006), 35 n. 58.

132. Trans. of Suetonius for the remainder of this chapter are adapted from LCL, unless noted.

133. E.g., Mattingly, *British Museum*, 1:368–93; cf. nos. 12 [= plate 60.22], 27–29 [= plate 61.4–6], 119 [plate 62.7]. Tacitus, *Hist.* 2.59 narrates the pageantry surrounding his young son, Germanicus.

134. A natural dynastic succession appealed to the Roman military mind-set, as typified in Josephus's speech-in-character by Vespasian's troops: "The best safeguard of peace lies in

a legitimate succession of rulers." Josephus, *BJ* 4.596–97: μέγιστον γὰρ δὴ πρὸς ἀσφάλειαν εἰρήνηςεῖναι τὰς γνησίους τῶν βασιλέων διαδοχάς.

135. Tacitus, *Hist.* 2.77. Trans. LCL.

136. Ando, *Imperial Ideology*, 24.

137. Plutarch, *Otho* 3.1–2.

138. Cassius Dio, *Roman History* 53.18.2: τὴν τοῦ γένους σφῶν διαδοχήν.

139. For the Julio-Claudian period, see Rose, *Dynastic Commemoration*. For individual emperors and dynasties, see the series, *Das römische Herrscherbild* (Berlin: Mann).

140. William Metcalf, personal interview, April 5, 2005.

141. For the beginnings of imperial adoption with Julius Caesar and Octavian, see the end of chap. 2.

142. Josephus, *BJ* 2.25.

143. William Metcalf, personal communication, April 5, 2005.

144. Rose, *Dynastic Commemoration*, 9.

145. Ibid., 14. Recall the tension caused by Porcius Latro in his declamation about adoption in the presence of Augustus and Agrippa (Elder Seneca, *Controversiae* 2.4.12).

146. Rose, *Dynastic Commemoration*, 14.

147. Ibid., 14.

148. For analysis and images of the compital altars, see Michel Hano, "A l'origine du culte impérial"; Galinsky, *Augustan Culture*, 300–12; and Gradel, *Emperor Worship*, 116–28.

149. Paul Zanker, *The Power of Images in the Age of Augustus* (trans. Alan Shapiro; Ann Arbor: University of Michigan Press, 1988), 130–34.

150. See Lott, *Neighborhoods*, 120–5.

151. Lott, *Neighborhoods*, 125–6. Gaius and Lucius were also honored in Athens at this time. On top of the Roman Market's "West Gate," most of which is still standing today, there was an equestrian statue of Lucius Caesar dedicated by "the people" of Athens to "Lucius Caesar, son of the Emperor Son of God Augustus Caesar." The "son of god" is part of the title of Augustus, not Lucius: Ὁ Δῆμος Λούκιον Καίσαρα Αὐτοκράτορος Θεοῦ Ὑοῦ Σεβαστοῦ Καίσαρος Ὑον (*IG* II² 3251; spelling defective). It seems that Gaius was also honored that year, and that the Athenian inscription to him as the "new Ares" was likely a dedication correlated to the transplantation of a temple of Ares to Athens, to honor Gaius's military tour of the East. He had left Rome from the Temple of Mars Ultor and would be honored in a similar fashion upon his arrival in Athens. For images and analysis, see Michael C. Hoff, "An Equestrian Statue of Lucius Caesar in Athens Reconsidered," *Archäologischer Anzeiger* (2001): 583–99.

152. Lott, *Neighborhoods*, 126.

153. Suetonius, *The Twelve Caesars* (trans. Robert Graves; rev. Michael Grant; London: Penguin, 1979), 139.

154. E.g., *RIC* 1, p. 103, coin 1 (= plate V.78).

155. Cf. Rose, *Dynastic Commemoration*, 20.

156. On the favorable omens surrounding the selection of Tiberius, see below.

157. Trans. of *Ann.* 12–13 adapted from Tacitus, *The Annals* (trans. Woodman).

158. Rose, *Dynastic Commemoration*, 42–3.

159. Ibid., 43.

160. Josephus, *BJ* 2.248–49. " . . . Nero, the successor of [Claudius'] rule, whom he adopted into the inheritance of his rule through the connivance of his wife Agrippina, although he had a legitimate son, Britannicus, by his former wife Messalina." Trans. my own.

Greek: . . . Νέρωνα τῆς ἀρχῆς διάδοχον, ὃν ταῖς Ἀγριππίνης τῆς γυναικὸς ἀπάταις ἐπὶ κληρονομίᾳ τῆς ἀρχῆς εἰσεποιήσατο καίπερ υἱὸν ἔχων γνήσιον Βρεττανικὸν ἐκ Μεσσαλίνης τῆς προτέρας γυναικὸς. Cf. *AJ* 20.150.

161. Ando does suggest that in the provinces and "the barracks," there was more faith in dynastic continuity than in constitutional debates or *leges de imperio*. Ando, *Imperial Ideology*, 33.

162. Hammond, "Transmission," 69.

163. Translations of the *Histories* are from the LCL.

164. Formal *leges curiatae* were promulgated for some other imperial adoptions: Octavian was most explicit (Appian, *Bell. civ.* 3.94) and convened a *lex curiata* to ratify all the rights he ought to have had as a son of Julius Caesar. Cf. Agrippa Postumus and Tiberius (Suet., *Aug.* 65.1); and Nero (Tac., *Ann.* 12.26.1).

165. Tacitus, *Hist.* 1.16: *sub Tiberio et Gaio et Claudio unius familiae quasi hereditas fuimus: loco libertatis erit quod eligi coepimus; et finita Iuliorum Claudiorumque domo optimum quemque adoptio inveniet. nam generari et nasci a principibus fortuitum, nec ultra aestimatur: adoptandi iudicium integrum et, si velis eligere, consensu monstratur.*

166. Elder Seneca, *Controversiae* 2.1.17: *adoptio fortunae remedium est.* The doctrine would be reiterated by Hadrian's speech at his deathbed adoption of Antoninus Pius: "Now there is a distinction between natural and adopted sons: for a begotten son (τὸ γεννώμενον) becomes whatever kind of person seems appropriate to the heavenly powers, but a man takes an adopted son (τὸ ποιούμενον) to himself through a deliberate selection. The result is that, through natural processes, a man is often given a deformed and incompetent son, but through a process of judgment, one of sound body and mind is certain to be chosen" (Dio 69.20.3). Trans. my own.

167. Otho was also concerned about *providentia*: if he would have been victorious over Vitellius at the battle of Betriacum, he would have adopted his nephew Salvius Cocceianus as his son and heir (Plutarch, *Otho* 16.2). This boy was executed over twenty years later (while consul) by Domitian, who was suspicious of him as a possible rival. Cf. Suetonius, *Dom.* 10.3; and P. A. Roche, "The Execution of L. Salvius Otho Cocceianus," *CQ* 53 (2003): 319–22.

168. Ando, *Imperial Ideology*, 34.

169. The storm is cited also by Plutarch, who states that "the act of adoption was inauspicious and was not favored or approved by the heavenly powers." *Galba* 23.2. Trans. LCL.

170. Ronald Syme notes resemblances between the political circumstances of the adoptions during 69 (Galba-Piso) and 97 (Nerva-Trajan). He describes Tacitus as primarily "a political historian" who is preoccupied less with events than with "the sources of power." The speech of Galba is thus one of "high policy" about adoption as a means of transmitting power. Ronald Syme, *Tacitus* (2 vols.; Oxford: Clarendon, 1958), 1:147, 153, 207.

171. Cassius Dio, *Roman History* 68.3.4: διὰ τὸ γῆρας οὕτω καταφρονούμενος. The phrasing is reminiscent of Plutarch's assessment of Galba thinking himself "despised not only on account of his old age but also his childlessness" (μὴ μόνον διὰ τὸ γῆρας ἀλλὰ καὶ διὰ τὴν ἀπαιδίαν καταφρονούμενος, Plutarch, *Galba* 19.1).

172. Cassius Dio, *Roman History* 68.3.4: Μᾶρκον Οὔλπιον Νέρουαν Τραϊανὸν ποιοῦμαι. The simplicity of the declaration echoes the speech given by Gaius Caligula to adopt Tiberius Gemellus, as recorded by Philo (*Legat.* 27) and noted earlier in this chapter. Note again the flexibility of the verbs used for adoption—here it is just the unprefixed verb ποιοῦμαι, used also by Dio to describe Galba's adoption of Piso (Cassius Dio, *Roman History* 63.5).

173. Hammond, "Transmission," 89.

174. It is also true that Pliny's positive portrayal of adoption should not be divorced from his own status as an adopted son (cf. Pliny, *Ep.* 5.8.5).

175. Fears, *Princeps*, 151. See also the literature cited there.

176. Translations of Pliny, *Panegyric*, are adapted from the LCL.

177. The connection between the two speeches has been noted already; e.g., Karl Büchner, "Tacitus und Plinius über Adoption des römischen Kaisers," *Rheinisches Museum für Philologie* 98 (1955): 289–312. On the relationship of the speeches, I concur with Fears: "Both Pliny and Tacitus drew from the common stock of political literature of the early principate, and for this reason there is little point to the question whether Pliny influenced Tacitus's language in this passage or vice-versa" (Fears, *Princeps*, 164).

178. Italics added. Latin: *oro et obtestor, si bene rem publicam, si ex utilitate omnium regit, primum, ut illum nepotibus nostris ac pronepotibus serves: deinde, ut quandoque successorem ei tribuas, quem genuerit, quem formaverit, similemque fecerit adoptato; aut, si hoc fato negatur, in consilio sis eligenti, monstresque aliquem, quem adoptari in Capitolio deceat.*

179. In the late-third or fourth century, the author of the "Life of Septimius Severus," who claims to be writing under the reign of Diocletian, praises adoption as a mode of succession (*SHA*, Septimius Severus, 20–21). Eusebius, on the other hand, would come to praise the begotten sons of Constantine, as I will discuss below in chap. 5.

■ Chapter 4

1. Candida R. Moss, "The Transfiguration: An Exercise in Markan Accommodation," *BibInt* 12 (2004): 69–89.

2. Moss, "Transfiguration," 70.

3. Ibid., 89.

4. I do not want to reinforce an artificial divide between "Jewish" and "Roman" listeners. I think the audience of Mark is diverse, and many of its members were culturally variegated in themselves. But imagining a listener attuned to Roman culture allows us to hear the text in new ways.

5. By *counter*-emperor, I do not mean simply that Jesus is depicted as *against* the emperor. I use "counter" in the sense of musical *counterpoint*, which is a musical figure or theme that is independent but also interdependent with another musical line. The counterpoint is constantly interacting with the other line and in some sense drawing its motif from the pervasive melody.

6. C. Clifton Black, "Was Mark a Roman Gospel?," *ExpT* 105 (1993): 36. Cf. C. Clifton Black, *Mark: Images of an Apostolic Interpreter* (Columbia: University of South Carolina Press, 1994).

7. Black, "Roman Gospel?," 39–40.

8. For a balanced treatment of these issues, see Adela Yarbro Collins, *Mark: A Commentary* (ed. Harold W. Attridge; Hermeneia; Philadelphia: Fortress Press, 2007), 7–10, 96–102.

9. See the full list at Robert H. Gundry, *Mark: A Commentary on His Apology for the Cross* (Grand Rapids: Eerdmans, 1993), 1044.

10. On these points, see Benjamin Wisner Bacon, *Is Mark a Roman Gospel?* (Cambridge, Mass.: Harvard University Press, 1919), 66–75; and John Donahue and Daniel Harrington, *The Gospel of Mark* (Sacra Pagina 2; Collegeville, Minn.: Liturgical Press, 2002), 40.

11. Black, "Roman Gospel?," 39.

12. Galilee was defended by Willi Marxsen, *Mark the Evangelist* (Nashville: Abingdon, 1969); and later by Hendrika N. Roskam, *The Purpose of the Gospel of Mark in Its Historical and Social Context* (NovTSup 114; Leiden; Boston: Brill, 2004). Syria is defended currently by Gerd Theissen, *The Gospels in Context* (trans. Linda M. Maloney; Minneapolis: Fortress Press, 1991), 236–49; and Joel Marcus, *Mark 1–8* (Anchor Bible Commentary 27; New York: Doubleday, 2000), 33–37.

13. Marcus, *Mark 1–8*, 33–34. Cf. Marcus, "The Jewish War and the *Sitz im Leben* of Mark," *JBL* 111 (1992): 441–62.

14. Ibid., 34.

15. Ibid., 34.

16. Francis J. Moloney, *The Gospel of Mark* (Peabody, Mass.: Hendrickson, 2002), 15.

17. Cf. Brian J. Incigneri, *The Gospel to the Romans* (Biblical Interpretation Series 65; Leiden; Boston: Brill, 2003), 138, and literature cited there about details of such communication in the first-century Empire.

18. Josephus, *B.J.* 7.37–40, 139–46.

19. Theissen, *Gospels*, 242, though he tries valiantly to explain away the absurdities.

20. The sixth-century hagiography of Barnabas even contains this surprising description of the relationship between Mark and Peter: when Peter went to Rome, "he took along Mark, *adopting him like a son*, and there he put together the Gospel narrative" (παρέλαβε μεθ' ἑαυτοῦ τὸν Μάρκον, τρόπον τίνα τεκνοποιήσας αὐτόν· ἐκεῖ συνέταξε τὴν εὐαγγελικὴν ἱστορίαν), from "Laudatio Barnabae," in *Hagiographica Cypria* (ed. Peter Van Deun and Jacques Noret; CCSG 26; Turnhout: Brepols, 1993), 106, lines 559–60. The hagiographer could be extrapolating from 1 Pet 5:13.

21. Compiled helpfully as "Testimonia patrum veterum" in Kurt Aland, *Synopsis Quattuor Evangeliorum* (rev. ed.; Stuttgart: Deutsche Bibelgesellschaft, 2001), 547–64. Analyzed at length in Black, *Mark*, 77–191.

22. The data is also reported in the "anti-Marcionite" and "Monarchian" prologues. In all this, only John Chrysostom diverts from the basic account—but he does not locate Mark in Syria, as one might expect, given that Chrysostom spent much of his life there. Rather, he claims Mark wrote in Alexandria, a statement scholars regard as a misunderstanding of Eusebius' report about Mark's preaching in Egypt. Eusebius had said that Mark was the first to be sent to Egypt "to preach the Gospel, which he also had written" (τὸ εὐαγγέλιον ὅ δὴ καὶ συνεγράψατο κηρῦξαι, *Hist. eccl.* 2.16).

23. A vast amount of literature has been produced about this text, which is not germane to the argument I make in this chapter.

24. The *Adumbrationes*, preserved in Latin, seems to be the same text as the lost Greek *Hypotypōseis* (Ὑποτυπώσεις).

25. Trans. my own. The text is from the edition of "Fragment 24" by Otto Stählin, GCS 17:206 = Aland, *Synopsis*, 555 = Berol. Phill. 1665. Two variants (neither of which is relevant for my argument) are preserved in Migne (*PG* 9:732). Latin: *Marcus Petri sectator, praedicante Petro Evangelium palam Romae coram quibusdam Caesareanis equitibus, et multa Christi testimonia proferente; petitus ab eis ut possent quae dicebantur memoriae commendare, scripsit ex his quae Petro dicta sunt, Evangelium quod secundum Marcum vocitatur.*

26. "Equites," *OCD*, 551.

27. R. Pesch, *Das Markusevangelium* (HTKNT II/1–2; 2 vols.; Freiburg: Herder, 1976–77); J. Ernst, *Das Evangleium nach Markus* (RNT; Regensburg: Pustet Verlag, 1981);

J. Gnilka, *Das Evangelium nach Markus* (5th ed.; EKKNT II/1–2; 2 vols.; Zürich/Neukirchen/ Vluyn: Benziger Verlag/Neukirchener Verlag, 1998). But a defender of Syrian provenance is Ludger Schenke, *Das Markusevangelium* (Stuttgart: Kohlhammer, 2005).

28. Martin Hengel, *Studies in the Gospel of Mark* (Philadelphia: Fortress, 1985), 28–30.

29. The interpretive practice of locating the Gospel of Mark in a specific time and place has been taken to its limit by Incigneri, *Gospel to the Romans*, which reads Mark as addressed to traumatized Roman Christians in late 71 c.e., after the triumphant return of Titus from Jerusalem. His interpretation has many fascinating moments, but it ultimately reads the Gospel of Mark too frequently as an allegory for current political events. Adam Winn, *The Purpose of Mark's Gospel* (WUNT II 245; Tübingen: Mohr Siebeck, 2008), was brought to my attention during this book's final revisions, and I was not yet able to assess its arguments.

30. John Ashton, *Understanding the Fourth Gospel* (Oxford: Clarendon, 1991), 198, after analyzing the debate over the provenance of the Gospel of John.

31. Yarbro Collins, *Mark*, 101.

32. Werner Eck, *Rom und Judaea: Fünf Vorträge zur Römischen Herrschaft in Palaestina* (Tübingen: Mohr Siebeck, 2007), 51, 236.

33. To supplement the general analysis of Clifford Ando, *Imperial Ideology and Provincial Loyalty in the Roman Empire* (Berkeley: University of California Press, 2000), 215–28, see the specific treatment of Carlos F. Noreña, "The Communication of the Emperor's Virtues," *JRS* 91 (2001): 146–68.

34. Fronto, *Ep.* 4.12: *usquequaque ubique imagines vestrae sint volgo propositae.*

35. Based on an approximate figure of 50 million residents in the Roman Empire in the mid-first century. See M. Pfanner, "Über das Herstellen von Porträts: Ein Beitrag zu Rationalisierungsmaßnahmen und Produktionsmechanismen von Massenware im späten Hellenismus und in der römischen Kaiserzeit," *Jahrbuch des deutschen archäologischen Instituts* 104 (1989): 178; cited in Ando, *Ideology*, 232.

36. There are over 300,000 Christian churches in the United States and about 300 million people. For this estimate of churches, see the Hartford Institute for Religious Research: http://hirr.hartsem.edu/index.html.

37. On the overall function of the portraits and other images, see Paul Zanker, *The Power of Images in the Age of Augustus* (trans. Alan Shapiro; Ann Arbor: University of Michigan Press, 1988).

38. Cf. Ando, *Ideology*, 392.

39. ἦρξεν δὲ τῶι κόσμωι τῶν δι' αὐτὸν εὐανγελί[ων ἡ γενέθλιος] τοῦ θεοῦ. *OGIS* 2:48–60, cited in Lily Ross Taylor, *The Divinity of the Roman Emperor* (Middletown, Conn.: American Philological Association, 1931), 273.

40. The connections were made as early as Julius Wellhausen, *Einleitung in die drei ersten Evangelien*, (2nd ed.; Berlin: G. Reimer, 1911), 98; and Ernst Lohmeyer, *Christuskult und Kaiserkult* (Tübingen: J. C. B. Mohr [Paul Siebeck], 1919), 24. They have been charted out by Craig A. Evans, "Mark's Incipit and the Priene Calendar Inscription: From Jewish Gospel to Greco-Roman Gospel," *Journal for the Study of Greco-Roman Christianity and Judaism* 1 (2000): 67–81.

41. On the textual problems with Mark 1:1, see Yarbro Collins, *Mark*, 130; eadem, "Establishing the Text: Mark 1:1," in *Texts and Contexts: The Function of Biblical Texts in Their Textual and Situational Contexts* (ed. Tord Fornberg and David Hellholm; Oslo: Scandinavian University Press, 1995), 111–27; N. Clayton Croy, "Where the Gospel Text Begins: A Non-Theological Interpretation of Mark 1:1," *NovT* 43 (2001): 105–27. There is

also a new papyrus witness, tentatively dated to the third century, lacking "Son of God," which will soon be published (probably by Geoffrey Smith) in *P.Oxy.*.

42. Josephus, *B.J.* 4.10.

43. Monika Bernett, *Der Kaiserkult in Judäa unter den Herodiern und Römern* (Tübingen: Mohr Siebeck, 2007). Cf. Joan E. Taylor, "Pontius Pilate and the Imperial Cult in Roman Judaea," *NTS* 52 (2006): 555–82.

44. In addition to these three temples (plus the Omrit temple), there is also a Roman temple being excavated at Hippos-Sussita (above the eastern shore of the Sea of Galilee). Reports at <http://hippos.haifa.ac.il/report.htm>. It is not yet known to whom the Roman temple there was dedicated, but the excavation director dates it to the principate of Augustus (late-first century B.C.E.), and it is possibly dedicated to him. It was built on a Hellenistic temple complex, and it was in turn supplanted by a Byzantine-era Christian Church (also undergoing excavation). Additionally, the forum at Hippos-Sussita features a *kalybe* shrine for emperor worship, dating from the late-second/early-third century C.E. and more in line with the other open shrine "Kalybe-structures" found along the eastern frontier. Arthur Segal and Michael Eisenberg, "Sussita-Hippos of the Decapolis: Town Planning and Architecture of a Roman-Byzantine City," *Near Eastern Archaeology* 70:2 (June 2007): 86–107; and Arthur Segal, "The 'Kalybe-Structures'—Temples for the Imperial Cult in Hauran and Trachon: An Historical-Architectural Analysis," found at http://www.tau.ac.il/arts/projects/PUB/assaph-art/assaph6/articles_assaph6/ArthurSegal.pdf.

45. Josephus, *B.J.* 1.403; *A.J.* 15.292–98. I have not been able to see this site for myself, due to instability in the region surrounding Nablus (West Bank). I rely on the archaeological reports from the first "Harvard Expedition" and the later "Joint Expedition." George A. Reisner, Clarence S. Fisher, and David G. Lyon, *Harvard Excavations at Samaria, 1908–1910* (2 vols.; Cambridge, Mass.: Harvard University Press, 1924), 1: 26–50, 1: 170–80, 2: plates 17–19. Some elements of the Herodian temple were excavated along with a headless statue (probably of Augustus?, 1: 176). An altar and stelae with votive inscriptions date from a Severan expansion of the temple complex. John W. Crowfoot, Kathleen M. Kenyon, and Eliezer L. Sukenik, *Samaria-Sebaste: Reports of the Work of the Joint Expedition in 1931–1933 and of the British Expedition in 1935, vol. 1: The Buildings at Samaria* (London: Palestine Exploration Fund, 1942), 123–32. Cf. the proposed temple reconstruction in Ehud Netzer, "The Augusteum at Samaria-Sebaste—A New Outlook," *Eretz-Israel* 19 (1987): 97–105 [Hebrew], 75* [English summary].

46. Josephus, *B.J.* 1.408–15; *A.J.* 15.331–41; Philo, *Legat.* 299–305. For descriptions and explanations from the excavation director, see Kenneth G. Holum, "The Temple Platform: Progress Report on the Excavations," in *Caesarea Papers 2: Herod's Temple, the Provincial Governor's Praetorium and Granaries, the Later Harbor, a Gold Coin Hoard, and Other Studies* (ed. Kenneth G. Holum, Avner Raban, and Joseph Patrich; JRASup 35; Portsmouth, RI: Journal of Roman Archaeology, 1999), 13–34. Though there are no extant inscriptions concerning Herod's temple, there was some kind of "Tiberieum" dedicated by Pontius Pilate, which may have been a temple, and the city did have "[severi] Augustales, an officially sanctioned association of wealthy freedman [sic], originating in Italy, who helped finance the imperial cult, including *ludi Augustales* honoring the emperors … To judge from the inscriptions, emperor worship figured prominently among Caesarea's public cults." Clayton Miles Lehmann and Kenneth G. Holum, *The Greek and Latin Inscriptions of Caesarea Maritima* (Joint Expedition to Caesarea Maritima 5; Boston: American Schools of Oriental Research, 2000), 17.

47. Josephus, *B.J.* 1.404–06; *A.J.* 15.363–64. Two sites at Banias have been proposed as the Temple of Augustus. For a summary of the *status quaestionis*, see the separate arguments of Andrea M. Berlin and Ehud Netzer in "Debate: Where was Herod's Temple to Augustus," *BAR* 29:5 (Sept/Oct 2003): 22–25. The consensus view, stated by the current National Parks placard at the site and reinforced by Andrea Berlin's argument, locates the temple directly in front of the grotto of Pan. The western wall of that building is partially preserved, and one can see niches carved in it, probably for statues of the imperial family. To access the ancient sanctuary of Pan, therefore, one would have had to pass through the Temple of Augustus. For an interpretation of the site according to the consensus view, see Andrea M. Berlin, "The Archaeology of Ritual: The Sanctuary of Pan at Banias/Caesarea Philippi," *BASOR* 315 (1999): 27–45. Ehud Netzer defends a different site at Banias, a partially excavated platform just west of the grotto, perched on the cliff. Cf. Ehud Netzer, "The Sanctuary of Pan at Banias," *Qadmoniot* 115 (1998): 18–25 [Hebrew]. Bernett follows Netzer's identification.

48. The excavators at Omrit argue that this temple is actually Herod's Temple of Augustus. J. Andrew Overman, Jack Olive, and Michael Nelson, "Discovering Herod's Shrine to Augustus: Mystery Temple Found at Omrit," *BAR* 29:2 (Mar/Apr 2003): 40–49, 67–68; cf. their argument in "Debate," 24. They base their conclusion on the architectural style of the Omrit temple, a tetraprostyle temple with dimensions and features corresponding to other Augustea in the Roman Empire. Berlin, however, weighs the literary evidence heavily—the descriptions of Josephus depict a closer proximity to the sanctuary complex at Banias itself. I await further publications from the Omrit excavation, but my current judgment is that there is a way to account for all the evidence (literary, archaeological, and numismatic), as adduced by Andrea Berlin, "Debate," 24. Herod's Temple of Augustus is one of the two sites at Banias (corresponding to Josephus's testimony), but that does *not* mean that the Omrit temple is not an imperial temple (corresponding to the archaeological evidence of Omrit). The Omrit temple would then be an imperial temple constructed by Herod's son Philip, a few decades later. The evidence of the coins of Herod Philip then would make more sense (cf. *RPC* 4951; *AJC* 2.245.6a). Previously, the clear depiction of a tetraprostyle Roman temple on Philip's coins was thought to have evoked his father's building of a temple for Augustus. However, it would have been a more common practice for Philip to have been advertising a building project of his own—the tetraprostyle temple at Omrit, dedicated to either Augustus or Tiberius. The shield depicted in front of the temple on Philip's coins of Tiberius would then be an allusion to Tiberius's intervention on behalf of the Jewish appeal (led by Herod's sons, Philip likely among them) regarding the golden shields that Pilate tried to set up in Jerusalem (Philo, *Legat.* 299–305; cf. Paul L. Maier, "The Episode of the Golden Shields at Jerusalem," *HTR* 62 [1969]: 109–21). In Berlin's words, "a more compelling argument could be made that this [Omrit] temple was a construction of Herod Philip, who raised this structure on the edge of his new city not only to mark his territory but also to make an architectural statement in keeping with that of his father." It could also have served as an expression of thanks for Tiberius's siding with the Jews against Pilate in the golden shields episode.

49. According to the excavators at Samaria-Sebaste, "the general plan of Herod's great temple is plain, and it can be realised what an imposing building it must have appeared, on the summit of the hill, with its great artificial platform and the temple towering above that." Kenyon, *Buildings at Samaria*, 126.

50. Her objections to the consensus are found in Bernett, *Kaiserkult in Judäa*, 1–15; quotation from Monika Bernett, "Roman Imperial Cult in the Galilee," in *Religion, Ethnicity,*

and Identity in Ancient Galilee (WUNT 210; ed. Jürgen Zangenberg, Harold Attridge, and Dale Martin; Tübingen: Mohr Siebeck, 2007), 341.

51. Bernett, *Kaiserkult in Judäa*, 354. Trans. my own.

52. Bernett, "Roman Imperial Cult," 341.

53. Judas the Galilean led a revolt against Roman occupation; he is mentioned in Acts 5:37 and described in Josephus, *A.J.* 18.1–10, 23.

54. I translate εὐδόκησα + ἐν in the baptismal voice as "pleased to choose," which will sound unfamiliar to most readers of English Bibles because the "well pleased" translation of the King James Version has influenced almost every subsequent English translation. See below for discussion.

55. For an example of the standard dogmatic rejection of an adoptionist reading, see James R. Edwards, "The Baptism of Jesus According to the Gospel of Mark," *JETS* 34 (1991): 55–7.

56. Adolph von Harnack, *History of Dogma* (7 vols.; 3rd ed.; trans. Neil Buchanan; Gloucester, Mass.: Peter Smith, 1976) discusses earliest Christology (1:183–204), the later Roman monarchian adoptionists (3:14–51), and the adoptionism of eighth-century Spain (5:278–92).

57. Dale B. Martin, *Slavery as Salvation: The Metaphor of Slavery in Pauline Christianity* (New Haven: Yale University Press, 1990).

58. Cf. Christiane Kunst, *Römische Adoption: Zur Strategie einer Familienorganisation* (Hennef: Marthe Clauss, 2005), especially 59–62.

59. On Theodotus and followers, see Bart D. Ehrman, *The Orthodox Corruption of Scripture* (Oxford: Oxford University Press, 1993), 47–54; and Winrich A. Löhr, "Theodotus der Lederarbeiter und Theodotus der Bankier—ein Beitrag zur römischen Theologiegeschichte des zweiten und dritten Jahrhunderts," *ZNW* 87 (1996): 101–25. For a cogent analysis of the so-called adoptionism of eighth-century Spain, see John C. Cavadini, *The Last Christology of the West: Adoptionism in Spain and Gaul, 785–820* (Philadelphia: University of Pennsylvania Press, 1993).

60. This general picture is supported by: Vincent Taylor, *The Gospel According to St. Mark* (London: MacMillan, 1959); C. E. B. Cranfield, *The Gospel According to St. Mark* (Cambridge: Cambridge University Press, 1963); Lane, *Gospel According to Mark*; Robert A. Guelich, *Mark 1–8:26* (Word Biblical Commentary 34A; Dallas: Word Books, 1989); Gundry, *Mark*; Marcus, *Mark 1–8*; Moloney, *Mark*; and R. T. France, *The Gospel of Mark* (New International Greek Testament Commentary; Grand Rapids: Eerdmans, 2002).

61. Marcus, *Mark 1–8*, 165.

62. There are, however, some Greek mss. of Isaiah which use εὐδοκέω to translate רצה (see France, *Gospel*, 82). See below on the ευδοκ- root.

63. Plutarch, *Galba* 7.3.

64. Cranfield, *Gospel*, 55.

65. Lane, *Gospel*, 58.

66. France, *Gospel*, 82.

67. Ehrman, *Orthodox Corruption*, 47–118.

68. Taylor, *Gospel*, 162.

69. Yarbro Collins, *Mark*, 150.

70. Donahue and Harrington, *Mark*, 67.

71. Ibid., 69.

72. Cf. chap. 5 below, on the patristic-era bifurcation of Jesus' divine sonship from that of Christians.

73. Marcus too draws the connection between Jesus' baptism and the divine sonship afforded to all Christians, however he does not think an adoptive interpretation follows from the connection (Marcus, *Mark 1–8*, 164–65). Without arguing for it, he presumes a distinction between Jesus' "real" sonship and Christians' sonship by adoption.

74. Quotations in this paragraph are from Eduard Schweizer, *The Good News According to Mark* (trans. Donald H. Madvig; Atlanta: John Knox, 1970), 40–1.

75. Schweizer, *Good News*, 356–7.

76. In the modern West, we normally think of adoption as a legal procedure, enforceable under the law, which transfers full parental authority from a biological parent or set of parents to another person or persons who gain(s) the full legal status of parent(s). Though the line between biological parents and adoptive parents can be fuzzy *emotionally* for all involved, the line is quite clear *legally*. The classic argument against the practice of adoption in ancient Judaism is Herbert Donner, "Adoption oder Legitimation? Erwägungen zur Adoption im Alten Testament auf dem Hintergrund der altorientalischen Rechte," *Oriens Antiquus* 8 (1969): 87–119. Donner's thesis has been skillfully critiqued, however, by James M. Scott, *Adoption as Sons of God: An Exegetical Investigation into the Background of ΥΙΟΘΕΣΙΑ in the Pauline Corpus* (WUNT II 48; Tübingen: Mohr Siebeck, 1992), especially 62–75. He argues that "the Jews recognized adoptions in the Old Testament; they knew of Roman adoptions; they used adoption in comparisons; and they probably even practiced adoption themselves" (75).

77. Surveys of adoption in ancient Judaism can be found in F. W. Knobloch, "Adoption," *ABD* 1:76–79; and Jeffrey Howard Tigay and Ben-Zion Schereschewsky, "Adoption," *Encyclopedia Judaica* (2nd ed.; 22 vols.; ed. Fred Skolnik; New York: Macmillan, 2007), 1:415–18. The continuing debate about adoption and Jewish identity is exhibited by both orthodox and reform perspectives: Melech Schachter, "Various Aspects of Adoption," in *Halacha and Contemporary Society* (ed. Alfred S. Cohen; New York: Ktav, 1984), 31–53; and Michael Gold, "Adoption: A New Problem for Jewish Law," *Judaism* 36 (1987): 443–50.

78. In addition to the biblical narratives treated here, one should also note the relationships considered adoptive by Josephus (Abram and Lot, *A.J.* 1.154; Jethro and Moses, *A.J.* 2.263, making Moses adopted on two different occasions) and Philo (Sarah and Ishmael, *Abr.* 250).

79. The word "as" in the English translation should not be construed as contrary to fact (took her "as if she were" his daughter) but as an actual fact (took her "to be" his daughter). The sense of these two narratives was clear enough to Jerome that these two examples contain the only use of the verb *adoptare* in the Latin Vulgate: *quem illa adoptavit in locum filii* (Exod 2:10); and *Mardocheus sibi eam adoptavit in filiam* (Esth 2:7).

80. Tigay, "Adoption," 1:416.

81. The modern scholarly answer is simple: this is a case of textual corruption. Though the MT and LXX contain "Michal," some Hebrew and Syriac manuscripts contain "Merab." Both ancient and modern readers identify the same problem but choose to deal with it much differently.

82. The word group כאילו stands behind the translation "as though." According to Marcus Jastrow, the combination כאילו connotes a situation contrary to fact. The foster-parent is considered "as though" he had begotten him, even though the reader knows that he did not. Thus it expresses well what we would call a "metaphorical" function, since metaphors function precisely to signify two things which both are and are not the same. On כאילו, see Marcus Jastrow, *A Dictionary of the Targumim, the Talmud Talmud and Yerushalmi, and the*

Midrashic Literature (2 vols.; New York: P. Shalom, 1967), 1:49a. On this functional definition of metaphor, see Paul Ricoeur, *Interpretation Theory: Discourse and the Surplus of Meaning* (Fort Worth: Texas Christian University Press, 1976), especially "Metaphor and Symbol," 45–69.

83. See *b. Meg.* 13a for a *tour de force* of etymology.

84. Another example stating this general principle comes from *Exod. Rab.* 46:5. A *mashal* there does not purport to solve an exegetical or halakhic problem, but rather it provides an imaginative parallel to illuminate how Israelites can claim a dual parentage from both Abraham and God (cf. the claims of "the Jews" in the John 8:39–41). What is important for our subject is its quotation of the general principle about fosterage: "he that brings up a child is called a father, and not he that gives birth."

85. For example, the "adoption ceremony" is presumed in E. A. Speiser, *Genesis* (AB 1; Garden City, N.Y.: Doubleday, 1981), 357. Cf. Isaac Mendelsohn, "A Ugaritic Parallel to the Adoption of Ephraim and Manasseh," *IEJ* 9 (1959): 180–83.

86. Cf. Gen 30:3; 50:23 for other references to sons on "the knees"; and B. Stade, "Auf Jemandes Knieen gebären," *ZAW* 6 (1886): 143–56.

87. This aligns with a thesis argued by Martin Jaffee, that the teacher-student relationship outweighed the parent-child relationship in late ancient discipleship communities. The teacher-student relationship, "at least in its ideal representations, supplanted and superseded even those of the patriarchal family. . . . The Mishnah teaches: 'Where a disciple finds a lost object of his father's and of his master's, the return of his master's takes precedence, for his father brought him into *this world*, but his master, who has taught him *wisdom*, brings him into *the coming world*'" (*m. B. Metzia* 2:11 / *t. B. Metzia* 2:30). Martin S. Jaffee, *Torah in the Mouth: Writing and Oral Tradition in Palestinian Judaism 200* B.C.E.—*400* C.E. (New York: Oxford University Press, 2001), 148.

88. Papyrus 8, lines 5, 8 and 9, in Emil G. Kraeling, ed., *The Brooklyn Museum Aramaic Papyri. New documents of the fifth century B.C. from the Jewish colony at Elephantine* (New Haven: Yale University Press, 1969), 224–31. For other adoption formulae from the Ancient Near East, see Shalom M. Paul, "Adoption Formulae: A Study of Cuneiform and Biblical Legal Clauses," *Maarav* 2 (1979–80): 173–85.

89. See the analysis in Harry J. Leon, *The Jews of Ancient Rome* (Philadelphia: Jewish Publication Society of America, 1960), 232–3 and inscription nos. 3, 21, 144, and 358.

90. For the concept of divine sonship in the Jewish mystical tradition, see Moshe Idel, *Ben: Sonship in Jewish Mysticism* (London: Continuum, 2008), esp. 1–107. He describes adoptive divine sonship as one of four types in Judaism (generation, emanation, adoption, and vocation, pp. 34–35).

91. The best analysis is Scott, *Adoption*, especially 221–70.

92. Joseph H. Hellerman has presented a cogent sociological analysis of the metaphor of the early church as a surrogate patrilineal kinship group. Joseph H. Hellerman, *The Ancient Church as Family* (Minneapolis: Fortress, 2001).

93. Latin: *Ita per saeculorum milia—incredibile dictu—gens aeterna est, in qua nemo nascitur.* The issue of celibacy among the Essenes is still debated, since there seem to have been non-celibate Essenes as well. Josephus calls them "another order" of Essenes (ἕτερον τάγμα, *B.J.* 2.160), and their existence may be corroborated by the Damascus Document (CD VII 6–7).

94. I am here adopting the Essene hypothesis of the Qumran community, though I acknowledge its detractors.

95. There are strong arguments in favor of this section of the *Hodayot* having been spoken/written by the Teacher of Righteousness. Cf. Michael C. Douglas, "Power and Praise in the Hodayot: A Literary-Critical Study of 1QH 9:1–18:14" (Ph.D. diss., The University of Chicago, 1998), esp. 144–72.

96. Translation is from Florentino García Martínez and Eibert J.C. Tigchelaar, eds., *The Dead Sea Scrolls Study Edition* (2 vols.; Leiden; Boston; Köln: Brill and Grand Rapids: Eerdmans, 1997–1998), 1:185, slightly modified.

97. As with the *Hodayot* generally, it is difficult to assess whether the speaker's prayer is individual and private, individual and yet representative of others' experiences, a communal and liturgical recitation, or something else altogether. Furthermore, the speaker's identification of God as adoptive father, mother, and wet-nurse does not preclude the speaker's depiction of himself in similar ways (1QHᵃ XV 20–22), if indeed it is the same speaker.

98. Though the king is most prominent, there were other individuals imagined as adopted sons of God. For example, Abraham is called εἰσποίητος υἱός ("adopted son") by Philo (*Sobr.* 56–57). If the aforementioned text from 1QH is a "Teacher Hymn," then it also proclaims individual divine sonship. I will not here enter the debate about the "son of God" text in 4Q246, which would take the argument far off course. Cf. Joseph A. Fitzmeyer, "4Q246: The 'Son of God' Document from Qumran," *Biblica* 74 (1993): 153–74; John J. Collins, "The 'Son of God' Text from Qumran," in *From Jesus to John: Essays on Jesus and the New Testament Christology in Honour of Marinus de Jonge* (ed. Martinus de Boer; Sheffield: JSOT Press, 1993), 65–82; James D.G. Dunn, "Son of God as Son of Man in the Dead Sea Scrolls: A Response to John Collins on 4Q246," in *Scrolls and the Scriptures* (ed. Stanley Porter and Craig Evans; Sheffield: Sheffield University Press, 1997), 198–210; and Karl A. Kuhn, "The 'One Like a Son of Man' Becomes the 'Son of God,'" *CBQ* 69 (2007): 22–42.

99. Gerald Cooke, "The Israelite King as Son of God," *ZAW* 73 (1961): 202–25; Sigmund Mowinckel, *He That Cometh. The Messiah Concept in the Old Testament and Later Judaism* (Nashville: Abingdon Press, 1955; repr. Grand Rapids: Eerdmans, 2005); Frank Moore Cross, *Canaanite Myth and Hebrew Epic* (Cambridge, Mass.: Harvard University Press, 1973), especially "The Ideologies of Kingship in the Era of the Empire: Conditional Covenant and Eternal Decree," 217–73; John J. Collins, *The Scepter and the Star: The Messiahs of the Dead Sea Scrolls and Other Ancient Literature* (New York: Doubleday, 1995); and Adela Yarbro Collins and John J. Collins, *King and Messiah as Son of God* (Grand Rapids: Eerdmans, 2008), 1–47.

100. The promise to David has a complex tradition history, analyzed deftly by William M. Schniedewind, *Society and the Promise to David: The Reception History of 2 Samuel 7:1–17* (Oxford: Oxford University Press, 1999).

101. Collins, *Scepter*, 23.

102. Cross, *Canaanite Myth*, 258.

103. Mowinckel, *He That Cometh*, 78. Cf. Martin Noth, "God, King and Nation," in *The Laws in the Pentateuch and Other Studies* (Philadelphia: Fortress Press, 1966), 172–3; and Yarbro Collins and Collins, *King and Messiah*, 10–15, 19–22.

104. Other scholars have looked to Egyptian royal ideology to illuminate divine sonship in Judaism, e.g., Joachim Kügler, *Pharao und Christus: religionsgeschichtliche Untersuchung zur Frage einer Verbindung zwischen altägyptischer Königstheologie und neutestamentlicher Christologie im Lukasevangelium* (Bodenheim: PHILO, 1997), which compares Egyptian divine sonship to the Christology of Luke.

105. Collins, *Scepter*, 167–8.

106. This survey is based in part on G. Schrenk, "εὐδοκέω, εὐδοκία," *TDNT* 2:738–51.

107. The *New Jerusalem Bible* translates it as "my favour rests on you." Although the *New Jersualem Bible* (1985) was translated directly from the original languages, it preserved some of the choices of the previous *Jerusalem Bible* (1961; English 1966), which was a French translation and was not influenced by the King James Version on this point.

108. I should also note that the Vulgate may have also influenced translators over the centuries. It often (though not exclusively) uses forms of *conplacere* to translate the word-group, e.g., the end of Mark 1:11 is rendered, *in te conplacui*.

109. Julius Wellhausen, *Das Evangelium Marci* (Berlin: Georg Reimer Verlag, 1909), 5. The parallel to the KJV would be the German translation, "an dir habe ich Wohlgefallen." The French is from *La Traduction Oecuménique de la Bible* (the "TOB," 1975–76).

110. The KJV uses "well pleased" for the examples in this paragraph, despite the clear contextual connotations of "choice" or "selection."

111. Cf. also 2 Macc 14:35 for another use of εὐδοκέω to grant the temple as a habitation.

112. The French *TOB* of the LXX renders it, "*pourtant le Seigneur ne les a pas préférés.*"

113. See citations in Schrenk, "εὐδοκέω, εὐδοκία," *TDNT* 2:739–40.

114. *P.Mich.* VIII 473.14.

115. *P.Oxy.* I 56.20.

116. *P.Lips.* 28.24. For the best edition, see L. Mitteis and U. Wilcken, eds., *Grundzüge und Chrestomathie der Papyruskunde* (Leipzig, 1912), no. 363.24. The fact that a *woman* here adopts a son confirms how adoptive practices in parts of the Roman Empire were based more on "common law" than the official legal codes.

117. Schrenk, "εὐδοκέω, εὐδοκία," *TDNT* 2:740–41.

118. Ibid., 2:740–41.

119. Ibid., 2:742.

120. Ibid., 2:742.

121. The use at 1 Cor 10:5 can also be viewed similarly. The emphasis there is not on how God was displeased with a previous state of affairs, but rather on how God intervened to choose to punish some of the Israelites. The connection to the "baptism" in this passage is likely a coincidence.

122. Gerhard Münderlein, "Die Erwählung durch das Pleroma: Bemerkungen zu Kol. i. 19," *NTS* 8 (1961): 264–76.

123. Ibid., 267. Trans. my own.

124. Ibid., 275. Trans. my own.

125. Ibid., 268. Trans. my own.

126. Ibid., 271–72. Trans. my own.

127. Schrenk, "εὐδοκέω, εὐδοκία," *TDNT* 2:743–44.

128. Ibid., 2:747.

129. For a different interpretation of the verbal connections between Mark and Ephesians, see Joel Marcus, *The Way of the Lord: Christological Exegesis of the Old Testament in the Gospel of Mark* (Louisville: Westminster/John Knox Press, 1992), 74; and the literature cited there.

130. Several ancient mss. do not end with "the beloved one" (τῷ ἠγαπημένῳ), but rather "his beloved son" (τῷ ἠγαπημένῳ υἱῷ αὐτοῦ); especially D* F G, the Old Latin (it), and Sahidic Coptic (sa).

131. These and other features of the Spirit are discussed in Fritzleo Lentzen-Deis, *Die Taufe Jesu nach den Synoptikern* (Frankfurt: Josef Knecht, 1970), 127–60.

132. See discussion of these in chap. 2.

133. The root use deals with members of a family, but it was also expanded: Romans imagined *genii* for the Roman senate, the Roman people, particular places, military legions, and individual gods.

134. This short definition of *numen* as "der ausgedrückte Wille einer Gottheit" is from *DNP* 8:1047–49.

135. It is thus related etymologically to the Greek νεῦμα, but not πνεῦμα.

136. Duncan Fishwick, *The Imperial Cult in the Latin West* (2 vols.; Leiden: Brill, 1987–92), 2:383.

137. There is not an etymological connection between Spirit (πνεῦμα) and *genius* or *numen*, despite the phonemic similarities of the latter (which is actually related to the Greek νεῦμα). The *genius* is often translated in Greek as τύχη. It is also possible that the early Christian connection of "Spirit" with "power" (πνεῦμα and δύναμις) would connect functionally to the pairing of *genius* and *numen*.

138. The relevant text of *CIL* 11.3303 is: *et ut natalibus Augusti et Ti. Caesarum, prius quam ad vescendum | decuriones irent, thure et vino genii eorum ad epulandum ara | numinis Augusti invitarentur |* . " . . . and so that on the birthdays of Augustus and Tiberius, before the council members go to eat, their *genii* should be invited with incense and wine to dine at the altar of the Augustan *numen*." See discussion in Fishwick, *Imperial Cult*, 2:380, and Ittai Gradel, *Emperor Worship and Roman Religion* (Oxford: Clarendon Press, 2002), 239–45.

139. Fishwick, *Imperial Cult*, 2:386–7. Despite this assessment, Fishwick still holds to a stark god/human dichotomy in his analysis.

140. These connections are all functional, as stated earlier. But there is at least one linguistic connection between the Spirit and the *spiritus* of the emperor. In Seneca's *De Clementia*, written to Nero, he elaborates on the stock metaphor of the political "body" in this way: the Roman people are an "immense multitude encircling the life of one man and ruled by his spirit [*spiritu*] . . . ; for he is the bond by which the republic stays together, the living breath [*spiritus vitalis*] which these many thousands draw" (Seneca, *Clem.* 1.3.5; 1.4.1). This image of the imperial *spiritus* is rather similar to the early Christian understanding of the Spirit as the unifying power of the divine family.

141. *Acts of Scillitan Martyrs*, 5; *Martyrdom of Apollonius* 3; *Martyrdom of Pionius* 18; *Martyrdom of Polycarp* 9–10; all compiled in Herbert Musurillo, *Acts of the Christian Martyrs* (Oxford: Clarendon Press, 1972). Cf. Keith Hopkins, *Conquerors and Slaves: Sociological Studies in Roman History* (Cambridge: Cambridge University Press, 1978), 227–8; and Fergus Millar, "The Imperial Cult and the Persecutions," in *Le Culte des Souverains dans l'Empire Romain* (ed. Willem den Boer; Entretiens sur l'antiquité classique 19; Vandœuvres-Genève: Fondation Hardt, 1973), 145–50.

142. W. D. Davies and Dale C. Allison, *The Gospel According to St. Matthew* (3 vols.; ICC; Edinburgh: T&T Clark, 1997) 1:330–4. To these we now add Edward P. Dixon, "Descending Spirit and Descending Gods: A 'Greek' Interpretation of the Spirit's 'Descent as a Dove' in Mark 1:10," *JBL* 128 (2009): 759–80, which interprets the dove in connection with the common Greek mythological topos of gods descending in human form.

143. See those listed in Stephen Gero, "The Spirit as a Dove at the Baptism of Jesus," *NovT* 18 (1976): 17–35.

144. E.g., Marcus, *Mark*; and Davies and Allison, *Matthew*. Some have also proposed an allusion to Noah's messenger bird (Gen 8:8–12), since the bird brings a sort of good news of salvation (see Davies and Allison, *Matthew*, 332). But this interpretation too has problems, discussed there and elsewhere.

145. The verb is used in another context to describe a bird (Deut 32:11), but elsewhere in the Hebrew Bible it portrays the shaking of bones (Jer 23:9). Another important passage is 4Q521, where the Lord's spirit "will hover upon the poor" (4Q521 1 II.6). The anointed one is also mentioned in this fragment, but the connection between the Lord and the anointed one is unclear. Furthermore, the spirit hovers here just as in Gen 1:2, but the issue for this chapter is to what degree that invokes a bird. 4Q521 gives no reason, apart from the verb, to interpret the spirit as a bird. Finally, the spirit here hovers on the poor, not the anointed one.

146. France, *Gospel*, 79.

147. See Othmar Keel, *Vögel als Boten* (Orbis Biblicus et Orientalis 14; Freiburg: Universitätsverlag Freiburg, 1977).

148. Suetonius, *Dom.* 6. For other eagle omens not covered in this chapter, see Suetonius, *Galba* 4, and *Vit.* 9.

149. Andrew Wallace-Hadrill, *Suetonius: The Scholar and His Caesars* (New Haven: Yale University Press, 1984), 192.

150. Wallace-Hadrill, *Suetonius*, 191.

151. Suetonius, *Claud.* 7.

152. Suetonius, *Aug.* 94.

153. Ibid., 97.

154. Ibid., 96.

155. On the difficulties of transferring charismatic authority, see Max Weber, *Economy and Society* (2 vols.; ed. and trans. Guenther Roth and Claus Wittich; Berkeley: University of California Press, 1978), 1:212–301; 2:1111–57.

156. Suetonius, *Tib.* 14.

157. Suetonius, *Vesp.* 4. The claim that the Judeans killed their governor is not corroborated by Josephus.

158. This almost certainly alludes to the capturing of a legionary eagle from the *XII Fulminata*, a Roman legion that suffered heavy losses in retreat (Josephus, *B.J.* 2.500–55, although he does not mention the lost eagle), whose remnant was later assigned to Titus for the assault on Jerusalem (Josephus, *B.J.* 5.41).

159. Suetonius, *Vesp.* 5.

160. Suetonius, *Aug.* 94.

161. This is a common trope: elsewhere in Suetonius, see *Vesp.* 5.

162. Annie Vigourt, *Les presages impériaux d'Auguste à Domitien* (Paris: De Boccard, 2001), 217. Cf. an anonymous *quadrans* with a bust of Venus and a dove on the reverse (*RIC* 2, p. 218, coins 24–25).

163. I have not documented here the use of eagles on Roman imperial coins and portraiture, but many examples could be offered to establish the widespread prevalence of the eagle in the physical images of imperial ideology. One coin type mentioned already in chap. 3 was the PROVIDENTIA DEORUM coin of Trajan, which depicts an eagle descending toward him. In Roman imperial ideology, *providentia* was the virtue often associated with an emperor's provision of sons/heirs to ensure a stable succession of power. *RIC* 2, p. 415, coin 589 (= plate XV.304); cf. *RIC* 2, p. 418, coin 602.

164. Tibullus, *Elegiae* 1.7.18, c. 27 B.C.E.. Latin: *Quid referam, ut volitet crebras intacta per urbes / Alba Palaestino sancta columba Syro?*

165. The presence of the dove in the worship and iconography of "the Syrian goddess" (likely Atargatis) is notable, but its meaning or function is not usually discernible (cf. Lucian, *De Dea Syria*, 14, 33, 54). On doves and pigeons in this area, see "Doves and Pigeons," *ABD* 6:1144–45.

166. E.g., *RPC* 2.2211.

167. Ovid, *Metam.* 1.504–07. Latin: *Nympha, precor, Penei, mane! non insequor hostis; / nympha, mane! sic agna lupum, sic cerva leonem, / sic aquilam penna fugiunt trepidante columbae, / hostes quaeque suos: amor est mihi causa sequendi.*

168. Horace, *Carm.* 4.4.29–32. Latin: *fortes creantur fortibus et bonis; / est in iuvencis, est in equis patrum / virtus, neque imbellem feroces / progenerant aquilae columbam.*

169. Another example occurs at Horace, *Epod.* 16.32–33, where the dove and the "bird of prey" (*milvus*) are contrasted.

170. In one of his letters to Marcus Aurelius, Fronto refers to "sheep and doves with wolves and eagles" (*oves et columbae cum lupis et aquilis, Ep.* 4.1) as part of a legend of Orpheus. The sheep-wolf and eagle-dove pairs symbolize archetypal enemies, which Fronto claims Marcus Aurelius has brought together in harmony. For a quite different use, see Pliny, *Ep.* 9.25, in which he calls his little letters "doves" as a contrast to his recipient's military standards ("eagles").

171. Josephus, *B.J.* 3.122–24. Trans. adapted from LCL.

172. There are myriad examples of how the eagle symbolized Roman military might. In a pivotal battle between the Romans and the Cherusci at the entrace to a forest, "the finest of auguries" appeared: eight eagles entering the forest. Tiberius, the commander, said, "Go and follow the Roman birds, the legions' very own divine powers!" (*sequerentur Romanas avis, propria legionum numina*; Tac. *Ann.* 2.17).

173. The author probably draws on the animal symbolism of a text like Ps 74: "Remember this, O Lord, how the enemy scoffs, and an impious people reviles your name. Do not deliver the soul of your dove to the wild animals; do not forget the life of your poor forever" (Ps 74:18–19). It is true that the animal here is a חור (turtle-dove), not a יונה (dove, pigeon), but the terminology oscillates, especially in translations of the Hebrew.

174. There are, of course, other references to Israel as a dove in the Bible and Jewish literature that do not directly inform my understanding of the eagle/dove trope. Nor have I incorporated Matthew's aphoristic simile in 10:16, portraying doves as "pure/innocent" (ἀκέραιος) or "most simple" (ἁπλούστατος, Codex D).

175. Trans. adapted from *OTP* 2:352. A more negative interpretation of such behavior is that the doves are timorous prey, as stated in *b. B. Qam.* 93a: "there is none among the birds more persecuted than doves."

176. Trans. adapted from *OTP* 2:22.

177. *Let. Aris.* 144–48. Trans. adapted from *OTP* 2:22.

178. The LXX states: βδέλυγμά ἐστιν—τὸν ἀετὸν . . . [etc.]. The proximity of these two words suggests a possible interpretation of Mark 13:14. The βδέλυγμα to which Mark refers could be the golden eagle set up over the temple by Herod. It would be difficult to argue definitively for this reading, but the historical event (combined with Mark's text) resonates with this passage of the Levitical law.

179. The story is not quite so simple, however. If one takes a simple tally of citations of the four Gospels in *Biblia Patristica*, one finds that the four Gospels are rather balanced in

citation until the end of the second century (Clement of Alexandria). Mark is in fourth place, but the differences are not large. Cf. Brenda Deen Schildgen, *Power and Prejudice: the Reception of the Gospel of Mark* (Detroit, Mich.: Wayne State University Press, 1998), 40. After the second century, however, Mark fades almost completely from the scene, such that not one of the third- or fourth-century commentators engages it on its own. The pattern corresponds with the christological trends among Christian theologians. After the second century, Christologies of divine begetting begin to dominate Christian discourse (cf. chap. 5 below).

180. Eusebius, *Hist. eccl.* 6.29. Trans. *NPNF*² 1:274–75.

181. Both Eusebius's *Life of Constantine* and the speech, *In Praise of Constantine*, suggest that he was at least attuned to and perhaps persuaded by the Roman political ideology of his day.

182. The description of this text as a "garland of legends" belongs to Vielhauer, cited in Wilhelm Schneemelcher, ed., *New Testament Apocrypha* (2 vols.; Louisville: Westminster John Knox, 2003), 1:435.

183. *Prot. Jas.* 9.1, trans. from Schneemelcher, *New Testament Apocrypha*, 1:429–30. Greek of last portion: καὶ ἰδοὺ περιστερὰ ἐξῆλθεν ἀπὸ τῆς ῥάβδου καὶ ἐπεστάθη ἐπὶ τὴν κεφαλὴν τοῦ Ἰωσήφ.

184. Gregory of Nazianzus, *Or.* 40.19 (*In sanctum baptisma, PG* 36:384).

185. The interpretation of the dove as colonial mimicry builds on—or rather, provides a theoretical foundation for—many of the astute observations about Mark and Roman power made by scholars such as Donald Senior, "With Swords and Clubs: The Setting of Mark's Community and His Critique of Abusive Power," *BTB* 17 (1987): 10–20; and John Donahue, "Windows and Mirrors: The Setting of Mark's Gospel," *CBQ* 57 (1995), 1–26. An intriguing parallel to this example of narrative mimicry is the report of the emperor Titus's death in rabbinic literature (*Lev. Rab.* 22:3), which ends with God's killing of Titus by means of a mosquito that transforms into a dove at the autopsy. For interpretation of the full version of this fascinating story as colonial mimicry, in part based on an eagle/dove trope, see Joshua Levinson, "'Tragedies Naturally Performed:' Fatal Charades, *Parodia Sacra*, and the Death of Titus," in *Jewish Culture and Society Under the Christian Roman Empire* (ed. Richard Kalmin and Seth Schwartz; Leuven: Peeters, 2003), 349–82.

186. Tat-Siong Benny Liew, "Tyranny, Boundary and Might: Colonial Mimicry in Mark's Gospel," *JSNT* 73 (1999): 13.

187. Homi K. Bhabha, *The Location of Culture* (London: Routledge, 1994), 86.

188. Bhabha, *Location*, 86.

189. The baptism "from heaven" is a circumlocution for "from God." See Moloney, *Gospel of Mark*, 231, and literature cited there.

190. Reference to Cassius Dio, *Roman History* 53.18.3; quotation from Mary Rose D'Angelo, "Abba and 'Father': Imperial Theology and the Jesus Traditions," *JBL* 111 (1992): 623. Philo also translates the imperial *potestas* with the word ἐξουσία (*Legat.* 28).

191. When I say that Mark is not focused on Davidic *descent* or Davidic *sonship*, I do not mean to discount the portrayal of Jesus in relationship to David as psalmist. Cf. Stephen P. Ahearne-Kroll, *The Psalms of Lament in Mark's Passion: Jesus' Davidic Suffering* (SNTSMS 142; Cambridge: Cambridge University Press, 2007).

192. Bacon, *Roman Gospel?*, 87.

193. Ibid., 89.

194. Despite the variant manuscript tradition attesting "the son of the carpenter and of Mary" (P⁴⁵ᵛⁱᵈ, *f*¹³, Old Latin, Bohairic, and Armenian), I agree with Nestle-Aland that the text

of the major codices is to be preferred. Cf. Raymond E. Brown, *The Birth of the Messiah* (New York: Doubleday, 1977), 537–39.

195. On the sonship status of Jesus in Matthew and Luke, see Brian M. Nolan, *The Royal Son of God: The Christology of Matthew 1–2 in the Setting of the Gospel* (Fribourg: Éditions universitaires; Göttingen: Vandenhoeck & Ruprecht, 1979); Donald J. Verseput, "The Role and Meaning of the 'Son of God' Title in Matthew's Gospel," *NTS* 33 (1987): 532–56; Yigal Levin, "Jesus, 'Son of God' and 'Son of David': The 'Adoption' of Jesus into the Davidic Line," *JSNT* 28 (2006): 415–42.

196. Tal Ilan, "'Man Born of Woman. . .' (Job 14:1) The Phenomenon of Men Bearing Metronymes at the Time of Jesus," *NovT* 34 (1992): 24. Cf. Brown, *Birth*, 537–41; and the contrasting previous positions of E. Stauffer, "Jeschu ben Mirjam (Mark 6:3)," in *Neotestamentica et Semitica: Studies in Honour of Matthew Black* (ed. E. Earle Ellis and Max Wilcox; Edinburgh: T & T Clark, 1969), 119–28, and H. K. McArthur, "'Son of Mary,'" *NovT* 15 (1973): 38–58.

197. In Roman adoptions, the adopted son did not usually get a new mother. Therefore, "son of Mary" is in line with the adoptive idea.

198. This teaching is not about Jesus' divine sonship but rather about that of other sons and daughters of God. In chap. 5, I discuss the relationship between the divine sonship of Christ and of Christians in early Christianity.

199. In the three related sayings from Matthew and Luke, Jesus describes what must be left behind, but he does not elaborate a second list of what will be received (Matt 8:21–22// Lk 9:59–62; Matt 10:34–36//Lk 12:51–53; Matt 10:37//Lk 14:26). Mark uniquely emphasizes the new family and its benefits.

200. These connections are suggested by Donahue and Harrington, *Mark*, 308.

201. In addition, only in this block of teaching, about entering the kingdom of God, does Jesus address the disciples as "children" (τέκνα, 10:24).

202. The point about having only one Father—the heavenly kind—is made less subtly by Matthew (23:9).

203. Scholars have called into question "the stereotype of the Roman father as an authoritarian figure wielding vast and oppressive disciplinary powers over his children," suggesting that the real relationships were less harsh or despotic than previously thought. Yet the powers legally granted to the *paterfamilias* were "awesome indeed," and the ideology of paternal sovereignty remained strong. Quotations from Richard Saller, "*Pietas*, Obligation and Authority in the Roman Family," in *Alte Geschichte und Wissenschaftsgeschichte: Festschrift für Karl Christ zum 65. Geburtstag* (ed. Peter Kneissl and Volker Losemann; Darmstadt: Wissenschaftliche Buchgesellschaft, 1988), 395 and 410.

204. In Nestle-Aland's edition, Peter confesses only that Jesus is the "Christ," but two early uncials do have a confession of divine sonship: "the Son of God" (א), or "the Son of the Living God" (W).

205. Cf. Earl S. Johnson, "Is Mark 15.39 the Key to Mark's Christology?" *JSNT* 31 (1987): 3–22; and the survey and analysis in Yarbro Collins, *Mark*, 764–71, who interprets the response of the centurion as dramatic irony (769).

206. Cf. Richard A. Horsley, *Jesus and Empire: The Kingdom of God and the New World Disorder* (Minneapolis: Fortress Press, 2002), 100–08; Stephen D. Moore, *Empire and Apocalypse: Postcolonialism and the New Testament* (Sheffield: Sheffield Phoenix Press, 2006), 24–32, especially literature cited at 25 no. 2; and Joshua Garroway, "The Invasion of a Mustard Seed: A Reading of Mark 5.1–20," *JSNT* 32 (2009): 57–75. For a thoroughgoing

postcolonial interpretation of Mark, see Simon Samuel, *A Postcolonial Reading of Mark's Story of Jesus* (Library of New Testament Studies 340; London; New York; T & T Clark, 2007).

207. The interpretation of these events as an "anti-triumph" and a "parabolic drama" are explored well in T. E. Schmidt, "Mark 15.16–32: The Crucifixion Narrative and the Roman Triumphal Procession," *NTS* 41 (1995): 1–18. Cf. W. Barnes Tatum, "Jesus' So-Called Triumphal Entry," *Forum* 1 (New Series, 1998): 129–144.

■ Chapter 5

1. When I discuss the "sonship" of Christians or Christian "divine sonship," I by no means exclude women from that category of filial relationship to God. There were obviously many influential and authoritative women in early Christianity, such as Mary, Mary Magdalene, the Samaritan Woman, Mary and Martha of Bethany, Prisca, Phoebe, Lydia, Thecla, Perpetua and Felicitas, Blandina, Priscilla and Maximilla, Macrina, Olympias, Melania the Elder and Younger, Marcella, Paula—and so many more that history does not allow us to see. I remain with the words "son" and "sonship," though, because the masculine terms enable me to portray more clearly the interaction in early Christian texts between the divine sonship of Jesus Christ and the filial relationship afforded to all Christians. This interplay of metaphors can be seen more easily with literal translations of "sons" or "sonship."

2. Raymond E. Brown, *The Birth of the Messiah* (New York: Doubleday, 1977), 29–32, 90 n. 68, 134 n. 6. He is not the first to argue this, but his formulation of it has had a wide influence.

3. Rom 1:3–4; Phil 2:8–9; Acts 2:32, 36; 5:31; 13:32–33. Although Brown does not elaborate here on his citation of Phil 2:8–9 as an example of this idea, his use of it clearly shows that he does not find the preexistence of Jesus Christ in the so-called Philippians "hymn." Cf. James D. G. Dunn, *Christology in the Making: A New Testament Inquiry into the Origins of the Doctrine of the Incarnation* (2nd ed.; Grand Rapids: Eerdmans, 1989), 114–25; and Karl-Josef Kuschel, *Born Before All Time? The Dispute Over Christ's Origin* (trans. John Bowden; London: SCM Press, 1992), 243–66. On the implications of the "hymn" designation, cf. Michael Peppard, "'Poetry, 'Hymns,' and 'Traditional Material' in New Testament Epistles or How to Do Things with Indentations," *JSNT* 30 (2008): 319–42.

4. Brown, *Birth*, 29 n. 14.

5. Ibid., 29.

6. There are dissenting opinions to this majority view, however. Cf. Francis Watson, "Is John's Christology Adoptionist?" in *The Glory of Christ in the New Testament: Studies in Christology in Memory of George Bradford Caird* (ed. L.D. Hurst and N.T. Wright; Oxford: Clarendon Press, 1987), 113–124; and recently, Gitte Buch-Hansen, "It Is the Spirit That Makes Alive: a Stoic Understanding of Pneuma in John" (Copenhagen diss., 2007), esp. 151–203.

7. Dunn, *Christology*, 61.

8. Ibid., 62.

9. For another use of the cubist idea in New Testament studies, see Harold W. Attridge, "The Cubist Principle in Johannine Imagery: John and the Reading of Images of Contemporary Platonism," in *Imagery in the Gospel of John: Terms, Forms, Themes, and Theology of Johannine Figurative Language* (ed. Jörg Frey, Jan G. Van der Watt, and Ruben Zimmermann; WUNT 200; Tübingen: Mohr Siebeck, 2006), 47–60.

10. An emphasis on Jesus' baptism is supported also by Peter's speech to Cornelius (Acts 10:38). On the Lukan variant in the manuscript tradition, see the excellent analysis in Bart D. Ehrman, *The Orthodox Corruption of Scripture* (Oxford: Oxford University Press, 1993), 62–67. On the Lukan variant in early liturgical traditions, see Kilian McDonnell, *The Baptism of Jesus in the Jordan: The Trinitarian and Cosmic Order of Salvation* (Collegeville, Minn.: Liturgical Press, 1996), 85–100. Also worthy of consideration is the theory that Luke originally began with the canonical chap. 3, a theory made more interesting by the ancient *testimonium* that the Gospel of Luke "began with the baptism of John" (from the appendix—of unknown origin—to Ephrem's *Commentary on the Diatessaron*).

11. Brown knows this (cf. *Birth*, 30 n. 15), but he still desires a chronological chart. I do not include the transfiguration in my list of Luke's divine sonship "moments" because he distinctively de-emphasizes the transfiguration as a sonship event. The divine voice there looks backwards—to the baptism, on my reading, but one could argue it refers also to the conception—when it says, "This is my son that has been chosen" (οὗτός ἐστιν ὁ υἱός μου ὁ ἐκλελεγμένος, 9:35).

12. Bousset comments similarly about divine sonship in the writings of both Paul and Luke: with respect to Paul's letters, "even where one talks of the resurrection of Jesus as his installation as Son of God or of the birth of the Son of God at the baptism, the assumption of a preexistent nature of Jesus is not flatly ruled out. Here conceptions which are for us apparently altogether different have, as it appears, existed peacefully side by side." Wilhelm Bousset, *Kyrios Christos: Geschichte des Christusglaubens von den Anfängen des Christentums bis Irenaeus* (4th ed; Göttingen: Vandenhoeck & Ruprecht, 1935); quotations from *Kyrios Christos* (trans. John E. Steely; Nashville: Abingdon, 1970), 337; cf. 338 on Luke.

13. For a survey of how Ps 2 is used by New Testament authors, see Jacques Dupont, "*Filius meus es Tu.* L'Interprétation de *Ps. II, 7,* dans le Nouveau Testament," *Recherches de Science Religieuse* 35 (1948): 522–43.

14. Recall that in ancient Hebrew there was no terminology for adoption as there was in Greek and Latin.

15. Harold W. Attridge, "The Psalms in Hebrews," in *The Psalms in the New Testament* (ed. Steve Moyise and Maarten J.J. Menken; London; New York: T & T Clark, 2004), 200. Cf. the excursus on sonship in Harold W. Attridge, *Hebrews* (ed. Helmut Koester; Hermeneia; Philadelphia: Fortress, 1989), 54–55.

16. E.g., Ernst Käsemann, *The Wandering People of God: An Investigation of the Letter to the Hebrews* (trans. Roy A. Harrisville and Irving L. Sandberg; Minneapolis: Augsburg, 1984), 99; *Das Wandernde Gottesvolk: Eine Untersuchung zum Hebräerbrief* (2nd ed.; FRLANT 55; Göttingen: Vandenhoeck & Ruprecht, 1957). Another helpful contribution is that of Dunn, *Christology*, 52–56, who reconciles different sonship ideas in Hebrews by interpreting its Platonic metaphysics—the Son of God did not have personal preexistence, but did have a formal preexistence (in the Platonic sense).

17. Attridge, *Hebrews*, 55. Cf. William R. G. Loader, *Sohn und Hoherpriester: Eine traditionsgeschichtliche Untersuchung zur Christologie des Hebräerbriefes* (WMANT 53; Neukirchen: Neukirchener, 1981), esp. 7–15, 118–19.

18. Luke's skill in this rhetorical presentation of Christianity has been aptly called "apologetic historiography." Gregory E. Sterling, *Historiography and Self-Definition: Josephos, Luke-Acts, and Apologetic Historiography* (Leiden; New York: Brill, 1992).

19. On Joseph as adoptive father in Matthew, see Yigal Levin, "Jesus, 'Son of God' and 'Son of David': The 'Adoption' of Jesus into the Davidic Line," *JSNT* 28 (2006): 415–42. Early

Christian interpreters also explained Joseph's presumed adoption of Jesus, and some even used adoption to explain *Joseph's* two fathers (a natural father in Matthew's list, an adoptive father in Luke's), e.g., Augustine, *Sermon 51* (*PL* 38: 348).

20. For a theological analysis along these same lines—distinguishing begotten from adopted in the New Testament—see Jean Richard, "Fils de Dieu. Reconsidération de l'interprétation adoptioniste," in *Le Christ Hier, Aujourd'hui et Demain: Colloque de christologie tenu à l'Université Laval* (ed. Raymond Laflamme and Michel Gervais; Québec: Les Presses de l'Université Laval, 1976), 431–65.

21. The most thorough studies of Paul's use of adoption metaphors are James M Scott, *Adoption as Sons of God: An Exegetical Investigation into the Background of ΥΙΟΘΕΣΙΑ in the Pauline Corpus* (WUNT II 48; Tübingen: Mohr Siebeck, 1992); and Brendan Byrne, S.J., *Sons of God – Seed of Abraham* (Rome: Biblical Institute Press, 1979). Both interpret Paul's language in connection with Jewish textual traditions and ideas. Scott's study is especially careful, and his argument (121–86) for interpreting a Moses/Exodus typology behind the example of Gal 4:1–7 is cogent. In my research, I emphasize the Greco-Roman resonance of the terms and concepts without necessarily dismissing the importance of other interpretations.

22. Understanding Roman adoption as the basis of Paul's metaphor is now quite common; for an early argument toward this end, see Francis Lyall, "Roman Law in the Writings of Paul—Adoption," *JBL* 88 (1969): 458–66.

23. James C. Walters, "Paul, Adoption, and Inheritance," in *Paul in the Greco-Roman World* (ed. J. Paul Sampley; Harrisburg: Trinity Press International, 2003), 42–76. For an excellent analysis of how patrilineal descent functions overall in Paul's "ethnic map," see Caroline Johnson Hodge, *If Sons, Then Heirs: A Study of Kinship and Ethnicity in the Letters of Paul* (Oxford; New York: Oxford University Press, 2007).

24. I try generally to avoid using the word "Christian" as a noun to describe this early period, since Christian identity was still in the beginning phases of being worked out; however, I use it here and elsewhere as an adjective that comprises relationship to God "in Christ." It is meant to distinguish when I am talking about Christian divine sonship from when I am talking about Jesus Christ's divine sonship.

25. Walters, "Adoption," 55.

26. The already-not yet understanding of adoption is captured well in Origen's commentary, which connects this text with 1 Cor 13:10–12: "We receive adoption, then, but that which is through a mirror and in a riddle. But when the things that are perfect come, then we shall attain adoption face to face" (Origen, *Comm. on Romans* 7.5.9). There is unfortunately no extant Greek manuscript, but only the Latin translation. English translation from *Origen, Commentary on the Epistle to the Romans, Books 6–10* (trans. Thomas P. Scheck; Fathers of the Church 104; Washington, D.C.: Catholic University of America Press, 2002).

27. For interpretation of this passage for a different purpose, see the section in chap. 4 on ευδοκ-.

28. For centuries *3 Corinthians* was known only as part of the Armenian biblical canon and through Ephrem's commentary on the Pauline Epistles. But in the twentieth century it was discovered in several manuscripts of *The Acts of Paul* in Coptic and Latin. For an English translation of the text in its literary context (*The Acts of Paul*) and a brief explanation of its transmission, see Wilhelm Schneemelcher, ed., *New Testament Apocrypha* (2 vols.; Louisville: Westminster John Knox, 2003), 2:217, 254–56. The extant Greek version was found among the Bodmer papyri: published with French translation by Michel Testuz,

Papyrus Bodmer X–XII (Cologny-Genève: Bibliotheca Bodmeriana, 1959), 9–45. A detailed treatment of the manuscripts and their contents is A. F. J. Klijn, "The Apocryphal Correspondence between Paul and the Corinthians," *Vigiliae Christianae* 17 (1963): 2–23.

29. The Bodmer papyrus has ἵνα ζωοποιηθῇ δ{ε}ιὰ τῆς υἱοθεσίας, and for υἱοθεσίας, the Latin manuscripts have either *adoptionem* or *filii creationem*. Testuz, *Papyrus Bodmer*, 36. This word lies in a lacuna of the Coptic manuscript.

30. See *Letter of the Corinthians to Paul* 2:13 (Schneemelcher, *New Testament Apocrypha* 2:254; Testuz, *Papyrus Bodmer*, 32).

31. There are seventeen references to Jesus as "son" in the traditional Pauline corpus (thirteen epistles), compared to over 200 references to Jesus as "Lord" (Dunn, *Christology*, 36–37). They are clustered in Romans (seven times) and Galatians (four times).

32. The only narrative Christology in Paul comes in Phil 2:6–11, but the emphasis there is the *lordship* of Jesus Christ, not his divine sonship.

33. The strophic presentation of the text is borrowed from Dunn, *Christology*, 41.

34. Dunn, *Christology*, 37–46. Yarbro Collins connects this sending to the sending of prophets in the Hebrew Bible; Adela Yarbro Collins and John J. Collins, *King and Messiah as Son of God* (Grand Rapids: Eerdmans, 2008), 107. Rom 8:3 also proclaims God's "sending" of his son unto death "in the likeness of sinful flesh"—a soteriological and eschatological commission from God. Rom 8:32 heightens God's compassion in "handing over" Jesus to die by calling him "his own son" (τοῦ ἰδίου υἱοῦ). The adjective ἴδιος undoubtedly emphasizes Jesus' close relationship to God before his death and resurrection. Although the word does not describe a particular process of acquiring sonship, it does express *in nuce* a distinction between the sonship of Christ and the sonship of Christians. In the third and fourth centuries, this distinction would come to be articulated through two different ways of acquiring sonship.

35. On the translation of ὁρισθέντος as "appointed," of κατά as instrumental, and of ἐξ as causal (and thus also temporal), see Scott, *Adoption*, 237–44. On Rom 1:4, cf. Dunn, *Christology*, 33–35; Collins and Collins, *King and Messiah*, 117–18; and especially the study of Davidic kingship echoes by Christopher J. Whitsett, "Son of God, Seed of David: Paul's Messianic Exegesis in Romans 2[sic]:3–4," *JBL* 119 (2000): 661–81. Robert Jewett also argues that the verb denotes adoptive sonship: "At the core of the original confession, therefore, is the affirmation of Jesus as the traditional Davidic Messiah, who was adopted and enthroned as the Son of God on the basis of his resurrection." But he states, in an argument that I do not understand, that Paul has modified this adoptive connotation by adding the phrases "concerning his son" and "in power" to the traditional formulation he had received. These "additions" imply "the preexistent Son of God." See Robert Jewett, *Romans* (Hermeneia; Minneapolis: Fortress, 2007), 104–07.

36. In addition to the Latin translators, several early Christian commentators understood the Greek to suggest an adoption enacted at the resurrection. See citations in Scott, *Adoption*, 221–23. Hurtado acknowledges that "in 1:4 the resurrection clearly seems to be seen as a salvation-historical event that places Jesus in a new position as the Son *in power*, appointed to rule on God's behalf," but he is convinced that the "sending" texts show that "for Paul Jesus is to be thought of as God's Son from the outset." L. W. Hurtado, "Jesus' Divine Sonship in Paul's Epistle to the Romans," in *Romans and the People of God* (ed. Sven K. Soderlund and N. T. Wright; Grand Rapids: Eerdmans, 1999), 228.

37. Old Latin and Vulgate versions; see Ehrman, *Orthodox Corruption*, 71–72.

38. Noted also by Scott, *Adoption*, 222 no. 6.

39. James D. G. Dunn, *The Theology of Paul the Apostle* (Grand Rapids: Eerdmans, 1997), 503.

40. See Scott, *Adoption*, 148–49. For the motif later, see Isa 43:1–7 and Jer 31:7–9. Origen, however, is reasonable to link the "adoption" of Israel to the time when it was granted its "inheritance" (Deut 32:8–9; Origen, *Comm. on Romans* 7.13.6).

41. Being "conformed to the image of his son" likely refers to his "death and subsequent glorification," as argued by Collins and Collins, *King and Messiah*, 121.

42. The term also occurs at Col 1:15 (perhaps implying preexistent begottenness), but at 1:18 it is clearly connected to the resurrection. In Heb 1:6 it perhaps implies preexistent begottenness, but at 12:23 it refers to an assembly of inhabitants in the heavenly Jerusalem. The use at Rev 1:5 is clearly connected to the resurrection.

43. The Hebrew בכור behind the Greek translation is also used figuratively in the Bible besides in this Psalm (cf. Ex 4:22; Isa 14:30; Jer 31:9; Job 18:3).

44. Cf. above, chap. 4, section on ευδοκ-.

45. *P. Lips.* 28.15.

46. A phrase adapted from Scott, *Adoption*, 252 no. 107.

47. On God as "father" in Paul's theology, see John L. White, "God's Paternity as Root Metaphor in Paul's Conception of Community," *Foundations and Facets Forum* 8 (1992): 271–95. On father theology in Romans in particular, see Marianne Meye Thompson, "'Mercy Upon All': God as Father in the Epistle to the Romans," in *Romans and the People of God* (ed. Sven K. Soderlund and N. T. Wright; Grand Rapids: Eerdmans, 1999), 203–16.

48. Scott, *Adoption*, 255.

49. Irenaeus, *Adv. Haer.* 3.20.2. Cf. Richard A. Norris, "Irenaeus' Use of Paul in His Polemic Against the Gnostics," in *Paul and the Legacies of Paul* (ed. William S. Babcock; Dallas: Southern Methodist University Press, 1990), 95.

50. But see below on a key textual variant in John 1:13.

51. Dionysius of Alexandria (*apud* Eusebius) must have understood Johannine begetting "again" to be another way of portraying "adoption," since he surprisingly refers to it with that word. To defend the authorship of John and 1 John by the same person, he offers a list of the similar terms and themes they share (in contradistinction to the Revelation of John, whose Johannine authorship Dionysius rejects). One theme that he thinks they share is "the adoptive sonship of God" (ἡ υἱοθεσία τοῦ θεοῦ), even though that word never appears in the Johannine corpus (Eusebius, *Hist. eccl.* 7.25.21).

52. The portrayal of wisdom in Wis 7:22 provides background.

53. The language is more explicit in 1 John 3:10. A dichotomous key is a modern taxonomic tool used in biology to organize plant and animal specimens into their correct species by analyzing their characteristics.

54. Sethians, Valentinians, and Ophites are examples of early Christian groups concerned with lineages of divine begetting that connected to special classes of Christians on earth. For the Sethians as descended from the primordial Seth, see Birger A. Pearson, "The Figure of Seth in Gnostic Literature," in *The Rediscovery of Gnosticism* (2 vols.; ed. Bentley Layton; Leiden: Brill, 1981), 2:472–514. For detailed interpretations of this among the Valentinians, see the studies of the *Gospel of Philip*, the *Tripartite Tractate*, and other sources for Valentinian protology, spermatology, and soteriology in Einar Thomassen, *The Spiritual Seed: The Church of the "Valentinians"* (NHMS 60; Leiden: Brill, 2006).

55. Early Latin sources with the singular are Irenaeus (*Adv. Haer.* 3.16.2; 3.19.2), Tertullian (*Carn. Chr.* 19, 24), and one Old Latin manuscript (b); the apocryphal *Epistula*

Apostolorum (chap. 3) has the singular in Coptic and Ethiopic. For modern citations and a thorough analysis of the issue, see Matthew Vellanickal, *The Divine Sonship of Christians in the Johannine Writings* (Analecta Biblica 72; Rome: Biblical Institute Press, 1977), 112–32, who favors the singular reading.

56. He interprets the singular to signify the miraculous birth of Jesus, and this works apologetically on two fronts. On one side, it defends the divine begetting of Jesus against the Christology of the Ebionites (Tertullian, *Carn. Chr.* 24); on the other, it tempers the Valentinian claim that they themselves were begotten of God (Tertullian, *Carn. Chr.* 19). Cf. Ehrman, *Orthodox Corruption*, 59, who favors the plural reading.

57. Vellanickal, *Divine Sonship*, 276–78. Cf. Ehrman, *Orthodox Corruption*, 70–71.

58. Cf. Judith Lieu, *I, II, & III John* (New Testament Library; Louisville; London: Westminster John Knox, 2008), 200.

59. A point noted also by Kuschel, *Born Before All Time?*, 383.

60. Vellancikal, *Divine Sonship*, 286.

61. On the history of translation and mistranslation for this word, see Dale Moody, "God's Only Son: The Translation of John 3:16 in the Revised Standard Version," *JBL* 72 (1953): 213–19.

62. E.g., Isaac is described thus by Josephus, *A.J.* 1.222, and Heb 11:17. It is true that Isaac was Abraham's only legitimate son, but to call him an "only-begotten" son would stretch the boundaries of what "begetting" normally means. There are many other examples from Greek texts, the most relevant of which are compiled and analyzed by Gerard Pendrick, "ΜΟΝΟΓΕΝΗΣ," *NTS* 41 (1995): 588–92.

63. Plutarch, *Moralia* 423A ("The Obsolesence of Oracles"). For a thorough discussion of the nonbiblical uses of the word in ancient Greek, see Pendrick, "ΜΟΝΟΓΕΝΗΣ," which is a persuasive rebuttal of those that claim begottenness is contained within the sense of the word (especially J. V. Dahms, "The Johannine Use of Monogenes Reconsidered," *NTS* 29 [1983]: 222–32).

64. Cf. Justin, *Dial.* 105.1, and discussion at Pendrick, "ΜΟΝΟΓΕΝΗΣ," 598.

65. Codex Vercellensis, which is normally cited as Old Latin (OL) manuscript (a).

66. Moody suggests that Jerome's translation was influenced by Gregory of Nazianzus, especially his *Oration 29* (*PG* 36: 74–103), during Jerome's stay in Constantinople (379–81 c.e.). Moody, "God's Only Son," 215.

67. His is the first known Latin translation of the 325 Nicene Creed: *natum ex patre unigenitum* (*PL* 10: 536). One Latin version of the Creed, quoted in the context of reporting on the 451 Council of Chalcedon, uses *unicus* to translate the 381 Niceno-Constantinopolitan Creed: *Filium Dei unicum* (*PL* 56: 532).

68. This is not to say that the adjective μονογενής modifies δόξα *grammatically*, which it obviously does not. It is a substantive adjective for which most translators supply "son," but I am calling attention to the lack of a defined begotten sonship of the Word in John's prologue.

69. The issues are treated in detail in Ehrman, *Orthodox Corruption*, 78–82. The best-attested variants are μονογενὴς θεός, ὁ μονογενὴς θεός, and ὁ μονογενὴς υἱός. Based on external criticism, Nestle-Aland prints the first of these, the anarthrous μονογενὴς θεός, which I also support. Ehrman agrees with that judgment of external evidence, but he argues for the third option, ὁ μονογενὴς υἱός, based on the grounds of internal criticism. He claims that it makes more sense for the text originally to have read "unique son," and that the variant "God" was "created to support a high Christology in the face of widespread claims. . .

that Christ was not God but merely a man, adopted by God. . . . This Alexandrian reading derives from an anti-adoptionistic context" (p. 82).

Though the resolution of this issue is not necessary for my argument about begotten-ness—and I dispute Ehrman's textual criticism with some trepidation—I do see the internal evidence differently. The Johannine prologue is not primarily about the "Christ," in Ehrman's words, nor is it about the "son," a word that does not otherwise appear. It is most explicitly about the Word/Light, and so it is internally consistent at the prologue's conclusion to recall its opening. John 1:18 recapitulates John 1:1 (the Word is θεός), just as it finishes the thought of 1:14 (where the Word is already linked uniquely to the Father). Furthermore, I would argue that an "anti-adoptionistic" change to this text works better in the direction *opposite* to what Ehrman proposed. When "son" is added to the prologue, it encourages a view of Jesus Christ's divine sonship as preexistent, "in the bosom of the Father." If "son" is *not* in the pro-logue, however, the Gospel of John is wide open to adoptionist interpretations—the first time Jesus is called "son of God" comes from John the Baptist, recalling Jesus' baptism (1:34).

70. Some of the difficulties presented by John's use of μονογενής can be ameliorated by postulating a theological development *within* the Johannine corpus. I have tried to treat the examples as contemporaneous and all meaning roughly the same thing, but others have shown the fruits of charting an "evolution" of meaning within the Johannine tradition, e.g., Michèle Morgen, "Le (Fils) *monogène* dans les écrits johanniques: Évolution des traditions et elaboration rédactionelle," *NTS* 53 (2007): 165–83.

71. Besides the father-son unity expressed in Jesus' prayer (17:1–25), he is also accused of "calling God his *own* Father" (ἴδιος), which his opponents interpret as equality to God the Father (5:18).

72. Cf. Vellanickal, *Divine Sonship*, 128.

73. See John Ashton, *Understanding the Fourth Gospel* (Oxford: Clarendon, 1991), 292–329; in which he relies also on the analysis of John's "*Sendungschristologie*" in Jan-Adolf Bühner, *Der Gesandte und sein Weg im vierten Evangelium* (Tübingen: Mohr, 1977).

74. Cf. my critique (chap. 1) of Hurtado's interpretation of divine sonship in John.

75. Vellanickal, *Divine Sonship*, 124.

76. In the dialogue with Pilate, he says, "It is for this that I have been begotten (γεγέννημαι), and for this I have come into the world: to testify to the truth" (John 18:37). Again, neither Jesus nor John gives us any clue as to the point in past time to which he refers. Even though the Nicene reading would see here his pre-temporal begetting and his later incarnation, the two expressions can also refer to Jesus' birth from Mary. In a different con-text in the Gospel of John, Jesus has already described a natural birth in these terms (ἐγεννήθη ἄνθρωπος εἰς τὸν κόσμον, 16:21).

77. Lieu, *I, II, & III John*, 230–31.

78. Paul begets new believers in Christ (1 Cor 4:5; Phlm 10), whose baptism is adoption (Gal 4:5; Rom 8:15), death (Rom 6:3), and resurrection (Rom 6:4). All these images (and more!) would come to flourish in early Christianity; cf. the source book by Maxwell Johnson, *Images of Baptism* (Chicago: Liturgy Training Publications, 2001).

79. Bart Ehrman, *The New Testament: A Historical Introduction to the Early Christian Writings* (4th ed.; New York; Oxford: Oxford University Press, 2008), 3.

80. Tertullian claims that they "did not think that Jesus was the Son of God" at all (*De praescript. Haer.* 33.11). For a good survey and analysis of the evidence about the Ebionites, see Oskar Skarsaune, "The Ebionites," in *Jewish Believers in Jesus* (ed. Oskar Skarsaune and Reidar Hvalvik; Peabody, Mass.: Hendrickson, 2007), 419–62.

81. Epiphanius, *Pan.* 30.13–14, esp. 30.13.7. Excerpts and English translations in Schneemelcher, *New Testament Apocrypha*, 1:166–71, esp. 1:169.3. Orthodox authors such as Augustine also defended both baptismal voices (*PL* 34: 1093).

82. A better example of a baptismal "adoption" in an apocryphal gospel might be the narration from the "Gospel of the Hebrews" (quoted by Jerome, *Comm. on Isa.* 4, on Isa 11:2): "And it came to pass when the Lord came up out of the water, the whole fount of the Holy Spirit descended upon him and rested on him and said to him: *My Son, in all the prophets was I waiting for you that you should come and I might rest in you. For you are my rest; you are my first-begotten Son that reigns forever*" (Schneemelcher, *New Testament Apocrypha*, 1:177.2, trans. adapted and italics added). Yet the imagery is actually more Johannine: it is a begetting again from above, as corroborated later by the Gospel's construal of the Holy Spirit as Jesus' "mother" (Schneemelcher, *New Testament Apocrypha*, 1:177.3) Father and Mother begat Jesus as son at his baptism.

83. Michael Goulder, "A Poor Man's Christology," *NTS* 45 (1999): 335.

84. For summaries of what we know about this group, see Ehrman, *Orthodox Corruption*, 51–52; Winrich A. Löhr, "Theodotus der Lederarbeiter und Theodotus der Bankier—ein Beitrag zur römischen Theologiegeschichte des zweiten und dritten Jahrhunderts," *ZNW* 87 (1996): 101–25; Peter Lampe, *From Paul to Valentinus: Christians at Rome in the First Two Centuries* (ed. Marshall D. Johnson; trans. Michael Steinhauser; Minneapolis: Fortress, 2003), 344–48.

85. Cf. Eusebius, *Hist. eccl.* 5.28, quoting an anonymous early-third-century source (5.28.7), which is often called the "Little Labyrinth." The charge about Scripture is assessed in Bart D. Ehrman, "The Theodotians as Corruptors of Scripture," *Studia Patristica* 25 (1993): 46–51.

86. Eusebius, *Hist. eccl.* 5.28.6. Greek: ... Θεόδοτον τὸν σκυτέα, τὸν ἀρχηγὸν καὶ πατέρα ταύτης τῆς ἀρνησιθέου ἀποστασίας ... πρῶτον εἰπόντα ψιλὸν ἄνθρωπον τὸν χριστόν.

87. Hippolytus, *Ref.* 7.35; cf. 10.23.

88. McDonnell, *Baptism*, 89.

89. In the selection of authors that follows, I have limited myself to major figures and texts that either use adoptive imagery in their portrayals of divine sonship or have been accused of doing so. Hence some major Christian theologians—notably proto-heterodox thinkers such as Valentinus—have been left out.

90. For a complementary analysis of how early Christian *ecclesiology* interacted with Roman images and models in the second century, see Allen Brent, *The Imperial Cult and the Development of Church Order: Concepts and Images of Authority in Paganism and Early Christianity before the Age of Cyprian* (Leiden: Brill, 1999).

91. This description of the portrayal of Hermas is from Osiek's commentary, which is the best English-language analysis of the text: Carolyn Osiek, *Shepherd of Hermas: A Commentary* (Hermeneia; Minneapolis: Fortress, 1999), 18, 23. On the social status of Hermas and its relationship to the text, cf. Carolyn Osiek, *Rich and Poor in the Shepherd of Hermas* (Washington, D.C.: Catholic University of America Press, 1983); Jeffers, "Influence of the Roman Family"; and Lampe, *From Paul to Valentinus*, 90–99.

92. The word "Christ" appears only in three manuscript variants (*Vis.* 2.2.8; 3.6.6; *Sim.* 9.18.1), which are not accepted by most scholars. Osiek, *Shepherd*, 34; cf. Molly Whittaker, ed., *Der Hirt des Hermas* (GCS; Berlin: Akadamie-Verlag, 1967), and now the latest critical edition: Martin Leutzsch, "Hirt des Hermas," in *Papiasfragmente. Hirt des Hermas* (ed. Ulrich H. J. Körtner and Martin Leutzsch; Schriften des Urchristentums 3; Darmstadt: Wissenschaftliche Buchgesellschaft, 1998), 107–497.

93. One recent attempt is Bogdan G. Bucur, "The Son of God and the Angelomorphic Holy Spirit: A Rereading of the Shepherd's Christology," *ZNW* 98 (2007): 120–42.

94. Osiek, *Shepherd*, 36, 35.

95. This passage is a main focus for Martin Dibelius, *Der Hirt des Hermas* (Tübingen: Mohr Siebeck, 1923), esp. 572–76; Luigi Cirillo, "La christologie pneumatique de la cinquième parabole du 'Pasteur' d'Hermas," *Revue de l'histoire des religions* 184 (1973): 25–48; Norbert Brox, *Der Hirt des Hermas* (Göttingen: Vandenhoeck & Ruprecht, 1991), 301–28, 485–95; Philippe Henne, *La Christologie chez Clément de Rome et dans le Pasteur d'Hermas* (Fribourg: Éditions Universitaires, 1992), 157–210; J. Christian Wilson, *Toward a Reassessment of the Shepherd of Hermas: Its Date and Pneumatology* (Lewiston, N.Y.: Mellen, 1993), 104–35; Bucur, "Son of God." But Osiek also emphasizes the statement of *Sim.* 9.1.1 ("The Holy Spirit is the Son of God"), which is difficult to harmonize with the doctrinal interpretations of *Sim.* 5. The Son of God is also portrayed as preexistent in *Sim.* 9.12.1–2.

96. This outline is similar to but more detailed than that of Osiek, *Shepherd*, 168.

97. The identification of the "son" with the Holy Spirit is absent from most Greek manuscripts, though it is accepted by most commentators. The restored text comes from a Latin ms.: *filius autem spiritus sanctus est*. Leutzsch, "Hirt des Hermas," 262. In terms of later Trinitarian doctrine, the restored text is certainly *lectio difficillima*.

98. From his review of Gebhardt and Harnack's 1877 edition of *The Shepherd*, cited in Brox, *Hirt des Hermas*, 6. Trans. my own.

99. Osiek, *Shepherd*, 178.

100. *Sim.* 5.6.2–4a. Trans. adapted from LCL (ed. Kirsopp Lake). Quotation marks are placed around verbal correspondences with the original parable. The final sentence (5.6.4a) is omitted from an important manuscript but accepted by most editors and commentators: *vides inquit dominum eum esse populi accepta a patre suo omni potestate*. Osiek proposes omission by homoioteleuton with the previous sentence. I have left out the *inquit* ("he said") in my translation.

101. The moniker was attached to *The Shepherd* through the influence of Adolph von Harnack, *History of Dogma* (7 vols.; 3rd ed.; trans. Neil Buchanan; Gloucester, Mass.: Peter Smith, 1976), 1:183–204, but most subsequent scholars that have treated the text in detail do not call it "adoptionist."

102. The parable might presume that the making of an heir implied adoption as son, since adoption was indeed the primary method of designating heirs. Most commentators also make this assumption. However, heirs could be designated without adoption, and the parable is careful not to call the slave a son, even after he has been granted inheritance.

103. For a different way of reckoning the text of *Sim.* 5, see Henne, *Christologie*, 157–210.

104. Osiek, *Shepherd*, 179.

105. *Sim.* 5.2; 5.5.2; 5.6.1; 5.6.4b.

106. *Sim.* 5.6.4b–7a. Trans. adapted from LCL and Osiek, *Shepherd*, 176. Quotation marks are placed around verbal correspondences with the original parable, including the verb "to serve" (δουλεύω), since it echoes the noun "slave" (δοῦλος). The idea that a slave does not have a "resting place" in the household, unless he becomes a son/heir, is similar to that expressed by Jesus in John 8:35.

107. Greek of *Sim.* 5.6.5a: τὸ πνεῦμα τὸ ἅγιον τὸ προόν τὸ κτίσαν πᾶσαν τὴν κτίσιν, κατῴκισεν ὁ θεὸς εἰς σάρκα, ἣν ἠβούλετο.

108. For a contrasting interpretation of the third interpretation, see Philippe Henne, "La Véritable Christologie de la *Cinquième Similitude* du *Pasteur* d'Hermas," *Revue des Sciences Philosophiques et Theologiques* 74 (1990): 182–204.

109. This point has been made, though in different words, by Aloys Grillmeier, *Christ in Christian Tradition* (2 vols.; 2nd ed.; trans. John Bowden; London: Mowbrays, 1975), 1:54; Brox, *Hirt des Hermas*, 486; Osiek, *Shepherd*, 36; Lage Pernveden, *The Concept of the Church in the Shepherd of Hermas* (Studia Theologica Lundensia 27; Lund: CWK Gleerup, 1966), 49–50; and Robert J. Hauck, "The Great Fast: Christology in the Shepherd of Hermas," *Anglican Theological Review* 75 (1993): 187–98.

110. This is also the emphasis given to the Arian controversy by Robert C. Gregg and Dennis E. Groh, *Early Arianism—A View of Salvation* (Philadelphia: Fortress Press, 1981), about which see below.

111. *Sim.* 5.6.7b. Trans. adapted from LCL.

112. The relevance of upward mobility in a household for the interpretation of this text is noted also by Martin Leutzsch, *Die Wahrnehmung sozialer Wirklichkeit im "Hirten des Hermas"* (Göttingen: Vandenhoeck & Ruprecht, 1989), 149–53.

113. Brox, *Hirt des Hermas*, 328. Brox further argues that Hermas was not a political thinker. I am inclined to agree, but his revelatory use of household imagery would have resonated in his particular sociopolitical context. Cf. Norbert Brox, "Hermas und eine »politische Metaphysik«?" in *Panchaia: Festschrift für Klaus Thraede* (ed. Manfred Wacht; Jahrbuch für Antike und Christentum 22; Münster: Aschendorffsche Verlagsbuchhandlung, 1995), 24–31.

114. Denise Kimber Buell, *Making Christians: Clement of Alexandria and the Rhetoric of Legitimacy* (Princeton: Princeton University Press, 1999). She expands this type of study to other early Christian authors in *Why This New Race: Ethnic Reasoning in Early Christianity* (New York: Columbia University Press, 2005).

115. Clement's use of adoption language has been briefly summarized in Carlo Nardi, *Il Battesimo in Clemente Alessandrino: Interpretazione di* Eclogae propheticae 1–26 (Studia Ephemeridis "Augustinianum"; Rome: Institutum Patristicum "Augustinianum," 1984), 157–62.

116. Clement of Alexandria, *Paed.* 1.5.21. τῶν ὅλων ὁ πατὴρ τοὺς εἰς αὐτὸν καταπεφευγότας προσίεται καὶ ἀναγεννήσας πνεύματι εἰς υἱοθεσίαν ἠπίους οἶδεν καὶ φιλεῖ τούτους μόνους καὶ βοηθεῖ καὶ ὑπερμαχεῖ καὶ διὰ τοῦτο ὀνομάζει παιδίον.

117. Clement of Alexandria, *Strom.* 6.8.68. τὰ ἁγιώτερα ἀποκαλύψαντος τοῖς γνησίως καὶ μὴ νόθως τῆς κυριακῆς υἱοθεσίας κληρονόμοις.

118. At *Strom.* 2.23.137, Clement uses the term in its fundamental sense, to describe the legitimate offspring of a marriage.

119. None before this, according to a full corpus search in TLG (*Thesaurus Linguae Graecae*). But the concepts are also linked in a Greek document, *P. Lips.* 28, the papyrus adoption contract quoted several times above.

120. Clement does not refer to Christians as God's γνήσιος sons or *children*. Christians are "legitimate children *of light*" (τέκνα φωτὸς γνήσια, *Prot.* 10.92.5), but Jesus Christ is the "legitimate child of God" (τέκνον γνήσιον, *Quis.* 36.2). The "legitimacy" of Christian divine sonship is constituted by their adoption as "legitimate" heirs.

121. I will not attempt to parse the difficult text, *Excerpta ex Theodoto*, in which Clement's views are often tough to distinguish from the Valentinian, Theodotus, whose cosmology he is depicting. The issue of adoptive and begotten sonship occurs at Clement of Alexandria, *Exc.* 33 and 67.

122. Clement of Alexandria, *Paed.* 1.12.98. μοι δοκεῖ αὐτὸς οὗτος πλάσαι μὲν τὸν ἄνθρωπον ἐκ χοός, ἀναγεννῆσαι δὲ ὕδατι, αὐξῆσαι δὲ πνεύματι, παιδαγωγῆσαι δὲ ῥήματι εἰς υἱοθεσίαν καὶ σωτερίαν, ἁγίαις ἐντολαῖς κατευθύνων.

123. For another clear connection of adoption with adulthood, cf. Clement of Alexandria, *Paed.* 1.6.33–34.

124. Clement of Alexandria, *Strom.* 1.27.173. θεοῦ δοῦλον μὲν τὰ πρῶτα, ἔπειτα δὲ πιστὸν γενέσθαι θεράποντα, φοβούμενον κύριον τὸν θεόν, εἰ δέ τις ἐπαναβαίη, τοῖς υἱοῖς ἐγκαταλέγεσθαι ... τοῦτον ἐγκατατατέντα τῇ ἐκλεκτῇ υἱοθεσίᾳ τῇ φίλῃ κεκλημένῃ τοῦ θεοῦ. The language at the end also resonates with the *amici* / φίλοι of a household's *paterfamilias*.

125. Clement of Alexandria, *Strom.* 2.16.75; *Paed.* 3.8.45.

126. Clement of Alexandria, *Strom.* 2.22.134.

127. Clement of Alexandria, *Strom.* 6.9.76. τὸν φίλον τοῦ θεοῦ, ὃν προώρισεν ὁ θεὸς πρὸ καταβολῆς κόσμου εἰς τὴν ἄκραν ἐγκαταλεγῆναι υἱοθεσίαν.

128. Clement of Alexandria, *Paed.* 1.6.26. αὐτίκα γοῦν βαπτιζομένῳ τῷ κυρίῳ ἀπ᾽ οὐρανῶν ἐπήχησε φωνὴ μάρτυς ἠγαπημένου, υἱός μου εἶ σὺ ἀγαπητός, ἐγὼ σήμερον γεγέννηκά σε. πυθώμεθα οὖν τῶν σοφῶν· σήμερον ἀναγεννηθεὶς ὁ χριστὸς ἤδη τέλειός ἐστιν ... ;

129. Clement of Alexandria, *Paed.* 1.6.26. τελειοῦται δὲ τῷ λουτρῷ μόνῳ καὶ τοῦ πνεύματος τῇ καθόδῳ ἁγιάζεται· οὕτως ἔχει. τὸ δὲ αὐτὸ συμβαίνει τοῦτο καὶ περὶ ἡμᾶς, ὧν γέγονεν ὑπογραφὴ ὁ κύριος· βαπτιζόμενοι φωτιζόμεθα, φωτιζόμενοι υἱοποιούμεθα, υἱοποιούμενοι τελειούμεθα, τελειούμενοι ἀπαθανατιζόμεθα· ἐγώ, φησίν, εἶπα, θεοί ἐστε καὶ υἱοὶ ὑψίστου πάντες.

130. Elsewhere, Clement describes Christ also as a "pattern" (ὑπόδειγμα) and as the subject of the verb "to model" (ὑποτυπώσασθαι, *Paed.* 1.12.98). This is the same section in which Clement refers to Christians as "becoming gods" or "being deified" (ἐκθεούμεθα), and the implication is that this action is part of the "model" established by Jesus Christ in his life.

131. Antonio Orbe, "Teología Bautismal de Clemente Alejandrino según Paed. I, 26, 3–27,2," *Gregorianum* 36 (1955): 440, 442. Trans. my own. Orbe argues that the different stages can be best understood as exegesis of a fuller (extra-canonical) depiction of the "events of the Jordan," such as are presumed by Justin Martyr, *Dial.* 88.

132. On the origin and development of the concept of divinization/deification in early Christianity, see Norman Russell, *The Doctrine of Deification in the Greek Patristic Tradition* (Oxford: Oxford University Press, 2004), who deals with the doctrine from ancient Israel and the Greco-Roman world all the way through to the end of the patristic era.

133. The interpetation of Psalm 82 is also related to the question of divinity and divine sonship in the Gospel of John (10:31–39), but for John, only the divinity and divine sonship of Jesus himself is at issue.

134. *ANF* 2:215.

135. Cf. a similar text on imitation of Christ and likeness to God at *Strom.* 6.14.114, which concludes as follows: "'For it is enough for the student to be like the teacher,' says the Teacher. Then as far as 'likeness to God' is concerned, whoever is appointed to adoptive sonship and friendship with God becomes so according to the joint inheritance of the lords and gods, if indeed, he be perfected according to the gospel, just as the Lord himself taught." Greek: ἀρκετὸν γὰρ τῷ μαθητῇ γενέσθαι ὡς ὁ διδάσκαλος, λέγει ὁ διδάσκαλος. καθ᾽ ὁμοίωσιν οὖν τοῦ θεοῦ ὁ εἰς υἱοθεσίαν καὶ φιλίαν τοῦ θεοῦ καταταγεὶς κατὰ τὴν συγκληρονομίαν τῶν κυρίων καὶ θεῶν γίνεται, ἐάν, καθὼς αὐτὸς ἐδίδαξεν ὁ κύριος, κατὰ τὸ εὐαγγέλιον τελειωθῇ.

136. Antonio Orbe, "¿San Ireneo adopcionista?" *Gregorianum* 65 (1984): 5–52.

137. Walter Kasper, *Jesus the Christ* (trans. V. Green; New York: Paulist Press, 1976), 234; trans. of *Jesus der Christus* (Mainz: Matthias-Grünewald Verlag, 1974).

138. Especially the voluminous work of Antonio Orbe, much of which is encapsulated in *Teología de San Ireneo* (4 vols.; vols. 1–3 from Madrid: La Editorial Catolica, 1985–88; vol. 4 from Madrid: Biblioteca de Autores Cristianos, 1996). A shorter treatment dealing with many of the texts I cover here is Bousset, *Kyrios*, 420–53.

139. Irenaeus, *Adv. Haer.* 4.8.1. Translations of Irenaeus are my own unless noted. Critical edition is Irénée de Lyon, *Contre les Hérésies* (5 vols.; ed. Adelin Rousseau *et al.*; Sources Chrétiennes 34, 100, 152–53, 210–11, 263–64, 293–94; Paris: du Cerf, 1952–82).

140. Cf. Irenaeus, *Adv. Haer.* 4.25.3 and 5.32.2.

141. Irenaeus, *Adv. Haer.* 4.11.1. Latin: . . . *aliquando quidem colloquente eo cum suo plasmate, aliquando autem dante legem, aliquando vero exprobrante, aliquando vero exhortante, ac deinceps liberante servum et adoptante in filium, et apto tempore incorruptelae hereditatem praestante ad perfectionem hominis.* In the context, what I have translated here as a statement is in the form of a question to the opponent.

142. Cf. the long exposition on the ascent of humanity to God at Irenaeus, *Adv. Haer.* 4.38.1–4. Cf. Robert F. Brown, "On the Necessary Imperfection of Creation: Irenaeus' *Adversus Haereses* IV, 38," *Scottish Journal of Theology* 28 (1975): 17–25; Miyako Namikawa, "La Paciencia del Crecimiento y la Maduración," *Estudios Eclesiásticos* 83 (2008): 51–85.

143. Cf. Irenaeus, *Adv. Haer.* 4.16.5 and 4.36.2.

144. Irenaeus, *Adv. Haer.* 4.33.4. A difficult text to interpret and translate: *Et quemadmodum homo transiet in Deum, si non Deus in hominem? Quemadmodum autem relinquent mortis generationem, si non in novam generationem mire et inopinate a Deo, in signum autem salutis datam, quae est ex Virgine, per fidem regenerentur? Vel quemadmodum adoptionem accipient a Deo, permanentes in hac genesi, quae est secundum hominem in hoc mundo?* A Greek fragment from Theodoret offers the first line of what I translated here from the Latin: ἢ πῶς ἄνθρωπος χωρήσει εἰς θεόν, εἰ μὴ ὁ θεὸς ἐχώρησεν εἰς ἄνθρωπον; (crit. ed. 4:2:810). On the interpretation of these lines, cf. Antonio Orbe, "En torno a los Ebionitas," *Augustinianum* 33 (1993): 315–37.

145. The introduction of "the Virgin" into the argument is primarily a response to the Ebionites' denial of Christ's miraculous origin. The relationship between the virgin birth and the two modes of Christian sonship is not spelled out by Irenaeus.

146. For Clement of Alexandria, the begetting again of Christians is prior to adoption. The same interpretation of Irenaeus might possibly be supported by his use of an adoptive idea in a different text (Irenaeus, *Adv. Haer.* 4.31.1) to explain how Lot was related to the children he had unwittingly begotten through his own daughters (Gen 19:30–38). Had he begotten them first, and then adopted them later? Irenaeus's typological exegesis is obscure, not least because the Latin translation has added an incorrect allegorical correspondence to its translation. The seduction-incest plot producing two family lines is interpreted as two *synagogae* or "groups" that have become adopted children to God as one Father. The Greek fragment is crucial to make sense of it (crit. ed., 4:1:83 and 4:2:790). Cf. Orbe, *Teología*, 4:428–40.

147. Irenaeus, *Adv. Haer.* 5.18.2. Again, the text is very concise and difficult to translate. Latin: *Pater enim conditionem simul et Verbum suum portat, et Verbum portatum a Patre praestat Spiritum omnibus quemadmodum vult Pater: quibusdam quidem secundum conditionem, quod est conditionis, quod est factum; quibusdam autem secundum adoptionem, quod est ex Deo, quod est generatio.*

148. He returns to the metaphor "again and again" (*più volte*), in the words of Elio Peretto, *La lettera ai Romani cc. 1–8 nell' Adversus Haereses d'Ireneo* (Quaderni di "Vetera Christianorum" 6; Bari: Istituto di Letteratura Cristiana Antica, 1971), 229. Cf. the analysis of Norris, "Irenaeus' Use of Paul," 89–98.

149. The LXX Greek is: ἐγὼ εἶπα Θεοί ἐστε καὶ υἱοὶ ὑψίστου πάντες. The interpretation of Psalm 82 in the second century has been expertly analyzed by Carl Mosser, "The Earliest Patristic Interpretations of Psalm 82, Jewish Antecedents, and the Origin of Deification," *JTS* 56 (2005): 30–74, esp. 41–54 on Irenaeus. He argues rightly that "the chief significance of the psalm was its declaration of divine sonship" (30).

150. Irenaeus, *Adv. Haer.* 3.6.1. Latin: *De Patre et Filio et de his qui adoptionem percepe-runt dicit; hi autem sunt Ecclesia: haec enim est synagoga Dei, quam Deus, hoc est Filius, ipse per semetipsum collegit.* The LXX Greek of 82(81):1a is: ὁ θεὸς ἔστη ἐν συναγωγῇ θεῶν.

151. Irenaeus, *Adv. Haer.* 3.6.1. Latin: *Quorum autem deorum? Quibus dicit: Ego dixi: Dii estis et filii Altissimi omnes, his scilicet qui adoptionis gratiam adepti sunt, per quam clama-mus: Abba Pater.*

152. In addition to Mosser, "Psalm 82," see Jacques Fantino, *La Théologie d'Irénée* (Paris: Cerf, 1994), 213–16.

153. Irenaeus, *Adv. Haer.* 4.Preface.4. Latin: *neminem alium Deum appellari a Scripturis, nisi Patrem omnium et Filium et eos qui adoptionem habent.*

154. Irenaeus, *Adv. Haer.* 3.16.3. Gal 4:4–5 is quoted just before this text. Latin: *Filius Dei hominis filius factus, ut per eum adoptionem percipiamus, portante homine et capiente et complectente Filium Dei.* On Irenaeus as interpreter of Paul, see Norris, "Irenaeus' Use of Paul"; Rolf Noormann, *Irenäus als Paulusinterpret* (WUNT II 66; Tübingen: Mohr Siebeck, 1994); Jeffrey D. Bingham, "Irenaeus's Reading of Romans 8," *Society of Biblical Literature Seminar Papers 2001* (2001): 131–50.

155. Irenaeus, *Adv. Haer.* 3.18.7. Latin: *Qua enim ratione filiorum adoptionis eius partici-pes esse possemus, nisi per Filium eam quae est ad ipsum recepissemus ab eo communionem, nisi verbum eius communicasset nobis caro factum?*

156. A version of the "exchange formula" is still present in the Roman Catholic Liturgy of the Eucharist. In preparing the cup, the priest says: *per huius aquae et vini mysterium eius efficiamur divinitatis consortes, qui humanitatis nostrae fieri dignatus est particeps*, or "By the mystery of this water and wine, may we come to share in the divinity of the one who deigned to partake of our humanity."

157. Kasper, *Jesus Christ*, 234.

158. Cf. Norris, "Irenaeus' Use of Paul," 97.

159. Irenaeus, *Adv. Haer.* 3.19.1. For detailed analysis of this text, see Orbe, "¿San Ireneo adopcionista?" and Noormann, *Irenäus*, 487–92. My trans. adapted from *ANF.* Latin: *Propter hoc enim Verbum Dei homo, et qui Filius Dei est Filius hominis factus est, <ut homo>, commixtus Verbo Dei et adoptionem percipiens, fiat filius Dei. Non enim poteramus aliter percipere incorruptelam et immortalitatem nisi aduniti fuissemus incorruptelae et immortalitati. Quemadmodum autem adunari possemus incorruptelae et immortalitati nisi prius incorruptela et immortalitas facta fuisset id quod et nos, ut absorberetur quod erat cor-ruptibile ab incorruptela et quod erat mortale ab immortalitate, uti filiorum adoptionem perciperemus?* A Greek version of the first sentence is extant from Theodoret: εἰς τοῦτο γὰρ ὁ Λόγος ἄνθρωπος καὶ Υἱὸς ἀνθρώπου ὁ Υἱὸς τοῦ Θεοῦ, ἵνα ὁ ἄνθρωπος χωρήσας τὸν Λόγον καὶ τὴν υἱοθεσίαν λαβὼν γένηται υἱὸς τοῦ Θεοῦ. Crit. ed. 3:2:374. The Latin *ut homo* is supplied from the Greek ἵνα ὁ ἄνθρωπος. The main difference between the two versions

is the verb used to describe how the human encounters the Word: in the Greek, the human "makes room for" the Word; in the Latin, the human is "joined with" the Word. Cf. Irenaeus, *Adv. Haer.* 4.33.4.

160. Cf. Irenaeus, *Adv. Haer.* 3.20.2, yet another elaboration of the exchange formula.

161. Irenaeus, *Adv. Haer.* 3.19.1. Trans. from the Greek of Theodoret: τοὺς μὴ δεξαμένους τὴν δωρεὰν τῆς υἱοθεσίας, ἀλλ᾽ ἀτιμάζοντας τὴν σάρκωσιν τῆς καθαρᾶς γεννήσεως τοῦ Λόγου τοῦ Θεοῦ καὶ ἀποστεροῦντας τὸν ἄνθρωπον τῆς εἰς τὸν Θεὸν ἀνόδου.

162. Irenaeus, *Adv. Haer.* 2.28.6. Trans. adapted from *ANF.* "Begetting" is *generatio*, and "born" is *natus*.

163. Norris, "Irenaeus' Use of Paul," 97.

164. Another example of a turn of phrase that would never again be repeated is the following description of how God is visible throughout salvation history. Its context draws on the language and imagery of John 1 and John 3. "For God is powerful in all things, having been seen indeed [in the past], *prophetically through the Spirit*, and then seen *adoptively through the Son*; and God shall also be seen *paternally in the kingdom of heaven*—the Spirit truly preparing the human to become a son of God, and the Son leading him to the Father, then the Father confers upon him incorruption for eternal life, which comes to every one from the fact of his seeing God" (Irenaeus, *Adv. Haer.* 4.20.5). It is difficult to imagine a later orthodox theologian writing the words, *per Filium adoptive*, even though the text probably means that God enacted the adoption of others through the Son. Cf. Orbe, *Teología*, 4: 288–89. The adverbial use of the adoptive metaphor would not be precise enough for later centuries.

165. It is important to recall that Irenaeus had the singular reading of John 1:13 (see above), which would catalyze the separation of sonships.

166. As I mentioned above, I have limited my inquiry to those who engage directly with adoptive imagery. The complex lineage systems of Valentinians, Sethians, and other Christian groups are unfortunately not able to be addressed here.

167. I will not deal with the murky topic of Paul of Samosata, bishop of Antioch (260–68), who often receives the label "adoptionist," because of our limited information about his views on divine sonship (cf. Eusebius, *Hist. eccl.* 7.27–30).

168. Peter Widdicombe, *The Fatherhood of God from Origen to Athanasius* (Oxford: Clarendon, 1994), 92.

169. In addition to the Latin and limited Greek fragments, I have consulted the English translation of G.W. Butterworth in *Origen, On First Principles* (trans. G.W. Butterworth; Gloucester, Mass.: Peter Smith, 1973).

170. Texts in this paragraph are from Origen, *De Princ.* 1.2.4 (*PL* 42: 1178). Relevant Latin excerpt: *quomodo ingenitus Deus Pater efficitur unigeniti Filii. Est ita namque aeterna ac sempiterna generatio, sicut splendor generatur ex luce. Non enim per adoptionem spiritus, Filius fit exstrinsecus: sed natura Filius est.*

171. The image is Middle Platonic, attested already in Numenius of Apamea (2nd c.). Numenius, *Fragments: Texte Établi et Traduit par Édouard des Places, S.J.* (trans. and ed. Édouard des Places; Paris: Les Belles Lettres, 1973), fr. 15. Origen subsequently cites Wis 7:25–26 and Heb 1:3 in the course of his argument.

172. Origen, *De Princ.* 4.4.1, for which there is a Greek fragment. He relies on the presentation of Wisdom in Prov 8:22.

173. Origen, *De Princ.* 1.2.4. Cf. Origen, *Comm. on John* 1.28, where the kingship of the Son of God is described as *kinship*—it is a natural trait and not one added-on. "Then [should

we say that] the kingship of the Son of God is something added-on and not congenitally his? How could it be that the firstborn of all creation does not *exist* as a king, but later must have *become* a king?" The terms for "added-on" and "congenital" are often used to describe plants in Greek. (ἆρ οὖν ἐπιγενητή ἐστιν ἡ τοῦ υἱοῦ τοῦ θεοῦ βασιλεία καὶ οὐ συμφυὴς αὐτῷ; καὶ πῶς οἷόν τε τὸν πρωτότοκον πάσης κτίσεως, οὐκ ὄντα βασιλέα, ὕστερον βασιλέα γεγονέναι;)

174. Origen, *Comm. on John* 1.29. Greek: ἀλλὰ διὰ τούτων πάντων οὐ σαφῶς ἡ εὐγένεια παρίσταται τοῦ υἱοῦ, ὅτε δὲ τὸ Υἱός μου εἶ σύ, ἐγὼ σήμερον γεγέννηκά σε λέγεται πρὸς αὐτὸν ὑπὸ τοῦ θεοῦ, ᾧ ἀεί ἐστι τὸ σήμερον . . . ἡμέρα ἐστὶν αὐτῷ σήμερον, ἐν ᾗ γεγέννηται ὁ υἱός· ἀρχῆς γενέσεως αὐτοῦ οὕτως οὐχ εὑρισκομένης ὡς οὐδὲ τῆς ἡμέρας.

175. Cf. Augustine's interpretation of Jesus' baptism, "*semper hodiernus est*" (*PL* 40: 255), cited also in McDonnell, *Baptism*, 98 no. 77.

176. Origen, *Peri Pascha* 41. There are some lacunae in this manuscript, but the key words ἐγεννήθησαν and υἱοθεσία are clear. The participle rendered as "we who came to be" is the partially reconstructed γεν[ομέ]νοις, which perhaps should instead be completed as γεννωμένοις, in line with the verb in the scriptural citation. Cf. critical edition in Origène, *Sur la Pâque: Traité inédit publié d'après un papyrus de Toura* (ed. Octave Guérard and Pierre Nautin; Christianisme Antique 2; Paris: Beauchesne, 1979), 235 no. 2. English translation available in: Origen, *Treatise on the Passover and Dialogue with Heraclides* (trans. and ed. Robert J. Daly; New York: Paulist, 1992), 50.

177. Origen, *Exp. in Prov.*, PG 17: 200–01. Relevant Greek excerpt: οἱ ἄγγελοι καὶ οἱ δίκαιοι ἄνθρωποι, ἀλλήλων εἰσὶν ἀδελφοί, τῷ τῆς υἱοθεσίας γεννώμενοι πνεύματι· τούτου γὰρ χάριν καὶ γεννῶνται ὑπὸ τῆς σοφίας, ἵνα ἀνθρώπους ὁδηγήσωσιν ἀπὸ κακίας εἰς ἀρετὴν, καὶ ἀπὸ ἀγνωσίας εἰς ἐπίγνωσιν Θεοῦ.

178. Origen, *Comm. on Romans* 7.9.3.

179. Another third-century theologian to champion the distinction in sonships was Methodius of Olympus, e.g., *Symposium*, Logos 8: Thecla 9.

180. E.g., Origen, *Comm. on John* 20.24–34; 32.21.

181. Origen, *Hom. in Jer.* 9.4 (*PG* 13: 357). Trans. in Widdicombe, *Fatherhood*, 98.

182. For example, Frances M. Young, *From Nicaea to Chalcedon* (Philadelphia: Fortress Press, 1983); Rowan Williams, *Arius: Heresy and Tradition* (London: SCM Press, 1987); R. P. C. Hanson, *The Search for the Christian Doctrine of God: The Arian Controversy 318–381* (Edinburgh: T. & T. Clark, 1988); Lewis Ayres, *Nicaea and its Legacy: An Approach to Fourth-Century Trinitarian Theology* (Oxford: Oxford University Press, 2004); Gregg and Groh, *Early Arianism.*

183. We do not have many of Arius's own words, of course. But if the teachings recorded in Athanasius, *De synodis* 15, are to be counted as those of Arius—as extracts from the *Thalia*, which many scholars do consider them to be—then one can see where the charge of adoptionism might have found a foothold. That text says, God "bore him into a Son for himself, τεκνοποιήσας him" (ἤνεγκεν εἰς υἱὸν ἑαυτῷ τόνδε τεκνοποιήσας). I leave the word τεκνοποιήσας untranslated because, although it normally means the making of a child through natural birth, there are rare uses of it in the middle voice for surrogate parenthood or adoption. Interestingly, the two biblical cases of its use for surrogate parenthood (Gen 16:2; 30:3) are held up by Athanasius as cases of "natural" offspring (*Or.* 1.38), and so perhaps he was not troubled by the verb in any form. More importantly, it contains the verbal root ποι-, which places the Son on the side of Becoming. The term may have invited the opponents of Arius to use adoptive metaphors to describe his Christology, even though he

had just previously described the Son as naturally begotten (τὸν τὴν φύσιν γεννητόν). Cf. Hanson, *Search*, 14; and Williams, *Arius*, 102, 259.

184. Cf. chapter 2 for some non-Christian sources. For a famous example from a Christian source, see Tertullian's quotable maxim: *Fiunt, non nascuntur, Christiani* ("Christians are made, not born"). Tertullian, *Apol.* 18.4.

185. The intended recipient of the letter, also named Alexander, cannot be identified for certain. Theodoret identifies him as Alexander of Byzantium, but it was more likely Alexander of Thessalonica. In any case, it was meant for a wider readership. Later on, Athanasius also accuses Arius of representing Christ's sonship as an adoption (e.g., Athanasius, *Or.* 1.38; 2.64; 3.9).

186. Greek text of Alexander of Alexandria, *Letter to Alexander*, available in *Athanasius Werke: Dritter Band, Erster Teil* (ed. Hans-Georg Opitz; Berlin and Leipzig: De Gruyter, 1934), Urkunde 14 (*apud* Theodoret, *Eccl. Hist.* 1.4). This quotation is from sections 28–29. Greek: ἐξ ἧς ἔστιν ἰδεῖν τὴν υἱότητα τοῦ σωτῆρος ἡμῶν οὐδεμίαν ἔχουσαν κοινωνίαν πρὸς τὴν τῶν λοιπῶν υἱότητα. ὃν τρόπον γὰρ ἡ ἄρρητος αὐτοῦ ὑπόστασις ἀσυγκρίτῳ ὑπεροχῇ ἐδείχθη ὑπερκειμένη πάντων οἷς αὐτὸς τὸ εἶναι ἐχαρίσατο, οὕτως καὶ ἡ υἱότης αὐτοῦ, κατὰ φύσιν τυγχάνουσα τῆς πατρικῆς θεότητος, ἀλέκτῳ ὑπεροχῇ διαφέρει τῶν δι' αὐτοῦ θέσει υἱοθετηθέντων. ὁ μὲν γὰρ ἀτρέπτου φύσεως τυγχάνει, τέλειος ὢν καὶ διὰ πάντων ἀνενδεής· οἱ δὲ τῇ εἰς ἑκάτερα τροπῇ ὑποκείμενοι τῆς παρὰ τούτου βοηθείας δέονται. I have consulted the English translation of *NPNF* in making my own.

187. I use the term "son-ness" to indicate the neologism υἱότης of the Nicene era. The orthodox side needed an abstraction to talk about the fact of Jesus Christ being God's son, and this static term of Being helped distinguish his sonship from the dynamic kind of Becoming (υἱοθεσία) that Christians possessed. Besides this occurrence, the noun υἱότης is attested in the text of Hippolytus's *Refutatio [Philosophoumena]*, a fact which may bolster the argument against the authenticity of that text's authorship by Hippolytus. The word also appears once in Origen, but there it refers to the "son-ness" that is "impressed" like an "image" upon "the saints" (εἰκὼν οὖν εἰκόνος οἱ ἅγιοι τυγχάνοντες, τῆς εἰκόνος οὔσης υἱοῦ, ἀπομάττονται υἱότητα, *PG* 11:485b). That is, it is functioning in precisely the *opposite* way to how it would be used later by Alexander of Alexandria. For Origen, son-ness connects Christians with Christ; for Alexander, son-ness distinguishes Christ's unique sonship from that of Christians. From the fourth century on, use of the word increases, in the way Alexander means it. Cf. below on Cyril of Jerusalem.

188. Clement of Alexandria, *Strom.* 2.16.75; *Paed.* 3.8.45; *Strom.* 2.22.134.

189. The "divided line" and the "myth of the cave" are parallel expressions of Platonic metaphysics in Plato, *Republic*, books 6 and 7.

190. Alexander, *Letter to Alexander* 31. Greek: ὁ κύριος ἡμῶν, φύσει τοῦ πατρὸς υἱὸς τυγχάνων, ὑπὸ πάντων προσκυνεῖται· οἱ δὲ ἀποθέμενοι τὸ πνεῦμα τῆς δουλείας, ἐξ ἀνδραγαθημάτων καὶ προκοπῆς τὸ τῆς υἱοθεσίας λαβόντες πνεῦμα, διὰ τοῦ φύσει υἱοῦ εὐεργετούμενοι γίγνονται αὐτοὶ θέσει υἱοί. Τὴν μὲν οὖν γνησίαν αὐτοῦ καὶ ἰδιότροπον καὶ φυσικὴν κατ' ἐξαίρετον υἱότητα ὁ Παῦλος οὕτως ἀπεφήνατο, περὶ θεοῦ εἰπών· ὅς γε τοῦ ἰδίου υἱοῦ οὐκ ἐφείσατο, ἀλλ' ὑπὲρ ἡμῶν δηλονότι τῶν μὴ φύσει υἱῶν παρέδωκεν αὐτόν. πρὸς γὰρ ἀντιδιαστολὴν τῶν οὐκ ἰδίων αὐτὸν ἴδιον υἱὸν ἔφησεν εἶναι.

191. Alexander, *Letter to Alexander* 34. Greek: οὐχὶ ἄντικρυς τῆς πατρικῆς μαιώσεως φυσικὴν ἐνδείκνυται υἱότητα, οὐ τρόπων ἐπιμελείᾳ καὶ προκοπῆς ἀσκήσει, ἀλλὰ φύσεως ἰδιώματι ταύτην λαχόντος; ὅθεν καὶ ἀμετάπτωτον ἔχει τὴν υἱότητα ὁ μονογενὴς υἱὸς τοῦ πατρός. τὴν δὲ τῶν λογικῶν υἱοθεσίαν, οὐ κατὰ φύσιν αὐτοῖς ὑπάρχουσαν ἀλλὰ τρόπων ἐπιτηδειότητι καὶ δωρεᾷ θεοῦ, καὶ μεταπτωτὴν.

192. Origen, however, did not think that one could regress from or lose the status of adoptive sonship. Christians can become better and better sons of God, but they cannot lose the status altogether. Cf. Widdicombe, *Fatherhood*, 104–05.

193. Gregg and Groh, *Early Arianism*, esp. 50–70.

194. Ibid., 70. The appeal of identification with Christ, of promotion to divine sonship with Christ, is still considered the attractive feature of adoptionistic Christologies for Christians. See the quite empathetic essay in a contemporary handbook of heresiography and apologetics: Rachel Muers, "Adoptionism: Is Jesus Christ the Son of God by Nature or by Adoption?" in *Heresies and How to Avoid Them* (ed. Ben Quash and Michael Ward; London: SPCK; Peabody, Mass.: Hendrickson, 2007), 50–58.

195. Gregg and Groh suggested that the sociopolitical context of adoption might have influenced the theological use of adoptive metaphors, but they did not pursue the point. Gregg and Groh, *Early Arianism*, 72 no. 45. My work is, in one sense, a large expansion of their footnote.

196. Peter Widdicombe, "The Fathers on the Father in the Gospel of John," *Semeia* 85 (1999): 116.

197. Widdicombe, *Fatherhood*, 238–39. His chapter, "Adoption, Salvation, and Life of Unity" (223–49), has deeply informed my own research on these matters, and the following paragraphs bear many similarities to his persuasive arguments there.

198. Athanasius, *Or.* 2.59. The entire argument is 2.57–72.

199. Athanasius, *Or.* 2.59. Discussed also at Widdicombe, *Fatherhood*, 240–41.

200. Athanasius, *Or.* 2.64.

201. Virginia Burrus, *Begotten, Not Made: Conceiving Manhood in Late Antiquity* (Stanford: Stanford University Press, 2000), 186.

202. Athanasius, *De Decretis* 31.

203. It is likely that Athanasius uses the adverb in a colloquial way, meaning something like "really," "certainly," "indeed," "of course," etc. But that does not much diminish the surprise at this juxtaposition.

204. Athanasius, *Or.* 1.9.

205. Widdicombe, *Fatherhood*, 241.

206. Timothy D. Barnes, *Constantine and Eusebius* (Cambridge, Mass.: Harvard University Press, 1981); Timothy D. Barnes, *Athanasius and Constantius: Theology and Politics in the Constantinian Empire* (Cambridge, Mass.: Harvard University Press, 1993). Cf. Friedrich Vittinghoff, "Staat, Kirche und Dynastie beim Tode Konstantins," in *L'Église et L'Empire au IVᵉ Siècle* (ed. Albrecht Dihle; Genève: Fondation Hardt, 1989), 1–34.

207. But see Grillmeier, *Christ in Christian Tradition*, 251–64; and Dale B. Martin, *Inventing Superstition* (Cambridge, Mass.: Harvard University Press, 2004), 217–25.

208. Athanasius, *Or.* 3.5. Since the statue is most certainly a "made" thing, Athanasius's choice of example was unusual. More fitting for the anti-Arian argument was Ephrem's analogy, which likens Father and Son to a tree and its fruit. P. J. Botha, "Ephrem's Comparison of the Father-Son Relationship to the Relationship Between a Tree and Its Fruit in His Hymns 'On Faith,'" *Acta Patristica et Byzantina* 4 (1993): 23–32. For other arguments based on imperial images from this era, cf. Basil, *Hom.* 24.4; *Spir.* 9.23; 18.45, and discussion in Jaroslav Pelikan, *The Spirit of Eastern Christendom (600–1700)* (Chicago: University of Chicago Press, 1977), 103.

209. The best place to interpret the relationship between Eusebius's political ideology and his theology is the speech, *In Praise of Constantine (Laud. Const.)*. The Greek edition—

essential to see the rhetorical play between the depictions of Constantine and God—is *Oratio de laudibus Constantini* in *Eusebius' Werke I* (ed. Ivar A. Heikel; GCS 7; Leipzig, 1902), 195–223. The English translation of *NPNF* must be avoided because it does not render the ambiguities of how the emperor and God are presented; in fact, it tries to eliminate them. Instead, use the excellent version of H. A. Drake, *In Praise of Constantine: A Historical Study and New Translation of Eusebius' Tricennial Orations* (Berkeley: University of California Press, 1976). For examples of Eusebius's connection between political ideology and theology, see *Laud. Const.* 0.2; 1.3; 2.1–5; 4.2–5.1; 6.21; 9.18; and especially 3.1–6.

210. Eusebius, *Vit. Const.* 1.1.2–3. Greek: τὸν μακάριον αὐτῇ συνόντα βασιλείᾳ ... ζῶντα δυνάμει. The best English translation is Eusebius, *Life of Constantine* (introduction, translation and commentary by Averil Cameron and Stuart G. Hall; Oxford: Clarendon, 1999).

211. Eusebius, *Vit. Const.* 1.3. Greek: τοὺς αὐτοῦ παῖδας οἷά τινας νέους λαμπτῆρας τῶν αὐτοῦ μαρμαρυγῶν συνορᾷ πληροῦντας τὸ πᾶν. Cf. Eusebius, *Laud. Const.* 3.4.

212. Constantine, *Letter to Arius and the Arians* 26 (Athanasius, *De decretis* 40 = Opitz, Urkunde 34). Greek: ὦ τῶν πάντων ἔχων τὸ κῦρος δέσποτα, ὦ τῆς μονήρους δυνάμεως πάτερ, διὰ τουτονὶ τὸν ἀνόσιον ὀνείδη τε καὶ μώλωπας καὶ μέντοι καὶ τραύματα καὶ ὀδύνας ἡ σὴ ἔχει ἐκκλησία. Ἄρειός σοι τόπον ἤδη προσαρμόζει καὶ μάλα γε εὐφυῶς ἐφ' οὗ καθιζάνων οἶμαι σύνοδον ἑαυτῷ ἢ παῖδα τὸν χριστὸν τὸν σὸν τὸν ἐκ σοῦ τὸν τῆς ἡμετέρας ἐπικουρίας ἀρχηγέτην θέσεως νόμῳ περιπεποίηται καὶ ἴσχει.

213. Eusebius, *Hist. eccl.* 10.9.4. Greek: ὁ τῶν ἀγαθῶν ἀρωγὸς πρόεισιν ἅμα παιδὶ Κρίσπῳ βασιλεῖ φιλανθρωποτάτῳ, σωτήριον δεξιὰν ἅπασιν τοῖς ἀπολλυμένοις ἐκτείνας. εἶθ' οἷα παμβασιλεῖ θεῷ θεοῦ τε παιδὶ σωτῆρι ἁπάντων ποδηγῷ καὶ συμμάχῳ χρώμενοι, πατὴρ ἅμα καὶ υἱός...

214. The emperor is the "image" (εἰκών) of God in Eusebius, *Laud. Const. passim.* But note that his political ideology seems to *precede* his theology (at least as they are presented logically) at *Laud. Const.* 3.6.

215. Another clear example of the orthodox view here represented by Augustine comes from Gregory of Nazianzus, *Ep. 101* (To Cledonius, Against Apollanaris): "If any assert that [Christ] was made perfect by works, or that after his Baptism, or after his Resurrection from the dead, he was counted worthy of an adoptive sonship, like those whom the Greeks interpolate as added to the ranks of the gods, let him be anathema. For that which has a beginning or progress or is made perfect is not God" (*Ep.* 101; *PG* 37: 180; *NPNF II* 7:440).

216. Augustine, *Enarrationes in Psalmos* (comment on Ps 89[88]:6), *PL* 37: 1124. The LXX and Vulgate versions of the psalm verse are: ὅτι τίς ἐν νεφέλαις ἰσωθήσεται τῷ κυρίῳ, καὶ τίς ὁμοιωθήσεται τῷ κυρίῳ ἐν υἱοῖς θεοῦ; and *Quoniam quis in nubibus aequabitur Domino; similis erit Deo in filiis Dei?* Latin original of commentary: *Ergo nemo in filiis Dei similis erit Filio Dei. Et ipse dictus est Filius Dei, et nos dicti sumus filii Dei; sed quis similis erit Domino in filiis Dei? Ille unicus, nos multi; ille unus, nos in illo unum; ille natus, nos adoptati; ille ab aeterno Filius genitus per naturam, nos a tempore facti per gratiam.*

217. Augustine, *Sermon 183* (on 1 John 4:2), *PL* 38: 990. Latin: *Quid dicis, Ariane? ... Factum dicis. Si factum dicis, Filium negas. Filium enim quaerimus natura, non gratia; Filium unicum, unigenitum, non adoptatum. Talem Filium quaerimus, tam verum Filium quaerimus.* Trans. adapted from *The Works of Saint Augustine: A Translation for the 21st Century: Sermons, Part III* (trans. Edmund Hill; Brooklyn, N.Y.: New City Press, 1990–2008), 339.

218. On these texts, a solid bibliography has emerged: for historical analyses, cf. Maxwell E. Johnson, *The Rites of Christian Initiation: Their Evolution and Interpretation* (Collegeville, Minn.: Liturgical Press, 1999), 89–124; Bryan D. Spinks, *Early and Medieval Rituals and Theologies of*

Baptism: From the New Testament to the Council of Trent (Hampshire: Ashgate, 2006), 38–67; Juliette Day, *The Baptismal Liturgy of Jerusalem: Fourth- and Fifth-Century Evidence from Palestine, Syria and Egypt* (Hampshire: Ashgate, 2007). None of these yet had access to Macarius's *Letter* (see below). For theological analysis of the early evidence, cf. McDonnell, *Baptism*.

219. *Didascalia Apostolorum* 9 (ed. Arthur Vööbus; CSCO 175–76, 179–80, 401–02, 407–08; Louvain: Secrétariat du CorpusSCO, 1979), 109 (Syriac). Trans. my own. Relevant Syriac (translit.) and Latin: *dbry ʾntʾnʾ ywmna yldtk / Filius meus es tu, ego hodie genui te … mṭl hnʾ ʾw br nšʾ hwyt ydʿ lʾpysqwpyk lhnwn dbʾydyhwn hwyt brʾ lʾlhʾ / Propterea, homo, agnosce episcopos tuos, per quos es filius Dei.*

220. The actual uttering of these words by the baptizer is interpreted by McDonnell (91–92) as historically accurate, though other historians are more cautious: it was "apparently recited as a formula" (Johnson, *Rites*, 1st ed., 42), "the formula … is uncertain" (Spinks, *Rituals and Theologies*, 19), and "possibly recited" (Johnson, *Rites*, 2007 rev. ed., 54). Baptism is also described as "begetting again" or "regeneration" in *Apostolic Tradition* 21.21, our other early liturgical source (Latin, Arabic and Ethiopic; the Bohairic differs). Paul F. Bradshaw, Maxwell E. Johnson, and L. Edward Phillips, *The Apostolic Tradition* (ed. Harold W. Attridge; Hermeneia; Minneapolis: Fortress, 2002), 118; Latin text available in Hippolyte de Rome, *La Tradition Apostolique* (2nd ed.; ed. Bernard Botte; Sources Chretiénnes 11; Paris: Les Éditions du Cerf, 1984), 88.

221. J.M. Harden, *The Ethiopic Didascalia* (London: SPCK; New York: Macmillan, 1920), 54.

222. *Didascalia Apostolorum* 9; Vööbus p. 103 and 110.

223. Abraham Terian, *Macarius of Jerusalem, Letter to the Armenians (A.D. 335): Introduction, Text, Translation, and Commentary* (Crestwood, N.Y.: St. Vladimir's Seminary Press, 2008). The text quoted here is from the oldest and most reliable version of the letter, preserved in the *Fragment in Anania of Shirak* 284.5–24, pp. 81–87.

224. The feast of Epiphany, the celebration of Jesus' baptism, is actually second only to Easter in antiquity. Though the extent of its celebration is uncertain, it predated the feast of the Nativity (or "Christmas"). Clement of Alexandria knew of the celebration of Epiphany, although neither of the dates he records as the ones proposed for the feast day line up with the date he records for Jesus' birth. He notes that the followers of Basilides mark the feast with an all-night vigil of readings (*Strom.* 1.21.145). For a compilation and historical analysis of the evidence for Epiphany and Nativity in early Christianity, see Hermann Usener, *Religionsgeschichtliche Untersuchungen. Erster Theil: Das Weihnachtsfest* (Bonn, 1889).

225. The later redactor (eleventh c.) of Macarius's letter deletes almost all of the author's explanations of the proper days for baptisms, eliminates the references to Christians as born/begotten of God, and at the end of the section introduces the adoption metaphor (cf. *Letter* 223.9–11, p. 87).

226. The baptism of Jesus was a troublesome *datum* for apologists of high Christological orthodoxy, as is well known, and remembrance of Jesus' baptism did not survive in any Christian creeds except one—the creed of the Armenian Church (cf. McDonnell, *Baptism*, 35–41). For another early text attempting to explain the relationship of the baptism of Christ and Christians, see Methodius of Olympus, *Symposium*, Logos 8.

227. On the various attempts to date Cyril's writings, see Day, *Baptismal Liturgy*, esp. 23–25. It is also possible that these lectures were refined each year and their present form should thus be regarded as late-fourth-century interpretations.

228. Cyril of Jerusalem, *Cat. Lect.* 3.14–15. Greek: Ἐὰν καὶ αὐτὸς ἔχῃς ἀνυπόκριτον εὐλάβειαν, κατέρχεται καὶ ἐπὶ σὲ τὸ Πνεῦμα τὸ ἅγιον, καὶ φωνή σοι πατρικὴ ἄνωθεν ἐπηχεῖ·

οὐχ, οὗτός ἐστιν ὁ υἱός μου, ἀλλ᾽ οὗτος νῦν γέγονεν υἱός μου. Ἐπ᾽ ἐκείνου μὲν γὰρ τὸ ἔστιν·
ἐπειδὴ ἐν ἀρχῇ ἦν ὁ Λόγος, καὶ ὁ Λόγος ἦν πρὸς τὸν Θεόν, καὶ Θεὸς ἦν ὁ Λόγος· ἐπ᾽ ἐκείνου
τὸ ἔστιν· ἐπειδὴ πάντοτέ ἐστιν υἱὸς Θεοῦ· ἐπὶ δὲ σοῦ τὸ νῦν γέγονεν· ἐπειδὴ οὐ κατὰ φύσιν
ἔχεις, ἀλλὰ κατὰ θέσιν τὴν υἱοθεσίαν λαμβάνεις· ἐκεῖνος ἀΐδιός ἐστι· σὺ δὲ ἐκ προκοπῆς
λαμβάνεις τὴν χάριν. Οὐκοῦν ἑτοίμασον τῆς ψυχῆς τὸ ἄγγος, ἵνα υἱὸς γένῃ Θεοῦ, καὶ
κληρονόμος μὲν Θεοῦ, συγκληρονόμος δὲ χριστοῦ.

229. This had by then become a common way of explaining why Jesus needed to be baptized.

230. Cyril of Jerusalem, *Cat. Lect.* 10.3, 10.5.

231. Cyril of Jerusalem, *Cat. Lect.* 7.7–8. For a longer analysis of Cyril's divine sonship language vis-à-vis Nicea, see Robert C. Gregg, "Cyril of Jerusalem and the Arians," in *Arianism: Historical and Theological Reassessments* (ed. Robert C. Gregg; Patristic Monograph Series 11; Philadelphia: Philadelphia Patristic Foundation, 1985), 85–109.

232. *Apostolic Constitutions* 2.32. Critical edition is Marcel Metzger, ed., *Les Constitutions Apostoliques* (Sources Chrétiennes 320, 329, 336; Paris: Cerf, 1985–87). Greek: υἱός μου εἶ σύ, ἐγὼ σήμερον γεγέννηκά σε. διὰ τοῦ ἐπισκόπου σου ὁ Θεὸς υἱοποιεῖταί σε, ἄνθρωπε.

233. *Didascalia Apostolorum* 9; Vööbus, p. 103: "the bishop is a servant of the word and mediator, but to you a teacher and your father, after God, who has begotten you (pl.) through the water" (*d᾽wldkwn byd my᾽/ per aquam regenerans*). *Apostolic Constitutions* 2.26: the bishop "is after God, your father, having begotten you (pl.) again through water and spirit into adoption" (δι᾽ ὕδατος καὶ πνεύματος ἀναγεννήσας ὑμᾶς εἰς υἱοθεσίαν).

234. He replaces the DA's description of bishops as "those who have begotten you again" with the phrase "your spiritual parents."

235. Cf. the use of the adoption metaphor with baptism later in the *AC*: 7.39–40, 7.43, 8.8.

236. *Apostolic Constitutions* 2.32. "Acknowledge then, O son …" Greek: γνώριζε οὖν, υἱέ …

237. On the christological significance of interpreting Jesus' baptism in the fourth century, see Robert L. Wilken, "The Interpretation of the Baptism of Jesus in the Later Fathers," *Studia Patristica* 11 (1972): 268–77.

238. The AC (2.32) makes this clear by adding Christ as *an object of belief* in its redaction of the DA. Instead of hearing the holy voice *like* Christ, being baptized and born *with* Christ, the Christian has come *to believe in* Christ.

■ Conclusion

1. John Chrysostom, *Hom. in Matt.* 12 (*PG* 57: 205–07). I will paraphrase the long homily and translate some key portions.

2. Greek: οὐδὲ γὰρ ἀπὸ κιβωτοῦ ἄνθρωπον ἐξάγει ἕνα, ἀλλὰ τὴν οἰκουμένην ἅπασαν εἰς τὸν οὐρανὸν ἀνάγει φανεῖσα, καὶ ἀντὶ θαλλοῦ ἐλαίας τὴν υἱοθεσίαν τῷ κοινῷ τῆς οἰκουμένης κομίζει γένει.

3. Greek: μὴ τοίνυν ἀχάριστος γίνου περὶ τὸν εὐεργέτην … ὅπου γὰρ υἱοθεσίας ἀξίωμα, ἐκεῖ καὶ ἡ τῶν κακῶν ἀναίρεσις, καὶ ἡ τῶν ἀγαθῶν ἁπάντων δόσις.

4. Cf. a similar moment in Ps-Hippolytus, *Discourse on Theophany* 6.

5. On adoptive sonship as "legitimate" (γνήσιος) for Chrysostom, cf. *Hom. in Eph.* 5.2 (*PG* 62: 39).

6. This is not the singular ἡ βασιλεία, but the plural τὰ βασίλεια (courts, palaces, imperial confines).

7. Greek: οὐδὲ γὰρ εἰ βασιλεύς τις τῶν ἐπὶ τῆς γῆς πτωχὸν ὄντα σε καὶ προσαιτοῦντα λαβών, υἱὸν ἐξαίφνης ἐποιήσατο, τὴν καλύβην καὶ τὴν εὐτέλειαν τῆς καλύβης τῆς σῆς ἐνενόησας ἄν· καίτοιγε οὐ πολὺ τὸ μέσον ἐκεῖ. μὴ τοίνυν μηδὲ ἐνταῦθα λογίζου τι τῶν προτέρων· καὶ γὰρ ἐπὶ πολλῷ μείζοσιν ἐκλήθης. ὅ τε γὰρ καλῶν, ὁ τῶν ἀγγέλων δεσπότης ἐστί· τά τε διδόμενα ἀγαθά, καὶ λόγον καὶ διάνοιαν ὑπερβαίνει πᾶσαν. οὐ γὰρ ἀπὸ γῆς εἰς γῆν σε μεθίστησι, καθάπερ ὁ βασιλεὺς, ἀλλ᾽ ἀπὸ γῆς εἰς οὐρανὸν, καὶ ἀπὸ φύσεως θνητῆς εἰς ἀθάνατον καὶ δόξαν ἄρρητον, τότε δυναμένην μόνον φανῆναι καλῶς, ὅταν αὐτῆς ἀπολαύσωμεν.

8. This is generally the case, and Chrysostom is no different (cf. *PG* 62: 622; 63: 491).

9. He uses a similar analogy in his instructions to catechumens; cf. St. John Chrysostom, *Baptismal Instructions* (trans. Paul W. Harkins; Ancient Christian Writers 31; Westminster, Md.: Newman Press; London: Longmans, Green, and Co., 1963), 89–90.

10. Greek: εἰ γὰρ ὁ παράδεισον λαχών, διὰ μίαν παρακοὴν τοσαῦτα μετὰ τὴν τιμὴν ὑπέστη δεινά· οἱ τὸν οὐρανὸν ἀπολαβόντες ἡμεῖς, καὶ τῷ μονογενεῖ γενόμενοι συγκληρονόμοι, τίνα ἕξομεν συγγνώμην, τῷ ὄφει μετὰ τὴν περιστερὰν προστρέχοντες;

■ Epilogue

1. This is an illustration by Eran Ben-Dov of the well-preserved shrine at Philippopolis, to which the shrine at Hippos-Sussita may be compared. Arthur Segal, "The Kalibe Buildings — Temples for the Worship of Emperors in Hauran and in Trachonitis — a Historical-Archaeological Analysis," *Qadmoniot* 34/1 [121] (2001): 60–66, image from p. 63 [Hebrew].

■ BIBLIOGRAPHY

Note: For ancient sources, I have tried to use the editions and translations most widely available in the United States: the Hebrew Bible, Septuagint and New Testament from Deutsche Bibelgesellschaft (Stuttgart); the Loeb Classical Library (Harvard University Press); *Patrologia Graeca* and *Latina*; Corpus Scriptorum; Sources Chrétiennes; *Thesaurus Linguae Graecae* (electronic); Library of Latin Texts (electronic). Ancient sources are listed below only if their editions or translations come from elsewhere.

Ahearne-Kroll, Stephen P. *The Psalms of Lament in Mark's Passion: Jesus' Davidic Suffering.* SNTSMS 142. Cambridge: Cambridge University Press, 2007.

Aland, Kurt. *Synopsis Quattuor Evangeliorum.* Rev. ed. Stuttgart: Deutsche Biblegesellschaft, 2001.

Alföldi, Andreas. *Der Vater des Vaterlandes im römischen Denken.* Darmstadt: Wissenschaftliche Buchgesellschaft, 1971.

Alföldy, Géza. "Subject and Ruler, Subjects and Methods: An Attempt at a Conclusion." Pages 254–61 in *Subject and Ruler.* Edited by Alistair Small.

Ando, Clifford. *Imperial Ideology and Provincial Loyalty in the Roman Empire.* Berkeley: University of California Press, 2000.

———. *The Matter of the Gods: Religion and the Roman Empire.* Berkeley: University of California Press, 2008.

Ashton, John. *Understanding the Fourth Gospel.* Oxford: Clarendon, 1991.

Athanassiadi, Polymnia, and Frede, Michael, eds. *Pagan Monotheism in Late Antiquity.* Oxford: Clarendon, 1999.

Attridge, Harold W. "The Cubist Principle in Johannine Imagery: John and the Reading of Images of Contemporary Platonism." Pages 47–60 in *Imagery in the Gospel of John: Terms, Forms, Themes, and Theology of Johannine Figurative Language.* Edited by Jörg Frey, Jan G. Van der Watt, and Ruben Zimmermann. WUNT 200. Tübingen: Mohr Siebeck, 2006.

———. "The Philosophical Critique of Religion under the Early Empire." *ANRW* 2.16.1 (1978): 45–78.

———. "The Psalms in Hebrews." Pages 197–212 in *The Psalms in the New Testament.* Edited by Steve Moyise and Maarten J.J. Menken. London; New York: T. & T. Clark, 2004.

———. *Hebrews.* Edited by Helmut Koester. Hermeneia. Philadelphia: Fortress, 1989.

Augustine. *The Works of Saint Augustine: A Translation for the 21st Century: Sermons, Part III.* Translated by Edmund Hill. Brooklyn: New City Press, 1992.

Ayres, Lewis. *Nicaea and its Legacy: An Approach to Fourth-Century Trinitarian Theology.* Oxford: Oxford University Press, 2004.

Bacon, Benjamin Wisner. *Is Mark a Roman Gospel?* Cambridge, Mass.: Harvard University Press, 1919.

Baird, William. *History of New Testament Research, Vol. 2.* Minneapolis: Fortress, 2003.

Barnes, Timothy D. *Athanasius and Constantius: Theology and Politics in the Constantinian Empire.* Cambridge, Mass.: Harvard University Press, 1993.

———. *Constantine and Eusebius.* Cambridge, Mass.: Harvard University Press, 1981.

Barrett, Anthony A. *Livia: First Lady of Imperial Rome.* New Haven: Yale University Press, 2004.

Bauckham, Richard. "The Sonship of the Historical Jesus in Christology." *Scottish Journal of Theology* 31 (1978): 245–60.

Bauer, Walter. *Rechtgläubigkeit und Ketzerei im ältesten Christentum.* Tübingen: Mohr, 1934. English version: *Orthodoxy and Heresy in Earliest Christianity.* Translated by a team from the Philadelphia Seminar on Christian Origins. Edited by Robert A. Kraft and Gerhard Krodel. Philadelphia: Fortress, 1971.

Beard, Mary. "Looking (Harder) for Roman Myth: Dumézil, Declamation and the Problems of Definition." Pages 44–64 in *Mythos in mythenloser Gesellschaft: Das Paradigma Roms.* Edited by Fritz Graf. Stuttgart: Teubner, 1993.

Beard, Mary, North, John, and Price, Simon. *Religions of Rome, Volume I: A History.* Cambridge: Cambridge University Press, 1998.

Béchard, Dean P. *The Scripture Documents: An Anthology of Official Catholic Teachings.* Collegeville, Minn.: Liturgical Press, 2002.

Bell, H. Idris. *Jews and Christians in Egypt.* London: Oxford University Press, 1924.

Berger, Adolf, Nicholas, Barry, and Treggiari, Susan M. "Adoption, Roman." *Oxford Classical Dictionary.* 3rd ed. Edited by Simon Hornblower and Antony Spawforth. Oxford; New York: Oxford University Press, 2003.

Berlin, Andrea M. "The Archaeology of Ritual: The Sanctuary of Pan at Banias/Caesarea Philippi." *BASOR* 315 (1999): 27–45.

Berlin, Andrea M., and Netzer, Ehud. "Debate: Where Was Herod's Temple to Augustus." *Biblical Archaeology Review* 29:5 (Sept/Oct 2003): 22–25.

Bernett, Monika. *Der Kaiserkult in Judäa unter den Herodiern und Römern: Untersuchungen zur politischen und religiösen Geschichte Judäas von 30 v. bis 66 n. Chr.* Tübingen: Mohr Siebeck, 2007.

———. "Roman Imperial Cult in the Galilee." Pages 337–56 in *Religion, Ethnicity, and Identity in Ancient Galilee.* WUNT 210. Edited by Jürgen Zangenberg, Harold Attridge, and Dale Martin. Tübingen: Mohr Siebeck, 2007.

Bhabha, Homi K. "Of Mimicry and Man: The Ambivalence of Colonial Discourse." Pages 85–92 in *The Location of Culture.* London: Routledge, 1994.

Bingham, Jeffrey D. "Irenaeus's Reading of Romans 8." *Society of Biblical Literature Seminar Papers 2001* (2001): 131–50.

Black, C. Clifton. *Mark: Images of an Apostolic Interpreter.* Columbia: University of South Carolina Press, 1994.

———. "Was Mark a Roman Gospel?" *Expository Times* 105 (1993): 36–40.

Bonner, S. F. *Roman Declamation in the Late Republic and Early Empire.* Liverpool: University Press of Liverpool, 1949.

Botha, P. J. "Ephrem's Comparison of the Father-Son Relationship to the Relationship Between a Tree and Its Fruit in His Hymns 'On Faith.'" *Acta Patristica et Byzantina* 4 (1993): 23–32.

Bourdieu, Pierre. *The Logic of Practice.* Translated by Richard Nice. Cambridge: Polity, 1990.

———. *Outline of a Theory of Practice.* Translated by Richard Nice. Cambridge: Cambridge University Press, 1977.

Bourdieu, Pierre, and Wacquant, Loïs J.D. *An Invitation to Reflexive Sociology.* Chicago: University of Chicago Press, 1992.

Bousset, Wilhelm. *Kyrios Christos: Geschichte des Christusglaubens von den Anfängen des Christentums bis Irenaeus.* 4th ed. Göttingen: Vandenhoeck & Ruprecht, 1935. English version: *Kyrios Christos.* Translated by John E. Steely. Nashville: Abingdon, 1970.

———. *Das Wesen der Religion: Dargestellt an ihrer Geschichte.* 3rd ed. Halle: Gebauer-Schwetschke, 1906. English version: *What is Religion?* Translated by F. B. Low. New York: G.B. Putnam, 1907.

Bowersock, G.W. "Greek Intellectuals and the Imperial Cult in the Second Century A.D." Pages 177–212 in *Le Culte des Souverains.* Edited by Willem den Boer.

Bradshaw, Paul F., Johnson, Maxwell E., and Phillips, L. Edward. *The Apostolic Tradition.* Edited by Harold W. Attridge. Hermeneia. Minneapolis: Fortress, 2002.

Brent, Allen. *The Imperial Cult and the Development of Church Order: Concepts and Images of Authority in Paganism and Early Christianity before the Age of Cyprian.* Leiden: Brill, 1999.

Brown, Raymond E. *The Birth of the Messiah.* New York: Doubleday, 1977.

Brown, Robert F. "On the Necessary Imperfection of Creation: Irenaeus' *Adversus Haereses* IV, 38." *Scottish Journal of Theology* 28 (1975): 17–25.

Brox, Norbert. "Hermas und eine »politische Metaphysik«?" Pages 24–31 in *Panchaia: Festschrift für Klaus Thraede.* Edited by Manfred Wacht. Jahrbuch für Antike und Christentum 22. Münster: Aschendorffsche Verlagsbuchhandlung, 1995.

———. *Der Hirt des Hermas.* Göttingen: Vandenhoeck & Ruprecht, 1991.

Bryan, Christopher. *Render to Caesar: Jesus, the Early Church, and the Roman Superpower.* New York: Oxford University Press, 2005.

Buch-Hansen, Gitte. "It Is the Spirit That Makes Alive: a Stoic Understanding of Pneuma in John." Ph.D. diss., Copenhagen, 2007.

Büchner, Karl. "Tacitus und Plinius über Adoption des römischen Kaisers." *Rheinisches Museum für Philologie* 98 (1955): 289–312.

Buckler, W. H. "Auguste, Zeus Patroos." *Revue de Philologie* 9 (3rd series, 1935): 177–88.

Bucur, Bogdan G. "The Son of God and the Angelomorphic Holy Spirit: A Rereading of the Shepherd's Christology." *ZNW* 98 (2007): 120–42.

Buell, Denise Kimber. *Making Christians: Clement of Alexandria and the Rhetoric of Legitimacy.* Princeton: Princeton University Press, 1999.

———. *Why This New Race: Ethnic Reasoning in Early Christianity.* New York: Columbia University Press, 2005.

Bühner, Jan-Adolf. *Der Gesandte und sein Weg im vierten Evangelium.* Tübingen: Mohr, 1977.

Bultmann, Rudolf. "Die Bedeutung der neuerschlossenen mandäischen und manichäischen Quellen für das Verständnis des Johannesevangeliums." Pages 10–35 in *Exegetica: Aufsätze zur Erforschung des Neuen Testaments.* Edited by Erich Dinkler. Tübingen: J.C.B. Mohr (Paul Siebeck), 1967.

Burrus, Virginia. *Begotten, Not Made: Conceiving Manhood in Late Antiquity.* Stanford, Calif: Stanford University Press, 2000.

Butterworth, G.W. *Origen On First Principles.* Gloucester, Mass.: Peter Smith, 1973.

Byrne, Brendan. *Sons of God – Seed of Abraham.* Rome: Biblical Institute Press, 1979.

Cameron, Averil. *Christianity and the Rhetoric of Empire: The Development of Christian Discourse.* Berkeley: University of California Press, 1991.

Cancick, Hubert, and Schneider, Helmuth. *Der Neue Pauly.* 16 vols. Stuttgart: J.B. Metzler, 1996–2003.

Casey, Maurice. "Lord Jesus Christ: A Reponse to Professor Hurtado." *JSNT* 27 (2004): 83–96.

Cavadini, John C. *The Last Christology of the West: Adoptionism in Spain and Gaul, 785–820.* Philadelphia: University of Pennsylvania Press, 1993.

Chancey, Mark A. *The Myth of a Gentile Galilee.* SNTSMS 118. Cambridge: Cambridge University Press, 2002.

Chaniotis, Angelos. "The Divinity of the Hellenistic Rulers." Pages 431–45 in *A Companion to the Hellenistic World*. Edited by Andrew Erskine. Malden, Mass.; Oxford: Blackwell, 2003.

Cirillo, Luigi. "La christologie pneumatique de la cinquième parabole du 'Pasteur' d'Hermas." *Revue de l'histoire des religions* 184 (1973): 25–48.

Clark, Gillian. *Divine Qualities: Cult and Community in Republican Rome.* Oxford: Oxford University Press, 2007.

Clauss, Manfred. "*Deus praesens*: der römische Kaiser als Gott." *Klio* 78 (1996): 400–33.

———. *Kaiser und Gott: Herrscherkult im römischen Reich.* Stuttgart; Leipzig: Tuebner, 1999.

Collins, John J. *The Scepter and the Star: The Messiahs of the Dead Sea Scrolls and Other Ancient Literature.* New York: Doubleday, 1995.

———. "The 'Son of God' Text from Qumran." Pages 65–82 in *From Jesus to John: Essays on Jesus and the New Testament Christology in Honour of Marinus de Jonge*. Edited by Martinus de Boer. Sheffield: JSOT Press, 1993.

Colpe, Carsten. *Die religionsgeschichtliche Schule: Darstellung und Kritik ihres Bildes vom gnostichen Erlösermythus.* FRLANT 78. Göttingen: Vandenhoeck & Ruprecht, 1961.

Cooke, Gerald. "The Israelite King as Son of God." *ZAW* 73 (1961): 202–25.

Corbier, Mireille. "Divorce and Adoption as Roman Familial Strategies (*Le Divorce et l'adoption 'en plus'*)." Pages 47–78 in *Marriage, Divorce, and Children in Ancient Rome*. Edited by Beryl Rawson.

Corbin, Henry. *Le Paradoxe du Monotheisme.* Paris: Éditions de l'Herne, 1981.

Cranfield, C. E. B. *The Gospel According to St. Mark.* Cambridge: Cambridge University Press, 1963.

Cross, Frank Moore. *Canaanite Myth and Hebrew Epic.* Cambridge, Mass.: Harvard University Press, 1973.

Crossan, John Dominic, and Reed, Jonathan L. *Excavating Jesus: Beneath the Stones, Behind the Texts.* San Francisco: HarperSanFrancisco, 2001.

———. *In Search of Paul: How Jesus' Apostle Opposed Rome's Empire with God's Kingdom.* San Francisco: HarperSanFrancisco, 2004.

Crowfoot, John W., Kenyon, Kathleen M., and Sukenik, Eliezer L. *Samaria-Sebaste: Reports of the Work of the Joint Expedition in 1931–1933 and of the British Expedition in 1935, vol. 1: The Buildings at Samaria.* London: Palestine Exploration Fund, 1942.

Croy, N. Clayton. "Where the Gospel Text Begins: A Non-Theological Interpretation of Mark 1:1." *NovT* 43 (2001): 105–27.

Curchin, Leonard A. "Cult and Celt: Indigenous Participation in Emperor Worship." Pages 143–52 in *Subject and Ruler*. Edited by Alistair Small.

Cuss, Dominique. *Imperial Cult and Honorary Terms in the New Testament.* Fribourg: University Press, 1974.

D'Angelo, Mary Rose. "Abba and 'Father': Imperial Theology and the Jesus Traditions." *JBL* 111 (1992): 611–30.

Dahms, J. V. "The Johannine Use of Monogenes Reconsidered." *NTS* 29 (1983): 222–32.

Davies, W. D., and Allison, Dale C. *The Gospel According to St. Matthew.* 3 vols. International Critical Commentary. Edinburgh: T&T Clark, 1997.

Day, Juliette. *The Baptismal Liturgy of Jerusalem: Fourth- and Fifth-Century Evidence from Palestine, Syria and Egypt.* Hampshire: Ashgate, 2007.

de Blois, Lukas, Funke, Peter, and Hahn, Johannes, eds. *The Impact of Imperial Rome on Religions, Ritual, and Religious Life in the Roman Empire: Proceedings of the Fifth International Network, Münster, June 30–July 4, 2004.* Leiden: Brill, 2006.

de Jong, Janneke. "Egyptian Papyri and 'Divinity' of the Roman Emperor." Pages 239–52 in *The Impact of Imperial Rome on Religions, Ritual, and Religious Life in the Roman Empire: Proceedings of the Fifth International Network, Münster, June 30–July 4, 2004.* Edited by Lukas de Blois, Peter Funke, and Johannes Hahn. Leiden: Brill, 2006.

Deissmann, Adolf. *Licht vom Osten: das Neue Testament und die neuentdeckten Texte der hellenistisch-römischen Welt.* 3rd ed. Tübingen: Mohr, 1909.

den Boer, Willem, ed. *Le Culte des Souverains dans l'Empire Romain.* Entretiens sur l'antiquitÈ classique 19. VandúuvresGeneÃve: Fondation Hardt, 1973.

Dennison, Charles G. "How Is Jesus the Son of God? Luke's Baptism Narrative and Christology." *Calvin Theological Journal* 17 (1982): 6–25.

Deutsch, Monroe E. "Caesar's Son and Heir." *California Publications in Classical Philology* 9:6 (1928): 149–200.

Dibelius, Martin. *Der Hirt des Hermas.* Tübingen: Mohr Siebeck, 1923.

⸻. *Rom und die Christen im ersten Jahrhundert. Vorgelegt am 10. Januar 1942.* Heidelberg: C. Winter, 1942.

Dixon, Suzanne. *The Roman Family.* Baltimore: Johns Hopkins University Press, 1992.

Donahue, John. "Windows and Mirrors: The Setting of Mark's Gospel." *CBQ* 57 (1995): 1–26.

Donahue, John, and Harrington, Daniel. *The Gospel of Mark.* Sacra Pagina 2. Collegeville, Minn.: Liturgical Press, 2002.

Donner, Herbert. "Adoption oder Legitimation? Erwägungen zur Adoption im Alten Testament auf dem Hintergrund der altorientalischen Rechte." *Oriens Antiquus* 8 (1969): 87–119.

Douglas, Michael C. "Power and Praise in the Hodayot: A Literary-Critical Study of 1QH 9:1–18:14." Ph.D. diss., The University of Chicago, 1998.

Drake, H. A. *In Praise of Constantine: A Historical Study and New Translation of Eusebius' Tricennial Orations.* Berkeley: University of California Press, 1976.

Dunn, James D. G. *Christology in the Making: A New Testament Inquiry into the Origins of the Doctrine of the Incarnation.* 2nd ed. Grand Rapids: Eerdmans, 1989.

⸻. "Son of God as Son of Man in the Dead Sea Scrolls: A Response to John Collins on 4Q246." Pages 198–210 in *Scrolls and the Scriptures.* Edited by Stanley Porter and Craig Evans. Sheffield: Sheffield University Press, 1997.

⸻. *The Theology of Paul the Apostle.* Grand Rapids: Eerdmans, 1997.

Dupont, Jacques. "*Filius meus es Tu.* L'Interprétation de *Ps. II, 7,* dans le Nouveau Testament." *Recherches de Science Religieuse* 35 (1948): 522–43.

Eck, Werner. *Rom und Judaea: Fünf Vorträge zur Römischen Herrschaft in Palaestina.* Tübingen: Mohr Siebeck, 2007.

Edwards, James R. "The Baptism of Jesus According to the Gospel of Mark." *Journal of the Evangelical Theological Society* 34 (1991): 43–57.

Ehrenberg, Victor, and Jones, A.H.M. *Documents Illustrating the Reigns of Augustus & Tiberius.* 2nd ed. Oxford: Clarendon, 1955.

Ernst, J. *Das Evangleium nach Markus.* Regensburger Neues Testament. Regensburg: Pustet Verlag, 1981.

Ehrman, Bart D. *The New Testament: A Historical Introduction to the Early Christian Writings.* 4th ed. New York; Oxford: Oxford University Press, 2008.

⸻. *The Orthodox Corruption of Scripture.* Oxford: Oxford University Press, 1993.

⸻. "The Theodotians as Corruptors of Scripture." *Studia Patristica* 25 (1993): 46–51.

Étienne, Robert. *Le Culte Impérial dans le péninsule ibérique d'Auguste à Dioclétien*. Paris: E. de Boccard, 1958.

———. "Du nouveau sur les débuts du culte impérial municipal dans la péninsule ibérique." Pages 153–64 in *Subject and Ruler*. Edited by Alistair Small.

Eusebius. *Life of Constantine*. Introduction, translation and commentary by Averil Cameron and Stuart G. Hall. Oxford: Clarendon, 1999.

Evans, Craig A. "Mark's Incipit and the Priene Calendar Inscription: From Jewish Gospel to Greco-Roman Gospel." *Journal for the Study of Greco-Roman Christianity and Judaism* 1 (2000): 67–81. Online: http://craigaevans.com/Priene%20art.pdf.

Eyben, Emiel. "Fathers and Sons." Pages 106–43 in *Marriage, Divorce, and Children in Ancient Rome*. Edited by Beryl Rawson.

Fantino, Jacques. *La Théologie d'Irénée*. Paris: Cerf, 1994.

Fears, J. Rufus. "Jupiter and Roman Imperial Ideology." *ANRW* II.17.1 (1981): 3–141.

———. *Princeps a diis electus: the Divine Election of the Emperor as a Political Concept at Rome*. Rome: American Academy in Rome, 1977.

Firmage, Edwin. "Zoology: Doves and Pigeons." *ABD* 6:1144–45.

Fishwick, Duncan. *The Imperial Cult in the Latin West*. 2 vols. Leiden: Brill, 1987–92.

Fitzmeyer, Joseph A. "4Q246: The 'Son of God' Document from Qumran." *Biblica* 74 (1993): 153–74.

Fletcher-Louis, Crispin H.T. *Luke-Acts: Angels, Christology, and Soteriology*. WUNT II 94. Tübingen: Mohr Siebeck, 1997.

———. "The Worship of Divine Humanity as God's Image and the Worship of Jesus." Pages 112–28 in *The Jewish Roots of Christological Monotheism*. Edited by Carey C. Newman, James R. Davila, and Gladys S. Lewis. JSJSup 63. Leiden: Brill, 1999.

Fowl, Stephen E. Review of Larry W. Hurtado, *Lord Jesus Christ*. *Modern Theology* 22 (2006): 152–54.

Fowler, W. Warde. *Roman Ideas of Deity*. London: Macmillan and Co., 1914.

France, R.T. *The Gospel of Mark*. New International Greek Testament Commentary. Grand Rapids: Eerdmans, 2002.

Fredriksen, Paula. "Mandatory Retirement: Ideas in the Study of Christian Origins Whose Time Has Come to Go." *Studies in Religion / Sciences Religieuses* 35/2 (2006): 231–46.

———. Review of Larry W. Hurtado, *Lord Jesus Christ*. *JECS* 12 (2004): 537–41.

———. "What 'Parting of the Ways'?" Pages 35–63 in *The Ways that Never Parted*. Edited by Adam Becker and Annette Yoshiko Reed. Tübingen: Mohr Siebeck, 2003.

Frey, Jörg. "The Relevance of the Roman Imperial Cult for the Book of Revelation: Exegetical and Hermeneutical Reflections on the Relation between the Seven Letters and the Visionary Main Part of the Book." Pages 231–55 in *The New Testament and Early Christian Literature in Greco-Roman Context: Studies in Honor of David E Aune*. Edited by John Fotopoulos. NovTSup 122. Leiden: Brill, 2006.

Friesen, Steven J. *Imperial Cults and the Apocalypse of John: Reading Revelation in the Ruins*. Oxford: Oxford University Press, 2001.

———. *Twice Neokoros: Ephesus, Asia and the Cult of the Flavian Imperial Family*. Leiden: Brill, 1993.

Frilingos, Christopher A. *Spectacles of Empire: Monsters, Martyrs, and the Book of Revelation*. Divinations. Philadelphia: University of Pennsylvania Press, 2004.

Galinsky, Karl. *Augustan Culture*. Princeton: Princeton University Press, 1996.

García Martínez, Florentino, and Tigchelaar, Eibert J.C., eds. *The Dead Sea Scrolls Study Edition*. 2 vols. Leiden; Boston; Köln: Brill and Grand Rapids: Eerdmans, 1997–1998.

Gardner, Jane F. *Family and* Familia *in Roman Law and Life*. Oxford: Clarendon, 1998.

Garroway, Joshua "The Invasion of a Mustard Seed: A Reading of Mark 5.1–20." *JSNT* 32 (2009): 57–75.

Gathercole, Simon J. *The Preexistent Son: Recovering the Christologies of Matthew, Mark, and Luke*. Grand Rapids: Eerdmans, 2006.

Geertz, Clifford. "Thick Description: Toward an Interpretive Theory of Culture." Pages 3–30 in *The Interpretation of Cultures: Selected Essays*. New York: Basic Books, 1973.

Gero, Stephen. "The Spirit as a Dove at the Baptism of Jesus." *NovT* 18 (1976): 17–35.

Gnilka, J. *Das Evangelium nach Markus*. 5th ed. 2 vols. Evangelisch-katholischer Kommentar zum Neuen Testament II/1–2. Zürich/Neukirchen/Vluyn: Benziger Verlag/Neukirchener Verlag, 1998.

Gold, Michael. "Adoption: A New Problem for Jewish Law." *Judaism* 36 (1987): 443–50.

Goldberg, Jonah. "Myth of Camelot." *National Review Online*. 1 February 2008. Cited 20 February 2009. Online: http://www.townhall.com/Columnists/JonahGoldberg/2008/02/01/the_myth_of_camelot.

Goody, Jack. "Adoption in Cross-Cultural Perspective." *Comparative Studies in Society and History* 11 (1969): 55–78.

Goulder, Michael. "A Poor Man's Christology." *NTS* 45 (1999): 332–48.

Gradel, Ittai. *Emperor Worship and Roman Religion*. Oxford: Clarendon Press, 2002.

Grant, Robert M. *Gods and the One God*. Philadelphia: Westminster Press, 1986.

Gregg, Robert C. "Cyril of Jerusalem and the Arians." Pages 85–109 in *Arianism: Historical and Theological Reassessments*. Edited by Robert C. Gregg. Patristic Monograph Series 11. Philadelphia: Philadelphia Patristic Foundation, 1985.

Gregg, Robert C., and Groh, Dennis E. *Early Arianism—A View of Salvation*. Philadelphia: Fortress Press, 1981.

Grillmeier, Aloys. *Christ in Christian Tradition*. 2nd ed. Translated by John Bowden. 2 vols. London: Mowbrays, 1975.

Guelich, Robert A. *Mark 1–8:26*. Word Biblical Commentary 34A. Dallas: Word Books, 1989.

Gunderson, Erik. *Declamation, Paternity, and Roman Identity*. Cambridge: Cambridge University Press, 2003.

Gundry, Robert H. *Mark: A Commentary on His Apology for the Cross*. Grand Rapids: Eerdmans, 1993.

Hahn, Ferdinand. *Christologische Hoheitstitel*. Göttingen: Vandenhoeck & Ruprecht, 1963. English version: *The Titles of Jesus in Christology*. Translated by Harold Knight and George Ogg. London: Lutterworth, 1969.

Habicht, Christian. "Die augusteische Zeit und das erste Jahrhundert nach Christi Geburt." Pages 41–88 in *Le Culte des Souverains*. Edited by Willem den Boer.

———. *Gottmenschentum und Griechische Städte*. 2nd ed. München: Beck, 1970.

Haight, Roger. *Jesus, Symbol of God*. Maryknoll, N.Y.: Orbis, 1999.

Hall, Clayton Morris. *Nicolaus of Damascus' Life of Augustus: A Historical Commentary Embodying a Translation*. Smith College Classical Studies 4; Northampton, Mass., 1923.

Hammond, Mason. *The Antonine Monarchy*. Rome: American Academy in Rome, 1959.

———. *The Augustan Principate in Theory and Practice During the Julio-Claudian Period*. Cambridge, Mass.: Harvard University Press, 1933.

_____. "The Transmission of Powers of the Roman Emperor from the Death of Nero in A.D. 68 to that of Alexander Severus in A.D. 235." *Memoirs of the American Academy in Rome* 24 (1956): 63–133.

Hänlein-Schäfer, Heidi. "Die Ikonographie des *Genius Augusti* im Kompital- und Hauskult der frühen Kaiserzeit." Pages 73–98 in *Subject and Ruler*. Edited by Alistair Small.

_____. *Veneratio Augusti: Eine Studie zu den Tempeln des ersten römischen Kaisers.* Archaeologica 39. Rome: Giorgio Bretschneider, 1985.

Hano, Michel. "A l'origine du culte impérial: les autels des Lares Augusti. Recherches sur les thèmes iconographiques et leur signification." *ANRW* 2.16.3 (1986): 2333–81.

Hanson, R. P. C. *The Search for the Christian Doctrine of God: The Arian Controversy 318–381.* Edinburgh: T. & T. Clark, 1988.

Harden, J. M. *The Ethiopic Didascalia.* London: SPCK; New York: Macmillan, 1920.

Harnack, Adolph. *History of Dogma.* Translated from the 3rd German edition by Neil Buchanan. 7 vols. Gloucester, Mass.: Peter Smith, 1976.

Hartford Institute for Religious Research. Online: http://hirr.hartsem.edu/index.html.

Harvey, Brian K. "Two Bases of Marcus Aurelius Caesar and the Roman Imperial Succession." *Historia: Zeitschrift für Alte Geschichte* 53 (2004): 46–60.

Hauck, Robert J. "The Great Fast: Christology in the Shepherd of Hermas." *Anglican Theological Review* 75 (1993): 187–98.

Heikel, Ivar A., ed. *Eusebius' Werke I.* GCS. Leipzig, 1902.

Hekster, Olivier. "All in the Family: The Appointment of Emperors Designate in the Second Century AD." Pages 35–49 in *Administration, Prosopography and Appointment Policies in the Roman Empire.* Edited by Lukas de Blois. Amsterdam: J.C. Gieben, 2001.

_____. "Descendants of Gods: Legendary Genealogies in the Roman Empire." Pages 24–35 in *Impact of Imperial Rome.* Edited by Lukas de Blois et al.

_____. "Honouring Ancestors: The Dynamic of Deification." Pages 95–110 in *Ritual Dynamics and Religious Change in the Roman Empire: Proceedings of the Eighth Workshop of the International Network Impact of Empire (Heidelberg, July 5–7, 2007).* Edited by Olivier Hekster, Sebastian Schmidt-Hofner, and Christian Witschel. Leiden: Brill, 2009.

Hellerman, Joseph H. *The Ancient Church as Family.* Minneapolis: Fortress, 2001.

Hengel, Martin. *Der Sohn Gottes, Die Entstehung der Christologie und die jüdisch-hellenistische Religionsgeschichte.* Tübingen: J.C.B. Mohr (Paul Siebeck), 1975. English version: *The Son of God.* Translated by John Bowden. London: SCM; Philadelphia: Fortress, 1977.

_____. *Studies in the Gospel of Mark.* Philadelphia: Fortress, 1985.

Henne, Philippe. "La Véritable Christologie de la *Cinquième Similitude* du *Pasteur* d'Hermas." *Revue des Sciences Philosophiques et Theologiques* 74 (1990): 182–204.

_____. *La Christologie chez Clément de Rome et dans le Pasteur d'Hermas.* Fribourg: Éditions Universitaires, 1992.

Henzen, Guil, ed. *Acta Fratrum Arvalium.* Berlin, 1874.

Herz, Peter. "Die Adoptivsöhne des Augustus und der Festkalender: Gedanken zu einer Inschrift aus Messene." *Klio* 75 (1993): 272–88.

_____. "Caesar and God: Recent Publications on Roman Imperial Cult." *JRA* 18 (2005): 638–48.

_____. "Emperors: Caring for the Empire and Their Successors." Pages 304–16 in *A Companion to Roman Religion.* Edited by Jörg Rüpke. Malden, Mass.: Blackwell, 2007.

_____. "Der römische Kaiser und der Kaiserkult: Gott oder primus inter pares?" Pages 115–40 in *Menschwerdung Gottes—Vergöttlichung von Menschen.* Edited by Dieter

Zeller. Novum Testamentum et Orbis Antiquus 7. Freiburg: Universitätsverlag; Göttingen: Vandenhoeck & Ruprecht, 1988.

Heyman, George. *The Power of Sacrifice: Roman and Christian Discourses in Conflict.* Washington, D.C.: Catholic University of America Press, 2007.

Hippolyte de Rome. *La Tradition Apostolique.* 2nd ed. Edited by Bernard Botte. Sources Chretiénnes 11. Paris: Les Éditions du Cerf, 1984.

Hodge, Caroline Johnson. *If Sons, Then Heirs: A Study of Kinship and Ethnicity in the Letters of Paul.* Oxford; New York: Oxford University Press, 2007.

Hoff, Michael C. "An Equestrian Statue of Lucius Caesar in Athens Reconsidered." *Archäologischer Anzeiger* (2001): 583–99.

Hölbl, Günther. *Altägypten im römischen Reich: der römische Pharao und seine Tempel.* 3 vols. Mainz: Philipp von Zabern, 2000–05.

Holum, Kenneth G. "The Temple Platform: Progress Report on the Excavations." Pages 13–34 in *Caesarea Papers 2: Herod's Temple, the Provincial Governor's Praetorium and Granaries, the Later Harbor, a Gold Coin Hoard, and Other Studies.* Edited by Kenneth G. Holum, Avner Raban, and Joseph Patrich. JRASup 35. Portsmouth, RI: Journal of Roman Archaeology, 1999.

Hopkins, Keith. *Conquerors and Slaves: Sociological Studies in Roman History.* Cambridge: Cambridge University Press, 1978.

––––––. *A World Full of Gods.* New York: Free Press, 2000.

Horbury, William. Review of Larry W. Hurtado, *Lord Jesus Christ. JTS* 56 (2005): 537–38.

Horsley, Richard A. *Jesus and Empire: The Kingdom of God and the New World Disorder.* Minneapolis: Fortress, 2002.

––––––, ed. *Paul and Empire: Religion and Power in Roman Imperial Society.* Harrisburg, Penn.: Trinity Press International, 1997.

Howgego, Christopher. *Ancient History from Coins.* London: Routledge, 1995.

Hurtado, Larry W. "Christ-Devotion in the First Two Centuries: Reflections and a Proposal." *Toronto Journal of Theology* 12 (1996): 17–33.

––––––. *How on Earth Did Jesus Become a God?* Grand Rapids: Eerdmans, 2005.

––––––. "Jesus' Divine Sonship in Paul's Epistle to the Romans." Pages 217–33 in *Romans and the People of God.* Edited by Sven K. Soderlund and N.T. Wright. Grand Rapids: Eerdmans, 1999.

––––––. *Lord Jesus Christ: Devotion to Jesus in Earliest Christianity.* Grand Rapids: Eerdmans, 2003.

––––––. "Son of God." Pages 900–06 in *Dictionary of Paul and His Letters.* Edited by G.F. Hawthorne et al. Downers Grove, Ill.: InterVarsity, 1997.

Huzar, Eleanor G. "Emperor Worship in Julio-Claudian Egypt." *ANRW* 2.18.5 (1995): 3092–3143.

Idel, Moshe. *Ben: Sonship in Jewish Mysticism.* London: Continuum, 2008.

Ilan, Tal. "'Man Born of Woman …' (Job 14:1) The Phenomenon of Men Bearing Metronymes at the Time of Jesus." *NovT* 34 (1992): 23–45.

Incigneri, Brian J. *The Gospel to the Romans.* Biblical Interpretation Series 65. Leiden; Boston: Brill, 2003.

Irénée de Lyon. *Contre les Hérésies.* 5 vols. Edited by Adelin Rousseau et al. Sources Chrétiennes 34, 100, 152–53, 210–11, 263–64, 293–94. Paris: du Cerf, 1952–82.

Jaffee, Martin S. *Torah in the Mouth: Writing and Oral Tradition in Palestinian Judaism 200 B.C.E–400 C.E.* New York: Oxford University Press, 2001.

Jastrow, Marcus. *A Dictionary of the Targumim, the Talmud Talmud and Yerushalmi, and the Midrashic Literature*. 2 vols. New York: P. Shalom, 1967.

Jeffers, James S. "The Influence of the Roman Family and Social Structures on Early Christianity in Rome." Pages 370–84 in *Society of Biblical Literature Seminar Papers 1988*. Edited by David J. Lull. Atlanta: Scholars Press, 1988.

Jeremias, Joachim. *New Testament Theology*. New York: Scribner, 1971.

Jewett, Robert. *Romans*. Edited by Eldon Jay Epp. Hermeneia. Minneapolis: Fortress, 2007.

John Chrysostom. *Baptismal Instructions*. Translated by Paul W. Harkins. Ancient Christian Writers 31. Westminster, Md.: Newman Press; London: Longmans, Green, and Co., 1963.

Johnson, Earl S. "Is Mark 15.39 the Key to Mark's Christology?" *JSNT* 31 (1987): 3–22.

Johnson, Luke Timothy. Review of Larry W. Hurtado, *Lord Jesus Christ*. *Scottish Journal of Theology* 59 (2006): 358–62.

Johnson, Maxwell. *Images of Baptism*. Chicago: Liturgy Training Publications, 2001.

———. *The Rites of Christian Initiation: Their Evolution and Interpretation*. Collegeville, Minn.: Liturgical Press, 1999.

Jones, D. L. "Christianity and the Roman Imperial Cult." *ANRW* 2.23.2 (1980): 1023–54.

Jüngel, Eberhard. "Metaphorische Wahrheit: Erwägungen zur theologischen Relevanz der Metapher als Beitrag zur Hermeneutik einer Narrativen Theologie." Pages 71–122 in *Metaphor: Zur Hermeneutik religiöser Sprache*. Edited by Paul Ricoeur and Eberhard Jüngel, with an introduction by Pierre Gisel. München: Chr. Kaiser Verlag, 1974.

Kantiréa, Maria. *Les dieux et les dieux augustes: Le culte impérial en Grèce sous les Julio-claudiens et les Flaviens: Etudes épigraphiques et archéologiques*. ΜΕΛΕΤΗΜΑΤΑ 50. Athens: Κέντρον Ἑλληνικῆς καὶ Ρωμαϊκῆς Ἀρχαιότητος τοῦ Ἐθνικοῦ Ἰδρύματος Ἐρευνῶν; Paris: Diffusion de Boccard, 2007.

Käsemann, Ernst. *Das Wandernde Gottesvolk: Eine Untersuchung zum Hebräerbrief*. 2nd ed. FRLANT 55. Göttingen: Vandenhoeck & Ruprecht, 1957. English version: *The Wandering People of God: An Investigation of the Letter to the Hebrews*. Translated by Roy A. Harrisville and Irving L. Sandberg. Minneapolis: Augsburg, 1984.

Kasper, Walter. *Jesus der Christus*. Mainz: Matthias-Grünewald Verlag, 1974. English version: *Jesus the Christ*. Translated by V. Green. New York: Paulist Press, 1976.

Keel, Othmar. *Vögel als Boten*. Orbis Biblicus et Orientalis 14. Freiburg: Universitätsverlag Freiburg, 1977.

Kern, Otto. *Die Inschriften von Magnesia am Mäander*. Berlin, 1900.

Kim, Seyoon. *Christ and Caesar: The Gospel and The Roman Empire in the Writings of Paul and Luke*. Grand Rapids: Eerdmans, 2008.

Kim, Tae Hun. "The Anarthrous *huios theou* in Mark 15:39 and the Roman Imperial Cult." *Biblica* 79 (1998): 221–41.

Kingsbury, Jack Dean. *The Christology of Mark's Gospel*. Philadelphia: Fortress, 1983.

———. *Matthew as Story*. 2nd ed. Minneapolis: Fortress, 1988.

Klauck, Hans-Josef. *Die religiöse Umwelt des Urchristentums II: Herrscher- und Kaiserkult, Philosophie, Gnosis*. Kohlhammer-Studienbücher Theologie 9.2. Stuttgart: Kohlhammer, 1996.

Klijn, A.F.J. "The Apocryphal Correspondence between Paul and the Corinthians." *Vigiliae Christianae* 17 (1963): 2–23.

Knobloch, F.W. "Adoption." *ABD* 1:76–79.

Koester, Helmut. *Ancient Christian Gospels: Their History and Development*. Philadelphia: Trinity Press; London: SCM, 1990.

_____. *From Jesus to the Gospels: Interpreting the New Testament in Its Context.* Minneapolis: Fortress, 2007.

Kolb, Frank. *Herrscherideologie in der Spätantike.* Berlin: Akademie Verlag, 2001.

Kornemann, Ernst. "Ἄναξ καινὸς Ἀδριανός." *Klio* 7 (1907): 278–88.

Kornemann, Ernst, and Eger, Otto. *Griechische Papyri in Museum des oberhessischen Geschichtsvereins zu Giessen.* Leipzig and Berlin: Teubner, 1910–12.

Kraeling, Emil G., ed. *The Brooklyn Museum Aramaic Papyri. New Documents of the Fifth Century B.C. from the Jewish Colony at Elephantine.* New Haven: Yale University Press, 1969.

Kristof, Nicholas D. "The Dynastic Question." *The New York Times.* 31 January 2008. Accessed 20 February 2009. Online: http://www.nytimes.com/2008/01/31/opinion/31kristof.html.

Kügler, Joachim. *Pharao und Christus: religionsgeschichtliche Untersuchung zur Frage einer Verbindung zwischen altägyptischer Königstheologie und neutestamentlicher Christologie im Lukasevangelium.* Bodenheim: PHILO, 1997.

Kuhn, Karl A. "The 'One Like a Son of Man' Becomes the 'Son of God.'" *CBQ* 69 (2007): 22–42.

Kunst, Christiane. *Römische Adoption: Zur Strategie einer Familienorganisation.* Hennef: Marthe Clauss, 2005.

Kurylowicz, Marek. "Adoption on the Evidence of the Papyri." *Journal of Juristic Papyrology* 19 (1983): 61–75.

Kuschel, Karl-Josef. *Geboren vor aller Zeit? Der Streit um Christi Ursprung.* München: Piper, 1990. English version: *Born Before All Time? The Dispute over Christ's Origin.* Translated by John Bowden. London: SCM Press, 1992.

Lampe, Peter. *From Paul to Valentinus: Christians at Rome in the First Two Centuries.* Edited by Marshall D. Johnson. Translated by Michael Steinhauser. Minneapolis: Fortress, 2003.

Lane, William L. *The Gospel According to Mark.* Grand Rapids: Eerdmans, 1974.

Lassen, Eva Marie. "The Roman Family: Ideal and Metaphor." Pages 103–20 in *Constructing Early Christian Families.* Edited by Halvor Moxnes.

_____. "The Use of the Father Image in Imperial Propaganda and 1 Corinthians 4:14–21." *Tyndale Bulletin* 42 (1991): 127–36.

Latte, Kurt. *Römische Religionsgeschichte.* München: C.H. Beck, 1960.

Lehmann, Clayton Miles, and Holum, Kenneth G. *The Greek and Latin Inscriptions of Caesarea Maritima.* Joint Expedition to Caesarea Maritima 5. Boston: American Schools of Oriental Research, 2000.

Lentzen-Deis, Fritzleo. *Die Taufe Jesu nach den Synoptikern.* Frankfurt: Josef Knecht, 1970.

Leon, Harry J. *The Jews of Ancient Rome.* Philadelphia: Jewish Publication Society of America, 1960.

Leutzsch, Martin. "Hirt des Hermas." Pages 107–497 in *Papiasfragmente. Hirt des Hermas.* Edited by Ulrich H.J. Körtner and Martin Leutzsch. Schriften des Urchristentums 3. Darmstadt: Wissenschaftliche Buchgesellschaft, 1998.

_____. *Die Wahrnehmung sozialer Wirklichkeit im "Hirten des Hermas."* Göttingen: Vandenhoeck & Ruprecht, 1989.

Levin, Yigal. "Jesus, 'Son of God' and 'Son of David': The 'Adoption' of Jesus into the Davidic Line." *JSNT* 28 (2006): 415–42.

Levinson, Joshua. "'Tragedies Naturally Performed:' Fatal Charades, *Parodia Sacra*, and the Death of Titus" Pages 349–82 in *Jewish Culture and Society Under the Christian Roman Empire.* Edited by Richard Kalmin and Seth Schwartz. Leuven: Peeters, 2003.

Liebeschuetz, J. H. W. G. *Continuity and Change in Roman Religion*. Oxford: Oxford University Press, 1979.

Lierman, John. *The New Testament Moses: Christian Perceptions of Moses and Israel in the Setting of Jewish Religion*. WUNT II 173. Tübingen: Mohr Siebeck, 2004.

Liertz, Uta-Maria. *Studien zu Kaiserkult und Kaiserverehrung in den germanischen Provinzen und in Gallia Belgica zur römischen Kaiserzeit*. Rome: Institutum Romanum Finlandiae, 1998.

Liew, Tat-Siong Benny. "Tyranny, Boundary and Might: Colonial Mimicry in Mark's Gospel." *JSNT* 73 (1999): 7–31.

Levin, Yigal. "Jesus, 'Son of God' and 'Son of David': The 'Adoption' of Jesus into the Davidic Line." *JSNT* 28 (2006): 415–42.

Lieu, Judith. *I, II, & III John*. New Testament Library. Louisville; London: Westminster John Knox, 2008.

Lindsay, Hugh. "Adoption and Its Function in Cross-Cultural Contexts." Pages 190–204 in *Childhood, Class, and Kin in the Roman World*. Edited by Suzanne Dixon. London: Routledge, 2001.

——. *Adoption in the Roman World*. Cambridge; New York: Cambridge University Press, 2009.

Loader, William R. G. "The Apocalyptic Model of Sonship: Its Origin and Development in New Testament Tradition." *JBL* 97 (1978): 525–54.

——. *Sohn und Hoherpriester: Eine traditionsgeschichtliche Untersuchung zur Christologie des Hebräerbriefes*. Neukirchen: Neukirchener, 1981.

Lohmeyer, Ernst. *Christuskult und Kaiserkult*. Tübingen: J.C.B. Mohr (Paul Siebeck), 1919.

Löhr, Winrich A. "Theodotus der Lederarbeiter und Theodotus der Bankier—ein Beitrag zur römischen Theologiegeschichte des zweiten und dritten Jahrhunderts," *ZNW* 87 (1996): 101–25.

Lott, J. Bert. *The Neighborhoods of Augustan Rome*. Cambridge: Cambridge University Press, 2004.

Lyall, Francis. "Roman Law in the Writings of Paul—Adoption." *JBL* 88 (1969): 458–66.

Macchiavelli, Niccolò. *Discourses on Livy*. Translated by Julia Conaway Bondanella and Peter Bondanella. The World's Classics. Oxford; New York: Oxford University Press, 1997.

Maier, Paul L. "The Episode of the Golden Shields at Jerusalem." *HTR* 62 (1969): 109–21.

Marcus, Joel. "The Jewish War and the *Sitz im Leben* of Mark." *JBL* 111 (1992): 441–62.

——. *Mark 1–8*. Anchor Bible 27. New York: Doubleday, 2000.

——. *The Way of the Lord: Christological Exegesis of the Old Testament in the Gospel of Mark*. Louisville: Westminster/John Knox Press, 1992.

Marshall, I. Howard. "The Divine Sonship of Jesus." *Interpretation* 21 (1967): 87–103.

Martin, Dale B. *Inventing Superstition*. Cambridge, Mass.: Harvard University Press, 2004.

——. *Slavery as Salvation: The Metaphor of Slavery in Pauline Christianity*. New Haven: Yale University Press, 1990.

Marxsen, Willi. *Mark the Evangelist*. Nashville: Abingdon, 1969.

Mattingly, Harold, ed. *Coins of the Roman Empire in the British Museum*. 3 vols. London: British Museum, 1965.

McArthur, H. K. "'Son of Mary.'" *NovT* 15 (1973): 38–58.

McDonnell, Kilian. *The Baptism of Jesus in the Jordan: The Trinitarian and Cosmic Order of Salvation*. Collegeville, Minn.: Liturgical Press, 1996.

Meeks, Wayne A. "Moses as God and King." Pages 354–71 in *Religion in Antiquity: Essays in Memory of Erwin Ramsdell Goodenough*. Edited by Jacob Neusner. Studies in the History of Religions 14. Leiden: Brill, 1968.

Meggitt, Justin. "Taking the Emperor's Clothes Seriously: The New Testament and The Roman Emperor." Pages 143–70 in *The Quest for Wisdom: Essays in Honour of Philip Budd*. Edited by C. Joynes. Cambridge: Orchard Academic, 2002. Online: http://www .religion-online.org/showarticle.asp?title=3278.

Mellor, Ronald. "The Goddess Roma." *ANRW* 2.17.2 (1981): 950–1030.

Mendelsohn, Isaac. "A Ugaritic Parallel to the Adoption of Ephraim and Manasseh." *IEJ* 9 (1959): 180–83.

Metzger, Marcel, ed. *Les Constitutions Apostoliques*. Sources Chrétiennes 320, 329, 336. Paris: Cerf, 1985–87.

Millar, Fergus. "The Imperial Cult and the Persecutions." Pages 143–75 in *Le Culte des Souverains*. Edited by Willem den Boer.

Mitchell, Margaret M., and Young, Frances M. *The Cambridge History of Christianity*. 9 vols. Cambridge: Cambridge University Press, 2006.

Mitteis, L., and Wilcken, U., eds. *Grundzüge und Chrestomathie der Papyruskunde*. Leipzig, 1912.

Moloney, Francis J. *The Gospel of Mark*. Peabody, Mass.: Hendrickson, 2002.

Momigliano, Arnaldo. "The Theological Efforts of the Roman Upper Classes in the First Century BC." *Classical Philology* 79 (1984): 199–211.

Moody, Dale. "God's Only Son: The Translation of John 3:16 in the Revised Standard Version." *JBL* 72 (1953): 213–19.

Moore, Stephen D. *Empire and Apocalypse: Postcolonialism and the New Testament*. Sheffield: Sheffield Phoenix Press, 2006.

———. *Literary Criticism and the Gospels*. New Haven: Yale University Press, 1989.

Morgen, Michèle. "Le (Fils) *monogène* dans les écrits johanniques: Évolution des traditions et elaboration rédactionelle." *NTS* 53 (2007): 165–83.

Moss, Candida R. *The Other Christs: Imitating Jesus in Ancient Christian Ideologies of Martyrdom*. New York: Oxford University Press, 2010.

———. "The Transfiguration: An Exercise in Markan Accommodation." *Biblical Interpretation* 12 (2004): 69–89.

Mosser, Carl. "The Earliest Patristic Interpretations of Psalm 82, Jewish Antecedents, and the Origin of Deification." *JTS* 56 (2005): 30–74.

Mowery, Robert. "Son of God in Roman Imperial Titles and Matthew." *Biblica* 83 (2002): 100–110.

Mowinckel, Sigmund. *He That Cometh. The Messiah Concept in the Old Testament and Later Judaism*. Nashville: Abingdon Press, 1955; repr. Grand Rapids: Eerdmans, 2005.

Moxnes, Halvor, ed. *Constructing Early Christian Families: Family as Social Reality and Metaphor*. London; New York: Routledge, 1997.

———. "What Is Family?" Pages 13–41 in *Constructing Early Christian Families*. Edited by Halvor Moxnes.

Muers, Rachel. "Adoptionism: Is Jesus Christ the Son of God by Nature or by Adoption?" Pages 50–58 in *Heresies and How to Avoid Them*. Edited by Ben Quash and Michael Ward. London: SPCK; Peabody, Mass.: Hendrickson, 2007.

Münderlein, Gerhard. "Die Erwählung durch das Pleroma: Bemerkungen zu Kol. i. 19." *NTS* 8 (1961): 264–76.

Musurillo, Herbert. *Acts of the Christian Martyrs*. Oxford: Clarendon Press, 1972.

Namikawa, Miyako. "La Paciencia del Crecimiento y la Maduración." *Estudios Eclesiásticos* 83 (2008): 51–85.

Nardi, Carlo. *Il Battesimo in Clemente Alessandrino: Interpretazione di* Eclogae propheticae 1–26. Studia Ephemeridis "Augustinianum." Rome: Institutum Patristicum "Augustinianum," 1984.

Needham, Rodney. *Belief, Language, and Experience.* Chicago: University of Chicago Press, 1972.

Nesselhauf, Herbert. "Die Adoption des römischen Kaisers." *Hermes* 83 (1955): 477–95.

Netzer, Ehud. "The Augusteum at Samaria-Sebaste—A New Outlook." *Eretz-Israel* 19 (1987): 97–105 [Hebrew], 75* [English summary].

―――. "The Sanctuary of Pan at Banias." *Qadmoniot* 115 (1998): 18–25 [Hebrew]. Nielsen, Hanne Sigismund. "*Alumnus*: A Term of Relation Denoting Quasi-Adoption." *Classica et Mediaevalia* 38 (1987): 141–88.

―――. "Quasi-Kin, Quasi-Adoption and the Roman Family." Pages 249–62 in *Adoption et Fosterage.* Edited by Mireille Corbier. Paris: De Boccard, 1999.

Nilsson, Martin. *Geschichte der griechischen Religion.* 2 vols. 2nd ed. München: C.H. Beck, 1961.

Nock, Arthur Darby. *Essays on Religion and the Ancient World.* 2 vols. Edited by Zeph Stewart. Cambridge, Mass.: Harvard University Press, 1972.

Nolan, Brian M. *The Royal Son of God: The Christology of Matthew 1–2 in the Setting of the Gospel.* Fribourg: Editions universitaires; Göttingen: Vandenhoeck & Ruprecht, 1979.

Nolland, John. *The Gospel of Matthew: A Commentary on the Greek Text.* NIGTC. Grand Rapids: Eerdmans; Bletchley: Paternoster Press, 2005.

―――. "No Son-of-God Christology in Matthew 1.18–25." *JSNT* 62 (1996): 3–12.

Nongbri, Brent. "Dislodging 'Embedded' Religion: A Brief Note on a Scholarly Trope." *Numen* 55 (2008): 440–60.

Noormann, Rolf. *Irenäus als Paulusinterpret.* WUNT II 66. Tübingen: Mohr Siebeck, 1994.

Noreña, Carlos F. "The Communication of the Emperor's Virtues." *JRS* 91 (2001): 146–68.

Norris, Richard A. "Irenaeus' Use of Paul in His Polemic Against the Gnostics." Pages 78–98 in *Paul and the Legacies of Paul.* Edited by William S. Babcock. Dallas: Southern Methodist University Press, 1990.

Noth, Martin. *The Laws in the Pentateuch and Other Studies.* Philadelphia: Fortress Press, 1966.

Numenius. *Fragments: Texte Établi et Traduit par Édouard des Places, S.J.* Translated and edited by Édouard des Places. Paris: Les Belles Lettres, 1973.

Oakes, Peter. "Re-mapping the Universe: Paul and the Emperor in 1 Thessalonians and Philippians." *JSNT* 27 (2005): 301–22.

Opitz, Hans-Georg, ed. *Athanasius Werke.* Berlin and Leipzig: De Gruyter, 1934–.

Orbe, Antonio. "En torno a los Ebionitas." *Augustinianum* 33 (1993): 315–37.

―――. "¿San Ireneo adopcionista?" *Gregorianum* 65 (1984): 5–52.

―――. "Teología Bautismal de Clemente Alejandrino según Paed. I, 26,3–27,2." *Gregorianum* 36 (1955): 410–48.

―――. *Teología de San Ireneo.* 4 vols. Madrid: La Editorial Catolica, 1985–88 (vols. 1–3). Madrid: Biblioteca de Autores Cristianos, 1996 (vol. 4).

Origen. *Commentary on the Epistle to the Romans, Books 6–10.* Translated by Thomas P. Scheck. Fathers of the Church 104. Washington, D.C.: Catholic University of America Press, 2002.

―――. *Sur la Pâque: Traité inédit publié d'après un papyrus de Toura.* Edited by Octave Guérard and Pierre Nautin. Christianisme Antique 2. Paris: Beauchesne, 1979.

―――. *Treatise on the Passover and Dialogue with Heraclides.* Translated and edited by Robert J. Daly. New York: Paulist, 1992.

Osiek, Carolyn. *Rich and Poor in the Shepherd of Hermas*. Washington, D.C.: Catholic University of America Press, 1983.

———. *Shepherd of Hermas: A Commentary*. Edited by Helmut Koester. Hermeneia. Minneapolis: Fortress, 1999.

Otto, Rudolf. *The Idea of the Holy*. Translated by John W. Harvey. London: Humphrey Milford; Oxford University Press, 1925.

Overman, J. Andrew, Olive, Jack, and Nelson, Michael, "Discovering Herod's Shrine to Augustus: Mystery Temple Found at Omrit." *Biblical Archaeology Review* 29:2 (Mar/Apr 2003): 40–49, 67–68.

Paul, Shalom M. "Adoption Formulae: A Study of Cuneiform and Biblical Legal Clauses." *Maarav* 2 (1979–80): 173–85.

Pearson, Birger A. "The Figure of Seth in Gnostic Literature." Pages 472–514 in vol. 2 of *The Rediscovery of Gnosticism*. 2 vols. Edited by Bentley Layton. Leiden: Brill, 1981.

Pelikan, Jaroslav *The Spirit of Eastern Christendom (600–1700)*. Chicago: University of Chicago Press, 1977.

Pelikan, Jaroslav, and Hotchkiss, Valerie, eds. *Creeds and Confessions of Faith in the Christian Tradition*. 4 vols. New Haven and London: Yale University Press, 2003.

Pendrick, Gerard. "ΜΟΝΟΓΕΝΗΣ." *NTS* 41 (1995): 587–600.

Peppard, Michael. "'Poetry,'Hymns,' and 'Traditional Material' in New Testament Epistles or How to Do Things with Indentations." *JSNT* 30 (2008): 319–42.

Peretto, Elio. *La lettera ai Romani cc. 1–8 nell' Adversus Haereses d'Ireneo*. Quaderni di "Vetera Christianorum" 6. Bari: Istituto di Letteratura Cristiana Antica, 1971.

Pernveden, Lage. *The Concept of the Church in the Shepherd of Hermas*. Studia Theologica Lundensia 27. Lund: CWK Gleerup, 1966.

Pesch, R. *Das Markusevangelium*. 2 vols. Herders theologischer Kommentar zum Neuen Testament II/1–2. Freiburg: Herder, 1976–77.

Pestman, P. W., ed. *The New Papyrological Primer*. 2nd ed. Leiden: Brill, 1994.

Pfanner, M. "Über das Herstellen von Porträts: Ein Beitrag zu Rationalisierungsmaßnahmen und Produktionsmechanismen von Massenware im späten Hellenismus und in der römischen Kaiserzeit." *Jahrbuch des Deutschen Archäologischen Instituts* 104 (1989): 157–257.

Phillips, C. R. "The Sociology of Religious Knowledge in the Roman Empire to A.D. 284." *ANRW* 2.16.2 (1986): 2697–2711.

Pleket, H. W. "An Aspect of the Emperor Cult: Imperial Mysteries." *HTR* 58 (1965): 331–47.

Pokorný, Petr. *Der Gottessohn: Literarische Übersicht und Fragestellung*. Zürich: Theologischer Verlag, 1971.

Pötscher, Walter. "'Numen' und 'numen Augusti.'" *ANRW* 2.16.1 (1978): 355–92.

Powell, Mark Alan. *What Is Narrative Criticism?* Minneapolis: Fortress, 1990.

Prévost, Marcel-Henri. *Les Adoptions politiques à Rome sous la République et le Principat*. Paris, 1949.

Price, Simon R. F. "Gods and Emperors: The Greek Language of the Roman Imperial Cult." *JHS* 104 (1984): 79–95.

———. *Rituals and Power: The Roman Imperial Cult in Asia Minor*. Cambridge: Cambridge University Press, 1984.

Rawson, Beryl, ed. *Marriage, Divorce, and Children in Ancient Rome*. Oxford: Clarendon, 1991.

Reid, J. S. "Roman Ideas of Deity," *JRS* 6 (1916): 170–84.

Reisner, George A., Fisher, Clarence S., and Lyon, David G. *Harvard Excavations at Samaria, 1908–1910*. 2 vols. Cambridge, Mass.: Harvard University Press, 1924.

Reitzenstein, Richard. *Die hellenistichen Mysterienreligionen: Nach ihren Grundgedanken und Wirkungen*. 3rd ed. Stuttgart: B.G. Teubner, 1927; repr., 1956). English version: *Hellenistic Mystery-Religions: Their Basic Ideas and Significance*. Translated by John E. Steely. Pittsburgh: Pickwick Press, 1987.

Reynolds, Joyce M. "Ruler-cult at Aphrodisias in the Late Republic and under the Julio-Claudian Emperors." Pages 41–50 in *Subject and Ruler*. Edited by Alistair Small.

Richard, Jean. "Fils de Dieu. Reconsidération de l'interprétation adoptioniste." Pages 431–65 in *Le Christ Hier, Aujourd'hui et Demain: Colloque de christologie tenu à l'Université Laval*. Edited by Raymond Laflamme and Michel Gervais. Québec: Les Presses de l'Université Laval, 1976.

Ricoeur, Paul. *Interpretation Theory: Discourse and the Surplus of Meaning*. Fort Worth: Texas Christian University Press, 1976.

Rives, James B. *Religion in the Roman Empire*. Malden, Mass.: Blackwell, 2007.

———. "Roman Religion Revived." *Phoenix* 52 (1998): 345–65.

Roche, P. A. "The Execution of L. Salvius Otho Cocceianus." *Classical Quarterly* 53 (2003): 319–22.

Rose, Charles Brian. *Dynastic Commemoration and Imperial Portraiture in the Julio-Claudian Period*. Cambridge: Cambridge University Press, 1997.

Roskam, Hendrika N. *The Purpose of the Gospel of Mark in Its Historical and Social Context*. NovTSup 114. Leiden; Boston: Brill, 2004.

Rüpke, Jörg. *Die Religion der Römer*. München: Beck, 2001. English version: *Religion of the Romans*. Translated by Richard Gordon. Cambridge: Polity, 2007.

Russell, Norman. *The Doctrine of Deification in the Greek Patristic Tradition*. Oxford: Oxford University Press, 2004.

Saller, Richard. "*Patria Potestas* and the Stereotype of the Roman Family." *Continuity and Change* 1 (1986): 7–22.

———. "Pietas, obligation, and authority in the Roman family." Pages 393–410 in *Alte Geschichte und Wissenschaftsgeschichte: Festschrift für Karl Christ zum 65. Geburtstag*. Edited by Peter Kneissl and Volker Losemann. Darmstadt: Wissenschaftliche Buchgesellschaft, 1988.

Samuel, Simon. *A Postcolonial Reading of Mark's Story of Jesus*. Library of New Testament Studies 340. London; New York: T. & T. Clark, 2007.

Sandmel, Samuel. "Parallelomania." *JBL* 81 (1962): 1–13.

Santero, J. M. "The 'Cultores Augusti' and the Private Worship of the Roman Emperor." *Athenaeum* 61 (1983): 111–25.

Schachter, Melech. "Various Aspects of Adoption." Pages 31–53 in *Halacha and Contemporary Society*. Edited by Alfred S. Cohen. New York: Ktav, 1984.

Scheid, John. *Commentarii Fratrum Arvalium qui supersunt*. Rome: École Française de Rome, 1998.

———. "Comprendre le culte dit impérial. Autour de deux livres récents." *L'Antiquité Classique* 73 (2004): 239–49.

——— *La Religion des Romans*. Paris: Armand Colin/Masson, 1998. English version: *An Introduction to Roman Religion*. Translated by Janet Lloyd. Bloomington: Indiana University Press, 2003.

———. *Romulus et ses frères: le collège des Frères Arvales, modèle du culte public dans la Rome des empereurs*. Rome: École Française de Rome, 1990.

Schenke, Ludger. *Das Markusevangelium*. Stuttgart: Kohlhammer, 2005.

Schildgen, Brenda Deen. *Power and Prejudice: The Reception of the Gospel of Mark*. Detroit: Wayne State University Press, 1998.

Schmidt, T. E. "Mark 15.16–32: The Crucifixion Narrative and the Roman Triumphal Procession." *NTS* 41 (1995): 1–18.

Schmitthenner, Walter. *Oktavian und das Testament Cäsars*. München: C.H. Beck, 1952.

Schneemelcher, Wilhelm, ed. *New Testament Apocrypha*. 2 vols. Louisville: Westminster John Knox, 2003.

Schniedewind, William M. *Society and the Promise to David. The Reception History of 2 Samuel 7:1–17*. Oxford: Oxford University Press, 1999.

Schrenk, G. "εὐδοκέω, εὐδοκία." *TDNT* 2:738–51.

Schweizer, Eduard. *The Good News According to Mark*. Translated by Donald H. Madvig. Atlanta: John Knox, 1970.

———. "Variety and Unity in the New Testament Proclamation of Jesus as the Son of God." *Australian Biblical Review* 15 (1967): 1–12.

Schwering, Walther. "*Deus* und *divus*. Eine semasiologische Studie als Ergänzung zum Artikel *divus* in Thesaurus linguae latinae." *Indogermanische Forschungen* 34 (1914–15): 1–44.

Scott, James M. *Adoption as Sons of God: An Exegetical Investigation into the Background of ΥΙΟΘΕΣΙΑ in the Pauline Corpus*. WUNT II 48. Tübingen: Mohr Siebeck, 1992.

Scott, Peter, and Cavanaugh, William T., eds. *The Blackwell Companion to Political Theology*. Malden, Mass.: Blackwell, 2004.

Segal, Arthur. "The Kalibe Buildings—Temples for the Worship of Emperors in Hauran and in Trachonitis—a Historical-Archaeological Analysis," *Qadmoniot* 34/1 [121] (2001): 60–66 [Hebrew].

———. "The 'Kalybe-Structures'—Temples for the Imperial Cult in Hauran and Trachon: An Historical-Architectural Analysis." Accessed 20 February 2009. Online: http://www.tau.ac.il/arts/projects/PUB/assaph-art/assaph6/articles_assaph6/ArthurSegal.pdf.

Segal, Arthur, and Eisenberg, Michael. "Sussita-Hippos of the Decapolis: Town Planning and Architecture of a Roman-Byzantine City." *Near Eastern Archaeology* 70:2 (2007): 86–107.

Senior, Donald. "With Swords and Clubs: The Setting of Mark's Community and His Critique of Abusive Power," *BTB* 17 (1987): 10–20.

Simpson, C. J. "Caligula's Cult: Immolation, Immortality, Intent." Pages 63–71 in *Subject and Ruler*. Edited by Alistair Small.

Skarsaune, Oskar. "The Ebionites." Pages 419–62 in *Jewish Believers in Jesus*. Edited by Oskar Skarsaune and Reidar Hvalvik. Peabody, Mass.: Hendrickson, 2007.

Skeat, T. C. "The Augustan Era in Egypt." *ZPE* 53 (1983): 241–44.

Small, Alistair, ed. *Subject and Ruler: The Cult of the Ruling Power in Classical Antiquity* Journal of Roman Archaeology Supplements 17. Ann Arbor: Journal of Roman Archaeology, 1996.

Smith, Martin S. "Greek Adoptive Formulae." *Classical Quarterly* 61 (1967): 302–10.

Smith, R. R. R. *Hellenistic Royal Portraits*. Oxford: Clarendon, 1988.

Speiser, E. A. *Genesis*. Anchor Bible 1. Garden City, N.Y.: Doubleday, 1981.

Spinks, Bryan D. *Early and Medieval Rituals and Theologies of Baptism: From the New Testament to the Council of Trent*. Hampshire: Ashgate, 2006.

Stade, B. "Auf Jemandes Knieen gebären." *ZAW* 6 (1886): 143–56.

Stanton, Graham N. *Jesus and Gospel*. Cambridge: Cambridge University Press, 2004.

Stauffer, E. "Jeschu ben Mirjam (Mk 6:3)." Pages 119–28 in *Neotestamentica et Semitica: Studies in Honour of Matthew Black*. Edited by E. Earle Ellis and Max Wilcox. Edinburgh: T. & T. Clark, 1969.

Sterling, Gregory E. *Historiography and Self-Definition: Josephos, Luke-Acts, and Apologetic Historiography.* Leiden; New York: Brill, 1992.

Suetonius, *The Twelve Caesars.* Translated by Robert Graves. Revised by Michael Grant. London: Penguin, 1979).

Sussman, Lewis A. *The Declamations of Calpurnius Flaccus.* Leiden: Brill, 1994.

———. *The Major Declamations Ascribed to Quintilian.* Frankfurt; New York: P. Lang, 1987.

———. "Sons and Fathers in the *Major Declamations* Ascribed to Quintilian." *Rhetorica* 13 (1995): 179–92.

Swancutt, Diana. *Pax Christi: Empire, Identity, and Protreptic Rhetoric in Paul's Letter to the Romans.* NovTSup. Leiden: Brill, forthcoming.

Syme, Ronald. *Tacitus.* 2 vols. Oxford: Clarendon, 1958.

Tacitus. *The Annals.* Translated by A. J. Woodman. Indianapolis: Hackett, 2004.

Tatum, W. Barnes. "Jesus' So-Called Triumphal Entry." *Forum* 1 (New Series, 1998): 129–144.

Taubenschlag, Raphael. *The Law of Greco-Roman Egypt in the Light of the Papyri, 332 B.C. – 640 A.D.* 2nd ed. Milano: Cisalpino-Goliardico, 1972.

Taylor, Joan E. "Pontius Pilate and the Imperial Cult in Roman Judaea." *NTS* 52 (2006): 555–82.

Taylor, Lily Ross. *The Divinity of the Roman Emperor.* Middletown, Conn.: American Philological Association, 1931.

Taylor, Vincent. *The Gospel According to St. Mark.* London: MacMillan, 1959.

Terian, Abraham. *Macarius of Jerusalem, Letter to the Armenians (A.D. 335): Introduction, Text, Translation, and Commentary.* Crestwood, N.Y.: St. Vladimir's Seminary Press, 2008.

Testuz, Michel. *Papyrus Bodmer X-XII.* Cologny-Genève: Bibliotheca Bodmeriana, 1959.

Theissen, Gerd. *The Gospels in Context.* Translated by Linda M. Maloney. Minneapolis: Fortress Press, 1991.

Thiede, Carsten Peter. *Jesus und Tiberius: Zwei Söhne Gottes.* München: Luchterhand, 2004.

Thomassen, Einar. *The Spiritual Seed: The Church of the "Valentinians."* NHMS 60. Leiden: Brill, 2006.

Thompson, Marianne Meye. "'Mercy Upon All': God as Father in the Epistle to the Romans." Pages 203–16 in *Romans and the People of God.* Edited by Sven K. Soderlund and N. T. Wright. Grand Rapids: Eerdmans, 1999.

Tigay, Jeffrey Howard, and Schereschewsky, Ben-Zion. "Adoption." Pages 415–18 in vol. 1 of *Encyclopedia Judaica.* 2nd ed. 22 vols. Edited by Fred Skolnik. New York: Macmillan, 2007.

Toynbee, J.M.C. Review of H.P. L'Orange, *Apotheosis in Ancient Portraiture. JRS* 38 (1948): 160–63.

———. "Ruler-apotheosis in ancient Rome." *Numismatic Chronicle* 7 (1947): 126–149.

Usener, Hermann. *Religionsgeschichtliche Untersuchungen. Erster Theil: Das Weihnachtsfest.* Bonn, 1889.

Van Deun, Peter, and Noret, Jacques, eds. *Hagiographica Cypria.* CCSG 26. Turnhout: Brepols, 1993.

Vellanickal, Matthew. *The Divine Sonship of Christians in the Johannine Writings.* Analecta Biblica 72. Rome: Biblical Institute Press, 1977.

Vermeule, Cornelius C. *Roman Imperial Art in Greece and Asia Minor.* Cambridge, Mass.: Harvard University Press, 1968.

Verseput, Donald J. "The Role and Meaning of the 'Son of God' Title in Matthew's Gospel." *NTS* 33 (1987): 532–56.

Vigourt, Annie. *Les presages impériaux d'Auguste à Domitien.* Paris: De Boccard, 2001.

Vittinghoff, Friedrich. "Staat, Kirche und Dynastie beim Tode Konstantins." Pages 1–34 in *L'Église et L'Empire au IVe Siècle*. Edited by Albrecht Dihle. Genève: Fondation Hardt, 1989.

Vööbus, Arthur, ed. *Didascalia Apostolorum*. CSCO 175–76, 179–80, 401–02, 407–08. Louvain: Secretariat du CorpusSCO, 1979.

Walbank, Frank W. "Könige als Götter: Überlegungen zum Herrscherkult von Alexander bis Augustus." *Chiron* 17 (1987): 365–82.

Wallace-Hadrill, Andrew. *Suetonius: the Scholar and His Caesars*. New Haven: Yale University Press, 1984.

Walters, James C. "Paul, Adoption, and Inheritance." Pages 42–76 in *Paul in the Greco-Roman World*. Edited by J. Paul Sampley. Harrisburg: Trinity Press International, 2003.

Watson, Alan. *The Law of the Ancient Romans*. Dallas: Southern Methodist University Press, 1970.

Watson, Francis. "Is John's Christology Adoptionist?" Pages 113–24 in *The Glory of Christ in the New Testament: Studies in Christology in Memory of George Bradford Caird*. Edited by L. D. Hurst and N. T. Wright. Oxford: Clarendon Press, 1987.

Weber, Max. *Economy and Society*. 2 vols. Edited and translated by Guenther Roth and Claus Wittich. Berkeley: University of California Press, 1978.

Weinreich, Otto. "Antikes Gottmenschentum." *Neue Jahrbücher für Wissenschaft und Jugendbildung* 2 (1926): 633–51. Repr. as pages 55–81 in *Römischer Kaiserkult*. Edited by Antonie Wlosok. Wege der Forschung 372. Darmstadt: Wissenschaftliche Buchgesellschaft, 1978.

Weinstock, Stefan. *Divus Julius*. Oxford: Clarendon, 1971.

Wellhausen, Julius. *Einleitung in die drei ersten Evangelien*. 2nd ed. Berlin: G. Reimer, 1911.

———. *Das Evangelium Marci*. Berlin: Georg Reimer Verlag, 1909.

White, John L. "God's Paternity as Root Metaphor in Paul's Conception of Community." *Foundations and Facets Forum* 8 (1992): 271–95.

Whitsett, Christopher J. "Son of God, Seed of David: Paul's Messianic Exegesis in Romans 2[*sic*]:3–4." *JBL* 119 (2000): 661–81.

Whittaker, Molly. *Der Hirt des Hermas*. GCS. Berlin: Akadamie-Verlag, 1967.

Widdicombe, Peter. *The Fatherhood of God from Origen to Athanasius*. Oxford: Clarendon, 1994.

———. "The Fathers on the Father in the Gospel of John." *Semeia* 85 (1999): 105–25.

Wiles, Maurice F. *Archetypal Heresy: Arianism Through the Centuries*. Oxford; New York: Clarendon, 1996.

Wilken, Robert L. "The Interpretation of the Baptism of Jesus in the Later Fathers." *Studia Patristica* 11 (1972): 268–77.

Williams, Rowan. *Arius: Heresy and Tradition*. London: SCM Press, 1987.

Wilson, J. Christian. *Toward a Reassessment of the Shepherd of Hermas: Its Date and Pneumatology*. Lewiston, N.Y.: Mellen, 1993.

Winn, Adam. *The Purpose of Mark's Gospel*. WUNT II 245. Tübingen: Mohr Siebeck, 2008.

Wiseman, T. P. "Domi Nobiles and the Roman Cultural Elite." Pages 298–306 in *Les «Bourgeoisies» municipales italiennes aux IIe et Ier siècles av. J.-C.* Edited by M. Cébeillac-Gervasoni. Paris: Éditions du Centre national de la recherche scientifique; Naples: Bibliothèque de l'Institut français de Naples, 1983.

Wissowa, Georg. *Religion und Kultus der Römer*. 2nd ed. München: C.H. Beck, 1912.

Wrede, Wilhelm. *Das Messiasgeheimnis in den Evangelien: Zugleich ein Beitrag zum Verständnis des Markusevangeliums*. Göttingen: Vandenhoeck & Ruprecht, 1901.

English version: *The Messianic Secret*. Translated by J. C. G. Greig. Cambridge: James Clarke, 1971.

Wren, Malcolm. "Sonship in Luke: The Advantage of a Literary Approach." *Scottish Journal of Theology* 37 (1984): 301–11.

Yamauchi, Edwin M. *Pre-Christian Gnosticism: A Survey of the Proposed Evidences*. Grand Rapids: Eerdmans, 1973.

Yarbro Collins, Adela. "Establishing the Text: Mark 1:1." Pages 111–27 in *Texts and Contexts: The Function of Biblical Texts in Their Textual and Situational Contexts*. Edited by Tord Fornberg and David Hellholm. Oslo: Scandinavian University Press, 1995.

———. "'How on Earth Did Jesus Become a God?' A Reply." Pages 55–66 in *Israel's God and Rebecca's Children: Christology and Community in Early Judaism and Christianity*. Edited by David B. Capes, April D. DeConick, Helen K. Bond, and Troy A. Miller. Waco: Baylor University Press, 2007.

———. *Mark: A Commentary*. Edited by Harold W. Attridge. Hermeneia. Philadelphia: Fortress Press, 2007.

———. "Mark and His Readers: The Son of God among Greeks and Romans." *HTR* 93 (2000): 85–100.

———. "Mark and His Readers: The Son of God among Jews." *HTR* 92 (1999): 393–408.

———. "Psalms, Phil. 2:6–11, and the Origins of Christology." *Biblical Interpretation* 11 (2003): 361–72.

———. "The Worship of Jesus and the Imperial Cult." Pages 234–57 in *The Jewish Roots of Christological Monotheism: Papers from the St. Andrews Conference on the Historical Origins of the Worship of Jesus*. Edited by Carey C. Newman, James R. Davila, and Gladys S. Lewis. Leiden: Brill, 1999.

Yarbro Collins, Adela, and Collins, John J. *King and Messiah as Son of God*. Grand Rapids: Eerdmans, 2008.

Young, Frances M. *From Nicaea to Chalcedon*. Philadelphia: Fortress Press, 1983.

———. *The Making of the Creeds*. London: SCM Press; Philadelphia: Trinity Press International, 1981.

Zanker, Paul. *The Power of Images in the Age of Augustus*. Translated by Alan Shapiro. Ann Arbor: University of Michigan Press, 1988.

Pan, sanctuary of, 24, 92, 216n47
Papias, 89
papyri
  adoption contracts, 53, 58, 109, 139
  Bodmer, 229n28, 230n29
  Elephantine, 102, 103
  Greek verb "to choose" in, 108–109, 112
  P.Brem., 72
  P.Giss. 3, 72
  P.Lips. 28, 139, 221n116, 236n119
  P.Oxy. 1453, 31, 45, 199n92
  P.Oxy. 3781, 72
  See also Dead Sea Scrolls
Passover, 161
paterfamilias, 113, 129, 222n140, 226n203
  See also family ideology; father-son relationships; imperial ideology
pater patriae, 50, 60–61, 125
  See also emperors; emperor worship/Roman religion
patria potestas, 50, 51, 125
  See also family ideology; father-son relationships
Paul
  Christian communities founded by, 103, 140
  travels of, 89
  See also Pauline Epistles
Pauline Epistles
  adoption metaphors in, 135–140, 146, 153, 157, 158, 162, 163–164, 171, 189n110, 203n37, 229n21, 230n36
  on adoption of Israelites, 138–139
  apocrypha, 137, 229n28
  baptism central to, 146
  Christ as "firstborn" in, 139–140, 171
  concept of Spirit in, 114
  family lineage of Jesus, 138, 141
  kinship language in, 127
  primitive Christology of, 20, 133, 137, 146, 230n32
  religionsgeschichtliche Schule analysis of, 15–16, 17
  resonance with Greco-Roman ideology, 135–136, 138, 140, 203n37, 229n21
  resurrection, 138, 158, 230n36

uniting Christ with Christians, 135, 139–140, 145, 158
  See also specific Epistles
Paullus Fabius Maximus, 92
Pelikan, Jaroslav, 7–8
Peter, 24, 87, 88, 89, 90, 126, 130, 213n20
Philip (Herod's son), 130
Piso, adoption by Galba, 59, 69, 79, 80–83, 84, 93, 96, 208n110, 211n169–172
Pius XII, 7–8
Platonism
  being vs. becoming, 11, 163, 170
  "divided line" vs. "myth of the cave," 163, 242n189
  and doctrine of Logos, 162
  influence on Nicene thought, 11, 12, 23, 30, 35, 132, 143, 163, 170
  in postmodern era, 31, 34
  and preexistent sonship, 134, 228n16
  See also Nicene era
Pliny the Younger, *Panegyric*, 74, 83–85
polytheism, 35, 193n17
postcolonial theory
  and colonial mimicry, 123–124, 130–131, 179, 196n51, 225n185
  uses of, 40, 187n71
princeps, 30, 43, 44, 62, 195n42

Q source, 22
Qumran, 103, 104, 108, 219n94
  See also Dead Sea Scrolls

religionsgeschichtliche Schule
  Bousset's analysis, 10, 15–17, 21, 22, 24, 26, 186n35, 186n51, 186n55
  Christianity as central "river" in, 15, 17, 24, 186n35–36, 187n65
  and Hellenistic data, 185n33–34
  key members of, 185n33
  key suppositions of, 15
  methodology, 15, 17, 185n34
  See also history-of-religion method
Resurrection, 20, 134, 135, 137, 138, 158, 230n36

■ INDEX OF ANCIENT SOURCES